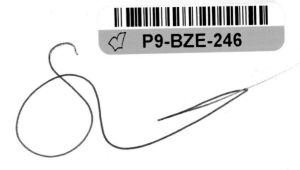

IF AT FIRST

IF AT FIRST

A Season with
the Mets

KEITH HERNANDEZ
AND MIKE BRYAN

McGraw-Hill Book Company

New York St. Louis San Francisco Hamburg Mexico Toronto

photo credits:
Chapter 1—© Thomas Victor 1986
Chapter 2—© duomo
Chapter 3—© duomo
Chapter 4—© duomo
Chapter 5—© duomo
Chapter 6—Wide World Photos

1 2 3 4 5 6 7 8 9 D O C D O C 8 7 6

ISBN 0-07-028345-1

LIBRARY OF CONGRESS CATALOGING-IN-PUBLICATION DATA

Hernandez, Keith.
   If at first.
   1. New York Mets (Baseball team)   I. Bryan, Mike.
II. Title.
GV875.N45H47   1986   796.357′64′097471   85-23371
ISBN 0-07-028345-1

BOOK DESIGN BY PATRICE FODERO

For Mom and Dad and brother Gary, for their love and support. And for these baseball people who were there when I needed them: Bob Kennedy Sr., Lou Brock, Ken Boyer, Joe Medwick, Rusty Staub, Willie Crawford, A. Ray Smith, Tony Santora, Dick Selma, Preston Gomez, Jim Kaat, and Gene Tenace.

K.H.

For Wyn and Bob, stalwart fans all these years.

M.B.

CONTENTS

1. New York, New York: *April 9–May 10*   1
2. On the Way: *May 11–May 28*   59
3. In a Dark Forest: *May 29–June 30*   103
4. Overnight Sensation: *July 1–August 1*   167
5. Strike Two: *August 2–September 3*   225
6. Hardball: *September 4–October 6*   279

ACKNOWLEDGMENTS

We thank Tom Quinn, our editor. The book was his idea, and he entrusted it to not one but two first-time book authors. And we thank his assistant, Susan Mayer, who handled with aplomb innumerable messages and details.

In the Met organization, Jay Horwitz and his public-relations staff, Dennis D'Agostino and Patricia Kirshey, were indispensable. Charlie Samuels, clubhouse man, handled logistical chores with good humor. Pitcher Eddie Lynch contributed wit and anecdotes at a number of our working lunches. Two other Met staffers merit special thanks: Jack Mullaney, the usher behind home plate, and Ed Tobin, the helpful official at window no. 1.

Agents Joe Spieler and Jack Childers did their jobs well. In addition, Joe was, as always, a first-rate critic and editor of the manuscript. The pickings were slim by the time it got to him, however: Patty Bryan is without peer when it comes to organizing a narrative.

Recognition should be given to two books that are valuable sources for facts and ideas, and might be responsible in some measure for the booming interest in big-league baseball. They are *The 1985 Elias Baseball Analyst,* by Seymour Siwoff, Steve Hirdt, and Peter Hirdt, and *The Bill James Baseball Abstract—1985.* (In addition, statistics on the 1985 season were made available by the Elias Sports Bureau.)

1. NEW YORK, NEW YORK

APRIL 9—NEW YORK CITY

No sheets, no towels, no blankets; not mine, at any rate—borrowed. One couch, two chairs, a table. No phone. On the tile floor in the kitchen, a sticky glaze of booze; on the carpet in the guest bedroom, a big stain of wiped-up something: An itinerant ball-playing friend, a guy who hasn't found an apartment yet, had a little party last night. In my bedroom, a mound of suitcases, duffel bags, and laundry the size of a street excavation. In the living room, a display of boxes, my possessions of the moment. The rest are back in St. Louis, with the woman from whom I'm getting a divorce, in the house that used to be my home. Where my three kids and the dog, Slider, live.

Opening Day at *Chez* Hernandez, the East Side co-op recently purchased by the New York Mets' popular first baseman—that's me. Fred Wilpon, one of the owners of the Mets, built the high-rise and lives in the penthouse. Yes, I got a good deal on my five rooms—which isn't to say they were cheap.

In an article in *The New York Times* about the new building, I was named as one of the celebrity residents. My name will be in scores of articles over the next six or seven months, and there's nothing unusual about that—in the sports section. But I know, and the fans don't, that later in the season my name may be on the front pages, too, and in articles that won't be about line drives and RBIs, or accompanied by photos of diving catches. They don't allow cameras in courtrooms.

The fans don't know what I testified to last month before the federal grand jury in Pittsburgh. The papers reported only that I missed a day of spring training in Florida to make the trip, and they reported the general thrust of the investigation—drug use by major-league ballplayers—and there the story rested. But if individuals are indicted for dealing cocaine and their cases go to trial, I may have to testify. In public. In the newspapers. On television.

I've used cocaine. I don't anymore. That period of my life didn't damage my career in baseball, but I made my own bed during those years—1980, '81, and '82—and this year I'll have to sleep in it with the whole world watching.

There will be other court appearances, too, in St. Louis, regarding the divorce.

Life at *Chez* Hernandez? It's not all going to be games and fun this year; mostly, however. On the ballfield, the bonds are taken off. I'm where I belong and feel truly at home. On the ballfield, I'm free.

This is more like it: Opening Day at *Chez* Mets, where 50,000 sold-out Shea Stadium fans expect Dwight Gooden and his teammates to shut out St. Louis and clinch the pennant today. The grizzled veterans on the Mets know better—in our minds, but our hearts aren't so sure, pumped up as they are by the hype and anticipation that have pursued us for six weeks in Florida and the few days we've been back in the Big Apple.

"Yo! Keith! It's your season!"

"Let's go, Mets!"

Passers-by on the streets and avenues, cabbies, store clerks: They all root for the Mets this year. Even the Vice President must be on our side. George Bush will throw out the first ball this afternoon. Backstage, a plump golden Lab is escorted around. She's sniffing for dynamite. The Vice President's "black box" sits in manager Davey Johnson's office, serving as a potent reminder that there are matters on earth more important than this baseball game, or any other. I know this to be true. It should be true. Nevertheless, cautionary wisdom doesn't seem relevant, or even appropriate, on Opening Day. Let us—players and fans—have our diversion.

Inappropriate but welcome is this cold, clammy air. The big sign beyond left field registers 37 degrees. The chill is a shock to our systems, but it wakes us up. At the spring training games in Florida, the snowbird fans dozing in the sunshine at the friendly little parks must assume that the major leaguers are enjoying an equally pleasant afternoon. But for myself, at least, as a veteran not competing for a job, spring training is 9-to-5 tedium. I'm bored. My swing should be ready after a couple of weeks of work, maybe three. My glove is ready from practically the first day.

If the air is cold, the game is for real. If the weather doesn't tell us, the fans at Shea this afternoon do. They're screaming with Dwight's every pitch in the first inning. Three times he goes to a 3-and-2 count before retiring the batter on a fly ball. Dwight blows on his right hand between deliveries. The batters have an easier time with this cold than the pitchers do. In warmer weather, a couple of those Cardinals probably strike out.

The Card starter is the self-proclaimed "one tough Domini-can," Joaquin Andujar. With one out in the first inning, an An-dujar fastball in on the hands breaks Mookie Wilson's bat—on a *bunt* attempt. That's frozen wood! Then Mookie singles, and I'm up for my first real at-bat of 1985. Andujar gets ahead of me 1-and-2, Mookie steals second, I foul off a pitch, take a deep breath and exhale a cloud of steam, then drive a single into center field off Andujar's bare hand. The RBI is a bonus; the idea on Opening Day is to get that first hit behind you. Zero-for-four . . . eight . . . twelve to begin a season? What could be worse?

After my hit our little rally prospers, and George Foster arrives at the plate with the bases loaded. He strikes out on three pitches. Some fans boo. He confides to me in the dugout that he was "overanxious." I'm not surprised.

In my year and a half with the Mets, George has never been a crowd favorite. In 1982, his first year with the team after his great years with Cincinnati, he didn't drive in the predicted runs with the predicted homers. The boos and the snide columns in the tabloids were difficult for George. He didn't help his cause by stating that he wouldn't go into the wall on fly balls, with the explanation that he couldn't help the team from the disabled list. Nor was it wise for him to arrive at the stadium in a limo. There was a reason for it—his wife arrived later in the family car, and they drove home in it—but the limo was bad public relations. George and Sheila, a lovely woman, eventually swapped cars.

Foster was, for a couple of years, one of the two unhappiest ballplayers I've known. The other one was Darrell Porter, catching for the Cards today. On Opening Day in St. Louis four years ago, he was booed unmercifully by 55,000 fans. His crime? Merely that he replaced the popular Ted Simmons. But Porter enjoyed a measure of sweet revenge when he was voted the Most Valuable Player in the World Series in 1982.

He and George—all of us—are first of all professional athletes. Some fans and writers wonder whether the rich and famous mod-ern ballplayers, with our guaranteed long-term contracts, care as much as the old-timers. Yes. We may care even more. No ballplayer gets to the major leagues without a serious streak of

competitiveness. The young guys coming up know what the re-
wards may be, and play their asses off to get a chance at the big
money. The players who have earned these contracts don't have
to worry anymore; we're free to play. Some free agents have
faltered after signing large contracts with new teams—trying too
hard.

Blood tells. Nobody on the Mets in 1985 wants to prove his
value more than George Foster. No thirty-six-year-old American
male is in better shape. George swung the bat beautifully all spring.
He'll be a big factor this season, you watch. Maybe the spectators
are surprised but I'm not, when in his second at-bat George drills
Andujar's pitch over the left-center field fence, giving the Mets a
3–2 lead.

Before my second at-bat, while I'm kneeling in the on-deck circle,
a stone the size of a ping-pong ball nails me in the back. Ballistics
tests confirm that it was hurled from the mezzanine. I like our
fans at Shea, but a few of them are the worst in the league about
getting on their own players and throwing crap on the field. Not
even the infamous bozos at Wrigley Field in Chicago can match
the New Yorkers. I'd rather play in front of 50,000 unruly fans
than 7,500 weak sisters anytime, but launching projectiles from
the stands is over the limit—especially in the first game of the
season! What can I already have done to piss them off?

Most of the time at Shea, however, the violence is contained
within the stands. The fourth inning today features the biggest
brawl at the stadium in years, according to pitcher Ed Lynch, who
has been here for years. An entire section in the blue loge seats
down the third-base line starts fighting. Baseball players tend to
be fight fans, so we watch these episodes with interest. I miss this
particular one because I'm back in the runway, smoking.

Okay, this astonishing revelation is off my chest. I go through
half a pack a game, sometimes an entire pack—but usually only
a couple of puffs per cigarette. Nothing but nerves. Tension. I
rarely smoke in my other life.

In the fifth, I enjoy the first good laugh of the season. Andujar
singles. I play behind him, as instructed by Davey from the bench,
even though I know he might steal. Davey knows he might steal.
He might do anything. He goes us one better by telling me, "I'm

going to steal this sonofabitch. Right now. This pitch." And he does—but doesn't score—so I can laugh. The one and only "Jack" Andujar.

Our one and only Doc Gooden is lifted after the sixth: It's too cold, too early in the year, and the franchise has already thrown a lot of pitches. We lead 5–2. Why risk an injury?

The fans here are knowledgeable; they understand, but are nevertheless dubious as Doug Sisk goes to the mound. Doug has the questionable habit of getting into trouble in order to get out of it—he throws too many balls and walks batters—and he promptly allows two Card runs in the seventh. He's fine in the eighth, but in the ninth he gives up the tying run. Johnson is booed when he comes out to the mound to get him, and Sisk is booed even louder as he walks off the field. In the first game of the campaign, Doug has already worn out his welcome. He's one of the fans' favorites to flog, and they'll take every opportunity, even ignoring today's difficult conditions.

He wears me out, too. I yell at Doug the whole time he's pitching. "Come on, throw the sonofabitch over!" Two innings of Sisk and I'm exhausted, but sometimes he responds to this harassment. In the spring, I informed catcher Gary Carter about this masochism. "Really?" Gary asked. Really.

In the ninth, after Doug hits Lonnie Smith with a pitch, Gary walks to the mound and chews him out. Doesn't do the trick, however. After striking out Terry Pendleton, Doug walks Jack Clark, forcing in that tying run.

I'm probably with the fans on this one. I would have taken Sisk out earlier. Second-guessing, it's one of the joys of baseball. The other team sports aren't as transparent and open for inspection. Baseball players are no different from the fans. We stand out there or sit on the bench and weigh the decisions. However, we *never* pass on our judgments to the manager. That privilege is reserved for the fans and sportswriters.

My thinking here is simple: What do we have Jesse Orosco for, anyway? And here he comes, perhaps one batter too late. While he makes his way across the outfield and throws his warm-up pitches, I leave the diamond for some warmth and a breather . . . so to speak.

It doesn't help. I almost blow the play for the third out, a one-hopper into the hole between me and Wally Backman. I get a bad jump on the ball and can't reach it. I jerk around expecting to see the ball and the game bouncing into right field, two runs scoring, but Backman ranges way to his left and gets to it. Now I have to hustle back to the bag for the throw.

In our half of the ninth, red-haired Daniel Joseph Staub bats. The fans call him Rusty. To the players, he's Orange. He's the only person in the stadium in short sleeves. His bat, however, is warm. He always sees to that, holding the wood up to the heaters in the ceiling of the dugout. Rusty takes his batting and everything else seriously. (*Example:* He hates smoking, including mine. In "Rusty's," his restaurant on Third Avenue, he tried some new-fangled ashtrays that suck up the exhaust. Battery-powered and short-lived, they proved too expensive.)

With first base open, Rusty is intentionally walked, but we can't push the pinch-runner around. The dugout is dying. After wasting a 5–2 lead we go into extra innings. Is the pennant already in jeopardy as twilight descends on the first game?

Hey, no sweat. The Cards don't score. Leading off our half of the tenth, I'm happy (in retrospect) to strike out so that Carter, the new kid on the block, the catcher supposed to be the last piece of the pennant-winning puzzle, can hit the homer heard round the five boroughs. No one on the team wants to prove his value more than Foster, but Gary certainly wants to prove his *as much*. He's in the same situation George was four years ago, but more so: We traded Hubie Brooks, a fan favorite and a great young ballplayer, to get Gary. And now he homers to win the first game. Joy erupts in the dugout and spills onto the field. The fans are beside themselves. Delight in the storybook ending! We wanted to win this one, badly. The game meant a lot more than it meant.

An hour later, Lynch, Danny Heep, and I pile into Rusty's van for the drive back to his restaurant, our depot. The players living in Manhattan ride with Staub to and from every game—with the exception of Ron Darling, who drives out with Tony Ferrara, one of the batting practice pitchers, or takes the subway. Last year, Orange utilized the restaurant's meat van. Blood flowed in the seams of the corrugated floor. We sat on crates. No wonder Darling didn't avail himself of the lift.

This year we've radically upgraded to a deluxe model with carpet and television, but Ronnie will still go his own way. Always has. Always will.

The city shines as we cross the Triborough Bridge from Queens. Some of the guys from the suburbs join us later, so it's about a dozen professional ballplayers who go out for dinner and fine wine at *Chez* Whatever, on the East Side. A banquet to celebrate our spotless record!

GAME 1—Mets 6
Cards 5

APRIL 11

Two days ago, the Vice President of the United States; today, Rodney Dangerfield throwing out the first ball at Opening Day II, another afternoon contest for those who couldn't get ducats for Tuesday's victory. On Diamondvision, the big TV screen in left field, they show Rodney's video, "It Ain't Easy Being Me"— expurgated, I'm told.

Expurgated. Look it up. The word shows up occasionally in the crossword puzzles, and the puzzles, oddly enough, have played a minor role in my baseball career. This harmless and beneficial pastime of mine wasn't appreciated by Whitey Herzog, the manager of the Cards who shipped me to the Mets in 1983. I worked the puzzle in the clubhouse before games, while he thought I should be palling around with teammates, providing leadership. I never bought it. Leadership on a team is 80 percent on the field and in the dugout. The other 20 percent is critical, but it's not an everyday, rah-rah thing. This isn't high school. We're not boys.

Davey Johnson agrees. With the Mets, I work my puzzle in peace, as do Staub, Lynch, and Darling. After the trade, Herzog made some disparaging remarks about me, and some fans at Shea retaliated with a banner draped over a railing: DON'T SAY A CROSS WORD ABOUT KEITH.

In 1983, it wasn't easy being the Mets. You can read a losing team a mile away—on the field, in the dugout, everywhere. The players are listless; they care about what's happening (blood tells), but they're either numbed into lethargy or, as a kind of defense mechanism, pretend they don't care. That was the Met team— expecting to lose. Riding to Shea Stadium on the St. Louis team bus in 1980, we Cardinals burst into laughter the first time we

saw the new publicity slogan mounted atop the stadium: THE MAGIC
IS BACK.

The Mets deserved and received no respect, and here I was,
coming over from the world champions to a team with four last-
place finishes in the previous six years, and the other two years
next-to-last. Banished. Shipped to the Siberia of baseball.

Hernandez and Herzog in the manager's office the evening
of the trade deadline, June 15, 1983:

We traded you.
Who to?
The Mets.
Who???
The New York Mets.
Who for?
Neil Allen and Rick Ownbey.
Is that all???

Before the Met deal, the rumor had floated that I was going
to Houston for Ray Knight and Vern Ruhle. I asked Bob Kennedy,
who was like a father to me in the St. Louis organization and is
one of the major reasons I'm playing baseball today, to tell Al
Rosen, the Astros' boss at that time, that I didn't want to play in
Houston. My mother's family lives nearby. Playing near family is
tough. I would simply have played out my option with the Astros
and left after one year.

That informal veto could not have pleased Whitey or the rest
of the Cardinal management. Fine, Keith, they said a couple of
weeks later. Take the Mets.

I cried in the shower. My agent rushed to the rescue. I wanted
to know if I retired, how much money would I have. He said not
enough. I still wasn't going to report. He literally packed my bags
and then cajoled me onto the plane to Montreal, where the Mets
were playing in four hours. I got to the field just before game
time. I went 2-for-4.

"Welcome to the Stems," Tom Seaver greeted me. That's "Mets"
spelled backward.

"Keith, you're my ticket out of here," exclaimed Dave Kingman, who was, indeed, soon gone from the Mets.

I was into self-pity; the morale on my new outfit didn't help
me fight it off. In that situation, with the team twenty games out
in June and going nowhere—and not even my team, really, be-

cause I had no intention of staying—the temptation was very much to play for myself and my statistics, in preparation for declaring free agency at the end of 1984.

A ballplayer can rationalize this attitude because stats are, after all, RBIs, and they help the team. But it's not the same thing as playing *for* the team. You play for the team *over and above* playing for stats. Or you don't. The difference is intangible but unmistakable.

While playing for a terrible team, an athlete is sometimes left with nothing but pride in his own performance; sometimes, however, there's the example of others. Specifically, it was Ed Lynch that year. How could I mope around at first base when Eddie was pitching his guts out, often in hopeless causes? He ended the year 10–10; mostly guts.

I tried my best to get with the program in New York, and succeeded somewhat. I hit about .310 for the last half of the year. I pulled up the dismal average I had dragged over from the Cards, finishing the year at .297—but with only 63 RBIs.

Frank Cashen, the Mets' general manager, realized that I wasn't thrilled with my new circumstances. He also knew the Mets would have nothing to show for the trade if I became a free agent.

"Tell us after the year, Keith, how you feel," he said. "Give me two weeks before the winter meetings. If you want, we'll trade you. We don't want to lose you for nothing."

That was fair. I owed it to them. The decision was perhaps the most difficult of my life. The city itself had nothing to do with it. Money had nothing to do with it. The state of the ballclub was my chief consideration. I wouldn't have signed with a sure loser for any sum. The Mets had played better the second half, when we could have laid down. We had Darryl Strawberry, who hit twenty-six homers in a little over 400 at-bats, and Jesse Orosco, who I felt was a real stopper, leading the team with thirteen victories and seventeen saves. My father, a former minor-leaguer with baseball connections all over, checked with scouts around the league and reported back about some great young arms in the minors, just about ready.

I decided the Mets had a chance to be a better ballclub in 1984, maybe fourth place, but I also feared I would be signing up for six years of sixth place—dead last. It was a scary thought.

Dad and Gary, my brother, lobbied for the Mets. They thought

I could help these rising stars. I was uncertain, despite my public pronouncements about how much I loved the city. I did like the city, but that summer I was living with my family in the suburbs. In the end, I gambled. After making any number of wrong decisions over the years, I decided to go against my natural instinct. I wanted to leave, so I stayed instead.

I had never met Dwight Gooden or Ron Darling.

And here we are, a year later, bona-fide contenders. Dwight started Tuesday's Opening Day. Ronnie follows him this afternoon. They are two of the reasons most of the pundits are picking us to finish first or second in the division. For the record right now (and I won't erase this in October): I cautiously pick the Cubs in our division, because they beat us last year and improved over the winter. But we improved, too. But we have to prove it.

In the National League West I'll go with the San Diego Padres to repeat. I don't know much about the American League, except that I don't believe the Yankees are very good.

The fans pelt Dangerfield with fruit and tennis balls as he throws out the honorary first pitch. Rodney has made millions, I suppose, earning no respect, but no ballplayer wants to emulate that career, believe me. What a change for the Mets since June of 1983. It's a helluva lot more fun playing for a winning ballclub. Tuesday's victory didn't clinch the pennant, it turns out, but still we're the toast of the town. I got special consideration yesterday when I bought my telephones. I got a wonderful smile from the clerk at Bloomingdale's—while paying full fare, of course, for the shower curtain.

The team is silently begging for Darling to have a good outing today against the Cards. After his first starts in Florida were discouraging, he pitched better in two games, but then he was rained out after five innings of his final tune-up. We need him this year— all year—like he was for the first half of 1984. When Ronnie wasn't invited to the All-Star game with his 10–3 record last year, he was disappointed. Right after the break, he took two tough no-decisions. If he had won them, I believe, he would have gone on to win twenty games, or close to it. I believe that. Instead, he fell off and finished 12–9.

Ballplayers are fragile. In 1978, my second full year with the Cards, I was almost leading the league in hitting before the All-

Star game (.323, 48 RBIs), but was left off the National League team in favor of Steve Garvey and Pete Rose, those hardy perennials. I was pissed and tailed off terribly the second half of the season. I finished at .255. To go from .323 to .255 is to not hit at all.

I did not quit—I was trying—but I just couldn't relinquish my disappointment; simple immaturity, I suppose—I was twenty-four years old. I didn't make the All-Star team in 1979, either, the year I was subsequently voted the league's Most Valuable Player, or a couple of other years I deserved it. I've been to the game three times; it should have been five. Darling and I have talked about the frustration.

"Turn it around," I advised him, by taking this attitude: "Ignore me, assholes, and I'll show you."

Darling didn't quit last year, either. Far from it, but he felt (and still feels) that he's performing in Dwight's lengthy shadow, and what does he have to do to emerge as a star in his own right. And now he might be wondering whether the hitters finally caught up with him last August and September. His confidence has to be shaky.

We want him to get off to a blazing start. He does, giving up only one run in seven innings, on four hits, so the congratulations are heartfelt when he's lifted for a pinch hitter in the seventh. We're tied 1–1, so it's another no-decision for Ron "No-Decision" Darling, as he was aptly labeled last year. (Another reason for a luckless pitcher to worry: Why don't they score any runs for me?)

We go into extra innings. The key play in the game may be a mere called strike in the Cards' tenth. Baseball is subtle.

Orosco walks Ozzie Smith to open the inning. Ivan DeJesus bats for their pitcher, John Tudor (I'm not sorry to see you depart, John, with your nasty left-handed stuff). The count goes to 2-and-1 on DeJesus before umpire Jim Quick calls the next pitch, a fastball, strike two.

Holding Smith on first, I say quietly to him (not wanting Ed Runge, umpiring behind us, to hear; umps are like the players, they stick together), "That pitch was low. He hasn't called it a strike all game. Thank God he calls it now."

Smith mutters, "No shit."

With two strikes, DeJesus can't safely bunt and Herzog can't safely play the hit-and-run (risking a strikeout protecting the runner on a bad pitch), so DeJesus swings away and flies out. A single one out later doesn't score Ozzie from first base. In effect, the called strike probably saves us a run.

The Shea fans can't get on Doug Sisk this game because he comes in and gets the third out in the tenth. They almost have a golden opportunity, however, to express displeasure with another of their "favorites," Ron Gardenhire. I don't know where the animosity comes from—sometime before I showed up—but the fans can't wait for Gardie to do something wrong. Nor do I understand, because he's a good hustling player.

Gardenhire pinch-hits in the tenth, pops out, and stays in to play shortstop. In the eleventh, Jack Clark hits a wicked grounder right at him, and Gardie plays it perfectly, staying in front of the ball, taking the in-between hop off his chest, grabbing it and throwing to me for the out. But the moment the ball bounces off his chest, the fans start to growl. I hear the reaction even as I concentrate on the play. They're ready to hose him down. Then as he throws to first, they have to change their tune and cheer.

Arrrggghhgh . . . yeeeeaaah!!! Standing on the bag, I have to laugh. Hell, I love to laugh.

Pitching for us in the eleventh is Roger McDowell, a rookie with a sinkerball in his first major-league appearance. The Cards go up and down in order, with two ground balls (the obvious clue to the effectiveness of the sinkerball) and a strikeout. Early in the season, these accomplishments are not so small. They make a young team feel better about the uncertain future.

Leading off for us, I'm thinking "hit, any hit." If I get one to crank out of the park, fine, but that's not my job—definitely not with power hitters Carter, Foster, and Strawberry following me this season. I get my sixth hard single in two games. Carter singles. Foster is walked intentionally. The sacks are drunk (*lingo:* bases loaded).

The cruel fans shout, "We want Neil! We want Neil!" That's Neil Allen, of course, the Card reliever who threw Gary his home run pitch on Tuesday and, coincidentally, the guy who went to the Cards in the Hernandez deal. A ballplayer watches fairly closely the career of any player he's traded for. Without knocking Neil in any way, I'm glad the Mets got the best of that exchange.

Herzog brings in Allen. He's the Cards' designated stopper this year, since they lost Bruce Sutter to free agency. Whitey has to demonstrate confidence. Danny Heep, pinch-hitting, takes the count to 3-and-2, fouls off a couple of pitches, then walks. I score. We win. The fans go wild. It's another happy clubhouse, calmer than on Opening Day but relieved that Darling pitched well, happy that we are, if only for a couple of days, apparently as good as the city wants us to be.

GAME 2—Mets 2
Cards 1

APRIL 12

Cincinnati in town, and that means Pete Rose and the ghost of Ty Cobb. Here I am closing in on my 1,500th hit—pretty good after eight full years—and Rose has collected over 4,000 and is going strong at age forty-four. And managing his team.

Can you really manage and play on the field? Only with help from your coaches. It's not possible to keep your head in the game situation of the moment, which changes with every batter, and also juggle strategies and line up contingencies two innings down the road. Pete has help.

Unfortunately for the Reds, they're playing the red-hot Mets. We can't lose. Carter wins this game with another homer, this one in the fourth inning. We win 1–0, and it's Bruce Berenyi's turn for an encouraging pitching performance. One hit in seven innings, that's *encouraging* for a pitcher with a chronically sore shoulder.

The fans are anxious when Sisk takes over in the eighth and walks the first man on four pitches. A smooth 1-6-3 double play saves him. The ninth is straightforward on paper, but in fact, that's a nasty, knuckling liner Dave Parker hits to right field with Rose on first. Strawberry battles it all the way and makes the catch off his knees. Probably a game saver.

Were the fans paying attention when Darryl stole third in the fourth inning, with two out and the pitcher at the plate? What was the point of the play? With his speed, he's no closer to scoring on a single. If he's thrown out, the pitcher leads off the next inning, something we try to avoid. A young player's mental error.

I didn't have many concerns about this team coming into spring training; Darryl was at the top of my short list. I watched Howard Johnson at third base because he's a new man from the other league; Ray Knight, also at third, because he has a variety of ailments; and Darryl, because of his work habits.

The cliché is true: Darryl has unlimited potential. With our lineup, he could drive in 150 runs (yes!) with 40-plus homers and a .300-plus average. He's the only potential Triple Crown winner in the National League. To get there, he'll have to become more selective of pitches. That should come.

Darryl is also the most frustrating man I've ever played with. In batting practice last year, he'd sometimes give up and take lazy, worthless swings. BP puts a player into more slumps than any other factor. We get about forty swings, so a bad habit can establish itself quickly. It's vital to work on cultivating the smooth, level, disciplined swing; everything a line drive or, at worst, on the ground.

I never try to hit a home run. A slugger like Darryl might, at the end of a BP session, try to pole a few. Last year, he sometimes tried to hit all of them out. While the early bird fans "Ooohhed" and "Aaahhed," I cringed. Several times, I stepped in and said, "Straw, they don't pay you to hit home runs in batting practice."

Too often, Darryl was either swinging for the fences or barely swinging at all. When a player has so much talent, teammates care. The opposition cares. Around midseason, Bill Madlock of the Pirates came to me and asked, "What the fuck is wrong with Strawberry?" As a four-time batting champion, Madlock, too, was pained to watch Darryl practice. I told Bill I had talked with Darryl many times. "Why don't you try?" I suggested, and he did.

It's not that I'm a saint. It's that Straw should have cared more about his talent. He should have cared more about the team. There were a couple of times when he got down 1-and-2 to a tough pitcher, and he gave in. I could see the look in his eyes. I know the feeling, we all do, but we have to battle—and none of Darryl's batting practice swings would benefit him against a hard slider on the outside corner at the knees. That pitch can't be hit for a homer.

Watching him became a drain on me. I took it personally. I, too, had a lot of trouble breaking into the big leagues, but I never quit. Put it this way: I'll quit before I quit. And to see Darryl pissing away his talent, I had to do something. Finally, in September, after biting my tongue for a month or more, I decided it might be best to shake him up. I went public and told the reporters after a game that Darryl had quit on himself and his team. After concluding my lecture, I walked over to Strawberry's cubicle. He was sitting on the stool.

"Straw, there'll be a story coming out tomorrow. I just want to tell you before it breaks. I said a few things. Now, how they'll write it and what kind of headline they put on it, I don't know. But I just want you to know now."

"Okay," he said.

I told Foster what I'd said. George agreed with my thoughts, but doubted whether I should have told the reporters.

Maybe I shouldn't have. I couldn't sleep that night. The newspapers ran the story big, of course. Even though I don't believe Darryl holds the episode against me, I question the wisdom of my outburst to this day. However, I know this: Strawberry played like a madman for the rest of 1984. He worked like the devil this spring. He made a helluva catch tonight.

In the post-game clubhouse, my uniform is barely off before a pretty reporter starts in with a set of questions. She's alone; the thundering herd is off with the obvious interviewees, Berenyi and Carter. Sitting in my skivvies, I answer her politely. Ballplayers don't think twice now about women in the locker room. Usually, we clothe ourselves with a towel. Sometimes we blow it off. Back in the late '70s, however, when the courts first opened the clubhouse doors, players were resentful. The invasion by the press immediately after every game was bad enough, but having to deal with women in that situation was worse. The wives weren't happy, either.

Many of the women we had never seen and would never see again. They just wanted to be in on history and scope out the jocks. I decided I wanted to be in on history, too. The Cards were playing in New York when the ruling went into effect, so my first confrontation was in the visitors' clubhouse at Shea. As players and reporters conversed with darting eyes, I disappeared around a corner, got up on my hands and paraded back through the clubhouse upside down, buck naked . . . flag at half-mast. The guys loved it. The women were nonplussed. I still consider it my best clubhouse stunt.

Tonight, my interviewer leaves the clubhouse right after our conversation. She talks to no one else; I start wondering. Is there a message here? Perhaps, although no reporter has explicitly tried to pick me up before. But I'm eligible, they know. We'll see whether she returns.

GAME 3—Mets 1
Reds 0

APRIL 13

Two days ago we won in part because an umpire called a strike on a low fastball. Today we win because Cesar Cedeno twice fails to get down a sacrifice bunt in the ninth inning with runners first and second, nobody out, score tied at one. Swinging on two strikes, he hits into a double play.

Pay attention out there to the ballgame; every pitch; the little things win and lose games, day after day.

Big things, too: Darryl homers in the ninth. How sweet for all concerned—Darryl, the team, the fans. The crowd this afternoon doesn't cheer quite as loud and long for Darryl as it did for Carter's two game-winners earlier in the week. That's fair enough. Carter is new in town, full of pizzazz and chutzpah and perfect for New York. Another Tug McGraw. Strawberry, on the other hand, is languid and laid back and doesn't appear to give the fans as much as Carter does, so they don't give it back.

The fans gave it back to me in 1974. Playing winter ball in Puerto Rico for the Ponce team, I was an object of their wrath because I didn't speak Spanish. Despite my surname Hernandez and my nickname "Mex," I'm not one of the "official" Hispanic players. My father's parents came over from Spain early in the century; my mother's family is Scottish, living in south Texas. However, any explanation of my heritage and thoroughly middle-class American upbringing in the suburbs of San Francisco was considered by the Puerto Ricans a denial of my real roots. They wanted me to be Hispanic.

I didn't help matters by drinking a lot and hitting terribly. After four great games, my average fell to .170. I didn't want to be there, but the Cards had told me I wouldn't make the big club without a good winter season.

On a two-day break, Ellis Valentine and I raced to San Juan for a forty-eight-hour drunk. I body surfed 100 yards offshore.

There's no good reason why I didn't drown. It rained on the day of the next game, so Ellis and I assumed a postponement. Back at our hotel, we turned on the radio. Baseball was on the air. Oh, who's playing? Ponce!

The next day, the fans tore into me. I was sick with *turista,* had lost ten pounds and had had enough of winter ball, period. I stepped out of the box and grabbed my crotch in the traditional lewd gesture that needs no translation. Then I struck out. The fans howled with joy. Then I asked Ken Boyer, who was managing Ponce that season, to talk to the Cardinals' general manager, Bing Devine, and get me the hell out of there. It was doing no good. Boyer—one of the great men in my life—agreed. Devine agreed.

Ten years later, here I am in New York City, the melting pot where the fans couldn't care less about my heritage—provided I hit.

GAME 4—Mets 2

Reds 1

APRIL 14

We win again, with Carter's homer in the sixth inning the big blow. That's three in five games for The Kid. It's a 3-and-2 pitch. Jay Tibbs shakes off Bilardello's sign, then comes in with a change-up of some sort. That selection surprises Carter, because a hitter doesn't expect off-speed stuff on 3-and-2, but with the slow pitch Gary has time to regroup. His hands do the rest. From the elbows down, this is where it's at for a hitter: strong hands, wrists, and forearms; strong and quick.

I'm hitless. I was hitless yesterday. I was hitless the night before. After our first two games, I was 6-for-10; now I'm 6-for-20. I feel strong and quick enough, but I'm not thinking clearly at the plate, for some reason I can't figure out. I'm not even thinking clearly in the on-deck circle. This afternoon, I swing my bat into coach Bobby Valentine's cheek. Fortunately it isn't a full swing, and it doesn't catch him solidly, but it's scary.

Rusty experiences a different kind of anxiety in the clubhouse after the game. As serious as Orange is about everything, he's even more serious about flying. Here's the problem: We're playing in Pittsburgh tomorrow night, so the team will fly there early in the day. (As a rule, we'll also fly to Montreal on the day of a night game; Philly is a bus ride; all other destinations require leaving the day or the night before.)

But Staub hates to fly, so he gives himself more time to recover by leaving for Pittsburgh or Montreal the night before. But tonight the cloud cover is low, and he's not about to fly in these conditions. So he'll have to fly with us tomorrow, after all, and he's unhappy about it.

The rest of the Mets feel pretty good. Five out of five is acceptable. In just his second start, Dwight has already rounded into form: no runs, four hits, ten Ks.

GAME 5—Mets 4
Reds 0

APRIL 15—PITTSBURGH

Poor Rusty. Today is worse for flying than last night was, and we're delayed an hour and a half before departing. Then a wreck on the freeway in Pittsburgh forces the bus driver to take a series of back roads to the hotel downtown. Rusty doesn't even have time for a nap before he's back on the bus for the ride to Three Rivers Stadium. And Foster, who also intensely dislikes flying, has a migraine.

I'm unhappy, too. On the road again for another season, tired of it already. For several years now, every road trip has seemed like it lasted a month. It's a battle for me out here. I'm afraid my record indicates as much. Last year, I hit .366 at home, only .259 on the road. The "friendly confines" theory doesn't account for that discrepancy.

I win the skirmish tonight, getting a couple of hits and an RBI, but it isn't nearly enough. We're sluggish, leave eleven men on base, and lose.

Our best chance comes with me at the plate in the seventh inning, runners on second and third, two out. Chuck Tanner brings in his best left-hander, one of the best in the league, John Candelaria. He pops me up with a hellacious slider. In the ninth inning, Pirates up by three, nobody on base, The Candy Man throws me an inside fastball, a pitch I can hit. He's just serving one up. Here, hit it. With complete confidence in his stuff this evening, he knows he can get anyone out if he has to. I get the single, he retires the side.

Left-hander Bill Latham starts the game for us, in his first major-league appearance. He gets hit hard. I wouldn't bet he's around in a few months—not because he isn't good, but because he isn't ready. Latham is a finesse pitcher, and it takes a lot of time to develop these fine skills. When a breaking-ball pitcher is off his game, which relies on painting the black (*lingo:* hitting the corners of the plate), he'll get murdered on pitches over the plate, up in the strike zone. A hard thrower like Gooden, on the other hand, is more likely to get by with less than his best stuff. He can simply throw the ball by many of the batters.

Later, Davey tells reporters that he thought Sisk would be ready in the bullpen sooner than he was in the fourth inning. Because he wasn't, the Pirates got a key hit off the struggling Latham. Then Doug came in and pitched well.

How often does a manager win or lose a game with his decisions? I recall reading that none other than George Steinbrenner believes a half-dozen times a year. That's enough to win or lose a championship, but I believe the figure is higher.

Most managers get screwed in the accounting, regardless, because it's easier—and more fun—to assess blame than give credit. The manager probably gets a black mark for lifting the starting pitcher if the reliever gives up a homer, but does he get a star if he keeps the starter in and the guy retires the side in the ninth? No. It's a no-win job. No thank you.

GAME 6—Pirates 4

Mets 1

APRIL 16

In the ninth inning this evening, John Candelaria has something to lose—the game. It's tied 1–1, Mookie's on third with a triple as I come up with nobody out. In this sacrifice-fly situation, infield drawn in for the play at the plate, I should prevail at least 70 percent of the time. Even against the best pitcher, the odds are with me.

I'm lying in the high weeds. When he has to get me out, Candelaria throws hard sliders outside. Why shouldn't he try it now? I look for the outside pitch and here it is as his first offering. I hit the ball fairly hard to the center fielder, Mookie trots home with the winning run and I get my first game-winning RBI (GWRBI).

It's a stat of dubious worth, I must concede, even though I lead the league with 70-plus since the computation was initiated in 1980. The GWRBI is granted to the player who drives in the run that puts his team ahead for good. The first RBI of a 10–9 victory is the GWRBI if the team is never tied. It's almost inevitable that a good hitter batting third on a good team will lead in this category, not so much for truly clutch hitting as for driving in the first run quite a few times. It's important to drive in the first run, but to label it a game-winner? Dumb.

I'll take the sacrifice fly tonight, but if I'm hitting really well, I'll drive Candelaria's pitch into the gap for a double. The sacrifice fly is more a good piece of strategy than a good piece of hitting, but that's fine with me. I love the cat-and-mouse of hitting—even if I am, technically, the mouse. Besides, I don't look at it that way. I try to turn the tables. Dad drummed into me: "Be like a tiger up there!"

I've always enjoyed hitting more against left-handers than right-handers, even though, theoretically, the lefties should give me, a left-handed batter, more trouble. Every hitter has to protect the outside of the plate, so as a left-handed hitter I'm most vulnerable to the left-hander's breaking ball on the outside corner, a pitch that moves away from me. Conversely, the right-handed hitter has more trouble with right-handed pitchers.

It's often repeated that the "guess hitter" doesn't last long in the major leagues. That's correct only if the reference is to guessing the *pitch*—fastball, curve, slider, etc.—as opposed to the zone. If the batter guesses fastball but gets a curve, he might recover, because the curve is the slower pitch. If he guesses curve but gets the hard fastball, forget it. Good hitters don't guess very often, and almost never with two strikes. If I do, I'm either playing an irresistible hunch or I'm having so much trouble with this pitcher, I figure the gamble is worth it.

Zoning is a different matter, however. Lou Brock worked with me on my zoning strategy against lefties (it wouldn't serve its purpose against right-handers). With no strikes or one strike against a left-hander, I will usually play a zone, looking either inside or out. If I guess inside, I can handle anything—hard stuff or off-speed—out to the far four inches of the plate. Take that pitch. If I guess outside, I can handle anything except the inside corner. Take that pitch. It took me a couple of years to learn to lay off the pitch I wasn't zoning for. With two strikes, everything changes. I have to protect inside, outside, up, down and around.

Strangely, perhaps, I don't want to *know* either the pitch or the zone. If I knew the pitch, I'd have a tendency to relax. Better for me is the split-second decision. And regarding the zone: What if the pitcher misses his target? I trust my reflexes more than his control.

Guys have told me they know the catcher's signs, or a pitcher's idiosyncrasies that give away the pitch; I tell them I'm not interested; some hitters, however, want to know everything. In St. Louis, we had the signs from Ron Hodges when he caught games for the Mets in 1981. He flashed them too low and didn't hide his fingers with his mitt. That year, I made one exception to my rule: I wanted to know when Ed Lynch was throwing his change-up.

While Brock worked with me on zoning against lefties, he also suggested that I move closer to the plate against them, thus acquiring the outside corner as my territory. "They'll try to beat you inside," he warned. "Look for the inside pitch." I did, they threw it and I hit it. Now, after all these years, they know I'm ready.

At the same time Brock was moving me in on the plate against lefties, Ken Boyer was moving me *off* the plate against right-handers because I was having trouble with their inside pitch, particularly the hard slider. Boyer thought it was crazy for me to adopt Brock's suggestion because I would have to learn, in effect, two strike zones. It was a valid concern, but for some reason I never had a problem making the adjustment. I automatically account for my distance from the plate, which can vary from as little as three inches against certain left-handers to as much as a foot and a half against right-handers.

The reason the score is tied 1–1 when I come up in the ninth is that Darling finally tires in the eighth, walks the first three hitters and gives up a run, after allowing only one hit for the night. I can't overemphasize the lift these performances by the young pitchers give the team, but it's another no-decision for Ronnie. If he chooses, however, he can look at it this way: If it hadn't been for a great stop by Howard Johnson at third base in the eighth, we would have fallen behind.

How in the world did HoJo come to the Mets from the Tigers

with a reputation for stone hands? That's the mystery of the year, so far. He has already made a bunch of good stops, and hasn't fumbled any. The irony is that he hasn't lived up to his reputation of being a fine hitter. He told me at the start of this trip he's glad to be on the road, away from the pressure at Shea.

When Howard comes up for his first at-bat tonight, Carter yells out, "Come on, HoJo! Swing the battie-wattie." The bench could be photographed for an E. F. Hutton ad: a dead silence, a long look, then widespread laughter. Carter must still be talking to his three kids. HoJo gets a hit.

As we head into the field, I yell down the dugout, "Come on, Gary! Let's go fieldie-wieldie."

Funnie-wunnie? Maybe you had to be there, but so it goes with the loose ballclub.

These low-scoring games we're playing are no surprise— although fourteen strikeouts for us against DeLeon tonight is a little much. Early in the season, the pitchers are ahead of the hitters; they're as good as they're going to get; our best days are still to come. Also, half the Mets are sick right now with some bug.

Strawberry caps off our lackluster batting by posting the team's first sombrero of the year. That's 0-for-4, with four strikeouts. Five strikeouts is the rare and not coveted golden sombrero. A mere three is the hat trick.

Hitters clearly recall their sombreros. I've had four in the big leagues, the first one off Tom Seaver in 1975, a year I started with the Cards before being sent down. Two of the strikeouts were with the bases loaded. I almost cried.

Candelaria did it to me in 1979, when I was hot and winning the batting championship. I was overmatched that day.

The two I can still taste were late in the following season. After a collision with Bill Buckner at first base, a mild concussion kept me out of three games. I tried to come back too soon and my first game was a sombrero against Bert Blyleven. I went 3-for-24 for the week.

A few weeks later we faced Bill Gullickson in Montreal. It was 28 degrees in late September and the wind chill factor was 5. I was trailing the same Buckner by two points for the batting title, and I wanted my second crown in a row. The Cards were out of the race, so I had nothing to do at the time but hit.

I was frozen at the plate; four times Gullickson sent me back to the dugout to thaw.

I still get angry recalling that collision. It cost me the title.

We're fortunate to strike out fourteen times, yet win the game. The victory frees up the squad. We razz Straw a little; he takes it fine. The level of needling in these situations depends on whether .we win or lose the game. Winning is license for a lot of things. The rest of our energy after dodging a bullet seems to be directed at Tom "Mooch" O'Toole, the visiting clubhouse man in Pittsburgh, a nice man but saddled with the worst post-game spread in the league. His food is terrible; the worst in organized baseball, and if you know what it's like in the minor leagues. . . .

Lynch remarks that his meal is the world's first sugarless gum sandwich, and Carter's good-natured ribbing upsets Mooch. He hides behind a grin, but I see the real emotion.

Half a dozen fight fans on the Mets watch the Hagler-Hearns bout on closed circuit. I know Hagler will win, and I collect $50 from a teammate for my perspicacity. If I were a betting man, it would have been a grand. Hagler has heart.

GAME 7—Mets 2
Pirates 1

APRIL 17

Besides the food, Pittsburgh has the worst organist in organized baseball and the PA announcer sounds like the narrator of the Yogi Bear cartoons. Maybe 25,000 fans show up for the three games with the Mets—total!—and they're not very interested. The paper is full of speculation regarding who will buy the team and where it will be moved. What a shame, recalling the Pirate ballclubs of just half a dozen years ago, from the Stargell and Parker era and, before that, the Clemente teams. Something could turn it all around in a year or two, however. The Mets have proved that.

Frankly, it's difficult playing in a vacated Three Rivers Stadium after hosting 30,000 and more at Shea. Everything works against us—including the Pirate pitching staff, the best in the league!

But to show how unpredictable the national pastime is, we come into the game in a batting slump of sorts, facing a good pitcher, Larry McWilliams, and we pound him and his successors for thirteen hits and ten runs. Nevertheless, it's an ugly game, as Met pitchers give up ten walks, and the two teams combine for twenty runners left on base. Almost three and a half hours of misplay. If this game had been what Abner Doubleday had in mind, baseball never would have made it.

Among other indignities tonight, we commit our first error of the season, a throwing mistake by Chapman. It's partly my fault. In the fourth inning, Jason Thompson is batting and I'm playing deep: He's a left-handed power hitter who can't run, and the field is Astroturf. On Thompson's ground ball to Chapman, I don't really bust my ass to get to first, knowing how slow Thompson is, so Kelvin has to throw at a moving target. I tell him later with a big grin that I'll take the error if he can convince the official scorer.

The worst is the bottom of the fifth inning, when we're already leading 8–1 but Berenyi can't get the third out to qualify for the victory. It's obvious that his arm is hurting, but I don't think he's told anyone. He has no business pitching. Get some treatment, Bruce. With two outs in the fifth, five consecutive batters get on: walk, single, walk, single, walk. Davey waits and hopes with the rest of us, but after the third walk, he gives up and relieves his pitcher.

They score three runs in the inning, we get one more, then they score two off Sisk. Finally, in the seventh, Staub drives in Rafael Santana with a pinch double. Even in a wild game, we know when a hit has finally done the trick. This is the hit—the game-winner, if you will, even though Kelvin Chapman gets the official GWRBI for a single in the first.

Davey congratulates Staub after the game, and Rusty replies, "Yeah, we kept pounding the nails in the coffin, but they kept trying to push out."

So long, Pittsburgh. I know you're listed at the top of the list of "livable American cities." You're still at the bottom of *playable* American cities.

GAME 8—Mets 10
Pirates 6

APRIL 19—PHILADELPHIA

About fifteen Mets showed up yesterday, Thursday, for an optional workout on the off day in Philadelphia. I took extra batting practice. If I were in a good groove, I might have taken in a movie instead. An optional workout is just that: an opportunity for guys who feel they need to work on this or that—usually hitting.

George Steinbrenner has made a big deal, or so the reporters say, of an optional workout to which only a handful of his Yankee players came. George said the showing was an insult to Yogi Berra, the manager. Hell, it was the team's first week back in the city after opening on the road! Players are just getting settled in, setting up accounts, maybe even locating apartments (I know one itinerant Met who hasn't found a place yet; my couch won't work for the whole season). Steinbrenner is, once again, way off base. Without taking a poll, I'll bet there's not one Met who would rather be performing in Yankee pinstripes. On the other hand . . .

"He muscled that pitch over the infield"—that's the phrase announcers use to describe a soft line drive on an inside pitch that the hitter can't hit with the sweet spot. The leverage of the bat isn't of much use; the muscled liner is the best we can do. That's the swing by Hernandez that wins tonight's game against the Phillies.

Steve Carlton and Gooden are out of the game; Carlton with seven, Dwight with eight scoreless innings. I'm up in the ninth inning. Wally Backman, who has singled as the pinch hitter for Doc, is on second after a sacrifice bunt. With the count 1-and-2, Don Carman throws me a fastball that rides in on my hands. I muscle the ball over the first baseman. A hitter, at least this one, can take as much pleasure in such a hit as in a homer—not just because it wins the game, but because it's the best that can be done with that particular pitch. I hit the pitcher's pitch. The swing might be a much better piece of hitting, technically, than a homer off the hanging curve right over the plate.

GAME 9—Mets 1
Phillies 0

APRIL 20

"You blew it, Terry," is all I can say to Terry Tata, the umpire at first who calls Juan Samuel safe in the fourth inning. I'm not usually so blunt, but Samuel was out by half a step on the relay from second base on the double play. It should have been the third out of the inning. Instead, the next hitter, Jeff Stone, hits a three-run homer. We never recover.

During batting practice, Stone came up to me, seeking strategies against left-handed pitching. He's a nice kid; we talked about the subject, a favorite of mine. Then he goes 3-for-4 in the game, 2 homers, 5 RBIs. All against Lynch, who's a right-hander.

The Philly starter, John Denny, is one of the more deceiving pitchers in the league. It appears he could throw the ball through a brick wall, but he's not really that fast. In fact, his sinker appears to slow down as it reaches the strike zone. I assume this is impossible, but so it appears. In addition, the pitch sinks "late"—thus I hit ground balls in two of my first three tries. In the eighth, I move up a little in the box, hoping to catch the ball before it sinks. I succeed, rifling a line drive to right field. Fun and games at the plate. There's no comparison, for me, between fielding and hitting: Fielding is all instincts and reflexes; hitting is the real challenge, because talent is not enough.

A three-run rally for the Mets in the ninth falls short, but it's a good try. A good sign.

GAME 10—Phillies 7
Mets 6

APRIL 21

Now it's in all the papers about how I helped Jeff Stone hit two homers and defeat my own team. Lynch, the victim of those homers, chides me at lunch.

"Benedict Arnold!"

I suppose he's kidding, although he isn't interested in my explanation that Stone was seeking aid against left-handers.

Jeff, we don't usually announce these tutorials to the press.

Today's game picks up where we left off yesterday afternoon. I had feared coming into Philadelphia that we were catching this team at the wrong time. A good club, they had won only one game. They're due to break out. Gooden was able to forestall the inevitable in the first game of the series, but the rest of the staff is swept away. Darling is the victim today. About half of us still have a bug, and Ronnie is pitching with a fever. He's creamed. Sisk is creamed, again, and I'm worried about him now.

Our play in the field hurts both pitchers. Mookie drops a fly ball by Tim Corcoran after a long sprint, and two runs score. Then Corcoran scores on an error by Gardenhire. Ray Knight fumbles a double-play ball.

I believe it can be safely said that the bloom is off the season. Now we're like everyone else.

For the record in this year of the Rose, I collect hit No. 1,500, a single in the fourth inning. I wanted a hard hit for the occasion, but it's a blooper. I wanted to do it in St. Louis, where we play tomorrow night, but I wasn't going to go hitless today just for that "revenge." The ball is retrieved and I'll give it to Bob Bauman, the trainer emeritus in St. Louis who has made beautiful trophies of other balls I consider important in my career.

Leaving the hotel for the flight west, we're besieged by autograph hounds. This is unusual on the road, but it was clear all weekend that a lot of Met fans had come down the turnpike for the games. I hope they keep to themselves what they saw today.

GAME 11—Phillies 10
Mets 6

APRIL 22—ST. LOUIS

Three a.m. Thigh throbbing, I wake up in the hotel and I blame Kent Tekulve, who hit me with a pitch in the ninth yesterday in Philly. I hobble down the hall to the ice machine and wrap up a cold pack and don't get much sleep the rest of the night.

Ten a.m. Wide awake, I might as well read about the world according to Mike Lupica and the boys—the New York press. Some players pore all over the New York papers every day; stories, columns, and tidbits. Not me. I just hunt and peck. I played in the game; I know what happened. Just the facts, ma'am, is all I'm interested in. Therefore I usually stick with the box scores and the wire-service reports on the other games. *U.S.A. Today* is perfect for this purpose. Lupica's column in the *Daily News* is the only one I read with any regularity. His judgments are well-considered, for the most part.

Sports journalism isn't written for the professional athlete. It's written for the average fan—and the writers' own gratification. In effect, the beat writers who follow the team daily serve as a second set of "men in blue"—at least in New York, where the sports headline on the back page of the two tabloids (CAN THEY BE THIS BAD???) probably sells as many papers as the screaming headline on the front page.

We play the games and the umps on the field call us safe or out. The umps in the newspapers and on TV go a step further: They label us good or bad, worthy or disgraceful. Their opinions don't interest me. That's why I don't read the men in blue.

Until this year. Because I'm working on this book, and because it's only through the press that most of the fans get a picture of the Mets, I'll have to pay more attention in 1985 to what they write. If I believe they're getting it wrong, I'll report on the reporters.

Some of the players hang out with writers and broadcasters. I never do. It's a mistake. How can a writer be a trusted friend when the ballplayer is, first and foremost, a source?

Do not get me wrong. I have a good working relationship with almost all the New York writers, who have treated me fairly since the day I arrived. If I have a gripe, it's that they went *overboard* with their enthusiastic welcome in 1983. That year, the Mets had little leadership. Foster is too quiet, plus it's tough to be the leader from the outfield. Likewise, it's tough for a pitcher to lead the team, playing every fifth game, so Tom Seaver wasn't a candidate. Hubie Brooks was worried about being traded (with good reason, as it turned out). Rusty is too damn blunt, without diplomacy.

The press decided to make Hernandez the leader. Some reports made it sound as though I was grasping for the team leadership. I wasn't. Now that we're a much better team, with major stars, the campaign is off. I appreciated their respect, but it was embarrassing at times.

At 10:00 a.m. this morning the big story is the gripes of Davey Johnson and the rebuttals from Darling and Sisk. Ah, yes, the season is under way for real now. Johnson points out that Darling is relying too much on his fastball; he isn't happy that Sisk isn't happy about not being used in short relief.

Regarding Darling, I agree with Davey: This isn't Triple A. No fastball by itself—not even Dwight's or Nolan Ryan's—is good enough in the major leagues. Other pitches have to set it up. Part of the problem now is that Ronnie and Carter are still getting used to each other. Gary is still learning what Ronnie throws best in different situations.

Regarding Sisk: He's definitely unhappy, not the life of the locker room this year. He's moping, and he insists he has to work more, otherwise his sinking fastball stays up, where it's vulnerable. This is probably true. Another problem Doug has this year is that the batters are waiting until the ump calls that sinker for a strike. Make him bring it up in the strike zone. Last year, they were swinging at pitches that were balls almost in the dirt.

I don't know which comes first with Doug, the moping or the ineffective pitching, but he needs to get straightened out.

Pitching is one of our problems. Hitting is another. We could look at this as good news: We're winning without putting it all together. Imagine what will happen when we do.

Because Berenyi's sore shoulder requires at least another day's rest, Calvin Schiraldi gets his first major-league start tonight and is pleasantly surprised by the six-run lead we stake him to early. Davey gets six good innings out of Schiraldi.

We're victimized by a terrible call in our half of the seventh. The tag on a play at third misses me by a foot, as the TV replay clearly shows, but Eric Gregg calls me out. Fat Albert, as we call him, was lazy on that play—completely out of position. He was behind the bag and Terry Pendleton, the Card third baseman, was inside the baseline; Gregg couldn't see the tag. He should have hustled around for the angle. It's a good thing we win the game.

The Cards score in the seventh when Wilson misplays a single to center. It's funny about him: A good outfielder, Mookie can nevertheless misplay balls with the "best" of them. Why? It's not a lack of concentration. The catcher Gene Tenace came up with the best explanation I've heard: Ballplayers "vapor lock" and this phrase means whatever you judge it to mean. Who knows what happens? We vapor lock, all of us, a few times a year. But for Mookie, this is twice in two games.

But a hustling Strawberry backs up the play to keep the hitter, Vince Coleman, on second base. Then McDowell, who has taken over for Schiraldi, picks off the speedster! Whew! The staff has been wonderful with the pickoffs.

But once again they have trouble closing out the other team. A cause for concern.

GAME 12—Mets 7
Cards 6

APRIL 23

The newest Yankee star, Rickey Henderson, says this morning in all the newspapers, "I don't need no press now, man." We know how you feel, Rickey, but don't paint yourself into a corner. Not in New York. This ain't Oakland. These guys are serious.

Bruce Berenyi is scheduled to pitch tonight with his extra-rested right shoulder. Carter was behind the plate in his last start in Pittsburgh, when Bruce gave up eight walks in five innings (not quite five; he couldn't get that third out). A lot of those pitches were in the dirt, so before the game tonight Carter buckles chest protectors and shin guards all over his frame, arms, and legs, and presents himself to the pitcher in the clubhouse.

"Okay, Bruce, I'm ready!"

It's a good way to loosen Bruce up. He must be concerned after that last outing. It's one thing to get hit hard; it's another entirely not to be able to throw a strike, any strike. So play around with the problem. Have some fun.

Alas, Bruce is gone after two innings. Clearly his shoulder is in bad shape. This hurts. When he's healthy, Bruce is one of the top five fastballers in our league. And how does it feel when a career hinges on an arm that always hurts—as Bruce testifies his always has? That fear would drive me bananas. A hitter does not have an equivalent nightmare.

In the fourth inning, a bogus balk eventually scores Ozzie Smith. Granted, it was a la-de-da move to first by Tom Gorman, who's in for Berenyi, but it was not a balk as the rule is usually interpreted. There's the rub: The balk call is the most subjective, unevenly enforced rule in baseball. The pitcher is supposed to pause one second after his stretch. Few of them do, so few that the pitchers who do pause thereby throw off the hitter's timing.

Rain delays the game for well over an hour, and we play cards and get stiff. The downpour would postpone any game on real grass, but not on the artificial rug in St. Louis—one of many reasons to dislike the stuff.

Astroturf and its derivatives are great for hitters and, perhaps in contradiction, fielders taking ground balls, but the rug is bad for the game.

Those great diving catches you see in replays? Look closely: They're almost always on real grass. Diving on Astroturf takes the skin off from elbow to wrist. Outfielders won't try these catches unless it's absolutely critical. Some of them wear long-sleeved jerseys under their uniforms—even in St. Louis in the summer.

On the rug, infielders don't have to play the ball, or charge for the short hop. We wait for it to come to us with a perfect bounce. The only problem is with the seams, and because we know where they are, we live in fear of them.

This rug in St. Louis has a seam running directly in front of my fielding position at first base. In the first game of the 1982 World Series, the bases were loaded with two out when Ben Ogilvie hit a one-hop bullet at me. The ball hit the seam and skidded into my shin. Error, first baseman: E-3.

Rugs belong on bald heads. They're bad for baseball—especially when one makes us wait a couple of hours to lose.

GAME 13—Cards 8
Mets 3

APRIL 24

We're sitting on four bad games in a row, of which we were fortunate to win one. The prophets of doom in the press are enjoying themselves. I suggest to Bobby Valentine, our third-base coach whose fractured cheek is fine, that perhaps it's time for the first team meeting of the young year. But Bobby reports that Davey doesn't want one. He doesn't panic. He knows we're still half-sick. He knows we were bound to cool off after winning eight of our first nine.

No meeting. We respond with another loss in a day game, and it hurts worse because Gooden is the loser. He now has a career 1–7 record under the sun, with a high ERA. One theory is that the hitters pick up his fastball better in the daylight; this could be true, but many hitters are nevertheless like me. I prefer to play at night. Dwight's record in day games is a fluke.

I find it strange that Davey rests Carter this afternoon, with tomorrow an off day, and starts Clint Hurdle in his first major-league game as a catcher—against the fastest team in the league. Foster, too, is out of the game, after he strains a knee running on the wet rug before the game. So we face their best man, Andujar, with something of a Chinese lineup. However, Danny Heep, playing for George, gets two of our five hits, and Hurdle one of the others.

I have total admiration for Clint Hurdle, Most Valuable Player in Triple A in 1977, *Sports Illustrated* cover boy, productive right fielder in 1980 with Kansas City when they won the pennant. A back injury slowed his career, and he was dropped to the minors with the reputation of being somewhat wild and crazy. Now he's back in the majors as a catcher, a born-again Christian, a helluva nice man. I admire how Clint has straightened out his life and come back to the big leagues. It's one thing to go down and come back up before you're truly established in the majors; many of us have done that. It's much tougher to go back to the minors *after* you're established, and then return to the majors.

Also, Clint is one of the best guys on the bench, always in the game, full of high spirits.

The Cards' first run, in the seventh inning, scores on a single by Van Slyke. Doc's pitch saws off the bat, but these breaks are running against us now. Dwight is lifted for a pinch hitter after giving up another run in the seventh, and McDowell is roughed up for three runs in the eighth.

Five bad games in a row. And, in the seventh inning, my 5,000th career at-bat. It's a 6–3 putout on the scorecard.

Because it's a day game, I have the rare opportunity to take my two older daughters out for dinner. They haven't seen any of the games. Jessi will be twelve tomorrow, and Melissa is five. The little baby, Mary, is just a year old, so she stays at home.

Jessi, the birthday girl, chooses a Japanese restaurant. Melissa is concerned about this Japanese place, remembering her fear from a couple of years ago about a Chinese restaurant. Somehow she had it in her mind then that the Chinese people were going to be different. She was pleasantly surprised to learn they're just like the rest of us. But tonight she has the same concern about these Japanese people she's about to meet. Again we have a lot of fun.

I see myself in this little girl, a spitfire. Energy boiling over. Jessi is more like her mother, quiet and subdued.

I miss the kids.

GAME 14—Cards 5
Mets 1

APRIL 26—NEW YORK CITY

One of the best-pitched ballgames I've ever witnessed, and just what this struggling ballclub needs. Darling is tremendous. You know the phrase about "handcuffing the hitters." These Pirates are bound and gagged. Ronnie strikes out eleven, seven of them looking at the pitch, usually the slow curve. Steve Kemp gets a hat trick, all on called strikes.

We score in six different innings and run Jose DeLeon out of the game. It's our most solid game of the year, and the most important win since the first one. It will shush the press temporarily.

Wally Backman goes 5-for-5. Now is as good a time as any to admit that I misjudged Wally in spring training last year. I didn't think he could hit well enough to play for the Mets. I should know it's impossible to judge a player in that pressurized situation. You're not seeing the real ballplayer. A couple of springs I hit a buck and change (*baseball parlance:* an average under .200; also known as an "interstate average"). But I jumped to conclusions about Wally.

This year he came to camp with the opposite problem: Having made the team and assured of his platooned position at second, along with Kelvin Chapman, Wally was having trouble concentrating. He asked me about it and I told him I had had the same problem for several years. I promised him that the cooler weather would get the adrenaline pumping. It's pumping for Wally tonight.

On Diamondvision, the Mets announce that Dwight will be at the Doubleday bookstore on Fifth Avenue next Monday to autograph his book. Wonder whether they'll do the same next year for me? Doubtful. Doubleday isn't my publisher.

In the fourth inning, the first jet of the day zooms over—almost the first of the year. We've been lucky. For those of you who have never been to Shea Stadium—well, you wouldn't believe it. We're located right under the takeoff pattern for La Guardia airport. With the wrong wind, the planes, dozens of them, thunder directly over the stadium with ear-splitting regularity. I still remember my shock at discovering this when I first played here. Flying I don't mind, but I don't at all like *playing* underneath the

damn planes. I won't say they worry me—but I do have my escape
route planned should a flight falter in midair.

I make light of the subject—sometimes in a game when a plane
forces me to step out of the batter's box, I'll raise my bat, take
aim, and pull the trigger a couple of times—but seriously, why
are 50,000 fans sitting at the end of a runway? I find it strange
that the New York Jets football team, which used to play here,
was named *in honor* of this dangerous situation.

In the sixth, I'm up with the sacks drunk and Chuck Tanner
calls in Al Holland, who just came over from Philadelphia in the
Tekulve deal. Holland used to be a dangerous pitcher with a hard
fastball, but he's lost velocity, and when a one-pitch pitcher loses
that pitch, he's in trouble. Holland is going to have to use his curve
and become a pitcher if he's going to last much longer. Waiting
for him to warm up, I discuss tactics with Staub, who knows as
much about hitting and pitchers as anyone. We agree that Holland
will come right after me with his heat on the first pitch. I lie in
the high weeds and here it comes, right on time, and I drive it
into center for a sacrifice fly.

In the seventh, I run over to the stands for a foul pop-up, out
past the dugout. The ball is out of play, but imagine my surprise
as I turn back to the field and discover Carter standing right by
me—way, way down the line, from his point of view. He grins
and quips, "You're supposed to dive in for that." I grin and quip,
"What are you doing down here, Gary? I thought you had bad
knees."

Frankly, I call this excessive hustle. Gary is not going to help
me on that play, and he's too close to me anyway. We could get
tangled up. But Gary plays this way. You wouldn't want to change
it any more than you would want Mookie Wilson to swing at fewer
bad pitches.

Good hustle: In the ninth, game iced down, rookie John Christensen races a mile in right field for a diving catch near the line.
It helps save Darling's shutout. The kid can't buy a hit and he's
hustling like this in the field. Inspiration for the grizzled veterans.

After those bad games on the road, this has been one to enjoy
playing and watching. Often, it's more thrilling to watch a pitcher
like Darling throw a great game, mixing up his deliveries in the
manner of a Don Sutton, than it is to stand by as a pitcher blows

it by everyone. (Although I hope to watch Gooden blow it by about 250 batters this year.) And I take this game as the sign that Carter and Darling are on the same wavelength regarding pitch selection.

They'll never be on the same wavelength as personalities. Ronnie is cool and diffident. Most of the guys don't pick up the beat of his drummer. He went to Yale and can prove it in his conversation. He wears the ultra-latest clothes. As I said, he's the only guy who lives in Manhattan who doesn't come to the park in Rusty's van. He's sort of a loner. He's my good friend.

Now for the bad news: Bruce Berenyi and Mookie Wilson are both out indefinitely with their sore shoulders. Bruce's situation is frightening. Mookie's is infuriating, because it should never have happened, and I'll tell you why.

In 1984 spring training, coach (and former manager) Frank Howard was working with the outfielders. On one of the very first days of training, he had them throwing full bore. On one of these throws, Mookie hurt his arm. He knew it. It has never been the same and I believe it was wrong to have him—or anyone—throwing 100 percent so early in the spring. Now he has a problem that won't go away and this team is about to pay the price.

GAME 15—Mets 6
Pirates 0

APRIL 27

From the most satisfying win to the most frustrating loss.

Eddie Lynch said at lunch the other day, "Being a major-league pitcher must be the best job in the world. Working every fifth day." I wonder if he still believes that.

Ed gives up no runs, three hits in seven innings, leaves the game for Jesse Orosco with a two-run lead—and Jesse blows it, mainly with a throw into left field trying for a force at third. The worst play of our young season. Instead of runners on first and second, one out, it's one run in, runners at second and third, none out. Jesse gives up two more hits and runs. The Pirates win, 3–2.

In the post-game interviews, Davey says that Lynch said in the dugout that he was "done." Lynch tells the reporters he didn't say anything like that. The clubhouse is deathly quiet, with the reporters moving in their herd from Johnson to Orosco to Lynch.

At least Jesse is talking today. A couple of times last year, he ducked the reporters after a bad game. Mel Stottlemyre, the pitching coach, advised Jesse that if he wanted to share his joy after a good game, he had to share the bitterness after a bad one.

I agree, but it's tough being diplomatic after a game like this. Jesse is disgusted with himself. We all know it. We all *saw* it. He pitched his glove fifteen feet into the air while his bad throw rolled down the line and the Pirate runners kept going.

It's one of those afternoons when it's easy for the players to forget that our endeavor is just a game. Perhaps ironically, "gamer" is the phrase we use for players who want to win as though more than a game is at stake. The Mets have twenty-five gamers. These losses literally thrown away are the most frustrating. We regret the games we blow; we forget the games the other team blew.

After going 4-for-4 at the plate, I dawdle in the shower and the herd is gone by the time I return to my locker. I have the feeling that there's a concerted effort this year to share the wealth regarding interviews. Last year, it took at least forty-five minutes for me to finish the interviews and get a shower. Rusty had to delay the departure of his Manhattan Express to accommodate me. This year, the press doesn't gather round after every game. The city slickers are getting away earlier. Do I miss all the attention? I do not. There will be plenty to go around as the season moves along.

Pirate Program Notes: Their starting pitcher today, Larry McWilliams, has the strangest delivery in baseball. He doesn't use a windup. He just stands with his left foot on the rubber, arm hanging down, ball exposed. Then he urgently jerks his right foot almost up to his thigh, strides, and throws. Pitching from the stretch, he's just as ungainly. Batting, he's the worst in the business. He had good velocity on his pitches last year, but he isn't throwing hard today.

Pirate second baseman Johnny Ray gets his glove on one of my hits, without diving. With a dive he'd have stopped the ball and thrown me out. A sign to me that the Pirates are a team in trouble: players going through the motions.

Tony Pena, on the other hand, is their catcher who doesn't know what that phrase means. He'll try anything. He almost picks me off first base, gunning the ball from his unusual sitting position behind the plate. In fact, I wouldn't have griped if the ump had thumbed me out.

GAME 16—Pirates 3
Mets 2

APRIL 28

I forgot last night—early this morning—to set my clock back for daylight savings, so instead of my normal one-hour lead time, I'm barely awake when Staub pulls up with the van at 9:45 a.m. Beep-beep. It's the concierge calling.

On Sunday mornings only, Rusty provides this special door-to-door service; my place is fairly close to the restaurant, and the traffic is light. The catch is that he drives out extra-early for a Mass held for the players. Although baptized as a Catholic (Dad's religion; Mom is Southern Baptist), I don't go to these services, so I don't usually go with the guys on Sunday. I cab out later. This morning, however, I'll ride with them and try to get a nap on the training table. I'm hung over.

And so wouldn't you know it? On this day when my mouth is so dry I'm forced to chew gum for one of the few times in my career, when I'm eating ice cream for energy (nutritionists might scoff), we play eighteen innings. The longest, most amazing eighteen innings of my life: I'm hitless, but with four walks, two intentional; both teams blow bases-loaded, no-out situations; a total of twenty-seven men are left on base. The Mets go sixteen innings without a run following Straw's grand slam in the first.

Hits for the game:

Winning team, Mets: 6
Losing team, Pirates: 18

Such are the vicissitudes of baseball.

Carter goes 0-for-6 but arguably wins the game in the field: blocking the plate twice to tag out runners; scrambling after a wild pitch and flipping on target to Orosco covering home to nail the runner in the ninth; tumbling into the stands to grab a foul ball in the sixteenth.

In the seventh, Joe Sambito makes his first appearance as a New York Met. He joined us a couple of days ago, after a tryout. Born in Brooklyn, raised in Queens, Joe is happy as heck to be with us—and why not? His career is on the line. He hasn't pitched in a meaningful situation in a couple of years, after an elbow operation while he was with the Astros. Three years ago, he was one of the best in the league. Today. . . .

He's tight, that's obvious. Bill Madlock singles with two out. I ask him at first if Joe is throwing hard. From my vantage, it doesn't appear so.

"No," Madlock agrees.

Sambito goes out for a pinch hitter, and Sisk replaces him in the eighth, giving up two walks but retiring the side. In the ninth he gives up two more walks, and then balks, and Davey has seen enough. When he comes out of the dugout to call for Jesse Orosco, the 35,000 fans hose down the manager, Sisk, and Orosco.

It's an old cliché, but I wish the fans had to perform whatever it is they do for a living in front of 35,000 boobirds, just once. But to hell with it. It goes with the territory.

What a tough situation for Jesse, coming off yesterday's debacle, but he strikes out Ray looking, gets Madlock to pop to third, and tags out Belliard trying to score on the wild pitch.

Also in that inning, a balk is called on *me* by Harry Wendelstedt. Here's what happens: Holding Belliard on first, I take a few steps in toward the plate on a bunt situation, then jump back to take Orosco's throw over. "Balk!" yells Harry. I jerk around and ask, "What do you mean?" He says there's a rule against dekeing out the runner like this. I tell him we had this as a set play in St. Louis for years. Wendelstedt replies that the rules committee has a meeting every year and decides what rules will be strictly enforced, and this year they've decided on this one, among others.

"I know it's stupid," he concludes, "but I have to enforce it."

Well, fine, but they should send out a memorandum with this information. And another memo regarding the "minimum of two minutes between half-innings" regulation. A couple of umps have stopwatches for verification!

The tenth inning is also eventful, with two balls hit to the warning track, but no runs—Hendrick out at the plate on a throw from Hurdle. I know Hendrick from our days in St. Louis, and it doesn't appear to me that he's running all out on the play. George wants out of Pittsburgh, and he's going to have to get tough to make it through this season, already shaping up as a long, losing one for the Pirates. Giving in doesn't make the summer go any faster. *Au contraire.*

Davey is shifting Hurdle and Staub in the outfield, right-left, left-right, depending on the batter, with Staub always playing the opposite field. Rusty doesn't look happy as he jogs back and forth, but he knows the strategy is correct. Hurdle, although not exactly speedy, has to be quicker than Orange, who is, after all, forty-one years old. But on one of the long fly balls in the inning, Rusty runs farther, faster than he has in years to make a great catch down the right field line.

Cecilio Guante is pitching for the Pirates when we load the bases in the twelfth, nobody out. Ray Knight is up, then me. I have a plan against Guante if that winning run is still on third. He's always tough on me, in large measure because his windup is so slow (the slowest in the league) it throws off my timing, but this afternoon I'll choke up on the bat and move up in the box. Knight, however, grounds into a 4-2-3 double play, leaving first base open. They walk me, naturally, to load them again. Irritating. Naturally I figure I'm the one to end the misery on this cool, damp day. I'll save my plan for another game.

As I'm approaching the plate in the fifteenth, Diamondvision announces that Yogi has been fired and Billy Martin has taken over the Yankees. I don't usually notice the messages posted on the big screen, but the moan from the fans, a lot of whom are still here, directs my attention. I bounce out. We're on the tread-mill now.

In the eighteenth inning, Tanner has pitcher Rick Rhoden pinch-hit for outfielder Doug Froebel. I don't care whether Rhoden is an excellent hitter, or whether Tanner is making the switch in order to get a right-handed hitter against our left-hander, Tom Gorman. The move isn't showing confidence in your young player. Rhoden makes an out.

In our half of the inning we finally win, in stylish fashion, on a ball right through Thompson's legs at first.

Five hours and twenty-one minutes after taking the field, the Mets leave it, bloodied, not too proud—except for Gorman, who pitched seven scoreless innings—but winners. Rusty "fines" Davey five bucks for all those forced marches in the outfield.

GAME 17—Mets 5
Pirates 4

APRIL 30

Word has spread that Davey, Frank Cashen, and Ed Lynch met for thirty minutes Sunday to discuss the contretemps that came out of the 3–2 loss Saturday, in which Lynch was pulled after telling Davey (or did he?) that he was "done." I don't know who said what. A ballclub is like any (big) family or office. There are going to be misunderstandings and disputes. The difference is that the average family or office doesn't have a crew of reporters hanging around, digging for stuff.

The Mets, cognizant of the problem this year because of the increased media attention from the first day of spring training, hired a PR lady to work with some of the players. She met with Orosco, Sisk, Gooden, Strawberry, maybe a couple of others, coaching them on how to talk to the reporters with diplomacy while watching out for those leading questions.

The media has the idea that we live by the sword, we die by the sword. A couple of times a reporter has said bluntly to me, "You're nothing without us." I say it's more the opposite. Am I supposed to be cheerful when, three minutes after a long, hard game, someone sticks a microphone right in my face and asks what went wrong out there? How do I feel about blowing the ballgame?

Irritated beyond my usual endurance to just such a query several years ago, I snapped, "Hey, man, I couldn't care less."

The reporters and broadcasters pick up this resentment, of course, so they lurk around the clubhouse, especially after a bad loss, feeling and acting unwanted. They get the official post mortem from Davey as he leans on the edge of the desk in his office, then they move down the hall to gang up on the culprits—safety in numbers. Some of them seem to relish the experience; others have compassion. It's no fun for us, but, like the booing, it goes with the territory, and these guys are just doing their jobs. But I resent the ones who relish it.

I feel great at the plate against left-handers, but only fair against righties. I know one reason. The left-handed batters on our team have dug a hole way back in the box during batting practice. My normal stance against right-handers puts my left foot just on the forward edge of that hole. This feels precarious, so I have to move either forward, away from the hole, or backwards into it. I don't like either choice, so I've asked Bobby Valentine to get the ground-keepers to dig a hole for me, just in front of the other one.

One of the guys asked me during BP to point out where I want the hole. This is much better. I don't hit that much better tonight, but one reason is knuckleballer Joe Niekro of the Astros. Nobody relishes hitting the Fred Astaire ball. About all you can do with the pitch is wait until the very last split-second and hope your hands react with the break of the pitch. There won't be time for any conscious decision-making. In the seventh, the hands react well and I lead off with a line-drive single to right. The hit is particularly satisfying because I don't like to lead off an inning; it doesn't leave me time to get my head together. Hurdle singles, then Strawberry swings for the fences on two knucklers. Then he flies out.

I score on Foster's double and the Astro's manager, Bobby Lillis, jerks Niekro. A big mistake in my book. With Heep up and a runner on third, when a sacrifice fly drives in the go-ahead run in a late inning, do you want a knuckler or a conventional pitcher? If I'm managing, I want the knuckler, even if he has given up some hits in the inning. But Lillis did this all last year—pulling Niekro around the seventh inning. I picked up the pattern from the box scores.

My "decision" to leave in Niekro looks good when Frank DePino gives up a hard single to Heep, on a 3-and-0 count; good, aggressive play-calling by Davey. The two runs are all Doc needs.

Hurdle plays tonight because Carter is beat up with a variety of strains and bruises; ribs are the latest problem. It's ominous for Gary to be in this shape so early in the season, but it's good to see his substitute, Hurdle, and the others doing the job. Danny Heep, with limited action, has by far the best RBI percentage on the team. And Christensen, a slow starter in the minors, so it figures to be the case up here, finally gets his first hit of the season tonight, and an RBI. We're getting production from the turds (*lingo:* nonstarters; Staub also calls them the F-troops).

After the game, I say to Strawberry, "Darryl, you can't swing for the fences against a knuckleballer when we're behind 1–0 in the late innings, with two guys on. Be patient." Something like that. He agrees.

GAME 18—Mets 4

Astros 1

May 1

The Mets are 12–6, tied for first with the Cubs. It's a good start, especially considering that we're not hitting consistently.

Hernandez's stats for April: .309 average, .405 on-base percentage, 12 RBIs, 0 HRs. (I had nine consecutive .300 months from the end of 1979 through 1980. I'm proud of that and would like to better it. April 1985 makes three in a row now, carrying over from last year.)

Tonight is not an acceptable start for the new month. For Doug Sisk, it's awful. The Astros bomb him for five hits and five runs in the ninth inning. The clock is ticking for Doug. He has lost the good sinking fastball. You know even before he gets in the game that Doug is in trouble: He doesn't walk directly to the mound from the bullpen anymore. Instead, he goes around under the stands and comes out from the dugout. I don't believe he wants to subject himself to the booing of the fans for that extra time it takes to cross right field. The booing is getting to him; perfectly understandable—but getting rattled is the kiss of death for a pitcher or a hitter. Nor does his evasive route get him away from two animals tonight, who sneak down from the upper reaches to stand at the railing by our dugout and scream at him the entire inning. Blasphemy like you've never heard. I don't know how I would react to this degree of widespread abuse. I've never experienced it.

GAME 19—Astros 10

Mets 3

MAY 3—CINCINNATI

Hats off to Ed Lynch, who, it can now be revealed, was the itinerant ballplayer bedding down on my couch for the first weeks of the season. Eddie has found a furnished place on Second Avenue. Also, he pitches a fine game tonight in Cincinnati, his first complete game in seventy-three starts, just the second in his four-plus years in the majors.

Kudos also for Len Dykstra, the kid just up from our Triple-A team, Tidewater, to fill in for Mookie Wilson. Dykstra homers in his second big league at-bat, off Mario Soto. What a pistol Dykstra is. One of these days he'll swallow his huge chaw in a moment of sheer joy. I wouldn't yet hazard a judgment on his career in the majors, but he looks good now.

And why not a tip of the cap to Hernandez, who finally hits a homer—in the first inning, a screaming shot over the right-center field wall. No, I wasn't worried that it hadn't happened for the first nineteen games, but I was *aware*. A friendly usher at Shea made sure I was on the last homestand. "Hey, Keith," he shouted at me during batting practice, "when you gonna hit your first homer?" He meant well, but it pissed me off. I don't go to the plate looking for homers. If I get a pitch I can drive, I try to do so. If it goes over the wall, terrific. Certainly on this team, with three bona-fide sluggers right behind me, thirty homers aren't required from me. My job is RBIs and a high on-base percentage.

This evening, I even try a bunt. Some fans might think I look foolish, but in the seventh inning with a 6–3 lead and nobody on, one out—why not? Esasky is playing back on the outfield "grass" down the third-base line, so if I lay the ball down fair, I walk to first. Plus, the attempt, if it goes foul, draws Esasky in a little, opening up the hole between short and third. Plus, I've always had trouble with Joe Price, who's on the mound. I wouldn't consider a bunt with a pitcher I hit well.

I foul it off.

GAME 20—Mets 9
Reds 4

MAY 4

Kentucky Derby Day, and before today's nationally televised base-ball game we draw horses out of a hat. Ron Gardenhire picks one of the favorites. Gardie has had trouble with his hamstrings throughout his career, and this unfortunate tendency is a target for ridicule. His nickname is Hammie. Leave it to Eddie Lynch to holler, "Forget that horse, he'll pull a hammie down the back-stretch!"

This is a harsh clubhouse, and a harsh clubhouse is a happy clubhouse, in my experience. The reason is simple: We're not going to joke with a player we're not comfortable with.

On this subject of legs: There's nothing worse for them than playing a day game after a night game. Any everyday player will agree. The legs are flat; hitting and fielding are slowed down. I'm not at that senior-veteran stage of my career when the manager will sit me down for the day game (a privilege merited by the thirty-six-year-old Foster), but I'm not ready for it like I was ten years ago.

On one list I've seen of the physical demands of various sports, baseball is almost on the bottom, ahead of only golf. On another list that includes "mental and other demands," baseball is way up, ahead of tennis, even with soccer. "Way up" is certainly where baseball should be, or even ahead of other sports, for this reason: We play almost every day for over seven months, including spring training. The mind never gets a break.

A baseball season is demanding on the legs and everything else. My legs are strong, and playing baseball wears them out: That's my evidence.

So why do the Reds feel so great this afternoon? A major league blowout is what we call the final score. These we accept with aplomb. They happen.

"Turn the page," in the immortal words of Jim Kaat.

"Shut up and deal," somebody else said.

The distressing point about this blowout is Sisk's performance. I'll never forget the look on his face after the pitch Esasky hits for a grand-slam homer. Pure devastation. Doug has hit rock bottom. Sometimes I feel my duty is to go to the mound and say something, anything, to a battered pitcher. In this instance, I know any encouragement would be superfluous. Doug may be on his way to Tidewater.

Roger McDowell starts the game, and we've learned a lesson, I believe. He's not a starting pitcher. He's thin and he's not strong; Roger tires after five innings. Put him in the bullpen as our right-handed short man.

"Look at Ron Guidry," you reply. "He's about the same build as McDowell and he's a great starter for the Yankees."

I don't know about Guidry. All I know is what I see regarding

McDowell. With Sisk on the ropes, Roger's our man in the bullpen from the right side.

After the game, Hernandez, Hurdle, Staub, and Charlie Samuels, the Mets clubhouse man, enjoy dinner at Johnny Bench's restaurant, "The Precinct." I, for one, am turning the pages and dealing as fast as I can. I get drunk. When I get drunk, I get loud. After the meal, our party proceeds upstairs to the bar, where Eddie Lynch joins us and reports on a conversation he has just overheard between a middle-aged man and woman who must have been seated next to the Met quartet at dinner. Lynch heard the lady complain, "I don't have to listen to that! I don't care if he is Keith Hernandez!"

GAME 21—Reds 14
Mets 2

MAY 5

A baseball talent like Dwight Gooden comes along once in a generation. Today he doesn't have his good stuff, but he still strikes out nine in seven innings, gives up seven hits, three walks, two runs. In a day game. The benefit to a ballclub of having a Doctor on the staff cannot be measured.

Alas, this is my worst game of the year, when my gold glove turns to iron pyrite. Those two runs besmirching Dwight's record should be charged to me. If I thought it would do any good, I would go to the scorer to get the "hit" changed to an error. I've done that before on a bad ruling, with results, but Cincy has always had generous scoring for the hitters; nothing will change.

With runners on first and second, Ron Oester hits a ground ball right behind the bag at first. It rolls like a bowling ball, no bounces, so my first thought is "foul ball, it hit Oester's foot in the batter's box." But no call is made, so I move to the ball and prepare for a backhanded stop. At the last moment, I change my mind and rotate my mitt back to the standard position for a straightforward scoop—too late. The ball rolls up my arm. Bases loaded. And they score this a hit! Absurd.

Dwight bears down, as is his habit, and strikes out Foley for the second out, but Van Gorder hits an 0–2 pitch for a ground-rule double, scoring the two runs. If I had fielded Oester's bowling ball, Doc gets out of the inning with the K of Foley. I tell Dwight as we trot into the dugout to blame those runs on me. He'll have none of it.

We're lucky on the ground-rule double. The Reds can blame their artificial turf. During the day, when the surface is hotter, balls bounce 10–15 feet higher—over the wall, in this instance, so the runners can advance only two bases. At night, that ball is off the fence, the third runner scores and the game is tied, 3–3.

If we're real lucky this year, we'll avoid games in the Astroturf stadiums on 100-degree days in August. Stories about the heat on turf are a dime a dozen, but they're all true! In St. Louis, where it gets up to 140 degrees on the surface, metal spikes have singed feet. Some players wear insulation pads in their shoes. I soaked my feet and shoes in ice water between innings. It's unreal.

But let's not worry about that already. It's barely May. We have other troubles. Kelvin Chapman continues to struggle—two errors today. The platooning of Kelvin and Wally Backman at second base worked fine last year; Kelvin was a great clutch hitter against left-handed pitching. He doesn't look like the same player in 1985. He's lost confidence on his throw to first. At the plate, he's swinging up on the high pitches; last year he was driving that ball with a level swing. I told him during spring training about the bad habit he was developing; Rusty has been hounding him. He's working on corrections, but he needs some kind of break, quickly, to get his confidence back.

Ray Knight, platooned at third against left-handers, can't get untracked, either. The other day he told me that he can't find a rhythm playing every third or fourth day, and that's as often as we face left-handers; Howard Johnson, facing the right-handers, gets more playing time. Ray said he might talk to Davey. There's no player more willing to sacrifice for his team than Knight, but Ray has been an everyday player for half a dozen years. His discomfort shows how difficult it is to make the transition to being a platoon player. The best platooners are the players who have known nothing else, like Gary Roenicke and John Lowenstein with the Orioles.

HoJo isn't hitting consistently, either, even with steadier work, so I would seriously consider giving Knight the job at third, day in, day out. We know he can hit, with a career average of .280. Taking over third base in Cincinnati after Rose went to Philadelphia, in 1979, he hit well over .300.

But we're still on our shakedown cruise. These personnel questions at second and third aren't the major concern. What's scary are the late innings we're enduring, game after game, it seems. This afternoon is no exception.

Orosco takes over for Gooden in the eighth, because Dwight has thrown a lot of pitches. We're clinging to a 3–2 lead. Gardenhire at shortstop lets a ball roll between his legs, but on the Reds' sacrifice attempt, I nail the runner at second.

It's true that I'm the best at this play, a throwback to my sprint-out pass days as a high school quarterback. Being left-handed is a great advantage here, because I scoop and throw in one motion. Also, I come down the line farther than the other first basemen and this might intimidate some batters, who know they have to bunt perfectly, right down the third-base line, or I'll throw out the runner at second. The danger is that the batter will hit away and ram one down my throat. I've never been hit, however, or even close to it. Anyway, I'm ready with precautionary measures. I get my glove directly in front of my face, and with my cup in front of my balls, I'm protected where it counts. He can have the rest of me.

After the putout at second, Jesse throws a wild pitch to advance a runner there anyway. Then he walks Tony Perez. Rose hits a ball to short center, but Dykstra breaks back. Realizing his mistake, he rushes in and makes a diving catch, and has the burn on his forearm to show for it.

We're living too dangerously.

After the game, I enter Davey Johnson's office and open the conversation this way: "Sid has struck out seventeen in Tidewater, right?" I'm referring to Sid Fernandez, the big left-hander who was going to be one of our five starters but had a terrible spring and wasn't brought north.

Davey replies that Sid needs a couple of more starts. I persist and suggest that we bring up Sid and use Roger McDowell as the short- or middle-relief man from the right side. Roger's a rookie, he didn't pitch at all last year because of an arm injury, and he's not physically strong. But for three or four innings, he's nasty. And he has guts. That's the definition of a good reliever.

Davey says, "It's a thought. I'll think about it."

I wouldn't approach many managers with such an outright suggestion, but Davey is remarkably open. He'll have a beer with the guys. He's of our ball-playing generation. At forty-two, he's only a year older than Rusty. The players don't feel that there's any gap between Davey's understanding of the game and ours. He's a modern ballplayer, therefore a modern manager.

GAME 22—Mets 3
Reds 2

MAY 6—NEW YORK CITY

An off day that may prove to be one of the more important days of the year. Sisk is gone. Sent down. Davey said part of the reason was to get him away from the crowds at Shea.

Carter goes out to the stadium for work on his cracked rib, left knee (hit by a foul ball Sunday), and sprained ankle (trying to protect his ribs, he didn't slide going into second base in Cincinnati, and so jammed the ankle with the sudden stop). I don't know how much more he can take. The training room looks like an NFL facility when Carter is in for his pre-game wrapping: ribs, ankle, left leg from mid-thigh to mid-calf.

Also, Dr. Parkes is looking at Mookie and Bruce Berenyi today, determining the status of their right shoulders. I fear that Mookie is going under the knife. Management is casting about for a veteran replacement. After yesterday's game in Cincinnati, Bobby Valentine asked me about Garry Maddox. He's available from Philadelphia for almost nothing, in terms of giving up players, but he carries a heavy salary. I say, "Do it." Maddox is a class act. His best days are behind him but he can play center field, and the change might do wonders for his bat. Instances are legion in which a veteran has been traded and immediately helped a club with his rejuvenated attitude. In football, L.A. Raider boss Al Davis practically has a policy of finding these players and getting them to produce.

The fact that Frank Cashen is even considering acquiring Maddox's salary tells me that the Met owners, Nelson Doubleday, Fred Wilpon, and company, want a winner this year and are willing to spend major money to get it.

Also, pitcher Joe Price of the Reds is available. He's always been bad news for me, but I think our own Sid Fernandez will get his chance soon.

Changes are coming, that's for sure. Also after yesterday's

game, Cashen came over to my locker, bow tie undone (he wears only bow ties, to my knowledge), shirt rumpled—distracted, in a word. We spoke for a minute at most, small talk, nothing about the personnel, then he sat down on the stool next to mine, assumed the position of The Thinker, began rubbing his forehead and didn't say a word for at least five minutes. It may have been much more. The wheels were spinning.

As the general manager of the Mets, Frank is the boss. Davey runs the show on the field, but the general manager is responsible for personnel decisions. Yesterday in the clubhouse, all the Mets honored Cashen's personal space with a careful margin. We circled around him, wondering what's up.

These injuries and platooning problems and sub-par performances are troublesome, but they're not critical—yet. It would be worse if this were July. We have time to get organized. We have depth of talent. Circle the wagons.

On his departure for Tidewater, Sisk made some remark, reported in the press, about how yet another pitching coach will get a crack at him. That complaint reverberates with many ballplayers.

Specifically, myself.

1975. I was the heir-apparent first baseman in St. Louis after hitting .351 in Tulsa the year before. The Cards had traded Joe Torre.

After a good spring I got off to a terrible start, hitting .230 after two weeks of the season. Harry "The Hat" Walker was working with the Card hitters, and for two weeks he coached me every day on hitting to the opposite field. That's how he hit; that's how he thought everyone should. But I had grown up hitting the ball where it was pitched: outside to left, inside to right. Dad threw thousands of pitches to me and made certain I hit to all fields. Now I was being told to hit everything to left. Walker's coaching, well-meaning as it was, set me back. It amazes me to realize how difficult it was to break the habits created by just two weeks of coaching by Harry "The Hat." It was three or four years before I was really comfortable pulling the ball again.

Red Schoendienst benched me, as he should have. Then I was sent down to Tulsa, and Ken Boyer, the manager there, worked with me all summer on pulling the ball. Boyer was the right man at the right time in my life. There have been several. I don't know where I would be now without them.

In June, playing in Tulsa and hitting well again, I blasted Red, Harry Walker, and Bing Devine, the general manager, in the newspaper, asserting that they hadn't given me a chance, that they were afraid of losing their jobs. Soon after that, Boyer came to my room in the motel in Denver and told me Devine was on the telephone. Bing yelled at me. I yelled back at him. My emotions occasionally defeat me now; they often got the better of me back then. I was hungry to play baseball in the big leagues.

I asked him if I had received a fair chance. He admitted I had not.

After the yelling, we had a worthwhile conversation. I admire him for that. In the end, he asked me to come straight to him, not the press, if I had a problem in the future.

Now I wonder what would have happened if they had kept me on the big team—working with Harry Walker on hitting everything to left field. Back in Tulsa, working with Ken Boyer, I hit .330 and lost the Triple A batting title on the last day of the season.

Being shipped to the minors is a blow to the ego and a confidence-crusher: You haven't made it in the majors. Some players respond to the challenge; others can't get it together.

In Sisk's case, I'm concerned that his main problem is the proverbial "tender elbow" that plagues so many pitchers, and which Doug first encountered last year. The elbow may be affecting his motion and thereby taking that sinking action out of his fastball. Carter says that even when the pitch is low in the strike zone, it's not sinking.

If Doug's problem is an injury, how will throwing at Tidewater do any good? He insists that the elbow is fine, but many pitchers don't want to admit to having arm problems.

MAY 7

I'm amazed by the report that Mookie is greatly improved and should start soon. I thought he was in real trouble—therefore we were in real trouble. I've always believed that Mookie is the most important player on the Mets, pitchers (Doc) aside. He's the catalyst.

I'm not so amazed that Carter, beat up as he is, hits a grand slam tonight off Bruce Sutter of the Braves. The "Gang of Four" the Mets traded for Gary is doing fine in Montreal, Hubie Brooks especially, but I'll still take Carter. He has hit four game-winning homers in twenty-three games, three of them in late or extra innings.

Wasn't I just wondering whether Ray Knight should be given the third-base job? Tonight, Howard Johnson beats out a beautiful drag bunt in the fourth, then slams his first homer of the year in the sixth off Braves starter Steve Bedrosian. Bedrosian was a reliever last year, and the word is that he tires by the middle innings. He does. I'm up after HoJo's homer and hit the ball to the wall in left center—for an out. The previous time at bat I drove it to the wall down the left field line, but foul. Usually such close ones don't make me angry. Tonight I'm pissed, with good reason.

I get two dozen bats in a shipment, and they last several months. This year, about half of my first batch felt light. I sifted through them and selected the heavier ones. But as the stock wore down, the lighter-feeling bats were all I had left, and I'd spend fifteen minutes trying to find one that felt at least decent. I can't remember feeling so strangely about a set of bats. I should have ordered a new batch immediately, but I didn't.

In batting practice before the last couple of games, the bat stung in my hands, even on a solid hit. Good contact that feels like it was hit on the hands is a sure sign of horseshit wood. This drive to the wall in the sixth inning is the last straw. That ball should have been out of here. I semi-storm into the clubhouse and tell Charlie Samuels that my bats are bad—too light. His Royal Figness gets pissed. "Fig" is our nickname for Charlie, in honor of his figlike body. When he gets angry and puffed up, I elevate my teasing accordingly. Your Royal Figness, these bats are too light. He agrees to weigh them.

In the seventh inning, when Atlanta manager Eddie Haas lifts Bedrosian for a pinch hitter in a possible sacrifice situation, game tied 1–1, Bedrosian throws his batting helmet and storms out of the dugout. I witness the scene from my fielding position, and I rather agree with Bedrosian. Let him bunt. Then Haas compounds his initial error with another one: using Chris Chambliss as the pinch hitter. I say wait until there's a runner in scoring position to use Chambliss, one of the best clutch hitters in the game. Chambliss strikes out.

In our half of the seventh, Strawberry, who has stolen second, runs right into the tag on a ground ball to the third baseman. The crowd grumbles, but these mistakes happen. Vapor lock.

Another great game for Darling. With nobody out in the eighth and the go-ahead run on second, game tied 1–1, he gets Dale Murphy on a weak fly to right, strikes out Bob Horner looking at an inside fastball at the knees, then paralyzes Terry Harper with a slow curve. Not bad, huh?

Nevertheless, Davey pulls him in the eighth for a pinch hitter with the score tied at one. We can feel it on the bench, and somebody says it aloud: "Let's get this one for Ronnie. He's pitched his ass off." If we don't score it's yet another no-decision.

And for the first time I recall, Ronnie doesn't wait out the game on the bench. He heads immediately for the clubhouse.

Mookie bats for him and walks, then Wally is safe on the pitcher's error and HoJo sacrifices the runners to second and third. I'm intentionally passed for the seventh time this year. It's a little frustrating because these are RBI opportunities lost, but when Carter establishes a steady hitting rhythm, they won't do it as much. But Bruce Sutter might; I've always hit him well. Under the circumstances, the pass is the right move—until Gary hits the grand slam.

Again we have trouble holding the lead in the ninth, but what a strikeout by Orosco on Dale Murphy, with two men on. Then Wally makes a good running catch of a blooper for the final out.

Hits for the game:

Winning team, Mets: 6
Losing team, Atlanta: 14

Such are the vicissitudes of baseball—for the second time this season. As a team we're hitting about .225. But have posted a 15–8 record. The Amazin' Mets.

I tell Ronnie I'm happy he gets the deserved victory, and he replies, "Me, too. It's okay if I pitch well and get a no-decision and we win, but the win is nice." How can a pitcher not be concerned about his record? That's what salaries are based on. Darling also admits he went straight into the clubhouse tonight to try to change his "no-decision" luck—and it worked.

Rusty has heard about my discussion with Charlie Samuels regarding the bats, and he assures me in the clubhouse that my bats are fine. Sometimes the ball just doesn't go out, he adds. Rusty is afraid I'm psyching myself about these bats—a subject on which he is the league's leading expert. Thoughtful and full of concern, that's Rusty. The Mets' surrogate father.

But I'm right this time. Charlie reports that about half of the remaining stock weigh a mere 30 ounces. Hell, nobody swings 30. Mookie swings our lightest bat, 31 ounces. Carter, Foster, and Strawberry usually swing 33. Foster's bat used to be much heavier. Dave Parker at one time swung a 38-ounce bat. The biggest I've heard of was Bobby Bonds' prehistoric club: 37 inches, 38 ounces.

I swing 32½. Charlie will immediately order another shipment from Louisville and tell them to get it right. He's amazed and says he'll never doubt me again. Well, I wouldn't go that far, Fig. Every good hitter knows bats.

For major leaguers the rule of thumb for a bat is that the length in inches shouldn't exceed the weight in ounces by more than two. Therefore, my 34½-inch bat should weigh at least 32½ ounces. My usual weight is at the lower limit to begin with. Anything less and the wood is weak; bad timber.

GAME 23—Mets 5
Braves 3

MAY 8

Key words. Every year the team has a key word. Last year it was "beech," Junior Ortiz's pronunciation of "bitch." Ortiz is a catcher now with the Pirates.

The word for 1985 has finally been picked: "Dickhead," compliments of Rusty.

Team songs. Every year the team has a team song. Last year it was "Ghostbusters." This year we've chosen "The Curley Shuffle."

You wonder why. Lynch, the Rodney Dangerfield of our mound staff because he doesn't get much respect, has a shutout going into the ninth inning tonight against Atlanta. The crowd is on its feet, rooting for him. While I'm throwing balls to the infielders, Eddie shouts, "Mex!" and points out to Diamondvision. There are the Three Stooges, screwing around in a video montage from their movies. The music is "The Curley Shuffle."

Eddie is grinning while he completes his warm-up pitches. I

know now he'll get his shutout. The Braves go meekly, one-two-three. The 20,000 fans go wild; so does the team, because this is the first shutout in Eddie's career. Nobody deserves it more than Lynch, who's twenty-nine years old and didn't even have a spot on the starting staff at the beginning of spring training. But no one worked harder, and he made the starting rotation.

So "The Curley Shuffle" becomes our team song. We ask Jay Horwitz, the Mets' PR man, to be certain the slapstick video plays before one of the late innings in every game.

And I hit my first homer of the year at Shea. Less than two years ago, I hit my first homer as a Met in the stadium. John Stuper was the pitcher for the Cardinals, and the crowd—a good crowd—kept cheering after I disappeared into the dugout. Rusty told me to take a curtain call. I said I wasn't going to. That's showing up the pitcher, in my opinion; I didn't know the fans in New York expected it. I guess they started what has become the tradition around the league.

Rusty explained, "This is New York. You're on stage. Besides, we can't finish the game until you do it." So I stepped out for the bow, but I'm still not comfortable with the custom. That said, I'll admit that homers are great for the ego; so is the cheering, and everybody loves to be stroked. And for whatever reason, the fans at Shea have stroked me from my first day on the job.

After my homer, I'm walked three times in a row; in the third inning, leading off. I needle Carter later, "Gary, they're walking me even leading off, to get to you."

They're also walking me because I have a fine eye for the strike zone. I figure this asset at the plate is good for maybe thirty points in the batting average. I can thank Dad for those points. After every one of the thousands of pitches he threw to me as a kid, he told me where it was, if there was any question at all. Outside, Keith. On the corner, too close to take with two strikes. On the corner but low. Just high. The importance of the strike zone was drilled into me. *Drilled in.* His pitches were left-handed, too, so no wonder I'm comfortable at the plate against left-handers.

Wilson's notoriously bad eye might cost him thirty points—except that he has to be aggressive at the plate, hacking at some bad pitches. Take away that go-for-broke free-swinging style and he wouldn't be Mookie. And he's back in the starting lineup tonight, after missing nine games. We have to have him. We were 6–3 in his absence, but I wouldn't want to try it for a season.

GAME 24—Mets 4
Braves 0

MAY 9

In the stands tonight is Shirley MacLaine. Growing up, I loved her! She's sitting two rows behind me for this Thursday-evening performance on Broadway of *Big River*. Also in the theater is Ruth Warrick, Orson Welles' first wife in *Citizen Kane*, and a star in the soap opera *All My Children*.

This will be my last night on the town for awhile. So far, the season has been a vacation: Mondays and Thursdays off. The real season starts tomorrow: sixty-three games (including a double-header) in the sixty-six days remaining before the All-Star break. Two of the four off days are West Coast travel days. The third requires a flight to Chicago. The fourth is an exhibition game against Tidewater in Virginia (or, in my case, a player rep's meeting in Chicago). In other words, no real days off until July 15— if then, depending on whether I make the National League squad.

But I look forward to the new pace, for two reasons. One, we can finally get into a hitting groove. Too many days off hurt a hitter's rhythm. Two, we get away from the day games, scheduled because of cool weather. I'm on record as favoring night games, even though they're supposed to be detrimental to the hitters. The stars come out at night, as Lou Brock has pointed out.

The newspapers this week are full of speculation about drugs and baseball. The Pittsburgh grand jury is about to announce some indictments, and they could be bad for the game. Our new commissioner, Peter Ueberroth, has announced a plan for mandatory drug testing for all employees of organized baseball—except the players, who have a separate union agreement. Ueberroth is pressuring the players' union to accept mandatory testing.

For now, no comment. I think Ueberroth is trying to get some leverage in the ongoing contract negotiations between the owners and players. It's contract time and the player reps will authorize a strike at our meeting in Chicago on May 23.

MAY 10

Back to work with Dwight, who is simply terrific, striking out thirteen and working on a no-hitter until the seventh inning, all before a nearly full house. Before one of the late innings, the PA system belts out the Sinatra version of the "New York, New York" song from the movie of that name. Play resumes and the recording stops—but the crowd keeps singing!

GAME 25—Mets 5
Phillies 0

2. ON THE WAY

MAY 11—NEW YORK CITY

I'm looking like managerial material: Sid Fernandez is back as a starting pitcher, Roger McDowell is in the bullpen. They combine for a one-hitter, striking out thirteen hapless Phillies (nine by Sid in just six innings). In a matter of one month at Tidewater, Sid has developed two new pitches, a change-up and a slider. I think it's a slider. It breaks more sharply than the curve. And he's throwing harder. And he seems to have more pep in him, a little more intensity. At heart, Sid is a teddy bear, and, though he's competitive on the mound, he's capable of getting pouty. Today he's like a tiger. The month in the minors may have accomplished more than improving his mechanics; it may have made him mad and mean. A pitcher has to be mean. It looks like Sid accepted the challenge when he was sent down.

I'll talk to him about living in Manhattan. I'm afraid the 'burbs will bore him to death. He's not the kind of guy who will get out and find something to do—if there is anything to do. In Manhattan, all he has to do is walk out the front door.

Our third shutout in a row. Pitching is carrying this team. The Mets aren't hitting. The Phillies aren't either. But we're winning, so we look good. They're losing, so they look bad. We—players, writers, fans—talk about the importance of the little things and getting the breaks and clutch pitching and hitting, but sometimes I wonder whether the truth isn't more simple. The main difference between the winners and the losers? Winning.

GAME 26—Mets 4
Phillies 0

MAY 12

Good news galore.

Headline on the front page of the sports section of *The Times:* "Drugs Seen as Peril to Game Itself." Keep reading and it's clear the piece is a Ueberroth vehicle. It's also clear that the drug question is going to be a main item for this baseball season.

Strawberry tore ligaments in his thumb yesterday making a diving catch on Ozzie Virgil's line drive, and the prognosis today is not good. Darryl needs surgery. We're not hitting and now we'll be not-hitting with less power.

This is the first real injury of Strawberry's career, and he's afraid. The doctor can operate either tomorrow or next week. Tomorrow, he can connect the original ligament in a relatively straightforward procedure that guarantees almost certain recovery. Waiting a week, however, means a more serious operation, because the torn ligament will have dried and shrunk, making a reconnection more difficult. A graft would be required. Either way, we'll lose the Straw for at least six weeks.

He wants a second opinion.

I talk with him after today's game, urging him to go with the best advice he has: Do it tomorrow. Get it over with, don't jeopardize your career.

His last words are, "I'm thinking. I'm thinking some more."

Then George Foster talks with him.

People who earn a living mainly with their heads have no idea of the athlete's paranoia about his or her body. In too many instances, this body and its talent is just about all we have. Take it away and we founder. And it can be taken away so easily.

In 1971, I passed up college (full rides to Cal Berkeley, Air Force, and Navy) to sign with the Cardinals. I was eighteen years old. On the last day of my first spring-training camp, in 1972, a throw from third base pulled me down the line, right into the runner coming into the bag. The collision broke my forearm. I was out six weeks. After a high school career hitting around .500 (not that unusual for a good schoolboy hitter, playing twice a week), I finished that year of A-ball in St. Petersburg hitting .256. That average was an eye-opener. The bone healed, but it was something else I could worry about. Negative thoughts have always been my worst enemy. Even now I'm surprised how quickly I can lose confidence; back then, I could lose it in a split-second.

In spring training the following year, 1973, I jammed my hand sliding into a base and couldn't lift the bat for a week. I had aggravated an old injury to my wrist, sustained as a kid by pole-vaulting off a dugout on the branch of a eucalyptus tree.

Invited to the big-league camp, I couldn't swing at all. Wearing a protective brace for the first six weeks of the season at Little Rock, Double A, I hit .179. I thought they might send me back to A-ball. I thought my career was finished. The tension was terrible.

With the brace off, it took two months to get my average up to .300. In late July, I went 6-for-8 in a doubleheader and went back to my apartment and figured it out: .300, at last. I collapsed. The strain of raising the average had been too much. Two and a half weeks later, my average was back down to .260. I was spent.

That was when Bob Kennedy, the farm director for the Cardinals, saved my career. He jumped me to Triple A! I joined Tulsa that summer when they were eight games under .500., languishing in third place in the American Association. I hit .333 and drove in thirty-five runs in thirty-three games to help the club in a stretch run. We won the championship against Des Moines; that first championship was as exciting as winning the World Series ten years later. I was not quite twenty years old.

In less than two months, I had gone from despair—and that's not exaggerating—to cockiness. Just this suddenly, I knew I could hit professional pitching. In the ninth inning of the second game against Des Moines, I hit a two-out, two-run homer off a slider on a full count against a left-hander to win the game. That hit helped turn my career around.

Then the following spring I tore cartilage in my right knee in a collision at first base, and lost six weeks to surgery. If I had been in my fragile frame of mind of a year or two earlier, I might have collapsed. But I came back to lead the American Association in hitting with .351.

There was no reason why Bob Kennedy should have moved me from Double A while I was in a slump, batting .260, to Triple A. If I had stayed in Little Rock, I would have hit .230. I might have been finished, or at least set back a couple of years. If one of those injuries hadn't healed, I might have been through. If, if, if. Well, so is everyone else's life, full of "ifs." Yes, but what if there's not much else to fall back on, *if?*

Sure Darryl is anxious. He has every right to be. If he weren't, I'd wonder why.

We need comic relief: When home plate ump Freddie Brocklander speeds down the line to cover a play at first base and takes a header fifteen feet from the bag, goes sprawling, the Mets strike up the band in the adjacent dugout and serenade him: "Bring on the dancing bears."

GAME 27—Mets 3
Phillies 2

MAY 13—ATLANTA

We flew commercial late yesterday afternoon to Atlanta, following the game with the Phillies. Ninety percent of our flights, perhaps more, are charters, but commercial isn't bad, especially now that the team buys up the entire right side of the airplane, allowing three tickets for every two players. This way we don't have to talk baseball with a fan; the seat in the middle of the row is empty. Management and the starting lineup merit first class. On the big 747s or DC-10s, which we might fly to the West Coast, all or almost all of the team fits into first or ambassador class.

I gripe about the travel, but it doesn't sound too bad, does it? Hell, I even spring for a suite in most of the hotels. The team pays for the double rate. I pick up the difference. It's worth it.

The Mets are shut out tonight for the first time this year—the last major-league team to be so humbled. Victimized is Eddie Lynch, who pitches another superb game.

In fact, the Mets are victimized. This makes the second game we've lost in large measure because of a bad call at first base. (The first was that double-play ball in Philadelphia, Game 10, when the third out at first base was called safe, and a homer followed. Lynch also pitched that game.)

In Atlanta the ball in question is hit into the hole to my right, Backman's left. We both go for it. Wally gets it. I look back at the mound, and Ed's still standing there. Now he reacts and races to cover first and Wally, after waiting a moment, feeds him the ball. On the replay, Dale Murphy is clearly out. But he's called safe, and scores the only run of the game.

In the dugout, Davey tears into me. "You're going over there too many times, Keith! You and Wally have to get together out there." He's pissed and I don't blame him. I should have been on first and the play wouldn't have been close enough for the ump to blow the call. The clubhouse joke is, "Anything up the middle, pitcher covers first." All right, all right. A few times I do range too far.

I've been in a fielding slump all year. We have them; they're just not as glaring as batting slumps, usually. But early last year Steve Sax, the second baseman for the Dodgers, had trouble making the ordinary throw to first base. Our Kelvin Chapman is uncertain in the field this year. I don't have any errors to show for my slump, but maybe that's the proof of the slump. I'm not getting to balls I normally reach. I haven't been picking up the ball well as it comes off the bat, so I haven't been getting a good jump. One play somewhere, I even broke the wrong way. It's one thing for an outfielder to break in or back by mistake, but for an infielder to break left instead of right?!

Have I lost a half-step, or is it just hiding somewhere? I don't know. I've been like this since April. If it goes on for a season, I'll have to accept the fact that I've slowed down a bit. A little tarnish on the golden glove.

I've talked to Bobby Valentine about it. He agrees that I'm a little slow now, and says not to worry. Bobby is what ballplayers need—a positive note. Always positive.

Unbelievably, Braves' manager Eddie Haas now has Chris Chambliss on the bench. I rate Chris above Dale Murphy as a clutch hitter, regardless of Murphy's unbelievable statistics so far this year. I rate Bob Horner above Murphy, too, as a clutch hitter, and Jack Clark, Steve Garvey, and Jose Cruz. Of course, you don't want to face any of them when they're hot. You don't want to face the worst major-league hitter when he's hot.

I appreciate what Haas is doing—telling Gerald Perry that the first-base job is his for the foreseeable future. Davey did the same thing last year with Backman and Chapman at second base, telling them, "It's your job." That's fine when you don't have anyone clearly superior on the bench, as the Mets did not last year at second base. But sitting down Chris Chambliss to develop a new man? As the opposition, I love it, even if Chris is moving on in years.

GAME 28—Braves 1
                 Mets 0

MAY 14

Horsing around during infield practice, I draw a line between Backman and myself and call our manager over. "Right here, Davey?" I ask. He laughs.

Davey Johnson is a good manager for this squad. He comes down on us when he should, he supports us, keeps his perspective. He has a life beyond baseball. Everyone needs a life beyond whatever it is they do for a living; however, leaving the game at the ballpark is easier said than done. Davey's stomach is ruined. He's way past the antacid-tablet stage. And chewing tobacco certainly can't help.

This Mickey Mouse 5:40 start is ridiculous, but Ted Turner's superstation has a basketball playoff game to broadcast later, so we have to face Rich Mahler in impossible conditions. I can barely see the pitch if it's above the waist. Forget reading the seams. On such a day we thank the Lord we don't take the collar (*lingo:* go hitless). My double in the third inning is a triumph.

In the Braves' half of the third, Brad Komminsk is caught stealing with Murphy at the plate, two outs. That's crazy and I say so to the Braves' first-base coach, Bobby Dews, a former minor-league manager. He's mum, but he agrees.

Calvin Schiraldi pitches a good game before he takes a line drive off the toe and goes out of the game. Enter Roger McDowell, and all he does is throw four and two-thirds perfect innings, striking out Murphy and three others. He may be the key man right now.

Where is Roger's wife? She has been along on every prior road trip, I believe. Then a couple of the guys started teasing Roger about outfitting her with an official Mets road uniform. I don't see her around this week.

Two more great plays by HoJo at third base, in the eighth inning. Diving to the right, he stops Komminsk's shot and throws him out, then he races in on Murphy's swinging bunt, gloves it and throws the slugger out, and Murphy isn't slow. Now I'm convinced Howard's reputation for poor fielding in Detroit was somebody's sabotage operation. Howard can field. We hang on to win.

I can't put my finger on it, but this game has lifted the team a notch. I feel some intangible "growth." We were shut out last night, we're playing in the lousiest park in the league (only my opinion, of course), guys are dropping with injuries every day, including our best home-run hitter, but we get clutch pitching, clutch hitting from Carter and Foster, and head to Houston on a high note.

Program Note: Darryl has joined the team. He accepted the wisdom of the quick operation; now it's done and deemed a complete success. Before his arrival, he said he had to be with the team. After this evening's game, however, he asks me to ask Davey if he can go home to California for his month-long recuperation. Absolutely not. "You can't go home and loaf, Darryl," I tell him. "You've got to run every day, with supervision. You've got to keep your head in baseball." I tell him I'd urge Davey *not* to send him home. We'll see what happens.

GAME 29—Mets 3
Braves 1

MAY 15—HOUSTON

Last year, Ron Darling and I were very close friends. This year, it hasn't been quite the same, and I haven't understood why. Tonight on the flight to Houston, I find out.

Background: Several times last winter, Ronnie was featured in the society pages of the papers, most notably for a well-publicized date with Madonna. He likes that acclaim and doesn't hide it, but I suggested to him at various times that he might try to stay out of the gossip columns. You get a label in this business, no matter how misleading, and it sticks. Management remembers. (Look who's calling the kettle black!)

If Ronnie didn't get the message from me, I believe he got it loud and clear at a promotional dinner on Long Island in January. He, myself, and some other players were there. Davey Johnson rose to give a little speech and his first words were, "I'm glad Ron Darling has been able to take time away from the New York social scene to join us."

Despite the good-natured laughter, it wasn't just a friendly joke. It was a message.

Davey knows as well as I do that Darling may play around for three nights after a starting assignment, but he's very careful for the next two preceding his starting assignment. He's in great shape for baseball, but he'll get a different reputation if he's not careful, and then he'll have to answer if he runs into a string of bad games.

During spring training, I said exactly this to one of the beat writers who follow the Mets. It was nothing I hadn't said to Ronnie.

Now, here we are on the charter flight from Atlanta to Houston, the team in a great mood. For the first time this year, I sit back in the ghetto. (On a charter flight, or a bus, that's the section in the back set aside for guys who want to horse around. The front is reserved for reading and sleeping. Before last year, I was mainly a ghetto-ite, but Bobby Valentine approached me at the beginning of the 1984 season and asked me to sit up front, to set an example. So I did last year, and so I have this year until the flight tonight.)

Ronnie is in the ghetto, too. The mood seems to be right, so I just put it to him straight. "Is something bugging you? You've been distant this year."

And he tells me that, according to this reporter, I'm unhappy because Ron Darling is playing around too much and getting out of shape and hurting the team. The guy had turned my words completely around, and Darling was justifiably upset that I was talking like this—he thought—behind his back. That's the reason he had been distant all year.

I had made no connection between my innocuous conversation with the reporter and the growing estrangement. Well, we set the record straight in a heart-to-heart reconciliation, and end up hugging.

Some writers just can't resist the temptation to stir shit up. This one disrupted a team and, more important, a good friendship.

The bus ride from Hobby Airport to the Shamrock Hilton in Houston is a zinger, verifying to me that the team has benefited immensely from the victory in Atlanta. Everyone on the bus is ready with a barb or two. Women and children off the streets!

In the game in Atlanta, Roger had screamed "Come on, Wally" as Backman went back on a pop fly for the final out. Such a play has not been Wally's forte, but he's getting better at it, and he made the catch. On the bus, I holler to Roger, "The way Wally goes back for the ball, I would have yelled too!"

Also in the game, Tom Gorman was warming in the bullpen, along with Wes Gardner. Gorman hadn't pitched since that great outing in the eighteen-inning marathon against the Pirates, weeks ago. The Atlanta scoreboard flashed, "Wes Gardner and a left-hander warming up."

Then it mistakenly substituted "Jesse Orosco" for "a left-hander." On the bus, someone yells out, "Gorfax, you haven't pitched in so long, they don't know who you are!"

Gorfax is a clever nickname. Gorman's "fast" ball is as slow as Sandy Koufax's was fast, so—presto! Gor-fax. Gorman is also called Johnny Mac, Jr., in honor of Johnny McNamara, the Boston manager who has perhaps the biggest nose in the game. Gorman's is good-sized, too. Mine is, too, and I took it on the chin in the Keith Hernandez look-alike contest staged by the broadcasters last year. The winner wore a Groucho Marx nose and moustache.

And so it goes for half an hour on the bus in Houston. In the bar at the hotel later, radio announcer Bob Murphy, who's been with the Mets since the beginning, is enjoying a nightcap with a couple of the guys. I observe what a great bus ride for the team, and Murphy replies, "Yes, but only when you're winning."

Wrong! Staying loose when you're losing is more important, and most important of all late in the season. In the first game of the Series in 1982, the ball hit that seam in the turf at St. Louis. E-3. In the second game, Molitor bunted and I ran for the bag before I got a good grip on the ball. They gave him a hit, but it was an error. Then I made a third error in the third game. "Gold Glove, my ass" they were teasing me, so I taped plastic forks to the fingers of both hands and stalked around the clubhouse in self-imposed ignominy. We had won the game; if we had lost, I might not have played around with the situation. Or I might have. Leave 'em laughing if you can.

In the Astrodome, it wouldn't be easy. The place is dead, and the mood in the stadium seeps into the players. My career average against the Astros is .235. I attribute part of this dismal figure to the Dome. And I think the dead atmosphere clings to the Astros even when they go on the road. The park hurts them, just as Candlestick hurts the Giants. As I understand it, they built the Dome to combat the two terrors of midsummer Houston: heat/humidity and mosquitoes. Understood, but they're paying too high a price for comfort. I suggest a compromise: Take off the lid to let some air in, and install mosquito netting over the hole.

Tonight, ironically, things are relatively lively—at least for me. First, a guy with a bullhorn (not a megaphone, a bullhorn) is sitting a few rows behind home plate, making crude remarks about my heritage. I wave him away, then tell Bruce Froemming behind the plate that if the guy gets on his horn while I'm hitting, I'm going to stop play until they throw him out. Froemming turns to the stands and yells at him to shut up. He does.

Then in the later innings, four guys behind our visitors' dugout on the third base side are riding my ass. After I ground out in the ninth, they holler, "Nice hustle, Hernandez! That's why Whitey traded your ass!"

I can't resist a sarcastic "Thanks" as I disappear into the dugout. I have Whitey, the White Rat, to thank for this rap I've carried around for a couple of years, although it's been getting better.

Bob Broeg, a writer in St. Louis, wrote in a book that I wasn't a team player and was a bad baserunner; I was a selfish player, he wrote. And he gave me a copy of the book. I didn't know what he'd written until I got to those pages. I tore them up and dumped the book into the trash. That's the only time I've really locked horns with the press. As a general rule, I acknowledge the wisdom of whoever first said, "Don't tangle with people who buy their ink by the barrel."

And when some fans read this stuff and accept it as gospel, I ignore them, too. Give 'em the top of your helmet is about all you can do. The fans at Shea never hassle me about hustling, because they see me play day in, day out.

Here's the objective truth (what else?) on the Hernandez hustle question. I hustle like hell when I need to. When I'm clearly out at first on a grounder, no, I don't sprint across the bag to break the tape. If Pete Rose wants to do this, fine, but my legs and ankles are sore enough, and I have miles to go before I sleep at the end of the season. As it is, I have to soak the legs many nights in a hot bath; late in the season, almost every night.

Besides, who are these gung-ho guys fooling? Some of the fans are easily duped, perhaps, but never the players. I've been called a ballplayer's ballplayer by managers, writers, and announcers I respect, and I'm proud of that designation: not a fan's ballplayer or management's ballplayer, but a player's player. They're the ones who know.

Find a player or anyone else who says Hernandez doesn't play for his team, and I'll listen, closely. But bring them to me. I don't want to read about it in a book first.

Doc loses his fastball tonight after the first inning, strikes out only one batter in six and a third innings (his lowest total ever), gives up eight hits—but wins the game because he keeps all this trouble to a manageable three runs, and because Orosco pitches great, striking out five of eight.

GAME 30—Mets 5
Astros 3

MAY 16

Because this is only a two-game series with the Astros, it's already getaway day in Houston. We're in and out of town in nothing flat, and I like it. Some of the guys gripe about the unpacking and packing of these short stays, but, to me, they mean I don't have time to get bored. The four-day, four-game series are the killers.

Coincidentally, the Cardinals are already in town for their series with the Astros starting tomorrow night, and they arrive at the Shamrock Hilton as the Mets are milling around waiting to leave on the bus for the Dome. We'll go straight to the airport and New York after the game. The Cards have the day off at the hotel, where they can enjoy the best swimming pool in the league. (Until I moved to New York, I hadn't thought about how much easier the travel is from St. Louis, the middle of the country. The Cards don't have any cross-continent endurance flights.)

Whitey walks over to greet me.

Keith.

Whitey.

Good to see you.

How's it going?

That kind of thing.

I believe Whitey intended to ship me to oblivion in 1983, and I get a measure of sweet revenge from having helped the Mets gain respectability, and more, in two quick years. But I still consider him the best field manager in our league. And could things have worked out better for me? Hell, I owe you a debt of gratitude, Whitey!

By 1980, I had been playing baseball competitively since I was ten years old—there was no playing baseball with my father unless it was competitive. I had been playing professionally since 1971. I had clawed—and I mean clawed—my way to the majors, been sent back to the minors, made it to the majors again. Dwight Gooden I wasn't, in either talent or temperament. Dwight is a genius for the game; I'm merely talented. At twenty years old, Dwight already has the maturity to deal with the game; it's taken me years to harness my rather wild energies. I'm still working on it.

I worked hard and made my talent pay off—with Gold Gloves, a batting title, and the MVP award in 1979. I was twenty-five years old.

It's been said many times before, and it's true in my case: The pressure to stay on top proved even greater than the pressure to get up there. I would not have believed it possible!

For ten years, all I had had was a career. I had *been* a career. It was the center of my existence—and the center of the existence of anyone who was around me much. Try it sometime; hard-driving professionals do, and they often give out.

At the All-Star break in 1980, my wife and I separated. Then we got back together and soon had a baby girl. All of a sudden, I was thinking about a life instead of just a career.

I survived 1980; in fact, I was second in the league in hitting. That's a tribute to raw talent.

In 1981, I gave out. That was the year of the first players' strike, and for the first time in memory, I had free time during the summer. I loved it. During all those seasons of baseball, I had forgotten the quiet pleasures of a warm summer weekend. The record shows I hit .306 for our 103 games, and drove in 48 runs, but it was a tough grind, especially after we came back from the strike.

Likewise 1982, even though I hit .299 with 94 RBIs and the Cardinals won the pennant and then the World Series against Milwaukee.

When Whitey moved me to the Mets the following June, I wasn't hitting at all. Whitey is a sharp judge of his personnel. Those little-town blues, as only Frank Sinatra can sing them? They were eating me alive. I can't really blame Herzog for trading me.

But to the Mets?? That's another matter. At the time, it was an insult. It has worked out well for me, but I'm still waiting for the last laugh.

The White Rat is probably in the stands tonight as Mike Scott and his new split-fingered fastball baffle us. Frank Cashen has to be concerned how long his patchwork lineup can stay the course. Mookie is playing, but with instructions to protect his shoulder. In other words, on a play requiring a hard throw, let the runner score. Can we win with a no-arm center fielder? We'll see, because we have to have Mookie in the batting order.

Danny Heep, formerly of the Astros, is filling in beautifully for Darryl. Danny is our best hitter right now. He has always said he can hit if he plays regularly. Many players have said that, but unfortunately most never get the chance to prove it. Danny is lucky: He's getting his chance this summer.

Mike Easler is the best hitter I've seen who couldn't get a chance. He hit .330 every year in Triple A, but somebody decided he didn't have it. Finally, the Pirates gave him his break when he was twenty-eight years old. Last year, he batted .313 for the Boston Red Sox. Heep, who also hit way over .300 every year in the minors, is twenty-eight this year.

Danny has a long swing, and long swingers tend to be streak hitters—if they're any good at all. A long swing is just that: The hands initiate the swing from a position far back and away from the body, so the arc is longer. The hitter has to start his swing earlier than the hitter who has a more compact stroke. Obviously, the earlier the swing begins, the less time the hitter has to watch the flight of the ball and compute vectors. His timing has to be perfect. A longer swing is susceptible to more and longer slumps.

Dad taught me a short stroke. It simply has to be more consistent over the long run, and a baseball season—much less a career—is a long, long run. There have been, however, some great long swings. Jimmy Wynn hit more home runs in the Astrodome than anyone, and he had one of the longest swings imaginable. George Foster has a long swing. Dale Murphy does pretty well with a long swing while striking out over a hundred times a year.

Sid Fernandez has a different kind of long swing, and it matches

Scott pitch for pitch tonight, after Jose Cruz drives in a run in the first inning. I'm not surprised at Sid's performance; as a lefty, he forces the several Astro switch-hitters to move to the right side of the plate; in every case, that's their weakest side.

But the one run in the first inning holds up. We're shut out for the second time in four games.

In the clubhouse afterwards, we cross paths with the Cardinals again, indirectly. Pete Prieto, the Astrodome clubhouse man for the visiting team, is installing the gear for the incoming Cards. This is my chance to put it to my friend Andujar. I noticed in the paper that he got a couple of singles and an RBI yesterday. That's excellent for a pitcher, but Jack has only scorn for "ping" hitters. He considers himself a power hitter, and goes to the plate hunting homers.

I get a marker and scrawl a note for Prieto to leave on Andujar's locker: "Jack. You can't hit. You're a Judy-hitting sonofabitch."

Andujar is one of the more unpredictable guys in baseball, as he proved in the first game of the year by announcing in advance his stolen-base attempt. He's also well-known for his belief that the game is mostly luck. He'd rather be lucky than good. I'd rather be good than lucky—except in those years when I thought I was basically unlucky, plagued by hard-hit balls right at somebody. Dad, an objective observer, of course, contends that I would have hit .330 last year with any luck. I have a hunch I may be in for frustration in 1985. So far it kind of seems that way. I certainly agree with Ralph Kiner, the former slugger who now announces the Met games, in scorning the notion that the good and bad breaks necessarily even out over a campaign, or a career.

Perhaps Andujar is correct in his assessment of the importance of luck. But if he is, you have to believe that he had bad luck for a number of years and then suddenly started getting lucky in 1982. That's when he started winning a lot of games. A better explanation is that the Astros, who traded Jack to St. Louis, just couldn't handle his temperamental self. One of Whitey's pluses is knowing how to handle players to get maximum performance from them.

Jack's and my most memorable evening was a strategically timed shit-faced drunk (and just a drunk) we threw in his hotel room in 1981. I was driving in some runs but it was a struggle. I decided to take a page from Dad's book. He doesn't drink, but recommends a one-night binge to break a disastrous slump. He would do it in his own playing days. The idea is to get so wasted you can't get tied up rehashing past mistakes, and you wake up with a clean slate—in a stupor, granted, but with a clean slate.

I was struggling and we had a doubleheader the next day against the Pirates and two tough pitchers. I needed to drink and I needed a buddy for the duration. Andujar volunteered. He had several days before his next start. We sat in his room until 6:00 a.m., listening to rock 'n' roll, drinking Scotch. That afternoon I went 6-for-8 and drove in seven runs.

My mistake was telling the reporters how I had done it. They wrote it up and I got flak from parents saying I was presenting a poor image. I agree. I should have kept my mouth shut.

The whole image of ballplayers as heavy drinkers is over-played. Quite a few, including myself, do drink a fair amount at times (on the road especially, in my case), but I see no correlation between this and performance. There are good players who do drink and bad players who don't.

On the road we have a lot of idle time at night. Am I supposed to go back to my hotel room like a good boy? I'd rather sit in the bar downstairs and have a few drinks with the guys, talk baseball, football, movies. Anything at all is better than watching late-night TV alone.

One of the major problems with the Mets when I came over in 1983 was a woeful lack of camaraderie. A small factor, I believe, was that management declared the hotel bar off limits.

Dead wrong! With the hotel bar off limits, the guys scatter to other bars or go to their rooms to wait out the night. In St. Louis, Whitey allowed the players in the bar but forbade himself or his coaches from joining in. Why the segregation?

Last year was Davey's first as a big-league manager, so Staub asked him in spring training what his policy on the hotel bar would be. He said, "It's open to everyone." The players started hanging out together, coming together as friends and, therefore, as a team.

Also early last year, in Philadelphia, I got together a bunch of players, over a dozen, and herded them to a club downtown. Darryl Strawberry and Hubie Brooks were two of the gang. The next day both dropped by my locker to tell me what a great time they'd had. Neither had realized we could all get together and have fun. A little libation is a small way the players can share their lives, but it shows up on the field. Don't ask me how, because I can't explain.

GAME 31—Astros 1
Mets 0

MAY 17—NEW YORK CITY

Every team figures to have a few "travel losses" on its schedule: awfully tough games because we're so tired from some horrendous scheduling.

Tonight is one of our travel losses—but we beat the Giants anyway! I arrive at my apartment at ten till six this morning, flip and flop for an hour or two, get up at noon, go out to the park—and play twelve innings!

In spring training, we'd do anything to avoid overtime, but not on your life tonight. This team fights. Ron Darling fights for nine innings, but he has an advantage. As tonight's starting pitcher, he was sent home early from Houston, a shrewd tactic commonly employed these days.

In the third inning, I get about as mad over a called strike as I'll get all year. Fatigue probably has something to do with my outburst. Lee Weyer, behind the plate, has the largest strike zone in the free world, and the pitchers know this. He's a high-ball ump, and awards them two inches off the corners to boot.

The first pitch this at-bat is low, very low, but he calls it for the pitcher. He never calls that pitch a strike. He didn't call it a strike in Atlanta. So I air him out: "You're a better ump than that, Lee. You call it a ball one day, a strike the next." He defends the call. I say, "Come on, Lee."

Then the next pitch is right where the first one was. I have to take it—too low to hit—and wait with trepidation. "Ball inside!" Inside! It was over the plate by inches but way low! So now I think to myself, "You're in trouble, pal. Start hacking."

And I hack a fly to center for the third out with a man in scoring position. Every batter tries not to let disputed calls rankle him, but sometimes they do.

We're game tonight, but sluggish. What a lift Ray Knight provides with his two-run homer in the seventh to tie the game, and maybe save us from a second-straight shutout. It's a long drive, too, and his wife Nancy Lopez, the great golfer, is in the stands to see it. Ray must have had that talk with Davey about playing time. He started two games in a row against right-handers in Houston. HoJo would normally get the call against them. Now Ray hits a big, big homer off Dave LaPoint. Is third base his job now?

The eighth inning is a proud moment for me, of sorts. Right now, I'll take any I can get. With a 2-and-0 count and Wilson on first—surprise! The catcher, Bob Brenly, calls a pitchout. Theory suggests he won't do this, because it makes the count three balls, with a walk impending. The Giants are guessing, and incorrectly: Mookie isn't going. Dumb guess.

Now, with the 3-and-0 count, they give me the fourth ball intentionally. I can only construe this as ultimate respect, and I appreciate it, because Mark Davis, a tough left-hander, is pitching, and my average is down around .280. Their decision also demonstrates the depth of Carter's slump. He's had maybe one good game since the grand slam ten days ago against Atlanta. To repeat, when he starts hitting consistently they won't be walking me. Right-hander Greg Minton comes in to get Gary on a pop-up.

But in the twelfth, Gary starts hitting. Fine relieving by Orosco and McDowell for Darling brings us to this point. Backman gets to first, I'm happy to move him along with a sharp single that would have been a hard double in the gap if I'm hitting well, then Carter drives in the winning run with a liner to right off Garrelts. All of this while it's raining.

How do you explain Gary? He's in the deepest slump of his career but still has delivered a couple of key hits. In the second, he took a seat next to me on the bench after striking out off Dave LaPoint. "I cannot hit him. I just can't do it. The only time I can is when he's stupid enough to throw the fastball."

Come on, Gary. Get positive! But he really is convinced that he can't hit LaPoint. In the fourth inning he tried to bunt for a base hit!

I'm pleased with my timely hit in the winning inning. I'm also pleased to have recovered the missing half-step in my fielding reflexes. Less than a week after I wonder what's going on, I make as good a stop as I've ever made, diving to my left in the first inning. On the next batter I race back on a pop fly and catch it over my shoulder running away from the plate. Is there an analogy here with those times I've broken out of a batting slump with a binge the night before, or while I'm sick? Could be. All I know is, it's good to have that half-step back.

The sad news today is that, as expected, Bobby Valentine is going over to the Texas Rangers as their manager. I hope they're paying him a lot for that thankless task. We'll miss Bobby's ebullient, positive personality, but Bud Harrelson has come up from managing in the minors in Columbia, South Carolina to take over coaching at third, and he knows what he's doing. Has he been a Met forever, or what?

Harrelson is blunt in his assessment of the two jobs. He prefers coaching up here. Managing in A–ball is one hard job. The manager does *everything*. Another reason I'll bet he's happy to be with the big club: Buddy has a shot at another World Series ring. I wish him luck.

By the way, watch Buddy run out to his coaching box. He skims along the grass. Watch all the different styles. They're interesting. Strawberry lopes. Willie McGee in St. Louis tilts forward. Ron "The Penguin" Cey in Chicago runs like one. Me, I'm just digging away.

Press Note: Backman was on first base in the last inning because Jeff Leonard dropped his line drive to left field. Clearly, he lost the ball in the lights. After the game, the gang of reporters has surrounded me, I'm very tired, and a guy asks, "The error? Did he make that error because the ball was wet?"

"What error?" I reply. "You mean the drive to Leonard? How was the ball going to get wet? It was in the air."

And I say it in a pretty surly manner. It's belittling to the man. I feel bad.

GAME 32—Mets 3
Giants 2

MAY 18

Since July of 1983, the Mets have won twenty-three of twenty-four extra-inning games. One of the game's popular statistical bibles points out that this streak began soon after I came over to the team and wonders whether there is more than coincidence here. Certainly, but so what? A streak like that requires luck, too. Tonight, ours runs out. The young Wes Gardner gives up six runs to the Giants in the tenth inning and all you can say is that it happens and to hell with it.

So make it twenty-three out of twenty-five. Unfortunately, we fail to cash in on a break given us by the schedule. This is our first night game on a Saturday. After flying home in the wee hours Friday morning and playing a game that night, we're delighted not to have the standard day game on Saturday. But we blow it. (My thinking about schedules can get pretty convoluted, I admit, but I'm always mulling hypothetical advantages and disadvantages. Am I a schedule freak?)

After the loss, we can look on the bright side: eight more fine innings from Lynch.

In the eighth, the Giants bring in Mark Davis, and he throws twenty consecutive curveballs—more than twenty. This isn't kosher, and we let him know from the bench.

"Mix in a heater!"

"Throw a fastball, why not?!"

My turn at bat comes, and a Little Leaguer could see I'll get curves, which I don't mind. I don't fear curves from lefties. I get one up in the strike zone that I can hit hard, but don't. That's another runner left in scoring position.

One critical play in the tenth opens the floodgates for San Francisco. With Alex Trevino on first with a lead-off single, Jose Uribe lays down a sacrifice bunt. Gardner fields the ball and throws to second—too late. Carter makes the call for him to throw there, but I know after glancing at the runner that the play will be late. But if I shout, "First! First!" what will happen? Gardner might freeze, I don't know. He hesitates anyway, I think, and maybe that's why the runner is safe. After the play, Gary and I exchange a glance. Oh, well, better to be aggressive.

Those little things. I'm not being a freak about them. As soundly as Gardner is subsequently bombed, it might have been different.

Davey has Knight playing third again, against another right-hander. It's his job now, I guess. In any event, he goes hitless. So do I; so does most of the squad. Our only consolation is that we're hitting a bit better against the opposition than they're hitting against us. In other words, pitching saves.

The National League is, thus far, a nonhitting league in 1985. One proof: eighteen two-hitters have been *lost* this year. Pitchers are dominating. In the American League, the hitters are creaming the ball, or so I read.

I don't know whether I'm a representative nonhitting National Leaguer, but I may have figured out one of my problems at the plate. I'm taking too many first pitches. I almost always take the first pitch of my first at-bat. I assume an attacking stance and stride, but I just don't swing. Often the pitch is a breaking ball, so I get a look at it, and often it misses, so I get ahead in the count.

In subsequent at-bats, I'll probably take the first pitch if I'm antsy in a big situation, and hope for a ball to calm me down. If it's a strike, tough luck. Tonight it occurs to me that I'm consistently seeing fastballs right down the middle on the first pitch. That tells me that the scouts have discovered I'm taking first pitches. I'll fool them soon.

GAME 33—Giants 8
Mets 2

MAY 19

It's a good one for me and the Mets, who win on Howard Johnson's clutch two-run single in the sixth inning. This comes after he has hit a couple of long drives foul. I rate it our second biggest clutch hit of the season, second only to Carter's homer to end that cold first game in April. What an irony that HoJo delivers in his first start in five games. *Now* what will Davey do about third base? The big hits in our last two victories have been struck, one apiece, by the two "candidates." My hunch is that he'll go back to the original platooning plan. Ray will just have to accept this, and he will, if HoJo hits, because Ray Knight plays for the team.

We win with a makeshift lineup: Carter and Foster get the day off, and Tom Gorman starts for the first time in a couple of years. Why? That line drive in Atlanta broke Calvin Schiraldi's toe. Calvin is out awhile. Gorfax pitches well after Jeff Leonard's two-run homer in the first inning. McDowell closes out in near perfection for three innings. If he keeps this up, he'll be the new Doug Sisk. Doug is getting belted at Tidewater, too.

There is no overstating the importance of the short reliever in the game as it's played today. Don't leave home without one. If I had a choice between a staff of five outstanding starters backed by a so-so bullpen, or five so-so starters backed by outstanding relievers, I'd take the latter. That's what we won with in St. Louis. That's what San Diego won with last year. The Mets have a chance of having the best of both worlds over the coming years: great starters backed by solid relievers. All our pitchers are young.

There's a full house today because it's cap day. Fine, but I urge management next year to distribute blue caps, not white ones. It's murder out there, and might as well be confetti on the field. A successful pickoff throw in the first could have just as easily whizzed over my shoulder. At the bag today, I'm playing zones—just like batting. Gary Rajsich's ground ball to me in the seventh disappears completely, hits near the heel of my glove and sticks; otherwise, E-3.

I shouldn't gripe about my paltry problems with the white caps. During HoJo's big at-bat with the bases loaded and the count 3-and-2, the 50,000 fans are *waving* them. Terrific concentration at the plate.

Finally, I feel I'm progressing at the plate. One pitch is my evidence: an outside pitch that I drive to left in the fourth for a hard single. That's all, but it's my first solid hit to left in a couple of weeks. I have to go there with the outside pitch. If I don't, I'm hurting.

Every slump or semislump is the same thing with me: I crouch too much, don't wait, get in front of the ball, and pull my right, lead shoulder out. In short, a batting slump is caused by hitting six inches too soon. However long it takes the ball to travel those six inches, that's how much too soon I've been swinging—a millisecond. Amazing to me that the body can be so finely in or out of tune.

In golfing parlance (which I can get away with only because you haven't seen me play that game), I'm not staying down on the ball. The outside pitch I pop up or roll weakly to the shortstop. The inside pitch I sometimes hit well, but just as often I bounce it to the second baseman.

To counteract the bad habit, I stand more upright today in batting practice. In the game, I crouch my legs but hold myself upright above the waist. This stance helps me wait that split second. And I feel it working. As I come around in the next few days, I'll slowly ease back into my tiger stance.

GAME 34—Mets 3
Giants 2

MAY 20

The Lord giveth; the Lord taketh away. Gary Carter's heroic moment on Opening Day has been replaced in the fans' immediate memory by his moment in the first inning of tonight's game against San Diego: bases loaded, nobody out, I've just walked on four straight pitches and Carter has received three more balls from Lamar Hoyt. On this 3-and-0 count, he swings at a low, outside pitch and hits into a 1-2-3 double play. Pitcher to catcher to first. Foster flies out. That ends it.

I know we're fucked. In any other inning, that failure is simply bad. In the first inning, it's ominous. Lamar Hoyt goes from a first-inning Budweiser to a four-hit shutout just like that.

Making it worse is our knowledge that, in his last start, Hoyt was bombed in the first frame. Before any game, I check out one statistic posted by the opposing pitcher: How many walks has he given up, in how many innings? Hoyt had given up only five walks in almost fifty innings, so nothing surprised me more than the four straight balls to me. Something is drastically wrong with his delivery. If I'm manager, Carter has the "take" sign on the three-ball count—especially considering that he's in a slump and will be naturally anxious to bust out of it in a big way. But Davey rolled the dice and they came up snake eyes.

Our subsequent pathetic showing—two hits in the final eight innings—has to be judged something of a letdown loss. Even Dwight may have suffered this letdown: The first man up for the Padres in the second inning hits a homer, and there are three more hits in the inning. The most galling of them is a hard single by Hoyt. It's his first hit in the major leagues because this is his first season in the National League; he came over from the White Sox of the damnable designated-hitter league. (Damnable, that is, until I'm old enough to be hired as one!)

When Hoyt arrives at first base, I inform him, "Lamar, it ain't that goddamn easy."

"I know. I just closed my eyes and swung where the ball was."

Should I try that?

The Mets are shut out for the third time in eight games. Atrocious hitting. But we won four of the other five games. This tells me more than the batting average. Every player, every team, has these streaks and slumps, and there's no explanation. We have to develop special skills of stoicism, but not resignation, to endure the slings and arrows.

If the Mets continue to play .500 ball during our allotted slumps, I change my mind: Mets win it all.

Notes from the infirmary: Cubs' ace Rick Sutcliffe tore a hamstring while running to first base and will miss quite a few weeks. This setback will help even things out between the two teams regarding injuries. I'm not worrying about the Cubs already—in fact, I don't want guys announcing prior to our night games how the Cubs did at Wrigley that afternoon—but it's impossible not to note such information, perhaps with a little satisfaction. We never wish another player ill, so we don't think about the player. We think about his team. Give no quarter.

Fernandez's Achilles tendon is inflamed. He can't pitch tomorrow night. Who can? Berenyi's arm at Tidewater is hurting and he's going to see yet another doctor.

And Sisk's elbow? Who knows, but Doug is returning to the club, to my surprise; he has been as ineffective at Tidewater as he was here. Making room for him on the roster is Wes Gardner, who was bombed by the Giants in the tenth inning on Friday.

GAME 35—Padres 2
Mets 0

MAY 21

Until the lineup cards are exchanged at home plate, the decision on postponement rests with the home team. In our case, with general manager Frank Cashen. Tonight, the rain is pouring from about six o'clock on, a deluge, so it would be perfectly fair and much to our benefit to call this game by the 7:35 starting time. Because of Fernandez's sore tendon, Rick Aguilera has been called from Tidewater to pitch just this one game; then he'll go back. The new man may throw a great one, but if you have your choice you don't try to break a semislump with a man making his first big-league start.

But we wait. After taking BP in the cage under the stands (a semiworthless exercise, in my opinion, because the hitter gets no sense of where the ball has gone in relation to fielders), we sit, we talk, we play cards, we fiddle (the crossword puzzle successfully completed long ago). By 8:30, I'm pissed. What are we doing here?! I find Davey in his office and suggest to him that the rain is a blessing. Maybe we won't have to use the kid. Davey agrees, and says he doesn't know what they're thinking "up there." Finally at nine o'clock the word comes. We go home. A wasted evening yields a good break.

MAY 22

Bruce Berenyi is cut on today for a "slight tear" in the rotator cuff in his shoulder. The words "rotator cuff" strike fear into the heart of any pitcher. I don't know the physiology of the shoulder, but I know it's hard to come back when the cuff is hurt. Mark "The Bird" Fidrych? Rotator cuff. Our own Mel Stottlemyer? Rotator cuff. Maybe Berenyi will return this year, but we might as well not count on it.

Last night's rainout gets us back to our "regular" starting rotation, but we can't capitalize. This ballgame is our toughest loss of the season. Leading 4–0 in the sixth, Darling suddenly loses his fastball (I can tell from my post) and Terry Kennedy caps off the Padres' inning with a three-run homer. The radar gun was recording Ronnie's heater at 91–92 mph for the first five innings. In the sixth, the pitch putters in at 84 mph.

TILT!

All you can do in this situation is hustle up the bullpen and hope your starter makes it through the inning. If he does, his velocity might well return the next inning. Davey doesn't want to find out, however, and pinch-hits for Darling in our half of the sixth.

McDowell pitches three nearly flawless innings with the game now tied, 4–4. But Roger has to go out for a pinch hitter in the ninth, Christensen strikes out in that roll, and the next inning the Padres get a couple of hits off Orosco and score.

Their bullpen—five of them—stops us cold. In the tenth I get two good cuts at Goose Gossage's fastball, then don't have a prayer on the best slider I've seen from him. A K for Keith. Nevertheless, I'm beginning to hit again. In batting practice and in the game (two hits) I'm swinging better than I have since the first week of the season. I'm back into my tiger stance. Every season I've been able to count on a couple of month-long streaks, sometimes longer, when I wear out the ball. I feel one coming. I regret that tomorrow is an off day. Let's keep this rhythm going.

The Padres are by far the best-looking team we've faced, with totally new personnel from five years ago. They're hitting so well that Garry Templeton, a fine hitter who almost won the title in 1982, is batting eighth in the order. He's a good friend. We talked before one of our games. He's unhappy about hitting eighth and told Dick Williams, the Padres' manager. Williams told him, "You don't walk enough."

In other words, "If you don't like batting eighth, tough."

Williams has a point. Mookie Wilson's weakness at the top of the Mets order is that he doesn't walk enough. Walking should jump a first- or second-place hitter's .280 or .290 batting average up to an on-base percentage of .350, minimum.

Davey had these statistics in mind when he shifted Mookie from first to second in the lineup, letting Backman go first and draw some walks.

A barely related point: Although my speed certainly doesn't make this team go, I grab a base tonight off the Padres' sleeping asses. Fans don't realize I stole nineteen bases in 1982, and was thrown out only eight times, up to the last six weeks of the season. Whitey wanted me to get one more steal the last month, so the Cardinals could be the first club in umpteen years to have five "speedsters" with twenty stolen bases.

In late August, I was thrown out twice with good jumps on the ball. The next time I was nailed by five yards. I gave up for the year.

Whitey was sorely disappointed, but I wasn't helping the club by getting thrown out. My legs were gone. Last year I was slowed at least a step by a pulled groin muscle, but now I feel fast again— well, faster. And I'll steal a few bases with canniness. Lull them to sleep: Get on base a couple of times, make no effort to steal, and the pitcher won't even glance over the third time I'm on. That's when I take off.

I'll advise Davey soon that I may run a little more if the opportunity is right and I can get a good jump. He'll say okay. But if I get thrown out twice in a row, I'll give up. My goal in this department? Seven more steals in my non-base-stealing career will give me 100.

Tonight's steal in the fifth does no good. I'm stranded.

Meanwhile, it seems as if the Padre runners at first base are right in my line of sight to home plate when I'm not holding them on. In this circumstance, I'm not averse to calling out, "One more step, please."

"Which way?"

"Your choice."

Sometimes he even moves. If he doesn't, I do.

GAME 36—Padres 5
Mets 4

MAY 23—CHICAGO

Last night, Rusty, myself, and a couple of other guys had dinner at an East Side restaurant. Then we stopped by "Rascals" and once again I got too loud; this time with a remark about a woman of excessive weight seated nearby. Rusty suggested I tone it down.

I snapped back, "If you don't like it, throw me out of *your* restaurant."

What the hell is wrong with me? Rusty considered me with justified chagrin, said simply, "Mex," and left the table. Next thing I know he's gone and the bill is paid.

While the team goes to Tidewater, Virginia for the obligatory exhibition game with our Triple A team, I fly to Chicago for the meeting of player representatives and the obligatory strike authorization. However, nothing will happen, mark my words, until we set a *date* and that date approaches. Only then will the owners get serious. They're certainly not serious with this latest proposal for a cap on team salaries. We'll never accept it, and if the owners don't believe it, we'll strike to prove it. (The Mets could not have made the Carter trade under the rule as proposed.)

MAY 24—NEW YORK

Joe Durso notes in today's *Times* that the Mets are five and five without Strawberry. This piece reinforces what I've always known: Darryl is the designated media darling, and that's fine with me. In 1983, I was cut in for some of the action; last year, Dwight; this year, Gary.

Sure, Darryl is a big loss. He's a game-breaker the opposing pitchers now don't have to worry about, but Heep has been hitting well in his absence—much better for average than Darryl's .215. In fact, Danny's about the only guy who has been hitting consistently. Carter, batting fourth, is probably hurt the most by Darryl's absence, because now the left-handed power isn't following him. They might be pitching around Gary. But we should and will win without Straw. Hernandez, Carter, Foster, and Heep can drive in plenty of runs for this pitching staff.

John Christensen has my sympathy. He has hit over .300 every year in the minors, but up here he'll play irregularly, mostly pinch hitting. It's no way to prove your worth. That's difficult enough with a steady job but impossible with these nickel-and-dime appearances.

Dealing with the fragile egos and careers of the promising minor leaguers is one of the most difficult tasks of a general manager, and one of the most important.

Len Dykstra is a real prospect, management has decided, and they don't want his confidence screwed up playing with the big club if he's not ready. And Davey is on record as opposing having young talent sit on the bench. That's the reason Dykstra has been up and down, depending on the status of Mookie's shoulder. Yet Davey has to have some young talent on the bench, so it's Christensen and Terry Blocker. Neither has contributed much. A lot of talented Triple A players haven't made it in the major leagues, and they never got a real chance. It's a sad thought, an unsettling one, because I could have been among their number.

1976: For the second year in a row, I came to the spring camp of the Cardinals as the favorite for the first-base job. The previous season was the Harry "The Hat" Walker disaster, but then I hit well and recovered with Ken Boyer in Tulsa. I believed I was ready in 1976.

But I got off to an even worse start than I had in 1975. I was benched. Fair enough. Then I made the mistake of insulting a sportswriter, and he got back at me, with repercussions. The infraction occurred at the team banquet, where I "mistook" the writer, Neil Russo, for a character in *One Flew Over the Cuckoo's Nest*.

I yelled to Hector Cruz, "Hector, there's Cheswick!"

Russo overheard me and was not amused. The following morning the headline of his column announced my benching, and he went on to suggest I be sent to the minors—again.

That story crushed me. To this day I like Neil Russo, but to this day I also recall my emotions after reading that payback column. I was buried.

Soon thereafter, I engaged in some more self-destructive behavior. The Cards rode on two buses, one for management and press, one for the players. In Philadelphia I snuck on the empty management bus with a woman and was obtaining—I wouldn't say enjoying, just obtaining—a sexual favor when Red Schoendienst and Preston Gomez climbed aboard. I incurred a $500 fine, a lot of money for me then, and the disfavor of the organization.

The Cardinals were twenty games out of first by mid-May that year, going nowhere, and they decided to platoon Ron Fairly and Ted Simmons at first base. They had traded for catcher Joe Ferguson, freeing Simmons from his catching duties.

I exploded. Storming into Red's office, I called him gutless. I was screaming. I was fighting for my life, the only one I knew.

How old was Fairly? Thirty-eight? How much sense did it make to play him in the hopeless situation of that season?

I demanded to know. Red's face turned completely red. To his immense credit, he walked right past me to his refrigerator and got a beer. He didn't offer me one. Seated behind his desk again, he said with remarkable calm, "I'm going to call Bing. Now just cool down."

Bing Devine, the general manager. Bing came down immediately from his office and gave me the honest explanation. He said they had to make the trade for Ferguson to look good, and it wouldn't look good if Simmons and Ferguson weren't both utilized.

At least he was honest. Look, I said, just give me the chance. Don't put me in for one day and if I go 0-for-4 I'm benched.

That's awful pressure in the sixth inning, hitless the first two times up. Bing acknowledged my point. He said he would continue with the platooning until the All-Star break, and if we hadn't made a run into the race, I would play the second half of the season or, at the end of the season, I could name three teams and they would try to trade me.

We didn't make a move, Red played me after the break and I hit .336 for three months, .289 for the year, driving in forty-six runs in the partial season.

If I hadn't exploded in Red's office, I would have remained buried all year. It took that to wake them up.

Batting practice is still good, the day off hasn't hurt the swing. Maybe I'm hot. But little things count in a batter's rhythm, and I'm not helped tonight in the first inning against the Dodgers when home-plate ump Doug "The Lord" Harvey decides to enforce the rule about one batter at a time in the on-deck circle. Wilson is leading off these days, and as Wally and I are out waving our bats, Harvey motions me back into the dugout.

When Backman steps to the plate, I call out to Harvey, "May I come out now?"

Yes you may. Backman strikes out.

May I step into the batter's box now?

Yes you may.

The Lord is a good ump and a proud ump but the only one who enforces this rule without being badgered into it by the opposing manager. I get a little pissed when a manager brings up a trivial point of order. Chickenshit gamesmanship, I call it. Joe Torre used to do that, when he was managing the Braves, and this year the White Rat did it.

I want to get out of the dugout early for a good reason. While Mookie hits, I swing the bat with the weighted doughnut to get loose. Then when Wally is up, I'm on my knee watching the pitches. If the umpire doesn't let me out one batter early, I have to warm up and study the pitcher at the same time. Not as good.

But I can't blame Doug Harvey for my 0-for-3 night. I swing well and hit the ball hard twice. Fans probably think it's frustrating to rifle the ball somewhere for an out, and it is, but I look at it this way, too: Better to line into an out than pop or bounce into that same out.

But in the third inning, I just blow it.

Orel Hershiser has been starting off our left-handed batters with a curve. (I watch extra closely how the pitcher throws to our left-handed hitters, often going into the clubhouse to watch these encounters on television. The center field camera tells all.)

I go to the plate in the third looking for another curve. Hershiser fires a fastball right down the middle, strike one. It's a pitch I should drive hard somewhere, but looking for the slower pitch, I'm frozen, and pissed, and the next pitch I roll meekly to first base.

Here's an instance in which I outthink myself. I decide to guess the pitch, and I guess wrong. I get to be the cat often enough at the plate, but this time Orel pounces on Keith. The episode ruins my whole night. I lie in bed thinking about that at-bat for fifteen minutes. Never again! (Bullshit.)

Hershiser is not a favorite with our team. He's what we call a real major leaguer, with all the pro moves out there, adjusting his cap, his arm, everything but the jewels (this would not be "real major leaguer" behavior, not on the mound). All this piddling takes time, and he can turn a no-hitter into a three-hour marathon. Tonight, however, he speeds up his act—until the third inning, when he realizes that the mound isn't right for him and, after digging on it awhile, calls for the ground crew. They trundle out with their tools and pound down the bad place. An irritated Eddie Lynch retaliates for us when he goes out to pitch. He digs everything up.

"Hey, Eddie, what are you going to plant?"

He starts to call out the crew, too, but settles for his own gardening.

We're trailing 4–1 when Davey calls on Doug Sisk in the eighth inning, his first appearance since returning from Tidewater. It's hard to believe, but I sense some sympathy from the fans, mixed in with the inevitable boos. He gets the Dodgers in order, then again in the ninth. I note, however, that four of the six outs are in the air. Not off a sinker, they're not. But, hell, they're out, they're out.

The same applies to us, however, and rallies in the eighth and ninth innings fall short. Our third loss in a row. And when was the last time the Mets lost with Mookie going 4-for-5?

GAME 37—Dodgers 4
Mets 3

MAY 25

I was playing for the Cardinals and taking my turn at the plate in a game against the Dodgers. The pitcher was a new guy in the league, and threw over to first five or six times in a row. Steve Yeager behind the plate yelled out, "Come on, Freddie, throw it here!"

"Freddie?!" I exclaimed.

"Sure," Yeager said through his mask. " 'Freddie' in English."

So Freddie Valenzuela it is. Anything Yeager says is good enough for me: He's a chain-smoking, coffee-drinking, keyed-up sonofabitch. I like him.

I don't think Freddie is any of these bad things. He certainly doesn't seem keyed up. You can't paint the black like he does with shaky fingers. What a Rembrandt (old baseball cliché, even though few batters know a Rembrandt from a Warhol).

Still, I hit Valenzuela pretty well. His long motion and high leg kick and big eyes staring up at the passing planes: All this bothers many hitters. Not me, because I don't see it. I don't look at the pitcher. I look at the zone above his shoulder where he'll release the ball. I'm vaguely aware of the preceding motion, but it bothers me only if it results in a delay. Any delay is a problem. The hitter starts an unconscious clock when the pitcher starts his windup, and he wants the ball to be released on time. Don Sutton really gave me trouble with his long, herky-jerky windup. The Pirates' Cecilio Guante, as I've mentioned, is too slow. Valenzuela throws right on time.

Today, it's Freddie against Dwight, and 40,000 fans show up for the confrontation. These are the two glamour pitchers in the league.

With Doug Harvey moving around to third base this afternoon, I'm back in the on-deck circle one batter too early—and I like it, and I drive a ball on one hop against the wall in left-center, scoring Chapman. That's my first RBI in eight games, and I'm hitting as well as anyone on the team. That shows how we're going.

Valenzuela against Christensen. Give this rookie a break! He's struggling and now has to face an array of fastballs (though they seem a little slow this afternoon), curves, sliders, and his infamous screwball—three speeds on that pitch. All of them on the black. Sometimes Freddie will go through the lineup the first time around throwing only one or two of the pitches in his repertoire, and then the next time through he'll use mostly the other two pitches. A veteran might be able to use this information, but Freddie is a veteran, too, and it's always a risk getting into a guessing game with him. Guessing or not guessing, most of the Mets are making outs today. Add the reputation/intimidation factor, which is of major consequence for rookies. I was awestruck the first time I faced Tom Seaver.

Christensen strikes out twice.

Gooden pitches well, of course, but the homer he gives up to Greg Brock in the fifth inning is all Valenzuela needs. After the inning, I ask Carter what the pitch was.

"Change-up."

I can't help reacting a little. "Change-up!"

"Sure," Gary says. "He's been throwing it well. This time it was out over the plate."

I get the feeling that Gary is a little defensive about the selection, so I assure him that I'm not second-guessing—and I'm not. I'm surprised, that's all. As it turns out, Davey second-guesses the pitch while talking to reporters after the game. I don't know. If it was effective earlier, why shouldn't it have worked with Brock?

The reason is simple: The black is everything. The only pitch in the big leagues that might survive over the middle of the plate is a good moving fastball—and a fair number of *them* will be abruptly turned around.

Mookie's arm in center probably costs us a run in the sixth, when Steve Sax scores on a hard single. Manny Mota, coaching at first, is telling the Dodgers to take the extra base on anything hit to center. I don't want to hear it.

Mota also believes he's stealing our signs. I let him think so, but actually we're just screwing them up.

The business starts in the first inning, with Chapman on first and me at bat. Buddy Harrelson flashes his signs. The way Davey has it set up, our hit-and-run sign is meaningful only if it's the last sign in the sequence.

Buddy runs through some meaningless gestures, then gives the hit-and-run sign, then starts to give another sign, then suddenly stops. I'm confused. Is the hit-and-run the last sign in the sequence? I look down at Kelvin on first base, he shrugs, so I run my hand across my chest, the hitter's request for the coach to start all over. This time it's clear: the hit-and-run is on. Chapman scores on my double.

Back in the dugout, Davey gripes, "Haven't you guys got the signs straight yet?"

"Davey," I reply, "Buddy started to give another sign."

"No he didn't."

"Yes he did, Davey."

Then, in the second inning, Johnson is thrown out at second, Santana with the bat on his shoulder. I ask HoJo if it was a hit-and-run. "No," he says, "straight steal."

The payoff: When I go out to first, Mota asks me, "Santana miss the hit-and-run?"

"Yeah."

Give me a break, Manny! Do you really believe I'm going to give you a tip on our signs?

After Gooden is pulled for a pinch hitter, Sisk comes in and gives up a three-run homer. Poor Dougie.

Four in a row.

GAME 38—Dodgers 6
Mets 2

MAY 26

No batting practice today, Sunday. Suit up by noon, take infield, play the game. I think it's a good move by Davey. When a team isn't hitting there are two options: extra BP or none at all.

I pass up Rusty's ride and walk onto Second Avenue to hail a cab.

"Shea Stadium."

"Pretty early, isn't it?"

"Yeah, I just mess around."

"I used to play, you know. I tell you what they got to do. They've got to suck up that $2 million contract."

I know he's referring to Foster. The boos have been louder and more numerous as George's average has slipped below .200.

"And that Hernandez. He goes out and stretches before the game, but don't play catch in front of the dugout. It's demoralizing to the team!"

I ease down in the seat, pull my cap lower and my collar higher, and darken the tint of my sunglasses. The monologue on the Mets, a nonstop twenty-minute virtuoso performance, entertains me all the way to the park. Now I understand the batting weakness of every member of the starting lineup, the flawed pitch in every starter's repertoire.

When I hand over the money, the best part of a double saw-buck, he looks at me.

"Anybody ever tell you you look like Keith Hernandez?"

"That's me."

He brightens.

"Why, you're the best player on the Mets!"

I love these crusty old-school advocates. According to them, no ballplayer of their generation ever missed a cutoff man or failed to run full-speed to first. What bullshit. They concede that present-day basketball and football players are better than their predecessors, but baseball players in their analysis are worse. It looks easy from the stands is all I can say.

If you want a real comparison, cut the leagues back to eight or ten teams, as it was in those good old days, and you'll see great baseball. Mostly you'll see great pitching.

"Why, pitchers used to always finish the game. If it went fifteen, we went fifteen."

That's right, and that's why the batters hit 50 homers, drove in 150 and averaged .350.

Expansion has diluted the pool of players, granted, but there are many more superb athletes now, primarily because of the arrival of the black and Hispanic players. Net result: Today's baseball players are better than their predecessors. Just like the basketball and football players, the swimmers, runners, leapers, lifters, and divers.

Thanks, cabbie, I've needed to get this off my chest. And by the way, Mac, I've seen a film of a Yankee World Series game in which Berra hits a bases-loaded one-hopper back to the pitcher. Yogi jogs toward first. Halfway down the line, he peels off and heads for the dugout. The World Series!

However, we, the New York Mets in 1985, haven't been playing better than the old-timers. Four in a row is getting dangerous. Ideally, a good team gets through a season with no more than three consecutive losses. (We managed that in St. Louis in 1982, until we had clinched the division in mid-September.)

And the little things are working against us in today's effort to break the streak. Ray Knight is home with some dizziness-inducing virus and Gardenhire is out, so we have no right-handed hitters on the bench to bring in against left-hander Rick Honeycutt. As we analyze the problem prior to the game, Rusty points out that the pennant-winning 1973 Mets also had bad injury problems, which they endured. Catcher Jerry Grote and shortstop Harrelson, among others, were out weeks apiece. A good omen, perhaps.

I don't recall a game in which I've made quite a few good plays and one really fine one—wrapped around two of the worst boners imaginable. Pick up the action in the third inning. Mariano Duncan drags a hard bunt to my right. I break for the ball, but realize that Sid Fernandez is still standing on the mound, a bystander, so now the only chance is for me to scramble back to cover first, hoping Chapman playing second can field the ball. On the field, however, I don't come up with this split-second decision. I continue for the ball and, in effect, deke out Chapman. Now when I pull back at the last moment, intending to let him field it, my decision is too late. Chapman, correctly, has headed for first to take my throw. The ball gets by both of us and Duncan goes into second base with the only bunt double I've ever witnessed, much less caused. A mental error—two, really, counting Fernandez's vapor lock—that won't show up in the scorebook.

Later in the inning, I dive to my right, catch a soft liner by R. J. "That's My Brand" Reynolds, and prevent Duncan from scoring.

A voice bellows from the stands, "You're a god, Keith! You're a god!"

Far from it, pal, as I prove in the fifth on a high pop off Marshall's bat. Thinking the ball is heading near the stands, I start rapidly in that direction. I slow up as it begins to drift back over the field, now start backpedaling as the ball inexplicably heads for fair territory, and finally I have to race to catch up with it. I conclude this routine with a last-moment lunge, to no avail: The ball drops fair.

I've run a circle from the baseline to the dugout and back again. The damn ball was mocking me. Bring on those dancing bears.

But we win and break the four-game skid with good pitching from Fernandez and, you guessed it, McDowell. Imagine that he didn't pitch at all last year, following arm surgery!

Quiz:

1. In the second inning, with one out and Christensen at the plate, Foster breaks for second on a 3-and-2 count. Christensen is struggling and strikes out a lot. Foster is slow. There's a good chance for a "strike 'em out, throw 'em out" double play to end the inning. Why does Davey send George?

2. In the third inning, with two outs, Duncan on third, Marshall on first, and Greg Brock batting, Marshall breaks for second. This is the first-and-third, two-out play. The idea is for the runner on first to get caught intentionally in a rundown but delay the tag until the runner on third crosses the plate; the run will count. It's a conservative, play-for-one-run strategy, something you might use against Gooden or Valenzuela. But why does Tommy Lasorda call for it with Greg Brock, the Dodgers' hottest power hitter, at the plate? Brock already has three homers in the series and a long out to center field in the first inning of this game.

3. Why *doesn't* Hernandez play catch in front of the dugout? The cabbie isn't the only one who has asked this question. Why does Hernandez do the minimum infield practice and then head for the clubhouse for a crossword puzzle or a card game, eschewing the camaraderie-building pre-game horseplay?

Answers:

1. Because that's the way Davey plays the game, at least early in the season. Be aggressive. Show confidence in your young players. (Christensen drew ball four.)

2. Because Fernandez on the mound used to be in the Dodger organization, and Lasorda knows he still has a lot to learn

about dealing with baserunners. I've seen Sid balk when the runner on first takes off; Lasorda probably figures he'll do the same today. He's hoping the surprise factor will cause a mistake, a pretty good bet. The play isn't in the front of my consciousness at the time, I must admit, not with Brock batting, and I'm certain Sid wasn't thinking about the possibility.

Then Mota yells to Marshall, "Go!"

At that moment, I can call for time or yell to Sid, "Step off!" Instead, I decide to watch Sid make the play. He does two of three things right. He steps off the rubber—no balk—and looks the runner at third back to the bag, preventing the runner from scoring. But he throws late to second base. Marshall is safe.

It's easy to analyze plays after the inning or game is over, but it's another matter entirely to make the right decision in a split-second with people yelling and screaming. One of the coaches will (or should) go over that play with Sid after the game. I think he handled the play well, considering how surprised we all were. And no matter, they didn't score.

3. I get warmed up in batting practice. While some of the guys are playing catch just prior to the game, I'm on the bench, sipping major-league coffee and smoking a cigarette. Sorry, old-timer, but this does not "demoralize" the team.

GAME 39—Mets 2

Dodgers 1

MAY 27

Here's how winning teams win games: Ray Knight, out for a couple of days with vertigo, plays second base tonight for the first time in seven years, and he doesn't find out about the assignment until thirty minutes before the game, after Chapman has come down with back spasms. (A hidden problem with platooning is revealed. When one man goes down, both go down. Chapman can't play because he's hurt; Backman can't play because he can't hit well from the right side of the plate.)

But Knight hits a three-run homer in the third, the club takes off, we win going away behind Darling.

What a pair Knight and I make on the right side of the diamond. The Loud Couple. Ray yaks as much out there as I do—more, and that's saying something.

A fan has started a "D" corner when Darling pitches, for the posting of his strikeouts, and Ron is recording them this year. Not because he's trying to, but because he's a solid pitcher in 1985. He's the Mets' most improved pitcher, and one of the most improved in the league, helped a great deal by Gary Carter, who is made to catch Ron Darling. I've always felt that Gary is great at calling a game with a pitcher who mixes heat with off-speed stuff, and Ron this year has developed a superb slow curve and change-up. Carter works them to perfection, and I haven't seen Ronnie waving off many signs.

So after losing twice to the Dodgers and standing 2–5 on the homestand, we win the final two games and come out of it 4–5. It doesn't look great, but it's important to come back. On every ballclub I've played for, an attitude develops early in the campaign: The team does or does not believe it will win. One or the other, nothing in between, and this belief is hard to change after it's established.

Injuries and all, the Mets believe we'll win.

Game 40—Mets 8
Dodgers 1

MAY 28—SAN FRANCISCO

Hello, Dad. Mom. Gary. Relatives, friends, and neighbors. I'm home!

Being home can be good and bad for Keith. It's always nice to see Juan and Juana (Gary and Keith's nicknames for John and Jackie, our folks). But at the ballgames at Candlestick Park, with Dad's eyes burning a hole in me at the plate (he always sits behind the third-base dugout for the best vantage), I have had some bad, bad series. I've had great ones, too, but when I'm struggling, it doesn't help to have the professor in the stands. I'm not alone in this regard. A lot of ballplayers who learned the game from their fathers have trouble playing in front of those determined eyes.

My baseball career and my father go hand in hand. It's impossible for me to think of one without the other. He had his own promising career as a first baseman in the Cardinal organization before he was beaned in Houston and his eyesight weakened. I suppose the psychologists would believe that he is vicariously living that lost career through me, his All-Star son. Perhaps. That's not my field. I know he has a passion for baseball, and he knows hitting, and he knows *my* hitting, and when I'm not hitting. . . .

He's a retired San Francisco fireman. He had long periods at the fire station and long periods at home. During those minivacations, Dad organized ballgames for all the kids in the neighborhood. Weekends, summers, and holidays: We played in the morning, took a lunch break, played in the afternoon. He pitched almost every inning.

I pitched and played center field in Little League; Gary, two years older, was the first baseman. I switched to first base after he went to a higher league; we were never on the same team after that. Mom made home movies of our Little League and Joe DiMaggio games, and the family reviewed the swings. Years later, when I was about twenty and playing in the lower echelons of the Cardinal farm system, Dad and I looked back at some of the old footage. He pointed at one of my swings as an eleven-year-old, and said, "That's when I knew you had a chance to be a major leaguer."

He took Gary and me to Candlestick to watch Willie McCovey hit. We made special trips to watch the good left-handed batters around the league, including Rusty Staub when he was with the Colt .45s. We sat behind the third-base dugout when we could.

When I was a sophomore in high school, Dad moved the family from Pacifica, where some kids were getting into trouble, to Millbrae, south of San Francisco. John and Jackie still live in that house. When the Mets play the Giants, I sleep in my old bedroom.

Capuchino High School enjoyed a major reputation in Bay Area schoolboy athletics. We were the Mustangs. Gary was a senior, and the first baseman on the varsity. I played on the frosh-soph team.

The first summer in Millbrae I didn't play baseball. I lifted weights instead, preparing for the football season, and told Dad I might give up baseball. He said I'd be making a mistake, but if that's what I wanted to do, fine. I was surprised how calmly he took my "decision." He handled the situation perfectly by not pushing me. The summer season away from the game rekindled my interest. I was ready to play again in the spring—as pitcher/first baseman on the varsity. Gary had advanced to Cal Berkeley.

Playing on the basketball team as well my senior year, I missed several of the early season baseball games. My second game back was a disaster. I wasn't throwing well on the mound. Hell, I wasn't ready! I had missed "spring training" entirely. Then I tried to pick off a runner and balked. The coach came out to get me— an unusual step in high school baseball. I went into the dugout to get my first baseman's mitt and was headed back to the field when he stopped me and said, "No. You're not trying. You're benched."

I remember his words verbatim. I had never felt so embarrassed. I walked out of the dugout, took off my uniform in the locker room and left it on the coach's desk. I quit.

A couple of games passed before I was told that the coach wanted to talk to me. He said, "I knew you'd come back, but the only way I'll let you back is if you apologize to me in front of your teammates."

"I can't do that," I replied, and walked out. Dad stood by me. A lot of years later, I still don't believe that the coach was dealing in the right way with a seventeen-year-old kid.

Earlier in the year I had been invited to Stanford for a weekend visit and had seen a list on which Hernandez was their number-two recruiting target for baseball. After I quit the high school team, I never heard from them again. The high school coach was a Stanford alumnus.

I played on a semipro team on the weekends that spring— 1971. In the summer I played in the Joe DiMaggio League, and a lot of pro scouts were in the stands for every game. I hit .500-plus, had a 9–1 pitching record, and struck out 150 in 70 innings. George Silvey, a vice president in the Cardinal organization, watched me pitch the championship game. I struck out nineteen in ten innings, but we lost the game, 2–1.

The scouts were shopping, but they weren't inclined to spend a draft selection on a kid who planned to go to college; Cal Berkeley, specifically, where Gary was a second-team All-American. When Dad told the scouts my price was $50,000 for turning pro instead, they backed off. Only St. Louis decided to take a chance. They chose me in the fortieth round of the June draft (I believe I was the 596th player selected), and in late August they offered $30,000 for my services. I didn't make the decision; Dad decided. I wanted to turn pro, but if he had said, "No, you're going to college," I would have gone to college. I had nothing to say about it. I had a "stage father."

The bonus money was set aside for college, in case I didn't make it in baseball. The odds were not in my favor.

Would I have gone through all those minor-league traumas and tantrums if I had gone to college before turning pro? Probably. College players should be more mature when they start in the minors, but they also have more pressure on them, because they have less time, they're older. Organizations rush them up the ladder quickly.

Dad has seen the best and the worst of his younger son's baseball career—amateur and pro—and he has seldom been without an opinion.

In 1974 at Tulsa, in Triple A, I was killing the ball—hitting as well as I ever have or ever will. I brought Dad to Denver. He had seen me play very little in my three years of minor-league ball, and I wasn't sending movies home. I wanted him to know my progress. And I wasn't nervous about the inspection; nothing could have deflated that swing and tempo. I would have showed it off to the Splendid Splinter, Stan the Man, Stretch McCovey—any of the greats.

Sure enough, I had twelve hits in the series. Dad heartily approved. Oh, sweet bird of youth.

My slumps, however, were a different story. It's difficult for him to wait quietly as I work my way out of a bad habit; it's difficult for me to listen to his judgments. I usually know what's wrong with my swing. I know how to correct it. We're both hard-headed. Dad and I have had terrific arguments.

The worst was during the World Series in 1982. For the first three games I was 0-for-12.

"I know what you're doing," Dad said.

I didn't feel that the World Series was the time for me to set about a major overhaul of my swing. My answer was sharp.

"If I go 0-for-28 in this series, Dad, I'll go 0-for-28. I don't want to know what I'm doing wrong. That's all there is to it."

He said, "If you don't want to hear it, you may not get a hit this whole series."

I just stared at him in disbelief. "Thanks, Dad."

In the fourth game I hit three ropes. They were caught, but I knew I was back. In the final three games I was 7-for-12 with a series-leading eight RBIs.

Last year, we had another major struggle. We didn't talk for two months. Finally I called him and said, "Dad, this is ridiculous. You're my father. I love you. Can't you just let me do it on my own?"

"Let me get your mother," he said.

As the world turns.

3. IN A DARK FOREST

MAY 29—SAN FRANCISCO

So it is with some trepidation that I play today, in the first of the short two-game set with the Giants. I've been hitting the ball better for the last four or five games, but I can't claim real confidence.

At least we're playing during the day. Anywhere else I prefer nights, but if you haven't sat for three hours in cold, windy, foggy Candlestick Park in the middle of the "summer," you haven't experienced baseball at its worst. The park is horrendously situated in one of the worst fog zones in San Francisco. Politics put it there, Dad tells me. They give out buttons to fans who make it through an extra-inning night game. It's brutal. Making it worse for the players, Candlestick is the only park in the league without access to the clubhouse from the dugout. We can't go down for hot, comforting coffee when we need it most.

The downside of the day game is the terrible sun field. Every field is the sun field for these noon starts; noon so that the game can end before 3 p.m., when the fog rolls in.

Knight playing third loses Gary Rajsich's foul pop in the first inning, and Rajsich capitalizes by slamming a two-run double and then scoring.

Another lost pop fly should cost us a run in the fifth inning, but doesn't. Rafael Santana loses Chili Davis' pop to shortstop. Rajsich hits another hard shot, this one into the right field corner. Davis should score easily from first—except that the ball rolls through a little gap in the cyclone fence. Thus, it's a ground-rule double, so Davis has to return to third base. Lynch strikes out Jeff Leonard to end the inning.

The fans bemoan the bad luck of the Giants; that gap in the wall cost them a run. I look at it differently: If Davis had been running all the way on his pop-up, he would have been on second after Santana lost it, and he would have scored on the ground-rule double. I'm not blaming Davis for not running hard, because I might not have either, but at Candlestick Park in the day, with the wind and the sun, we should run hard on anything in the air.

I can't report firsthand on the rest of the game. I'm thrown out of the contest. Here's what happened, in its entirety:

Jim Quick is the home-plate umpire. Quick and I have had no problems in the past. I'm 0-for-3 coming up in the eighth inning—two rollers and a pop fly—and am not all that happy. But I'm not looking for a fight, either. Not yet.

Mark Davis' first pitch is a fastball five inches inside (I don't exaggerate). I take the pitch without a second thought—then flinch when Quick yells, "Strike!"

"Damn it, that ball's inside" is my reply. The problem is that I deliver these words to the umpire's face. I could mutter them while I'm looking down at the plate or out at the pitcher and nobody has a problem, but I walk back to Quick for a face-to-face meeting. Then I repeat myself, in harsher language. He tells me to get back in the box.

Just a split-second before Davis' second pitch, I step out, asking for time. Quick glances at me, smirks, gets down on one knee and calls the pitch. It's so outside he has to say ball, but that doesn't matter to me. He should have called time. I'm furious, but I don't say a word to him. To myself I say, "You no-good prick."

I also know I'm going to get thrown out of the game. I'm going to let him have it after this at-bat, even if I hit a home run.

I foul off a couple of pitches, then take a slow curve on the inside corner for strike three. Fair enough, that's a good pitch. As soon as he rings me up, I walk off proclaiming, "I'm struck out. That was a strike. But you're a no-good motherfucker."

"What did you say?" Quick demands.

I repeat myself, and add, "You're a horseshit umpire, to boot."

And he barks, "Take that to the clubhouse."

And then I light into him with both barrels and have a good time doing it. I'm right in his face and get more enraged when Bill Robinson and Davey feel compelled to restrain me. Hell, I'm not going to hit the guy. Quick bumps me and I bump him back and he yells, "Don't you bump me!" Sometimes the umps are like the writers. They can dish it out, but give it back to them and they turn into crybabies.

The raging argument is a helluva show for the hometown fans, some of whom I happen to know.

Davey and Bill push me back toward the dugout. For this one day only at Candlestick I'm glad that I have to cross the diamond to get to the clubhouse down the right field line. As I pass Quick at a distance of fifteen feet, I call out, "Stick it up my ass, Quick. I'll get my hits without your help."

I could have said to Quick after the first pitch, "Jim, you blew

it. You're a better umpire than that. Let's bear down out here."
That's a good approach with the umps. It makes the point while
building up their egos. Instead, I lost my cool, and then when he
smirked while not granting the time out, well, he lit my fuse.

Already in the clubhouse is my good friend and our starting
pitcher. Ed Lynch had been lifted for a pinch hitter in the inning.
I have failed to mention that my tantrum interrupted a major
Met rally. Going into the eighth, we were down 3–0, but one run
was in as I came up, two men on, only one out. I made the second
out.

Lynch and I go through a six-pack and watch the game on
the clubhouse television. He hasn't given up hope for the inning,
yelling to Carter, "Get me off the hook!" Gary doubles in the tying
runs. Lynch ups the ante and yells to Foster, "Win this one for
me, George!" George delivers.

Eddie and I have a great time at the ballpark that inning, and
the next two, as we hold on to win. A most satisfying come-from-
behind victory, one of our few. A fine way to start the road trip.

Carter grabs me in the festive clubhouse, "You're my idol. I
heard every word of that."

GAME 41—Mets 4
Giants 3

MAY 30

The season is one-quarter over and those forty-one games have
flown by, for a simple reason: Despite our problems, we're 26–
15 and leading the division, a game in front of Montreal, one and
a half ahead of the Cubs. However, St. Louis, only five behind
after a slow start, is the team that finally has my attention: All
those singles hitters and baserunners united with slugger Jack
Clark, acquired this year from the Giants. He must feel as if he's
been let out of the Candlestick prison. I say watch out for the
Cardinals and the Cubs. Rusty fears the Expos.

The next six-plus weeks will be dicey for the Mets: We have
thirty-one road and only fourteen home games before the break.
That's because May was a "home" month, basically, and it has to
even out. So we're on the road until the break in mid-July; then
we're home for the last half of July and much of August; then
we're on the road much of September.

I look at the batting leaders. I'm not among them but I'm not worried. Some pretenders are on the list. I'll be there in the end. (On my optimistic days, I boast. On my downer days, I fret. It has always been a roller coaster for me.)

It's also voting time for the All-Star team. Frankly, my dear, I don't give a damn. As I said earlier, I'd rather be a player's player, and the players don't vote. Now that the fans have been given the ballot, the All-Star team is not as prestigious in our minds. Ask us. It won't matter to me if I don't make the team. I could use the three days off. The teams picked at the end of the year mean more, especially the *Sporting News* team, which is voted by the players.

Yesterday's rhubarb saga continues today. Throwing me out isn't the end of it with this umpiring crew. For the first three innings today, crew chief Paul Runge at second base glares at me as I throw balls to the infielders. I want to ask him what the hell he thinks this is—fifth grade? Going to report me to the principal? Hell, yesterday is over. I yelled at Quick. Jim yelled at me. He threw me out, which is his prerogative. I'll pay the $250 fine, or whatever it turns out to be, when Chub Feeney sends me the bill. Let's forget it and play ball on this beautiful afternoon. But Runge clearly wants to carry things over.

In the fourth inning, I walk on a full count, after checking my swing on ball four. Alex Trevino, the Giants' catcher, makes a big mistake. He should appeal to the third-base ump, Quick, who would thumb me out. How do I know? After that half-inning, Runge and Quick are conversing and I watch closely as I toss rollers. At one point, Quick gives the punch-him-out sign. You'll never convince me Runge hadn't asked, "If the catcher had appealed, would you have called Hernandez out?"

The sixth inning is the final straw—for Davey! Mookie is on second, Backman on first. The first pitch to me is a ball, very wide. The second pitch is borderline on the outside corner. Ed Engle calls out, "Baa—" and catches himself, or so it seems to me, as he remembers that this is Hernandez at the plate—call the pitch a damn strike if at all possible. It's too late on this pitch, however, so he makes up for his mistake on the next offering, which is approximately four inches off the ground. He calls it a strike.

The correct call would have made the count 3-and-0. Davey, seeing the pitch, assumed the count was three balls, and flashed the "take" sign to Harrelson at third. Then he saw that Buddy wasn't passing the sign along to me, and realized to his disbelief that the pitch had been called a strike. That made about four bogus "strike" calls against me for the day. I hadn't said a word on any of them. Davey (he confides all this to me later) decides to let this umpiring crew have it, one way or another.

If he had any doubts, they were erased on the ensuing play, my ground ball to second. It's a double play all the way, but just to make sure, Runge flags Backman for interference—sliding out of the base path to break up the double play. That infraction is called about once a year. Besides, Backman hadn't left the base path. Running to first, I was in perfect position to see the action. Runge just wanted to make certain that I hit into a double play: The batter as well as the runner is automatically out on that interference call.

Davey holds his tongue. In the eighth inning, he gets a better chance. Mookie chops a ball high over his and the catcher's head. He stays in the box, the ball comes down and the catcher tags him.

"Out!"

Out?? The ball was in foul territory. The catcher was standing in foul territory when he caught it. Davey charges from the dugout. Unfortunately, our manager is not great in rhubarbs. He just can't yell, so his verbal assault loses some impact. But he makes his points, and chief among them is the umps' attitude toward Hernandez.

"I have no respect for this crew now," he argues. "You have a vendetta against one of my players."

I appreciate this. Davey sticks up for me. He gets thrown out, he'll pay a fine, too, but all the players respect him for it. The platoon wants to see the general get down in the trenches when it's required.

It's a satisfying day in other respects, too. Foster, hitting hard now for three games, wins for us with a homer in the fifth. Gooden strikes out a season high fourteen, pitches out of two big jams (two on, nobody out), and strikes out two batters in the eighth, all three in the ninth.

But the game should have been tied 2–2. The Giants should have scored in the sixth. On a wild pitch that got at least twenty, maybe thirty feet away from Gary, Manny Trillo on third doesn't go home. He could have made it on his hands and knees. Again, the bad team finds a way to lose. That talent almost *defines* the bad team. We've won half a dozen games in the past month as a direct result of the other teams' mistakes. Just yesterday: Chili Davis' failure to get to second on the pop fly.

On the other hand, I can recall only one game that we've blatantly and literally thrown away—against the Pirates in late April, when Jesse threw the ball into left field while fielding a sacrifice bunt.

While everyone is congratulating the Doctor on the mound after the game, Gary stops me with the news that Engle was messing with him behind the plate, too. When Gary questioned a call, Engle retorted, "Shut the fuck up."

For the most part, I respect the umps. We make errors. They make errors. But I don't appreciate this drill sergeant's macho ego some of them assume. The big question now is the grapevine factor. Will this crew spread some nastiness against the Mets? We'll wait and see.

Am I being objective about all this? Absolutely.

, GAME 42—Mets 2
Giants 1

MAY 31—SAN DIEGO

Jack Murphy Stadium is my favorite park in the league (including Wrigley Field), and San Diego is my favorite town to play in. I'd like to finish my career here—even though it couldn't be less like Shea Stadium and Manhattan. The place is relaxed, the fans actually *sing* the national anthem in key, and the swallows sweep in at dusk, seeking moths. It's beautiful.

The stadium, by the way, is named in honor of a popular local sportswriter who died several years ago, the brother of Met announcer Bob Murphy. Among all the new arenas, it's the only one even close to being "intimate" in the manner of the old ballyards. The stands are near the field and the seats are steeply banked, pulling the fans closer to the players. The other new stadiums are sprawling. They're just that, stadiums as opposed to parks.

San Diego is a good place to forget about lawyers (my wife has recently hired a new one, so I have a new one, too) and indictments (seven were handed down in Pittsburgh today, for drug sales) and labor negotiations (a few players have suggested a boycott of the All-Star game, as a negotiating point).

Hardball '85.

Jack Murphy Stadium will also be a good place to start a new month. Hernandez is going to bat around .240 for May. So much for a worthwhile streak of consecutive months batting at least .300. There are weak and strong .240 averages. Mine is weak: 10 RBIs for the month.

More frustrating was the on-again, off-again batting rhythm. Several times I thought I was getting it together, only to start sputtering. Then I had the strong positive feeling as we left New York for this West Coast swing, to be followed by the disaster at Candlestick; 0-for-7, and not even a solidly hit ball. I stunk up the place. But if the team can turn a page, so can I.

A month ago I thought Mookie Wilson was going to bat second, then it looked like he wasn't going to be batting at all, then after giving the shoulder a rest he was leading off again. Today it's official: Mookie is the Mets' lead-off man, and to hell with the fact that he doesn't walk. I like Davey's decision (not that he's concerned whether I like it or not). Put up your most exciting player first.

In the eighth inning, Mookie homers to tie the game. Davey puts in Sisk to hold them. Doug should kiss his manager! Davey believes in him, period. That's a wonderful feeling to play ball with. The opposite is a killer.

The confidence and tutelage of a few men in the Cardinal organization saved my career.

1977. After I finally got a chance to play in 1976, following the All-Star break, hitting well over .300 for the last half, I thought the job was mine the following year. But Red Schoendienst was fired, and Vern Rapp was named the new manager. They hired him because he was tough and conservative, a throwback to the era of the Gashouse Gang. No facial hair, he decreed. I shaved my mustache. Bad enough, but nothing compared to the shock of his announcement to Roger Freed that Freed would get a chance to win the first-base job in 1977. It was only fair, I suppose, because Freed had been player of the year in Triple-A ball the year before. But now I had to prove myself all over again, for a manager who had never expressed any special confidence in me.

I was begging myself to get off to a good start that April. I had never enjoyed a decent, much less a good start in my life. Hitting .150 or .200 for the first couple of weeks would have sunk me.

Thank God, I hit four homers in the first ten games. I have no explanation. I finished the year at .291, fifteen homers and ninety-one RBIs.

The next year, 1978, I was second in the league in hitting at the All-Star break, got pissed when I didn't make the team, and was terrible thereafter. But Rapp was fired at midyear and Ken Boyer took over; the same Ken Boyer who had saved my batting swing in Tulsa, who had better things to worry about than my mustache, so I grew it again.

He stuck by me all year, even though I fell from .323 to .255. Maybe Vern Rapp would have put in Roger Freed.

At a sporting-goods convention a couple of years later, I talked with Ted Williams. He said 1978 was my sophomore slump. None of the other half-years had counted in this regard, he theorized. My first full year was 1977, so I was due for the slump in 1978.

Whatever. In 1979 I was once again very concerned about getting off to a good start. Will the real Keith Hernandez please step forward? The writers put that question.

I hit .232 that April.

The press rubbed its hands in glee:

Hernandez is a head case.
Great talent, but something missing somewhere.
He's his own worst enemy (an assertion I don't dispute).

My career was on the line—again. Ken Boyer took me aside and said, "Look, you're my third hitter every game this year. Don't worry about it. You're the man."

That's what I needed. I won the batting title and the MVP. Boyer had saved my career—again.

I sincerely hope Davey's confidence in Sisk yields the same results. For the pitcher. For the team.

It's just tough luck that Dougie loses this game, on a single, a sacrifice bunt, and another bunt. That second bunt, a drag by Carmelo Martinez with a runner on third and two outs, looks great because it works, but I still doubt the wisdom. It was an advantageous two-ball count, the man had hit three homers in his six previous at-bats. As Orange remarked later, "If you do it, you'd better be successful." A pop-up gets him chewed out. He's the hero, however, and Sisk is the loser.

But look at your scorecard. All ground balls but one. The sinker must be sinking.

I'm 0-for-4; for the West Coast, 0-for-11. After the game, Davey tells me I'm getting tomorrow off. You look flat, he says. Go out tonight and have some fun.

Reading his players is half the job of a manager, and Davey is right on target with me. I haven't switched to West Coast time yet, so I'm getting up at nine o'clock instead of my accustomed noon. My legs feel like rubber; hot baths aren't helping.

What is all this about my tired legs? Last summer was the first time I can remember my legs getting tired. It was in August after the ill-fated four-game series with the Cubs, which concluded with a doubleheader on Sunday. I felt great that day, but the next day the pins wouldn't support me. We were flying to St. Louis to start a series, and I told Davey that I needed a rest; that admission was a first for me. And now this year, tired already in June??

Tonight, Rusty, Sid Fernandez, and I go to "TGI Friday's," a local club, where I imbibe heavily and look for pity: so hot in New York, albeit briefly, so cold now on the road. Worse, this is the longest I've ever gone without the hot, hot streak. I thought it was starting back in New York; doesn't look like it now. I'm getting scared.

"Bullshit," says Rusty. I should know that Rusty is the last man to go to with self-pity. This is the man whose motto is: "Life's a bitch, then you die." It's Rusty's considered opinion, in this his twenty-third year in the majors, that self-pity is the greatest occupational hazard for athletes.

Quit feeling sorry for yourself, he goes on. Four months of the season remain. Way over a hundred games. The streaks will come. Patience.

But I have never been patient.

GAME 43—Padres 4
Mets 3

JUNE 1

Staub and I go to the new James Bond movie this afternoon. Walking to the car after the show, we pass a crippled man struggling to walk with his braces. Rusty gives me a pointed look. I know. Here I am with my career and security and future, trying to feel sorry for myself, while this fellow. . . .

At the stadium I try to talk Davey into playing me tonight and resting me tomorrow, Sunday. My reasoning is simple. Tonight we face Mark Thurmond, a lefty. With our platooning system, we're stronger against right-handed pitchers, one of whom throws tomorrow. Leave me in against the left-hander. We'll need the help.

Davey won't budge. I'm resting.

Davey, you're a genius. With Carter playing first and Hurdle behind the plate, the Mets come through with a 5–3 win. Hurdle always looks good in the few opportunities he has to play. I'd like to see him get more time.

Hurdle won't play much, however, because he's the number three catcher, and the number five or six outfielder. Outfielders we have—it's infielders we lack. Cashen still hasn't replaced the injured Gardenhire. I don't understand it.

As Whitey Herzog points out, injuries hurt the most by hurting the bench, not the starting lineup. Heep has been filling in just fine for Darryl—but now Heep isn't on the bench, so our bench suffers.

Pinch-hitting in the seventh, I don't have a prayer against Luis DeLeon. Pinch-hitting is difficult enough. It's worse for me because the only time I fill this role is when I'm being rested. I'm only rested when I'm flat. Ergo, I only pinch-hit when I'm not hitting well. Three strikes and I'm out.

A snowy owl drones over the park tonight, flying high and straight down the third-base line from beyond left field. It's ten times as large as the darting swallows, and seems uninterested in the moths; uninterested in us, too.

The provocative passage of the owl rivals a story told by my agent's partner (and son). He was watching a spring-training game in Florida when a towering foul pop landed on a light standard supporting a ramshackle nest. A large hawk lifted into the sky. The game stopped and players and fans looked up as the bird circled the perimeter of the field twice, slowly, and then returned to its vantage on top of the pole.

GAME 44—Mets 5
Padres 3

JUNE 2

Gary Hernandez went to Cal Berkeley for three years before he was drafted in June 1972, by St. Louis. He signed immediately and attended the rookie league camp in Sarasota, Florida that summer, while I was finishing my first year of A ball in St. Petersburg. Two years older than his brother, Gary was a year behind me in the Cardinals' minor-league system.

It was a tough summer for me and I was in a particularly bad slump when Gary got away from his duties to drive to St. Pete to watch me play. We talked before the game, then I went 3-for-4 with a home run.

It has always been this way. On the ballfield, I'm free; with Gary in the stands, I soar.

The brothers were roomies in the minor-league spring training camp in 1974. He went on to Modesto, I to Tulsa. He played one more year in the minors before leaving the game after the 1975 season. As reported, I had started out that year dismally with the big team, then was demoted to Tulsa, where I tore it up. Late in the season I rejoined the Cardinals. Soon thereafter, we were playing a series at Wrigley Field. Gary and a teammate, their season concluded, drove to Chicago to watch our games. He arrived at the park late, grabbed a ticket and rushed up the aisle just as the Cub pitcher was winding up for his delivery—to me. I hit a homer precisely as Gary reached the top of the aisle, from where he saw the play.

I can say it best with these four words: I love my brother. I wish we could be together all the time.

My soon-to-be former wife told me that Gary is jealous of my success in the game. After she said that a couple of times, I looked as carefully as I could for the signs. I didn't find them. I don't find them now. I don't think he is.

Gary is almost my opposite: calmer and more laid-back. He

has suggested to friends that one reason I made it as a major leaguer and he didn't is the nervous intensity that gets me in trouble but also drives me on. Perhaps. Gary was never as driven as I was, that's a fact, but he worked hard and had talent; those are facts, too. Who can say what happened? Who cares now? He has his family and career in the insurance business. I have my kids and career as a baseball player.

He's in the stands this afternoon after flying down from San Francisco, so I'm not the least surprised that I'm 3-for-4, a couple of rockets, everything to left field as pitched. But Gary has to share credit with Davey, who made me rest; and maybe with that man on the crutches, who delivered a cautionary message without saying a word or even looking at me; and maybe even with the snowy owl, who also wasn't interested in my problems.

Much more important than all this, perhaps the team is finally hitting in bunches. A three-run inning yesterday, another today, and a possibly bigger one ruined by some faulty baserunning, mainly mine. With Wally Backman on third, me on second, Carter grounds to third. In that situation, the runner on third has explicit instructions: Either go for the plate on any ground ball or go only if the ball gets through the infield. The runner on second cues off the runner on third, for obvious reasons.

Presumably on instructions, Backman races home and gets caught in a rundown. My job now is to sneak into third, and Carter all the way to second, perhaps, while Backman delays the putout. But as I approach third, the throw from the catcher to third baseman Nettles arrives in timely fashion. Right then, I should stop and retreat. They can't chase me because they have to deal with Backman between third and home. But I vapor lock and run right into the play at third. Nettles tags me and still has time to get the ball back to the catcher to continue Wally's rundown.

But Nettles drops the ball on a return throw, so Backman races toward home.

But Nettles alertly throws to second, nailing Carter.

But Backman crosses home plate before Carter is tagged, so his run counts.

Truly, a Chinese fire drill on the bases. The crowd buzzes for five minutes. There's a good bit of discussion in the dugout, too. The Mets score, but thanks only to the Padres' miscue and without any help at all from me. I'm a better baserunner than that. "Second grade, second semester" is Staub's aphorism for these mistakes.

In the eighth, it's an ump who vapor locks—Fred Brocklander at first base. Danny Heep's long drive over the wall down the right field line is fair by ten feet. But Brocklander calls it foul! Heep starts screaming, Bill Robinson coaching at first joins in, Davey races out. Give Brocklander credit—he asks home plate ump Ed Montague if he saw the ball better. Yes. Montague immediately overrules the call and awards Heep his homer. Now Dick Williams of the Padres lodges a complaint, but it's pro forma; his heart isn't in it, that's obvious. Everyone in the stadium but Brocklander knows the ball was fair.

Montague, by the way, has asked me about the beef with Quick, and Davey's accusation in San Francisco. Montague's crew is calling them fairly this weekend. The dispute is over with until the Mets draw the Runge crew, when I expect trouble. I could bother to find out when that will be, but won't.

And now what are the writers going to say about the absence of Strawberry? Heep continues to do the job, and when it counts in the game. The Straw gets his job back next month no matter what Heep is hitting or how many runs he has driven in, for the simple reason that Darryl may be one of the great players of the future, or the present. But will Davey sit Heep down while Foster is flirting with an interstate average? Will the Shea fans let him? Yes, the fans have a say in this matter, indirectly. They were one of the reasons Davey sent Sisk to Tidewater. Davey admitted it.

I think Davey will play George. Figure in that George won both games in San Francisco and one in this series with big hits. He'll hit this year, sometime. Also figure in that team-leading $2 million salary. It would be tough to sit him down. Davey could have it both ways and platoon him with Heep—George against lefties, Danny against right-handers—but that would be difficult because Heep would get more playing time than George, and besides, George is just as effective against righties as lefties.

Most important of all, perhaps: What a player Heep is to have on the bench. He hit four pinch home runs two years ago.

The other hero today is Sisk, with four scoreless innings, only one hit, and one walk, against a hot team. It will do wonders for his confidence—and maybe that's all he's lacking. Maybe the elbow is fine.

So now we're 4-of-5 on the road, with two of those victories solid games against the best team in the West. I'm hitting again— I know it!—and the bus ride up to L. A. is utterly pleasant . . . for a bus ride.

GAME 45—Mets 7
Padres 3

JUNE 3—LOS ANGELES

I'm cited in this week's *Sports Illustrated* as the fifth-best clubhouse tipper in the National League. I take no great pride in my $100 tip; on the contrary, the guys who leave $10 per day are cheapskates, pure and simple. The norm of around $40 for a three-game series is thin, too. All of us can afford better than that. Good clubhouse service is like having a valet. The clubhouse man unpacks our bags, washes uniforms and underclothes, polishes shoes and sets out the refreshments. My favorites among the guys are Jim Muhe right here at Dodger Stadium and Claude Lavoie in Montreal.

Come on, ballplayers. Your public is (now) watching.

They're watching tonight for four hours as the Mets lose a tough one against Orel Hershiser and his sinking fastball. I roll it on the ground in the first inning; walk in the fourth, with the distinct impression that Hershiser doesn't want to pitch to me with Wilson on second base; then drive his first pitch in the sixth down the line in left for a double to score Wilson and Backman. A satisfying hit. All day Orel had been pitching me inside or way outside. As I go to the plate in the sixth I'm thinking "inside," and have to fight off this preconception. Hershiser fooled me at Shea when I looked for the curve off him and got a good fastball to hit, but couldn't. Against left-handers I do prepare in terms of zones, but against right-handers I want a free and uncluttered mind, as the Buddhists teach.

In this inning I successfully clear my brain of the temptation to guess. I'm ready for anything, especially on the first pitch. I've been burned on enough of them lately. Hershiser's fastball is outside and I hit it there.

Mota coaching at first says later, "Nice piece of hitting."

I reply, "He got it up on me."

And Mota says, "Yeah, but you still have to hit it."

That's right, Manny, and you were perhaps the greatest pinch hitter ever. As difficult as our job is, we should feel good any time we hit the ball hard, even if it's right over the heart of the dish. Less than half a second is not much time to pick up, read the seams on, and swing at the easiest pitch in the world.

With the score tied at two in the ninth, I single off reliever Ken Howell. What was I saying awhile back about lulling the opposition to sleep? After Carter and Foster have been retired, Howell has forgotten all about my existence. Hell, I'm standing on second base when Heep swings—but he fouls it off. Returning to first, I holler to Yeager behind the plate, "I had that base!" He sneers. The aborted steal is made moot by Danny's homer, which is in turn made moot by the Dodgers' rally off Orosco.

My theory is that Jesse needs more innings. At work here is the Catch-22 of relieving: If the starters are doing well, the relievers don't get enough work, so when they are called on, they're not sharp. Great starting impedes great relieving.

In Jesse's case, there's an added Catch-22. He needs work, but too much work gives him a tender—that's always the description, "tender"—elbow.

After the Dodgers tie the game in the ninth (I gather from the newspapers that their comebacks have been even rarer than ours), both teams squander chances in the extra innings. Our best is in the eleventh. Backman on second, no outs, I get him to third on a ground ball to the right side that's actually a pretty good piece of hitting. I hit a rope foul on the second pitch, and the ball I ground to first is on the outside part of the plate, a two-strike pitch. Not an easy one to pull, but that's my job in the situation, with a runner on second and none out. Get him to third base. Whitey Herzog impressed on me the importance of that unofficial sacrifice.

But they walk Carter to set up a double play with Foster at the plate. George strikes out. Heep flies out to end the inning.

In the bottom of the twelfth, the Dodgers score the winning run when Santana throws the ball away; the game that got away. Not many have, from us, and that's why we're winning without doing much hitting.

Sisk is the victim in the inning. It's clear that Davey isn't going to use Joe Sambito in tight situations. How dispiriting this must be for Joe, who was so good three years ago. Then his arm went, and now nobody trusts it. It might be back, or, more likely, he might have developed into a different kind of pitcher, but he may never get the opportunity to prove it. The players on the team are aware of this and other ongoing dramas (like Sisk's) but we can't afford to dwell on them or get sentimental. We can dwell only on baseball.

It's interesting that Davey uses Christensen and Knight in pinch-hit situations against left-hander Steve Howe in the last inning, while Staub, our specialist in this department, sits on the bench. Davey wants the righty-lefty matchup, and he wants to show confidence in these two struggling players.

GAME 46—Dodgers 5
Mets 4

JUNE 4

The most exciting six outs of the season, without question, in the bottom of the eighth and the top of the ninth tonight.

Bases loaded, none out for the Dodgers against Dwight. The Doctor throws nine fastballs, shaking off Gary a couple of times. Greg Brock, who beat him ten days ago with a homer off a change-up at Shea, strikes out; Mike Sciosca pops up; Terry Whitfield strikes out, an overmatched hitter if I've seen one, and I've seen quite a few the last two years against Doc.

I've watched Gooden accomplish amazing things on the mound, but I figured the Dodgers had to score at least once after loading the bases with two hits and an intentional walk. It's difficult *not* to score. I was as amazed as the 50,000 fans who were cheering for their team but then, nine pitches later, were buzzing with excitement. They knew what they had witnessed. I've heard that Arnold Palmer in his heyday absolutely willed the ball into the cup. I had doubts, but no more. I've now seen Dwight Gooden exert that kind of domination with a baseball.

That half-inning is only half of the story. We counter in the ninth with an identical situation against Valenzuela. The score is tied, 1–1. I start the rally with a single to center. After a strikeout and two roll-outs for the evening, I'm fed up with Freddie's pitches and a big hole pawed in the batter's box. These are two good reasons to move up in the box: Get out of the hole and maybe catch a breaking ball before the break. I hit the slider.

Carter singles, Foster walks, and here we are, sacks drunk, no outs. Perfect symmetry.

The crowd is roaring again—but not for long, after Heep's sacrifice fly, Santana's single off Valenzuela's glove, and Gooden's single, his third of the night. Another tough-luck outing for Valenzuela, who is an improbable 5–6 with an interstate ERA. If it's consolation, and I imagine it is for Freddie, he loses to the best tonight.

Another official scorer fails to give me an error I deserve. I hope they don't think they're doing me any favors. Give me the damn error. I'll make my ten or so a year. There's no great honor in going through life without a mistake.

I don't even get my glove on this ball, a foul pop near but not too near the stands. The reason is simple: I hear Carter coming. Gary has a way of charging around back here, and we've come close to crashing a couple of times. His 225 pounds have my full respect. I've told him before, I'll probably tell him again, "Gary, give me some breathing room on the pop-ups."

But it's an error and should have been scored that way. After all, the "home book" rule isn't affected. The home book tradition decrees that the home player gets the benefit of the doubt on a close play. If he's the hitter, score the play a hit. If he's the fielder, score the play a hit. Well, on this foul ball the hitter isn't helped by withholding the error from me. Something else may be going on: The scorekeepers, who are local sportswriters, sometimes play favorites. I may have an angel in the press box tonight.

Program notes: Davey played Heep against Valenzuela, left-hander against left-hander. He has put aside the brief experiment of platooning Danny with Christensen in Strawberry's continuing absence. Heep is hitting too well and he deserves the job, and he comes through with the big sacrifice fly tonight.

Strawberry did receive that permission to recuperate out here. Los Angeles is his hometown. He's with the club this series.

GAME 47—Mets 4
Dodgers 1

JUNE 5

Melissa's birthday is today, and I don't get a phone call. She and her mother are on vacation somewhere in the Rocky Mountains, so I can't call her. I've told her mother that I'd be at the Biltmore Hotel, call me collect. No such luck.

Making his first start since April 22, Bob Welch baffles us, and the cheers for him get mixed up with others ringing through the stadium at inappropriate moments: The Lakers and Celtics are playing their championship series this evening. Half the fans have brought portable televisions. The other half is looking over shoulders. The ballplayers slip back into the clubhouse more often than normal, watching the basketball game, too. Lakers lose, Mets lose, I lose. I had Kareem and team. A bad day and night—and now we have to fly across the country.

GAME 48—Dodgers 2
Mets 1

JUNE 6—MIDAIR

In this day and age a coast-to-coast jet has to land to refuel? I thought that insult was reserved for hijackers. But our charter stops for gas in St. Louis, sometime around 4:00 a.m. Tanked up on a pint of Scotch and four hours of card-playing, I flame out royally and start screaming. (On commercial flights, we're restricted to beer and wine. We can have hard liquor on all charter flights except coast-to-coast. Except tonight: I sneak the pint on.)

I'm screaming at no one in particular—just setting my world on fire, that's all. Some of the players and their manager who are trying to sleep aren't too happy. Can't say that I blame them. Can't say that I'm very happy, either. As a team, aren't we supposed to share?!

Funny about this card-playing. Other years I've hated it. For ten major-league seasons I haven't played cards. This year I play all the time, hearts mostly, my deck in my hand as I walk through the clubhouse door. I don't know why.

We don't play for money, our little group of red asses: Hernandez, Christensen, McDowell, coach Vern Hoscheit, a couple of kibitzers.

I will not play for money, and that's one reason I've abstained in years past. Plenty of clubhouse fights, not with fists, necessarily, but with bad words and bad feelings, have broken out over card games. If I were a manager, no gambling among my players would be allowed. Tony Carullo, the clubhouse man for the visiting team at Shea, reports that $500 is sometimes on the table when San Diego comes to town. Dick Williams must know about it, and must therefore condone it. How can I question him? He's only won championships in both leagues. But I wouldn't allow it, and wouldn't play with teammates in a gambling game, when "with" becomes "against."

I get home at 10:00 a.m. Still, it's preferable to staying the night in Los Angeles and flying in today, our off day.

JUNE 7—NEW YORK CITY

Neither divorces, lawyers, nor publishing contracts can keep me from my appointed rounds during the baseball game. Quite honestly, these other matters very, very rarely cross my mind between the first and the fifty-fourth outs. Playing the game is my meditation, the chatter of the players my mantra. Lord knows I need one, as hyper as I am most of the time.

The scheduling this weekend couldn't be worse. Just back from the West Coast and the long flight, we have an eight o'clock game tonight, followed by an afternoon game tomorrow, Saturday, followed by the only Shea doubleheader of the year on Sunday— Banner Day, to boot, which assures an hour and a half between games. But the Cardinals play the same games, and they won't arrive in New York until today, thanks to the rather stingy policy of their management, saving a night of hotel bills. It was like that when I was there and it will stay like that as long as Whitey Herzog is the manager. Whitey argues that it doesn't hurt the team, and I must concede that in my years in St. Louis we won most of the games played only hours after we arrived in town. But he's also saving money.

The Cardinals are coming on fast, literally, with the two top base-stealers in the league, four of the top ten hitters, three of the leading RBI men, etc., etc., etc. Tommy Herr has more RBIs (49) than the Mets' leading batter (me) has hits. *That* is an amazing comparison.

Despite their offensive production, we lead them by five games. We're twelve games over .500; the Cards are only two games over. Our pitching is better and our defense is better (only ten unearned runs allowed, against forty-two for them). They win games 6–2, we win them 3– or 4–2. And they lose games 7–6. We rarely do.

However, don't construe this analysis as a defense of our hitting. We must start hitting or we're in trouble.

We do not start hitting tonight: In twelve innings, we manage just seven safeties for two runs. This against Kurt Kepshire for seven of the innings, and he came into the game with a 2–5 record and an ERA over 6.

But Darling yields only six hits in eight innings. The highlight of his performance is the eighth inning, his last. With Willie McGee on second and two outs, Ronnie gets Tommy Herr, who at .370 is about 100 points above his career average, after falling behind in the count, 3-and-0. Ronnie throws three fastballs and beats him. Outstanding.

Prediction: Willie McGee will end up the year way ahead of Herr in batting average. But .360, McGee's current average, when his career mark is .291? We'll check in October.

McDowell comes on and gets out of a bases-loaded, no-out dilemma in the ninth inning. The last play may prove to be the memorable one, and not as a positive note. With two outs and the bases still loaded, pinch hitter Steve Braun hits one into the hole between me and Chapman. Kelvin had pinch-hit for Backman in the eighth inning, when Whitey switched pitchers.

My failure to take into account Davey's substitution screws up the play, and worse. I move to my right for the ball, but don't get to it, so McDowell has to cover first and take Chapman's throw. If I had remembered that Chapman, not Backman, was playing second, I would not have broken for the ball. Kelvin has more range than Wally. I would have taken for granted that Kelvin would reach the ball. I would have headed for first.

McDowell would not have covered the bag or sprained his right ankle in the process. My mental lapse brings about McDowell's sprain. Now he's out of action. He pitches the tenth, but not with his usual form, and limps off.

I limp off with him. Right after a successful pickoff of Vince Coleman, Willie McGee spikes me on the bag as I take the throw on a grounder.

Drive a nail in next time, Willie! The worst spiking of my career, and first basemen get more spikes than any other position. The foot on the bag is vulnerable. We try to find the edge and the runners try to avoid stepping on us, but accidents are inevitable.

The game drags on toward midnight, the worst imaginable beginning to this series. McGee singles in the eleventh and apologizes profusely as we stand on the bag. A great guy, Willie, and a helluva hitter. But .360!?

In the twelfth, do I have to watch? Santana starts things with an error, Sisk gets a ground-ball out, then everything collapses. Five hits, six runs, and a second error later, we're finished; it's our worst inning of the year.

It's all or nothing with Doug these days. I understand why Davey continues to use him—we'll need Sisk later on, in the stretch—but I don't know of another manager who would stick with him this long. Add in the fact that Doug is pitching with some bad luck, too. The team may start thinking negatively when he comes in: "How will things go wrong this time?"

That would be the kiss of death. Davey's just going to have to stop going to him in the tight situations, for now at least.

But if Davey doesn't show that confidence, how will Doug be ready later in the year? Good point, Davey. If I had your job, I'd be devoted to *R-O-L-A-I-D-S,* too. I would not, however, dump tobacco juice into the cauldron! I tried that stuff once in Denver in 1973, got sick as a dog and swore off.

GAME 49—Cardinals 7
Mets 2

JUNE 8

Four a.m. More ice for the spiked third toe. Is this thing broken? At the ballpark they decide otherwise, but I can't play. The Mets collect three hits and lose to Tommy Herr's ninth-inning homer off Tom Gorman, after Ed Lynch has held the hottest-hitting team in baseball to two hits in eight innings.

The starters work only every fifth day, as Lynch points out in his conviction that he has the world's best job, but I suspect the frustration sometimes inflicted on that day carries over for the next four. Hitters at least have another crack at it the following game.

The Cardinals' basic lineup features five switch-hitters. Switch-hitting is supposed to be a great advantage, as "proved" by all the managers who juggle pitchers in order to obtain lefty-lefty, righty-righty matchups, and opposing managers who juggle batters to avoid same.

I'm not convinced. I know it would be a disadvantage for me. I hit left-handed pitching about as well as right, and I'm scared to death standing at the plate right-handed, and always have been. I'm a klutz from that side, without coordination; a tennis ball terrifies me.

A whiffle ball I can handle. Dad made me bat right-handed in whiffle-ball games because he was afraid the light plastic bat would lure me into uppercutting. If I was going to uppercut, he didn't want it to affect my left-handed swing. Likewise, he never let me play slow-pitch softball, in which an uppercut is required to hit the steeply descending ball. And of course I couldn't face the terror of the softball batting right-handed.

A golf swing is the ultimate uppercut, however, and I play that game left-handed. I don't worry about it. I don't play enough for anything to happen—in either sport.

Davey doesn't worry about putting me into lefty-lefty situations. He chooses me, bad toe and all, to pinch-hit for Lynch in the eighth, Christensen on first, two out. Left-hander John Tudor, who looks a lot better than his 2–7 record, avoids the plate with two pitches, then makes it official: He issues my third intentional walk from a left-handed pitcher. I'll take it as a compliment, and to hell with all the switch-hitting Cardinals.

Alas, a lefty, Tom Gorman, replaces right-hander Lynch in the ninth inning, so Herr simply steps around the plate and hits his homer from the right side.

We can handle the switch-hitting. If I envy anything about the Cardinals, it's their speed. Vince Coleman's legs would be worth fifty hits to me. So it seems intuitively, until quick math shows that fifty more hits would have jumped my average in 1984 from .311 to .402, highly unlikely.

Today's largely uneventful pitchers' duel proves too tedious for the fun-seeking fans. In the middle innings they generate their most coherent, enthusiastic, and long-lasting waves of the year, which wash around and around the stadium ad nauseam.

The fans miss a good, close contest; now we have lost one game to Cardinals' hitting and another to their pitching. Tomorrow is two games. We cannot lose them both. Cannot.

GAME 50—Cardinals 1
Mets 0

JUNE 9

I feel pretty safe saying that we cannot lose two because I know Doc is pitching one of our games. I wouldn't put that "cannot" burden on anyone else on the staff. We put it on Dwight regularly. Try it sometime when you're twenty years old. (I admired the lead in one of the Los Angeles newspapers following Doc's great game against Valenzuela. The writer said Gooden got out of the bases-loaded situation "about as easily as the average twenty-year-old breaks a date.")

I had almost forgotten, relations have been so quiet in the first two games: Umpiring is Paul Runge's crew. In today's first game Runge is on first, and Jim Quick behind the plate. Runge and I have a casual conversation. I need to determine whether I'm in hot water. Runge looks something like Clint Eastwood, so sometimes I call him Clint, and do today in jest. Quickly the conversation turns to Eastwood's new movie, *Pale Rider,* which we both hope to catch. Runge and I are fine. He's not a bad guy. I went overboard in my denunciations in San Francisco.

Quick behind the plate doesn't look at me as I come up for the first time, and we say nothing. His calling of balls and strikes is fair, and I get a hit off Bob Forsch.

There's no vendetta. I was paranoid.

We see another amazing Gooden performance. He doesn't have his strikeout speed (only four for eight innings), but in the third and eighth innings, speedsters Coleman and McGee are on with less than two outs—and both times Dwight gets Herr and Clark: fly ball, fly ball, strikeout, fly ball. I'll bet no other pitcher in the league has accomplished that this year.

And we score some runs for a change, for a relatively comfortable victory. It's amazing to me how a team will play better behind its ace. By all rights, Darling has earned that support from us, too, but he doesn't get it.

Herzog uses four pitchers in this game. We've now seen Horton, Campbell, and Dayley twice in the series. Herzog has made a decision about reliever Neil Allen: Don't use him.

In the second game today he has no reason to use any of his relievers. His batters bomb Schiraldi and then Sambito for eight runs and his one tough Dominican shuts us down on seven hits. There you are; teams supporting their aces. Andujar is now 11–1, many of those with big early leads.

The first inning should have been a premonition. The Cards try to blow Whitey's favorite play, runners on first and third, two out, etc., but we do a better job of blowing it and they score. Recall the plan: Jack Clark will break for second, drawing the throw from Schiraldi. During the rundown, Herr will score from third.

But Clark blows the play, running right up to Howard Johnson, who's playing shortstop. Tag him and we're out of it. But HoJo, playing a new position in order to give Santana a rest, reacts by the book: Ignoring Clark's proximity, he throws home—too late to get Herr.

HoJo is at shortstop only because we still don't have the spare middle infielder, and I still don't understand. Tell me that a trade is in the works.

For the Mets, the game is a systemwide failure. Two of our fielders—Heep and Terry Blocker—collide while running for a fly ball that goes for an inside-the-park grand-slam homer. On the mound, Joe Sambito.

So we lose three of four to the Cards at Shea, but I still believe we're a better team. Our pitchers weren't intimidated by their base stealers. We picked off a couple. I don't know whether the loose, clumpy infield has anything to do with it. It's certainly different than it was before the West Coast road trip. Some of the Cardinals say it's doctored. They say the infield in Atlanta was soaked. Hey, that's the game. Besides, Astroturf is the last word in doctored ballfields.

The Cards are a hotter team now, that's the difference between us; McGee is swinging a magic wand. Fourteen hits for them today, forty-one over the series, many of them bloops, dinks, six-hop grounders. The Cardinals may just be hitting lucky, and it's our misfortune to catch them now.

Before the second game of this doubleheader, after the hundreds of banners have been carried across the field, Hurdle,

Christensen, Santana, and Harrelson carry signs to the mound: YOU MAKE IT FUN, THANKS.

That's not quite accurate. It hasn't been fun lately. Some of the guys are getting what we call the red ass; they're mad; they want to start playing better, and now. The guy who surprises me is Carter. He's down on himself. I wouldn't have guessed it, but Gary may be like me in this regard: his own worse enemy at times. It's damned hard not to be when you're batting .230 or so, forty points below career.

Wally Backman is almost a basket case. His always tensely muscled face is frozen.

GAME 51—Mets 6
Cardinals 1

GAME 52—Cardinals 8
Mets 2

JUNE 10—PHILADELPHIA

We stink. The aroma of a team meeting is unmistakable. There are two kinds of meetings, ass-kickings and spirit-builders. Either one may be effective, although the ass-kicking can backfire. Vern Rapp in St. Louis held some destructive ass-kickings. He picked up the habit managing in Triple A in the Cincinnati organization, the most conservative in baseball, and he brought it over to the Cards in 1977. Both he and his meetings were intensely disliked. I wouldn't say we had a negative attitude; rather, we didn't have the positive attitude of "Let's *play* for this guy." Rapp lasted a year and a half.

An ass-kicking can be beneficial if the players really are not hustling and haven't realized it, and if they respect the manager who is pointing out this delinquency. But is Davey going to kick Wally Backman's or Gary Carter's ass? My God, they're busting them every day. They just can't hit right now. None of us can.

I prefer meetings called of, by, and for the players, without the manager. George, Rusty, and I organized one last year, when we had lost seven in a row. Everything said was positive. Rusty's five minutes were brilliant; he could be a manager, but doesn't want to do it. The team picked up—too late for the standings but not too late for our pride. Pride, really, must be the biggest motivator for professional ballplayers or bricklayers. Pride plus the competitive blood lust most ballplayers were born with (I don't know about bricklayers).

This team is definitely not quitting. Down 6–1 tonight in Philadelphia, we rally for one in the eighth, three in the ninth. Too little, too late.

We're simply in a terrible, teamwide slump. Backman has fallen into the .260s. Mookie, too. Carter is batting .231. Foster is still lower. Johnson, Knight, and Chapman are under .200. Nobody on the team, including Hernandez, is anywhere close to his career average. I keep coming back to the schedule: We were fine in California, winning five of eight, playing well against the best of the west, San Diego. Then the flight back, the tough series against St. Louis in which the dominoes started falling from both directions, a vicious circle: Runners don't get on, runners aren't driven in, runners don't get on.

When runners are in scoring position, the danger is that the RBI men start pressing. It's absolutely essential that the first and second hitters get on base, but Mookie, Wally, and Kelvin are slumping at the same time. A formula for disaster, as we're proving.

Here's how it goes. In the top of the sixth, when the game is still 1–1, Santana and Johnson get hits. With nobody out, Wilson scorches the ball—but right at Mike Schmidt (playing first base now for the revamped Phillies). A yard left or right and it's a triple, two RBIs.

In their seventh, after a leadoff walk by Sisk to Rick Schu (the new third baseman), Juan Samuel hits a high bouncer to Johnson at third, but HoJo loses it in the lights. Single. Both runners eventually score.

If Roger McDowell were healthy, he comes into the game, but he'll be out another week with his sprained ankle. Nobody is saying as much, but he's the main stopper now. Sisk gets bombed again tonight. Is Orosco's elbow tender or not?

I can come up with just three bright notes. Christensen hits his first major-league homer in the ninth inning. Hurdle has hit the ball hard, with one homer, in two recent starts, and he plays the outfield well. Heep is still hitting the ball hard.

I'm beginning to wonder about the Strawberry factor. Even though his numbers might not be any better than Danny's, is there some other factor working against us in Darryl's absence? Do we need him even if his replacement hits *.350*? Is his presence in the lineup necessary for the psych value against opposing pitchers? It could be.

Just so you'll know: Ray Knight starts against a right-hander tonight, so maybe Davey is again considering going with Ray all the way at third. Maybe Ray will respond with a solid bat. Somebody—Hernandez, Carter, Hurdle, Knight—has to, and fast.

GAME 53—Phillies 6
Mets 4

JUNE 11

Before the game, we're reasonably loose and relaxed, despite the bad streak. As a team leader, a veteran, my main job when things are bad is to stay loose, play around some before and after the game. Look loose, at least. As I told Bob Murphy in the hotel in Houston, the buses to and from the park should be jovial, or at least not stricken, in the worst of times, too. Last night I had to force it a little. Swinging the bat good, but no hits.

Tonight I keep plugging away. Usually I don't carry on a lot before the game, but the Phillie Phanatic makes it easier to play around. The players like this clown who rides around the artificial field on his three-wheeler before the game, baiting us. While I'm stretching in the outfield behind second base, my accustomed spot, he comes after me with the water hose. (The crew waters the patch of dirt around each base.) Carter, Hurdle, and Johnson come to my defense, driving him back, while I go for his cycle. He recovers and comes back after me. I flee.

The Phanatic is the best of the mascots, far better than Fred Bird in St. Louis, Youppi in Montreal, or the Pirate Parrot. San Francisco used to have a great one, Crazy Crab in his crustacean's outfit, but he has retired. He was into masochism, inviting the fans' wrath, and they obliged by pelting him with objects soft and hard. The crab took to wearing a football helmet.

Davey rests the slumping Wilson and installs Hurdle in right field, Heep moving to center, Foster in left—not the fleetest outfield in the league; in fact, the slowest by far, but we need hitting and might have to sacrifice some defense to get it.

In the first inning Backman singles and is thrown out stealing,

I single and am thrown out trying for two. An inauspicious beginning, and it's irrelevant that I was safe on the play.

And you know about the rest, because this is the slaughter to end all slaughters, or the laugher to end all laughers.

The final score: 26–7, you will recall.

It's difficult for a ballplayer to pin down exactly what he feels during a debacle. My reaction shifts between embarrassment and anger. I was angry in the first inning, when we were down 4–0, bases loaded, one out, and Calvin Schiraldi, on a 2-and-2 count against Luis Aguayo, hits him with the pitch. Inexcusable, really, even though Calvin was rushed into the game after Gorfax gave up four hits and two walks to the first seven hitters.

I spin away from the field as Aguayo walks to first. I'm pissed. One batter and one out later, Von Hayes hits his second homer of the inning, a grand slam, and now I figure this is just going to be the basic big-league blowout. Little do I know.

Seven more runs in the second. After two innings, 16–0. Well, alright, a major big-league blowout. I'm getting annoyed, but this should be about it. In the top of the third, Davey calls me over: "Get your at-bat, Mex, then I'll take you out." This is one of the privileges of being a ten-year veteran; they take you out in the hopeless causes. George Foster, however, stays in the whole game. I don't believe he's very happy about it, but the only spare outfielder is Mookie, and Davey can hardly replace a vet with a vet.

It would not be impossible at this stage to get back into the game, not in Veterans Stadium, which, for hitters, is one of the friendliest of all National League parks. The ball flies, as we have seen this evening, the grass is fake—so a lot of ground balls and high chops make it through—and the fence just looks like it's fifty feet closer than Shea's; so it is, in effect. It looks close, I suppose, because the stands encircle the field. Shea is open beyond the outfield, so there is nothing to deceive the eye. It looks like a long way, and it is.

Mike Schmidt and Veterans Stadium. What a mismatch; a pro in the Little Leagues.

Philly must realize that a comeback is possible. They have already played a 23–22 extravaganza this year, against the Cubs in Wrigley Field, another park in which no lead is too big.

So I take my bat against Charles Hudson and in fact we do have a little rally of our own going. Two runs in, two men on, and only one out when I come up. I rip the ball up the middle, but right off Hudson's cheek—the big, soft one on the right side. Could the ball at least bounce twenty feet away so the rally can keep going, and I can muster a hit out of this debacle?

Nooooooooooooooooo.

It has to drop softly right beside him, where he picks it up and flips to first.

Now I'm angry. ANGRY. The rally is just about dead and I'm robbed and the pent-up emotions erupt. I slam my batting helmet down, grab the glove and head for the clubhouse, had it with this goddamn game. Not until the Mets head out to the field after scoring one more run do I learn that I grabbed the wrong glove. After making the last out of the inning, Danny Heep waits near first base for someone to bring it to him. Nobody can find it. Lynch cries out, "Mex must have taken it!" He comes running into the clubhouse and finds it in my locker. I'm already in the shower.

Orange shows up shortly thereafter to inform me and Carter to be sure and stick around. Davey has announced that there will be a meeting after the game. The inevitable meeting has come, but it will have to be different now, following a loss like this.

I wouldn't have left the stadium, anyway. I probably could have gotten away with it—I'd have taken a cab back to the hotel regardless of the score, so they wouldn't have missed me on the bus—but I just wouldn't do it.

We score two more in the fourth, two more in the fifth (remember, it's not that easy to pitch with a huge lead, either), and Sisk holds them for two innings. It's 16–7 in the middle of the fifth.

In the bottom of the fifth the Phillies slam Sambito. Watching a career go down the drain is a sad sight. In fact, I quit watching. The clubhouse fills up as guys can't take it any longer in the dugout. The Phillies score five in this inning, another one in the sixth, and four more in the seventh, all off Joe. We call this hanging out to dry.

With one more inning to bat, they have twenty-six runs and thirty seems a real possibility, with time not running out fast enough. That number is on our minds. Somebody says it aloud.

"Please God, don't let them make it thirty."

As their runs pile up, my anger dissipates, and I decide this embarrassment might be a blessing. Let it clear the air. We've deserved it for weeks, after all; our pitchers are "getting the blame" tonight, but our hitters more than share the cumulative guilt.

Davey does a great job in the meeting: Don't forget this game, fellas. Remember it. We're too good a team to go on like this. Carry this memory on the field tomorrow and the next game and the next game.

Nobody gets his ass kicked. Nobody deserves it.

Frank Cashen looks shell-shocked.

GAME 54—Phillies 26
Mets 7

JUNE 12

Congratulations, team. We make this evening's *World News Tonight* on ABC. Pat Benatar sings "Hit Me With Your Best Shot" while a montage features balls rocketing off Phillie bats and Met pitchers in anguish. Darling, as tonight's starter, kept the log on Met pitches for the game. They totaled an incredible 238. That chart will be legendary.

The newspapers, local and national, are full of all the records the Phillies set last night: most this, most that, most everything. Who gives a damn? Might as well have won 1–zip, but this notoriety on the national news is what we get for being a New York City team. We must like it, because we try our damnedest to look bad and blow this game, too.

With a starting lineup featuring three batters under .200, we nevertheless have fourteen hits through the ninth inning. The Phillies have three hits, but the score is tied 3–3. The Mets get a runner to third base with nobody out in the fourth, fifth, and eighth innings, and a runner to third with just one out in the third and ninth innings. Not one of the five runners scores— impossible, I would have thought.

And our un-fleet-footed outfield finally catches up with us. For the second game in a row, Mookie isn't playing (I haven't asked about an injury, and nobody has informed me) and Heep is in center. He and Christensen, playing right field, mishandle a long fly. Heep misses it at the wall, and John is too close to the play, so the carom skips past him and back toward the infield.

The play goes for an inside-the-park homer, and three runs score. The Phillies lead 3–1 after four innings, and I have a queasy feeling.

In the fifth, with no outs and Knight and Chapman on second and third, I simply press at the plate. I'm crouching too low. I'm a tiger, but I'm not a thinking tiger. I hit the weakest little pop of my life to the third baseman.

In the seventh, I redeem myself with a two-out, bases-empty single. A real clutch blow. I'm so disgusted I don't even acknowledge Bill Robinson's standard greeting to successful hitters who stop at first base, a soft touching of fingers; the opposite of the high-five; the low-two.

All in all, the operative question for the second night in a row is "Can you believe this?" A lot of "fucks" are flying out of the Met dugout this night. I hear Backman's expletive all the way out at first base after I've stranded Darling on third. Wally isn't cussing me. We're all cussing ourselves.

Finally, in the eighth, we blow everything so badly that Davey loses his cool and kicks a stray batting helmet. It clatters down the dugout.

The inning starts beautifully, with Heep redeeming his play on the inside-the-park ball. His two-run screamer over the right field wall ties the game. I'm watching on TV in the clubhouse. Tekulve is pitching, underarm of course, and he tries to come inside to Danny. That's where Bo Diaz holds his mitt. But I see the ball tail back over the plate, and I shout out, "Hit it!" Danny does. He also makes three fine running catches after the miscue in the fourth. It's almost as if the Phillies are aiming it his way. Fuck them.

After the homer, Christensen redeems his own participation in the bungled play by doubling into the left field corner. He moves up on Santana's single. Now we're playing.

Now we blow the suicide squeeze. Right play, right time, wrong execution; none at all, really. Christensen, a pretty fast fellow for a big guy, is on third with one out. Backman's at the plate. Davey flashes the squeeze sign out to Buddy, who relays it to Wally and John. The squeeze is one signal requiring an acknowledgment from the batter, so the runner racing home won't have to duck a screaming line drive.

Backman gives his answer—but with an old sign, no longer operative. Christensen, puzzled, glances over at Buddy, who decides that Wally was intending to answer in the affirmative. Any answer was an affirmative answer, in effect. Harrelson tells Christensen to go. He goes. But Backman, confused at the plate, pulls back his bat at the last moment. Christensen is dead meat, halfway down the line.

Anybody blame Davey for booting the helmet? I think, "Oh, shit. With all this happening, we'll be lucky now to win this game."

At least our depleted pitching is holding up. Darling is fine for seven innings, Orosco holds them hitless in the eighth and ninth.

We go into extra innings and McDowell is unavailable. Apparently his sore ankle functions well enough from a windup, but not from the stretch. Given the recent performances by the rest of the bullpen, Davey has no choice but to entrust this critical game (growing more critical every inning as we blow chances in a demoralizing way) to a raw rookie. Rick Aguilera's major-league debut was rained out at Shea last month, but he gets his chance now.

Before Rick pitches to his first batter, I offer some calming words on the mound. Where the hell is Gary? He should be out here, too, saying something, anything, to the guy in his first game.

One . . . two . . . three. A southern Californian of Spanish heritage who attended Brigham Young for two years, Aguilera has guts.

We finally win the game in the eleventh. I start the inning with a triple to right-center, my first triple in over a year. On grass, it's a single; it's a single or a double if Garry Maddox dives to stop the ball in the outfield. In fact, my first hit of the game should have been stopped by Juan Samuel at second, but he didn't dive for the ball, either.

The line drive rolls to the wall and I look great belly-flopping into third. Actually, my legs have simply given out and I collapse.

Fans are surprised that a baseball player shows fatigue after running hard from home to third base, or from first base to home. It's only 270 feet, after all, not even the 100-yard dash. Let me make a couple of points. First, our bodies are conditioned for running short distances, stopping and starting, crouching, leaping, and diving. Watch one player closely in a ballgame. His legs have worked hard by the *eleventh* inning. Second, try running in steel cleats on Astroturf; it might as well be concrete. Ladies, play eleven innings in high heels and see how your legs and ankles feel. It's a fair analogy. Some players (Strawberry and Wilson) wear sneakers on Astroturf so they'll have an easier time of it on the basepaths and in the field. I need steel cleats in the batter's box dirt, so I suffer elsewhere. The legs collapse going into third base tonight and they're not ashamed of it.

And damned if they don't score. Damned if Santana doesn't offer me a drag off his cigarette in the runway immediately thereafter. "No—*huh huh huh*—thanks—*huh huh*—Rafael—*huh huh huh.*" Damned if Christensen doesn't conclude the four-run rally with his second homer in three games. (John wouldn't have been in the game if I were managing. In the fourth inning, runner on third, one out, I would have sent up Mookie to hit for him, a struggling rookie batting .135. Here's another example of Davey sticking by his chosen; plus, John has been hitting the ball better lately.)

Damned if Aguilera doesn't stop them cold for another inning.

Baseball. Damnedest game I ever saw.

If we had lost, I wouldn't have wanted to be around later. Had I not gotten three hits, I wouldn't have wanted to see Frank Cashen. He overheard me tell the hotel housekeeper this afternoon that she didn't need to change the sheets because I hadn't slept in the bed. Technically, that's a violation of our curfew— whenever it is.

I know when it is: two and a half hours after the game. It's unenforced.

GAME 55—Mets 7
Phillies 3

JUNE 13

"Keith, that ball was fair and you didn't run it out!"

My brain is referring to the pop fly to third base last night, bases loaded, fifth inning. I blacked out after the swing, the ultimate vapor lock, and must have been functionally "unconscious" when I grabbed the wrong glove. Only now, twelve hours later while dozing peacefully, does it hit me; at the time—nothing.

Before the game tonight Tim McCarver, one of the Met announcers, informs me that he knocked me pretty hard on the air. About a minute's worth, somebody else tells me, in this vein: "I'm sorry, Keith, you're a fine ballplayer but you have to run that ball out in the circumstances. You never know what's going to happen." I tell Tim he has nothing to apologize for. He says he isn't apologizing.

He has a job to announce the games as he sees them, and he saw me turn back toward the dugout on a fair ball. The announcers aren't cheerleaders. He ripped me and I deserved it.

The episode still amazes me. I black out with frustration and anger, then wake up with the scene replaying itself in complete detail in my brain. Weird.

Bonehead play of the year: Von Hayes is out attempting to steal *home* in the *first* inning, *Mike Schmidt* at the plate.

Lucky play of the year: Heep at third, Christensen on first, sixth inning, two outs. John is picked off at first but heads for second, Heep breaks for home and scores ahead of the throw. In effect, the guys inadvertently pull off the season's favorite scam.

Earlier in that inning, with Heep at the plate, I'm on third, Carter on second. One out. That's a situation ripe for a suicide squeeze with certain players. It would be unlikely with Heep and me as the principals, but who knows? But Danny doesn't even look down at Harrelson coaching at third. Buddy yells to him, "Danny, step out. Watch the signs!"

Give them something to think about on defense. Heep's carefully studying some bogus signs might draw the third baseman in a step, and that's a lost split-second of reaction time on a shot down the line. The bunt is not on, and after a couple of careful pitches for balls, Andersen walks Danny intentionally. That's respect for Heep, and he's earned it. Davey has said he'll find some place for Heep when Strawberry returns. This promise will give the other outfielders something to think about. Or the first baseman? Heep is also a first baseman.

Christensen singles with the bases loaded, so we go into the eighth inning leading 4–3. What happens next may haunt us for a while. It hurts a hundred times more than the silly blowout: Davey lifts Eddie Lynch after he gets the first out of the inning, bringing in Orosco to face left-handed Von Hayes. Hayes walks, then Glenn Wilson homers.

I don't second-guess the manager's decision. I didn't second-guess the same decision earlier in the year, when Jesse came in for Eddie, who was pitching well, and lost it. But I do think Davey will be more reluctant to make that change the next time, until Eddie actually gets into some trouble. Who wouldn't be?

Orosco swears there's nothing wrong with the arm. I've asked him, he says it's fine. But other pitchers report that the wing is "killing" him. I don't know. Jesse is under no particular obligation to tell me or the other players, but he should tell Davey if it hurts. He may have, and team management may want to keep the news from the press. In order to keep it from the press, they would have to keep it from the players. There aren't many secrets around here.

GAME 56—Phillies 5
Mets 4

JUNE 14—MONTREAL

One-thirty a.m., and the Mets entourage has just arrived at the hotel. Exhausted, I uncharacteristically elect to retire to my room while a dozen or so ballplayers head for the "*Chez* Paris" nightclub, a traditional diversion for the squad. There are no strip joints in my experience like Montreal's, and none of them matches "*Chez* Paris." It boasts a staff of thirty on stage. Sixty breasts. Nevertheless, I had not heard of the place in all my years with the Cardinals. I was almost embarrassed when I joined the Mets in 1983—"What, you've never heard of '*Chez* Paris'?!"

The following narrative is hearsay:

The Met contingent is enjoying the show when Doug Sisk and his fiancée walk in. The rule is unwritten and stern: Don't bring wives, fiancées, or girlfriends into the hotel bar or anywhere else players gather. Sisk does. (His fiancée, a very nice woman, is following the team everywhere. So is Orosco's wife. Fig, issue uniforms to the ladies.)

What follows the fiancée's entry is what I call the Dracula act. I've seen it before. All the players, among them some married guys, throw up their arms to hide. Sisk and his lady select a separate table. The Mets send bachelor Eddie Lynch as an emissary.

Sisk preempts Eddie, "I know what you're going to say, but I'm not leaving. I'll have a drink, then we'll leave."

But the interlopers stay until the lights go up at three a.m. The players hide behind their capes. Sisk stands up, waves, calls out, "Bye, guys," and leaves.

It's not a laughing matter to some of them. A couple are pissed. In the clubhouse this afternoon, informed of the episode, I clip out a newspaper picture of the recently exploded hijacked airliner in Lebanon, tack it onto the wall, and scribble as a caption, "Doug Sisk's fiancée's flight from Montreal after road trip."

In poor taste, I grant, but indicative of the seriousness of Sisk's transgression.

The following analysis is not hearsay:

The wives and other women associated with a baseball team can be a source of considerable trouble. I don't make this assertion because of a temporary misogyny caused by my impending divorce. The trouble is a fact.

The team itself has twenty-five different players with one common goal: playing together and winning. But what do the wives have in common? Not all of them know or care anything about baseball, or about the team, really. Instead, they care about their husbands' careers and their own status relative to that career. This "relative" status is part of the problem: Some of the wives have a serious problem establishing their own identity. During the seven-month season, the wife's life centers on her husband's baseball playing. In public, most people aren't interested in talking with her. I saw this clearly with my own wife when I would introduce her at parties, and she was promptly ignored after the obligatory exchange of pleasantries. The wife's situation is difficult.

Jealousy of the husband is a possible, even likely, response, both as a general reaction to the wife's second-class status and as a specific acknowledgment of the facts: Their husbands' "potentials" on the road are limitless. (Likewise, when we're on the road their "potentials" are limitless. Some of the wives fool around, too.)

Thus the unwritten rule about wives, fiancées, and girlfriends in the bars or clubs or wherever the players hang out. A player might be talking quite innocently with a woman, a wife comes in, sees, draws false conclusions, and spreads the word among the wives. Rumor is afoot and, very frankly, some of the ladies are quite willing to help it make the rounds.

Another rule requires that the players keep their mouths shut. A big destroyer of team unity is a player telling his wife what's going on on the road, if anything. I've witnessed more than one fistfight between a player who told his wife something and the player who was the subject of this information (which got back to him via his own wife, via the rumor mill). Keep your mouth shut. That's the rule.

Jealousy *among* the wives is also possible. I acknowledge their difficult situation but the resulting competitiveness can be petty. On some evenings the wives' section at the ballpark looks like the runway at a Milan fashion show.

Perhaps Sisk should have stayed home last night—this morning. Taking over for Gooden in the ninth, with the Mets leading 4–3, Doug walks the first two batters. They come around to score off Schiraldi and Orosco, and we've lost our second straight game in the last inning, and we waste three hits by Carter in his home-coming. The clubhouse is funereal, worst of the year. My joke pinned on the wall elicits no laughter. If Doug had saved the game, we would have had a lot of fun at his expense.

The announced reason for removing Dwight is that he had thrown over 140 pitches, while striking out eleven Expos. I understand, but couldn't he throw ten or fifteen more? This game is important.

It didn't occur to me in the spring to worry about our bullpen, but with McDowell still out, Orosco and Sisk struggling, that's our major problem now.

GAME 57—Expos 5
Mets 4

JUNE 15

Doug Gould's lead in *The Post* today reads, "Davey Johnson is going to restore Doug Sisk's confidence—even if it costs the Mets the pennant."

That's harsh, but not without a point. Davey is sticking with Sisk to a remarkable degree—even though he has admitted that Doug is not doing the job. But who else is there?

Gun-shy, Davey stays with Sid Fernandez tonight in the late innings, and we lose our third game in a row in the late innings, on a homer in the eighth, two hits in the ninth.

Fernandez is pitching well, but if McDowell is ready, I'll bet Davey goes with him.

We're hitting better and Carter is suddenly red hot, but most of us are still way below our career averages. Some of our key players are hurt; others may be but aren't saying. The breaks aren't doing us any favors. In short, it's an official slump—nine losses in eleven games.

Turn the page, I would calmly advise, except for one problem with Jim Kaat's useful wisdom: Turn enough pages this early in the story and the book is over with in August . . . or July.

GAME 58—Expos 3
Mets 2

JUNE 16

I feared as much after the loss in the first game of the series Friday night, but you never can tell, so I didn't say it. Now on Sunday evening, I might as well. I feared a sweep, and now it has happened. Suddenly we're in fourth place, but that's not as bad as it sounds, because after a dismal 1-and-6 road trip, we return to Shea only three games out. If McDowell had been available, we would have won three, maybe four of those six losses. The Cubs are struggling as much as we are. The tide is clearly with the fast Astroturf teams, Montreal and St. Louis.

It's an appropriate time to invoke the old adage: A team is never as good as it looks when it's winning, or as bad as it looks when it's losing. Therefore, my strategy right now, negative though it sounds, is for us to stay close until the All-Star break, a month away; no more than seven games back. That's all that's absolutely required out of the first half of the season.

We're losing the way we were winning a month ago—we're making the bonehead plays, the opposition is getting the clutch hits and the breaks. This game has textbook examples.

Mental error: Chapman doesn't score from third base on a double play. Another one: Santana doesn't get to second base quickly enough for a force on a ball hit to me, so I have to spin and throw to first—but Gorman doesn't get over to cover fast enough, so my throw directly over the bag sails wide of him. The scorer has to give someone an error, so I notch my first of the year. Fine. I deserved several others that weren't awarded.

Clutch hit: Andre Dawson pulls a low, outside pitch for a home run.

Break: A hard grounder by Dawson in the fifth is heading right for Backman and an easy inning-ending double play—but the ball hits a seam, jumps over him for a double, and two runs score. Then Dawson scores.

Meanwhile, facing a right-handed starter for the first time in five games, I hit five balls hard—but only one is a hit. In the third, with men on second and third and one out, I nail a liner to right field but Dawson catches it. Sac fly. Next time, with runners again on second and third, I hit a hard ball on the ground—but right to the shortstop. On the turf in Montreal, a hard grounder has to be right at somebody to be an out.

Honestly: I'm hitting in bad luck right now, and have been for most of the season. This is not to say that I'm being robbed of a .340 season. Bad luck can't ruin a season's batting average, but it can move that average to the lower end of a range. In October we'll see what my range is for 1985.

My lackluster average is dragging down this team. As the third-place hitter, I have all three offensive responsibilities: getting on base, moving the runners along, and driving runners in. If I'm not hitting, the runners aren't driven in, or even moved along for Gary or Darryl or George to drive in. That's why the third hitter is the most important batter in the lineup, in my opinion. Mike Lupica sometimes refers to me as the Mets' "main man." Any third hitter is his team's main man. That's why the all-around best hitter (average/power combination) hits third.

This afternoon, my one hit and the sacrifice fly aren't nearly enough. The Expos trounce us and, as sometimes happens after a series of bad losses and somber post-game recapitulations, horseplay breaks out as we pack up and head home. Animal Clubhouse. All that's missing is the old-fashioned food fight, but we're too mature for that!

Father's Day notes: Vance Law, the Expo second baseman, is on a five-game hitting tear and attributes it to a tip from his father, the fine pitcher Vernon Law, who was a *terrible* hitter. Darryl

Strawberry acquires his first son, Darryl Jr. I get a card from my kids. No phone call, so I call them, and my father, too.

GAME 59—Expos 7
Mets 2

JUNE 17—NEW YORK CITY

Well, here we are for the first highly anticipated series of the year, a four-game grudge match against the Cubs, who did us a grave injustice last year by winning seven out of eight in late July and August, outscoring us 32–19 in a four-game sweep at Wrigley. It's too early in 1985 for either team to be ruined, but neither club can afford a sweep. We're both losing: the Mets ten of twelve, the Cubs five in a row. The two tabloids have special analysis pages. Every columnist is writing about the series. Over 160,000 fans are expected for the four games.

The Cubs have to feel good about the first two pitching match-ups: Rick Sutcliffe tonight, Steve Trout tomorrow. Their 1–2 punch. We don't have Dwight until Wednesday, when our backs might be to the wall after two losses. But I feel good about Darling tonight. Ronnie is a different pitcher this year. What does he lack that Gooden has? A couple of inches on his fastball, and he can afford to be without those.

I'll take Darling over Sutcliffe, who unwisely said, or was quoted as saying, that he wouldn't trade any of the starting eight Cubs for his counterpart on the Mets. That wasn't smart. Don't rile us. Let sleeping dogs lie.

Would I trade some of the Mets for their counterparts on either of the other three contenders? Maybe I would, since all of us are below our career averages right now and most of the Cards, for example, are above theirs. But would I trade the Mets' starting eight for the Cubs' starting eight? Or the Cards'? Or the Expos'? No. I don't look position-by-position, because these analyses overlook a critical question: Where will the new man hit in the lineup? Teams don't simply need hitters; they need lead-off hitters, third-place hitters, cleanup hitters, etc. A swap of outfielders might look beneficial to Team A, but what if the guy coming over from Team B is a perfect leadoff man, and Team A has a leadoff man? What if Team A traded a fifth hitter, a role the man coming over can't fill? The analyses don't consider these factors, and they mean everything. I look at the team. I'll take the Mets.

However, I wouldn't stand pat, and I don't think our management wants to, either. I have a hunch Frank Cashen was trying to get Larry Parrish, third baseman for the Texas Rangers. Third base is hurting us more than any other position. HoJo and Knight's batting averages *added together* barely make .300. Bobby Valentine, the new Texas manager and former Met coach, might put in a good word for a trade bringing him young talent, but the Rangers probably wanted pitching—too much pitching. Now the trading deadline is past.

Tonight it doesn't matter. The 40,000-plus fans are pumped up and Ronnie and Gary give them what we—fans and team—are desperately seeking: a victory, a shutout, a big homer.

Darling for Sutcliffe, even-up? I'll take Darling, and I mean that seriously. However, Sutcliffe is tough, with that little hesitation at the top of his windup. It makes the hitters stride too soon, hence we're off balance. Then he whips in a nasty curve. He's the only pitcher in the league against whom I regularly change my stance. I stand more upright, a posture that makes me slow down my stride.

I work him to a full count in the first inning, and walk. Then I'm picked off. How embarrassing, as our first runner in the first game of the biggest series of the year. There's no excuse for it. Sutcliffe makes a good move just as I'm taking my last step toward second base. I don't recall the last time I was picked off.

In the third, I strike out with a full count. Beautiful. A punk down the line in right field is blistering me as I head back to the dugout. "You're making one and a half million and looking for walks, Hernandez, ya bum! You're not worth one and a half dollars!"

Fans in the mezzanine and upper decks, and television fans especially, don't realize the amount of jeering and less-abusive language the players are pelted with, usually as we're coming back to the dugout. It's a zoo, and we're the animals in the cages. Away from the park, too: In a midtown restaurant this afternoon, I'm quietly enjoying my meal at a table by the window. Suddenly a pack of kids is outside, yelling and pointing. I shoo them away. Is this rude of me? Do I have a higher obligation? No and no.

I handle the taunts at the park pretty well; occasionally I make the mistake of eye contact, as I do tonight, and thereby let myself in for another salvo. Last year in Chicago I lost control when I wasn't even the target. A fan was giving Bill Robinson a terrible time, and I pitched a jug of Gatorade at the guy. The creep ducked, and the splash soaked an innocent bystander sitting in the row behind.

Program Note: Mookie, 0-for-5 yesterday against right-hander Gullickson in Montreal, is on the bench today, and there's another change in his status: He'll play only against left-handers. His bad shoulder is bothering his swing from the left side. I said at the start that Mookie is the one player we could least afford to lose, not counting pitchers. Are we in trouble? I answer the question with a question: How can this development *help* the team?

However, Lenny Dykstra, who will play against right-handers, is a quick, scrappy base-stealer in the Mookie-mold, and Dykstra has a good eye. He'll draw some walks. If he hits, I believe we'll be okay.

Darling is almost flawless tonight. The play I note is the last out in the eighth inning, a comebacker to the mound. Ronnie takes the ball and fires it to me on the bag. *Fires* it, and I know why. He threw one away in Philadelphia by lobbing it over. To-night, he's taking no chances; no prisoners, either. He's mean on the mound. I expect him to glance at me as we head for the dugout after the play, but he doesn't. After three more outs he'll relax.

GAME 60—Mets 2
Cubs 0

JUNE 18

Boston has won fifteen of seventeen in the other league. Could we do that? Doubtful, but we could win twenty of twenty-five, especially with more games like tonight's. At long last, a classic offensive game with the first and second guys getting on base and the third, fourth, and fifth guys driving them in.

It takes some agony for me to help. I look awful in the first two at-bats against Trout, another left-hander: a K on three pitches with two men on, and a roller to short. After that ground out, I pass Bill Robinson coming in from the coach's box. He says, not harshly but with plenty of purpose, "Stop feeling sorry for yourself. Pick yourself up."

Damn right, Bill. I was slipping out there. Back at the plate in the fifth, two out, two on, I'm ready to hit. I may make an out, but not because my head is in a bad place. Trout helps me along by throwing the first two pitches for balls. Three weeks ago, he might have continued with careful pitches, willing to walk me because Carter was in a slump. But as I said then, they won't walk me when Gary starts hitting, and now he's hitting. Trout certainly doesn't want to load the bases for him. His third offering is on the outside edge, a good pitch, and I whack it to left for an RBI single. My first key hit in quite a while.

What a relief, and I can feel it from the crowd too, as they chant, "Keith! Keith! Keith!" I sometimes dwell on the jerks who ride me, but I can't complain about the great majority of the Mets' fans. They've always appreciated my play. The good guys outnumber the bad guys 100 to 1. Tonight, 1,000 to 1. "Guys" is used intentionally. The gals very, very rarely abuse the ballplayers.

My aggressive play carries into the eighth inning, on a Davey Lopes pop fly down the line. Carter charges up the line, but I charge in, too, screaming as loud as I can, "I got it! I got it! I got it!" By god, this one is mine. Maybe the fans don't know why I execute a nifty pirouette as I catch the ball. Hell, I'm dodging the big guy.

The chant in the ninth is "Ed-die! Ed-die! Ed-die!" and Lynch earns it. After a shaky first inning, he gives the Cubs nothing but scattered singles; not one walk. If he keeps up this level of work for the entire campaign, he could make the difference.

GAME 61—Mets 5
Cubs 1

JUNE 19

Bob Klapisch writes in *The Post,* "The Cubs bleed, too." And how. With an apparent advantage in their pitching rotation, they've lost the first two games, seven in a row, and now must face the Doctor.

I'm hurting right along with them—internally. Seven games on the rug in Philly and Montreal were too much for my lousy left ankle. The ligaments are shot; bone chips, too. I can pop that ankle just like a knuckle.

Tape it up, gulp three Ascriptin, and keep on truckin': That's my home remedy for tonight's game. But what about this morning at 7:30 a.m.? I'm finally moved into my place, after living out of the stack of boxes for a couple of months, but now the home above me is in transition. They're either tearing out the marble to put in parquet or tearing out the parquet to put in marble. I mean they're jackhammering. It's been going on for several weeks, but this morning I can't take it. Come on guys! The concierge hears from me . . . and I hear from him that the job will be completed in a couple of days. Great. Just when we go back on the road.

At noon the phone rings. It's Jim Kaat calling from the clubhouse in San Francisco, just saying hello, saw brother Gary yesterday, how's Keith doing? After a call from Kaat, Keith is fine. What a wonderful man, the pitching coach for the Reds, holder of the major-league longevity record for a pitcher: twenty-five years!

After several minutes, he rings off to obtain another cup of major-league coffee, as he calls it. This stuff is potent enough to wake the comatose. I enjoy four or five cups of brew before game time. Gets me perked up. Good friend Lynch does a pretty funny rendition of a perked-up Keith Hernandez: eyes shot open, arms extended at full reach, fingers splayed, a plugged-in Frankenstein. Fair enough. I'm not laid back, nor was meant to be. I look at guys like John Christensen with envy. John, one of the regulars in the card games, is so relaxed it's ridiculous. Slow smile, slow talk, slow everything. The scorepad reads "Mr. Warmth."

Before the game I tape a public-service announcement to be shown on Diamondvision, wherein I urge the fans to go easy on the drinking and fighting. It's become that bad at Shea Stadium, especially on Friday nights. If something isn't done, it will only get worse as the summer and the pennant race really heat up. There have been nights at Shea when I would have taken my kids out of the stadium. I hate to say that, and it's not good PR, but it's true. Worse PR would be to do nothing.

Beyond the problem in the stadium, how many thousands are driving home from the games plowed? My recommendations are straightforward: sell only 3.2 percent beer, with no sales at all after the sixth inning. Of course, it will never happen. Beer brings in big profits on a good night.

Tonight, I'm certain, is a very good night. When was the last time Shea was sold out on Wednesday? Other than playoff games, never. The crowd is the largest since 1977. Credit Dwight—and our two victories in the series. Gooden has even unnerved Cubs' manager Jim Frey, who picks this of all nights to rest two of his right-handed power hitters, Cey and Moreland. With Dernier out with an injury and Jody Davis sick, they're going with a makeshift lineup against the best pitcher in baseball. Why should they expect to score?

When Doc gets two strikes on Thad Bosley in the ninth inning, working on a shutout with two outs, but with runners on first and second and our lead merely one run, the roar from the stands is shattering. Shea is the loudest stadium in the league, anyway, and that's appropriate, because New York is the loudest city in the country. Just walking around town puts a buzz in the ears. A big crowd cheering at Shea pumps us up—I get goose pimples—but we can't hear ourselves think. The jackhammering this morning was muted by comparison. I don't give Thad much of a chance against Dwight right now, and I'm right. Doc posts his last K of the evening.

Have we won the pennant? I look for them to mob us on the field. No, we've only won three games from the Cubs—on a total of seventeen hits. We've won because of three complete games from the starters.

Wayne Gretzky was supposed to throw out the first ball tonight, but he arrived late. I meet him after the game. "Not a big guy" is my first impression. I'm taller and wider, and I'm no palooka. All the padding makes the hockey guys look bigger. (Regarding which, a friend's wife has this recommendation: Make them play without the padding. That would stop the violence. Yeah, but I like all that slamming around on the ice.)

When Gretzky finally arrives in the stands behind home plate, a welcome is flashed on Diamondvision, and the Long Island fans boo. They can boo all they want, he's still the greatest pro athlete of this era. The greatest of the great.

Basketball: Larry Bird, or Magic Johnson.

Football: Harder to pick, but I might go with Joe Montana, and not because he plays for San Francisco; because he wins.

Baseball: Eddie Murray, Orioles first baseman, and I nominate him without having seen him play, except in the All-Star game, which doesn't count. I don't have to watch him play. I see the numbers go up every season. A good fielder, too.

Murray is the greatest of the starting eight players in either league. Pitchers have to be considered separately. It's early, but I have few doubts that Dwight will be the superlative of this era. The greatest pitcher with at least five years to his credit: Steve Carlton of the Phillies.

GAME 62—Mets 1
Cubs 0

JUNE 20

Thank you, Davey. The ankle badly needs a day's rest. At season's end, it may need the surgeon's knife.

So it's a day on the bench for me as Foster hits a grand slam in the third—a two-out grand slam, after Ray Fontenot pitches around Carter. The fans will love George, for an inning or two. It's a tough season on him. He knows the pressure is on; he has only this year and one more on his contract, and that might be it for his career; and he knows that with Heep playing so well in Strawberry's absence, something may have to give when Strawberry returns. And he does strike out a lot, and always has. But he's playing hard in the field and has won four or five games with home runs.

What happens all day on the bench? You try hard to keep your head in the game, banter with the guys, exude optimism. I have an uncontrollable urge to go into the clubhouse and watch the pitching on television—especially today, with the left-hander Fontenot. But it's important to be on the bench most of the time, so I scurry back and forth—the tunnel connecting clubhouse and dugout at Shea must be thirty yards long—and hope most of all for a blowout. That way there's no possibility I'll be used. I take my R & R seriously.

One thing about not playing: You get a lot of time on the bench to think. Mookie is thrown out stealing in the first inning, and I realize we don't have a running game. We swipe the occasional base, but we're the slowest team in the league. If I were a general manager, I'd do what Whitey has done with the Cards: build a team around speedy singles-hitters. When the home park is turf, there's no question that this is the right strategy. The singles-hitters are miraculously transformed by the fast, bouncy outfield surface into doubles- and triples-hitters. The White Rat and his team have made me a believer.

Another point, one which has eluded most observers: The pitching in the National League is in transition from the old power-based style of relying on the fastball and slider to an off-speed and finesse style. (The Met staff is an anomaly in this regard. We feature power pitchers, with the exception of Lynch.) Batters don't get as many home runs off the John Tudors of the league. We have to have great patience, and a fast, controlled swing. Al Oliver, a great player in both leagues, told me that American League pitching is harder to hit, because the dink-type pitchers have proliferated there in recent years. This testimony is contradicted thus far in 1985 by the statistics in the two leagues, which show that the American Leaguers are hitting much better than we are. Or maybe they're just better hitters, but I doubt that.

At any rate, it makes sense to me that the contact hitters and basestealers of the Cardinals are driving the league batty.

But the Mets can do it the old-fashioned way if George keeps hitting homers. Immediately after his blow, Christensen hits one, our first back-to-back homers of the year, and our biggest inning. Mr. Warmth has always had the reputation of getting off to poor starts, and he has proved it again this year. One night not long ago, after it became apparent that John was finally hitting, Cashen got off a good quip in the clubhouse. "John," Frank said, "why don't you hold out until June next year, and we won't have to pay your salary for the lost months?" Just joking, I suppose.

The fans scream "Sweep! Sweep! Sweep!" in the ninth inning as McDowell, finally back after two weeks resting his sprained ankle, mops up for Fernandez. Sid doesn't want to come out, but Davey makes a good call on this, in my opinion. Sid has lost some heartbreakers lately; don't let him let another one get away.

The sweep is hard to believe. The Cubs don't look that bad. They certainly haven't stopped trying—but their losing streak stands now at nine. Very serious stuff. Sutcliffe's remark before the first game didn't help them.

Richard Nixon, a big baseball fan, must also find the sweep hard to believe. He's in an elite box somewhere, and comes down to the clubhouse after the game with his grandson Christopher. The little boy is awed, and peeks out from beneath his Mets cap at the ballplayers, his heroes. All I'm wearing when Nixon appears is a wraparound, but now's my chance to thank him for the book *Lee and Grant*, which he sent me last August, warmly inscribed with thanks for my "indispensable leadership" on the Mets. I never got around to sending him a thank-you note. I return later, more appropriately clothed, for a picture; a photographer has set up his lights for this purpose; the Mets line up.

Eddie Lynch is photographed—then goes off to shave.

The reporters pay scant attention to the former President; they're off covering the late-breaking METS SWEEP!! story. They finished with Nixon eleven years ago.

Nixon quips to Carter, "You certainly know how to handle the press. I didn't know much about that."

Like a lot of citizens, I have mixed feelings about his tenure, but I do know that number 352 in the 1971 military draft lottery—Nixon's lottery—saved me a lot of grief.

The deal is that pro ballplayers get to join the National Guard. Sounds great, but two weeks of summer duty and all those weekends is bad for a young player. I was delighted to get out of it, and didn't consider that attitude unpatriotic.

(I know of one exception to the general rule that ballplayers are placed with the Guard. Charley Finley, owner of the Oakland A's, received a phone call from platoon sergeant George Hendrick, who was in the A's organization.

"Know where I am, Charley?" George asked. "Saigon!"

A week later, he was back in the States.)

I ask Arthur Richman, who handles our travel arrangements, among other duties, to try to set up a dinner with Nixon. I'd enjoy it; he might, too. We're both Civil War buffs. We'll talk about it and baseball.

GAME 63—Mets 5
                    Cubs 3

JUNE 21

Over 175,000 fans witnessed the Cubs series: the biggest four days in Shea Stadium history. I wonder how many would show up to see the Mets' Triple A players, in the event of a strike? That's a balloon floated today by Dick Young in his *Daily News* column. About 175 is my guess.

There's also a story about the Mets players' "verdict" on Gary Carter, relating to the problems he had with some of the Expos. Is he having those problems with some of the Mets? CARTER JURY: NOT GUILTY is the headline, and the story quotes players as being pleased with Gary's contribution on and off the field. This is a nonstory, of interest perhaps to some of the readers but only potential trouble for the team. Why not HERNANDEZ JURY: NOT GUILTY? Or————GUILTY? There are some guys here, I suppose, who feel I get out of hand now and then. I do. But what can they say? What should they say? These stories alienate the subjects.

In one of the other boroughs, Rickey Henderson is tearing apart the American League, but I get the impression that he's operating in a media vacuum. I'll bet he never expected to come to New York and be ignored.

John Candelaria has waived a trade-veto clause in his contract with the Pirates. Three clubs are interested. Wish the Mets were one of them. That man can pitch, as a starter or reliever.

With the Cubs dispatched, the Expos are in town for another big series. If any of the four teams now in the running in the N.L. East falls back, I think it will be Montreal, but I'm not betting on it.

Two good signs for us: Rick Aguilera starts and pitches five pretty good innings, and Sisk closes out with three perfect ones. My god, what a year for him. Good, bad. Up, down. My ten-year career telescoped in three months!

GAME 64—Mets 6
Expos 3

JUNE 22

After five straight big wins, a heartbreaker. We come from behind on Staub's pinch three-run homer, only to lose it when Jesse picks up a bunt on which he has no play, a ball that would have rolled foul. Oh, these mental mistakes! They happen to all of us, and they kill every time. This episode turns the game around.

GAME 65—Expos 5
Mets 4

JUNE 23

The Expos win again, and again we give it to them. I firmly believe in the "carryover effect"; one terrible ballgame often leads to another one. Davey publicly disagrees; I suppose he has to.

I hit the ball well enough, but nothing drops. That makes me 3-for-21 on the homestand. Through all my struggling with the bat for two months, I've been able to scrape up enough hits, some of them timely, to avoid the appearance of an out-and-out disastrous slump. Now it's getting truly serious. Nothing is happening for me. If our third-place hitter doesn't improve, the Mets can't win this year.

GAME 66—Expos 5
Mets 1

JUNE 24—CHICAGO

How's this for an "off day"? My eleven o'clock flight to Chicago is canceled. I squeeze on another one an hour later, the flight takes two and a half hours. I meet with Jack Childers, my agent, and lawyers Gerhard Petzall and Jim Shoemake for four hours at a hotel at O'Hare airport, plotting strategy for a court appearance on Friday in St. Louis.

Things could be worse. They are for Joe Sambito, who has been shipped to Tidewater. It was inevitable. He needs to pitch. I talked with him briefly after the news was delivered. He took it well enough, but he knows the odds he now faces.

I've never figured this out: Americans believe that businessmen, entrepreneurs, actors, you name it, should sell their talents for the highest price, but somehow they forget that a good ballplayer's talent is as rare and fragile as most talents—more so—and yet we're not supposed to sell to the highest bidder. We're supposed to accept some salary the owners dictate, as we did and they did for seventy-five years. The fans forget about all the Joe Sambitos, whose careers blaze for two or three years, and then something happens and they're underemployed, or unemployed.

I get angry thinking about it.

It's impossible to get angry reading *USA Today*, the good-news

paper, so I turn to it and discover none other than my friend
Ronnie Darling citing his five favorite New York City restaurants.
Nice of him to put "Rusty's" in second place. I give Orange's shop
a high ranking, too, along with "Isle of Capri" on the same avenue,
about ten blocks south. A good bit of the work on this saga is
being accomplished at these two restaurants.

Best restaurant cities around the National League are easy to
name: New York, Chicago, Montreal, and Houston (for the Mex-
ican food).

The Shamrock Hilton in Houston is also my favorite hotel,
followed by the Sheraton Harbor Island in San Diego (alas, we're
not staying there this year), the Sheraton Centre in Montreal, and
the Hershey in Philadelphia.

Philadelphia is without question the most underrated great
city in the country. It's a jewel.

Did I believe I was finally moved into my co-op? Wrong. The
interior designer, Ray Hoehne, is working on the place this week,
in my absence. It seems I didn't have everything properly posi-
tioned. What's new?

JUNE 25

Speaking of *USA Today*, I want a little chat with their reporter.
He has the bad habit of hanging around the edge of the group
as I talk to the New York beat reporters, then he misquotes me.
I've asked the fellows to point out this guy, the next time he's
around. He and I need to get something straight.

I said the Cardinals will be tough "if their bullpen holds up."

Here it's printed, "if they get their bullpen together."

There's a difference, pal. The first statement is true, their
bullpen has been good, without Bruce Sutter and with Neil Allen
in the doghouse; the second statement is derogatory and might
just make them mad, and we're headed to St. Louis at the end of
the week. And I didn't say it.

I'm touchy these days, I admit it. I'm slumping, I'm divorcing,
I'm angry. None of the players has said anything, but Arthur
Richman said, "Keithy, Keithy, you're not the same Keithy. Is
anything wrong?" I like Arthur, so he can get away with that usage
of the diminutive. And, yes, there is something wrong. Plenty. I

walk around town this morning, trying to burn off some of the anger, without much luck . . . until I get to Wrigley Field.

What a beautiful ballyard, what a hitter's heaven (way over .300 for me for my career), and what a nice touch above the center field scoreboard: The pennants of the National League teams are raised in ascending order of the standings that day. In the East this afternoon, the Expos flutter on top, but we'll check the pennants on our last trip in here, in late September. Actually, the pennants today aren't fluttering; they're whipping straight out from right to left. The wind won't help me, and I like it this way at Wrigley. The combination of a wind blowing *in* and the traditional very high grass that slows down ground balls makes me concentrate. With the wind blowing *out,* you feel like a fly ball is a homer, and that's a dangerous feeling for a line-drive hitter.

On the apartment roofs across the street beyond left and right fields, the fans rise for the national anthem. They sing along with the paying fans during the seventh-inning stretch as Harry Caray, the famous Cub announcer, leans out of his press box to lead the faithful in "Take Me Out to the Ball Game."

I wouldn't be surprised if they're standing at attention *in* their apartments, too, during the anthem and the stretch. The neighborhood is part of the game, and the game is part of the neighborhood. Last fall, a building inspector limited rooftop attendance, for safety reasons, but at least the authorities don't collect taxes for the view. They do assess the mom-and-pop parking concessions all around the park. My agent whose operation is based nearby, pulls his big car into one of these; often we'll drive off together to have dinner.

These rabid Cub fans don't want lights. On this burning national issue, I disagree with them. The Cubs want to play only eighteen or so night games, plus playoffs. If that's what it takes to keep baseball at Wrigley—do it! Compromise before it's too late. I don't want to play on yet another rug.

But tradition is the rule at Wrigley. No video screen, no rock music, no mascot, and *no waves.* About the only concession to modern times I see is Marla Collins, the pretty girl who runs the balls out to the home-plate umpire. Turns out Marla and I have something in common: our agent.

The baseball passion of the "near North side" has its downside. While Shea fans are the toughest on their own favorites, the Cubbies' stalwarts are the hardest on the opposition. The abuse can be awful, on and off the field. A zealot once conked Pete Rose on the head with a souvenir bat. As a consequence of this and other episodes, the visiting team's bus pulls up right next to the exit gate from the clubhouse, with the open door of the bus almost touching the wall. This way, the fans can't get directly at us.

As abusive as they are to the opposition, the Cub fans are loyal to their heroes. With their team on a twelve-game losing streak (after losing four in New York, they were swept away in St. Louis), a packed house gives their Cubbies a clamorous, heartfelt standing ovation this afternoon. In another Hernandez misquote, *USA Today* asserts that this is "the biggest game of the year." For the Mets, the biggest game of the year was Darling's victory over Sutcliffe a week ago.

I would have thought a long losing streak impossible for the Cubs—too much pitching, too much hitting—but here it is, and they do execute poorly a couple of times today, on the bases and in the field. We return the favor in the eighth. We're leading 3–2 with Gooden batting and Hurdle on third base. Frey calls for a pitchout and, indeed, Davey has the suicide squeeze on; Hurdle is dead.

Amazing that Davey stays with Dwight in that situation; with only one out, a sacrifice fly scores the insurance run. In this era of the reliever, that's showing extraordinary confidence in your starter, but why not when you're working with a prodigy?

Nothing remains to be said about Doc's pitching, but the last out of the ballgame is a quietly remarkable demonstration of his genius for the *game*. With two out and a man on first, Billy Hatcher, a right-handed hitter, cues one toward me at first. The ball behaves erratically; it's a sidewinder. With a sidewinding grounder, I want to get in front of the ball and block it, if nothing else. I succeed in getting my mitt on this one, but the ball bounces off to my right. Only five feet from the bag when I handle it initially, I have to dive away to pick it up now. I can't get back in time! Hatcher is fast. Here's Dwight's genius: He's covering first. I shovel the ball to him for the final out.

There aren't five pitchers in baseball who would have recognized the danger on that play and run to cover the bag. All would break instinctively, but almost all would then slow up, seeing that

I'm practically on the bag as I wait for the ball—and of course Hernandez couldn't misplay it if he tried to! Dwight knows better. His *instinct* makes the play.

I'm hitless again, even though I do get that bogus GWRBI in the first inning, after Moreland has lost Dykstra's fly in the infamous Wrigley sun field in right. I manage to get the ball in the air for the sacrifice fly. Usually I go to the plate in this situation confident I'll get the runner in, but I'm swinging so poorly now that all I can do is go up hacking. I consider myself lucky to contribute at all. The real GWRBI goes to Howard Johnson, who hits one onto the street in the fourth inning.

In my own mind, I've been slumping for a month or more, but nobody is saying anything. This afternoon, for the first time, a couple of reporters (Marty Noble of *Newsday* and Bob Klapisch of *The Post*) ask me what's wrong. I don't resent the question—it's about time—and I tell them the truth. I stink. And I'm tired of stinking. I'm tired, period. My head's tired, my body's tired. This is one of those occasions when a day off seems to have actually slowed down my legs. Two straight days off always helps, but just one sometimes hurts. I don't know why. Today, the pins are dead, so I try to compensate at the plate with more quickness in my upper body. This plan never works because my right shoulder flies open; that fly out to center for the sacrifice fly is about as far as the ball will go with such a swing. Pathetic. On top of that, I discard my good eye—my great eye, let's be honest—and swing at marginal pitches. The pitchers and catchers recognize this, and work me *off* the corners, not on them, and I swing at those impossible pitches. The few good pitches I see I'm unprepared for.

To Noble and Klapisch I say merely, "I stink."

A reporter I don't know asks me what I think about the Cardinals. "I don't give a fuck about the Cardinals," I reply truthfully, with a cold stare at him, and he scuttles off.

After the game I drive with Gary Matthews to his apartment downtown. The Sarge is a good pal of mine who went through a difficult divorce last year. His three sons are in town for the series.

Gary and I have a long, long talk. His analysis of my torpor: Last year, after signing the big contract with the Mets, I had something to prove. That intensity carried me through the first year of my marital separation. But in this second year of the split-up, Matthews says, it's more difficult to generate that intensity, harder to come to the park with a clear head. Yet another sophomore slump, in a way.

It doesn't feel that way to me, but maybe he's right. To myself, I seem just as intense on the ballfield; I'm not conscious of carrying a lot of bad baggage with me to the plate. I still feel free out there, but maybe this is a delusion.

His kids walk with me to the elevator in the high-rise building, and the oldest boy, Gary Jr., about the same age as my Jessi, reaches up and hugs me and says, "I love you."

I'm in bed at eleven, exhausted—but still wide awake three hours later.

GAME 67—Mets 3
Cubs 2

JUNE 26

On top of it all, kids are calling in the early a.m.: "Mr. Hernandez, I just want to—"

SLAM! Goddamn it! They're supposed to be taking messages at the desk. No caller gets through in Chicago, that's the rule, because we had a big problem here last year, at another hotel. A radio station identified that hotel, implicitly urging retaliation by local kids for the inhospitality of New York kids, who had called the Cub players at all hours. So we were pestered last year, and that's one reason we've switched to the Sheraton Plaza this year. But here come the calls again.

Word gets around (helped greatly by the Mets' *Information Guide,* which lists our hotels). Kids and older guys are hanging around outside the hotel entrance this week, but not an unusual number—a dozen or so. I won't sign baseball cards for forty-year-old guys. Grow up, fellas. Besides, I suspect they're sharks, scalping the autographed cards (although why would any kid buy an unverified autograph?).

USA Today features an analysis of the weak hitting in the National League this year, taking note of all the good new pitchers, new pitches, and a bigger strike zone.

I go with Mike Schmidt's remark: "It'll all even out. Give us time." As I've mentioned, the National League is in transition, and it's taking the hitters time to adjust to the finesse pitching we're seeing more of, exemplified by the pitch of the eighties: the split-fingered fastball.

This pitch has the action of a hard forkball. It drops sharply at the plate, sometimes as much as a knuckler. In case you're interested: For the straight fastball, the middle and index fingers are on top of the ball, almost touching; for the forkball, these two fingers are spread about as far apart as possible, gripping the ball on the sides; the split-fingered fastball splits the difference. The fingers have to be long and strong. Bruce Sutter, who perfected the pitch, also pushes with his thumb as he releases the ball. In his follow-through, his fingers form a fist, and the thumb sticks out between the first two fingers.

The major problem for the hitters with the split-fingered pitch is that, like the fastball, its spin is not clearly defined, so it can be mistaken for the fastball. Other pitches have signature spins: The slider is a small, tight circular spin; the curve spins over the top; the screwball is a big circle turning in reverse.

The spin of the seams is the batter's best clue to the pitch. If a batter can't read them and make judgments accordingly, he can't hit in the major leagues. An interesting related point is the question of whether we see the ball as it approaches the bat. An article in a scientific journal some years back argued that we don't. The human eye, it asserted, simply cannot move fast enough.

Maybe the human eye doesn't, but mine does.

It's my *legs* that can't keep up. If they don't wake up, I won't need to concern myself with reading seams. I won't hit anything. Steve Garland works hard on my calves this afternoon, digging in with his knowledgeable fingers. I need help, let's face it. After batting practice, I still need help. I don't do much with these 75–80 mph straight balls. (To make up for the slower speed of the BP pitches, some hitters, including Rusty, move up in the box, so the net time for the pitch to arrive is about the same as for a real fastball. I stay back, but I might ask the guys to throw harder, if I feel they can. Some of the BP pitchers are freelancers, working for $35 an hour, I believe; in New York, a couple of them work at both Shea and Yankee stadiums.)

This afternoon, the odds are with the Cubs. We've beaten them an improbable five times in a row; another loss for them would set a team-record fourteen in a row. A bad team would be due to win. A good team like the Cubs is way overdue, and we're not playing so hot ourselves. Plus they're mad at Backman, who made a mistake yesterday evening by telling the press that the Cub bench looked dead in the loss to Gooden. If Sutcliffe's remark last week riled us up, Wally has returned the favor at Wrigley.

Staub is working his puzzle in the clubhouse when I put the newspaper quote in front of his face. He drops the crossword in dismay. In batting practice, the Cubs work Wally over.

"You've been in the league two years, and you're telling us how to win??"

Alas, the Cubs win. With the Mets leading 3–1 in the sixth inning, Sid Fernandez gives up consecutive singles to Sandberg and Matthews (the latter a fisted bloop to center). Davey calls in McDowell, and he gets two quick strikes on Keith Moreland, who can't get the bunt down. Then he drives McDowell's third pitch over the wall, and that turns out to be the game.

I wish you were a better bunter, Moreland.

In the next inning, Sandberg ices the victory with another homer. On Roger's next pitch, he sends Matthews to the dirt— or at least Gary goes to the dirt. Then Sarge makes a move toward the mound, and the fielders move in that direction to intercede, but Sarge isn't too serious. Roger walks him.

I greet Gary at first base. "I know what you're doing, Sarge. You're trying to stir up the troops."

"Yeah, I know," he replies. "The pitch wasn't even close."

Carter, starting the game in right field, is 4-for-4 on the day. He has lifted his average fifty points in the last few weeks and provided most of our offense. I'm headed the other way: average down to .264, hitless again today against Ray Fontenot, the lefty I was able to study on television on my day off last week, but that doesn't help a bit today; can't get the ball out of the infield.

A friend remarks, "Imagine how the team will go when you start hitting!" I appreciate that. He might have said "if."

Davey tells the reporters today that the missing Strawberry is the key man in this batting order; not Carter, not Hernandez, not Mookie. In part, Davey, like any good manager, is talking for purposes of Darryl's self-esteem, but the thin man is returning to the lineup momentarily, and we'll find out whether he can be the rising star that lifts all the struggling Mets.

It's a shame that a neat play by Fernandez and Hernandez in the first inning doesn't help win the game.

With Sid pitching and a runner on first, I sometimes call for him to throw over, signaling with my left hand, which I hide on the field side of my body so the first-base coach can't see it; the runner, Sandberg, is watching Sid. Fernandez throws over, then to the plate, then to first again—and again, nailing Sandberg, who has broken for second. The opposing clubs know Sid doesn't hold runners well. Pretty soon they'll realize Hernandez is trying to help him learn. A satisfying play at the time; not much in retrospect.

GAME 68—Cubs 7
Mets 3

JUNE 27

A few reporters are stirring up trouble about Carter's fourth hit yesterday, in the ninth inning, when he was thrown out trying to stretch a ball off the wall into a double, in order to complete the cycle: single, double, triple, homer. Jack Lang of the *Daily News* beats them to the punch. He states flat out in his report that the play was "self-serving," since the team was down by four runs at the time. This is not good.

Today, I have the unenviable assignment of breaking a slump against Sutcliffe. I don't, but I can take some encouragement from a couple of decently hit balls on which I am semirobbed—in the eighth inning, on a very important play. Good friend Matthews grabs a sinking liner just off the grass in left field, and throws to first to double off Backman. A game-turning play.

In Philadelphia two weeks ago, I got fed up and went berserk; blacked out. Today, what's the use? Clearly, higher powers are controlling my fate. I grab Rusty, the good Catholic, and inveigh, "Lord, I know I've sinned. I've broken up with my wife and lost my kids. I've done other things wrong. But slacken up. I repent."

First man up in the Cubs' half of the inning is Matthews. Flying out to right field, he has to circle me as he trots back to his dugout. "Thanks a lot, asshole," I growl. "You just made me 0-for-Chicago." If a hitter can't produce in Wrigley, where the hell can he? A slumping hitter asks himself this question. And the answer is, when I start hitting, not even the Astrodome will be able to hold me down.

Tradition at Wrigley dictates that fans throw all opposition home runs back onto the field. (Last year during the pennant race, they broadened the rule, and rejected at least twenty balls the Mets tossed up, friendly-like, during batting practice.) The rule, ironclad, is tough on a fan who may have waited for years to get a baseball. It's tougher, however, to refuse. Hurdle belts one for us in the seventh into some new seats installed in the right field corner. After a few moments, the fans out there are screaming, "Throw it back! Throw it back!" The game goes on, so does the commotion. They want that obnoxious ball banished. Finally, after our half of the inning is over, the ball sails back onto the grass during Harry Caray's song. Pure peer pressure.

Doug Harvey succumbs to another kind of pressure in that inning. With Sisk in for us, Frey asks The Lord to check the ball and Sisk's glove. He doesn't find anything. I don't mean this sarcastically, but one look at Dougie's record this year would verify he hasn't been juicing the ball. It's a bush move by Frey, and I holler at him as he trudges off.

Best quip from a player: After Foster takes Sutcliffe deep, very deep, over the left field wall in the seventh inning, Danny Heep inquires, "Did they serve dinner on that flight?"

Best quip from a Wrigley fan, directed at Ray Knight after he went out for the third time on Wednesday: "Hey Ray! At least there's one athlete in the family . . . *Naaaaancy!!!*" This guy doesn't know about Knight's boxing background but, for sure, Ms. Lopez is enjoying a better year than her husband.

GAME 69—Cubs 4
Mets 2

JUNE 28—ST. LOUIS

The Cards are the talk of the league. I'm the talk of St. Louis, not regarding my slump or my divorce (for six hours today, I'm in the courthouse as the lawyers argue over money), but my "illegal left foot." It's the main subject on a popular call-in radio program. Holding a runner on the bag, my left foot is several feet foul, my right foot on the edge of the base. More important, my glove is right on the base. I get an instant tag.

The Cards (Whitey?) have filed a protest with the league office. Indeed, the rules do state that both feet of all players except the catcher must be inside the baselines. However, as Harry Wendelstedt told me earlier in the year, there are rules and there are rules. If the umps are instructed to declare my foot illegal, our pickoff play will be hurt. I won't get as quick a tag. Whitey's main idea, though, is to mess with our heads. My foot was illegal when I played for him in St. Louis.

I'm exhausted after the day in court. I hit the ball that way, too, managing only an infield single off John Tudor. Announcers are fond of asserting that just such a fluke hit can snap a batter out of a slump. I'm dubious. A hitter can be 1-for-20 but not in a slump, or 5-for-20 and slumping. The hitter knows how he feels at the plate, how well he's seeing the ball. For myself, I'll know this slump is coming to an end when I drive an outside pitch into left field. Right now, I'm afraid to wait on the pitch, so I swing early (often at bad pitches) and jerk the ball weakly to the right side. Same old story.

However, the fluke hit has to help the attitude a little because it is a potential run on the bases. I'll take the fluke, but it won't break me out of this career-worst slump. I don't score.

The Cards win. We're worried. We see this Cardinal team hitting and running, and read all the writers hailing the superiority of the Astroturf-brand of offensive baseball: speed, speed, and speed (although it's not a new concept; Houston has had this kind of team for years; they're just not as good). We compare this formula for success with our team, one of the slowest around.

The tension almost explodes tonight in the second inning, after Ed Lynch gives up a two-run single to the Cardinals' eighth-place hitter, Tom Nieto. First base is open, the pitcher is batting next. Put Nieto on, certainly don't give him anything tasty. Eddie knows this but makes a mistake. After the inning, Foster confronts him in the dugout and says, in effect, "Next time, with runners on base, remember who's up next." I'm a good friend of Ed's and I'd never say that to him. He doesn't need it; he knows he made a bad mistake. Maybe George is pissed because he was thrown out at second, trying to stretch a single.

Lynch takes offense. He and Foster exchange some sharp words. I take the episode to be symptomatic. We're tight. We're losing. We're tired of it.

The good news is that Strawberry is back, after forty-three games in which we were 20–23. If we turn it around now, for whatever reason, the press will acclaim Darryl.

If we do turn it around with solid but not spectacular help from him, I'll be puzzled, because Danny Heep has filled in well for Straw, hitting considerably better than Darryl was hitting before he got hurt. It might prove that Darryl's mere presence in the batting order, regardless of his performance, is an asset. Certainly Mookie's mere presence is an asset, but now that the Straw is back, the powers-that-be are seriously considering a drastic midseason remedy for Wilson's shoulder—surgery.

Darryl will be on the starting All-Star team, regardless. The fans have voted for him even in his absence. They voted for him last year. It amazes me how quickly he has caught on as a favorite; the process usually takes several years. In Darryl's case, I attribute this acclaim to the vivid impression he makes with his unusual name, his remarkable build (six foot six, 190 pounds), and those towering home runs, which are unforgettable.

Darryl's first throw from the field nails Van Slyke at third base, but a baserunning error, failing to advance to third on a long fly, may cost us a run. Talking to the press after the game, Davey is blunt in his criticism. (A manager may talk to his players without ever talking to them, if he so desires.) I take this criticism to be a very intentional priming of Darryl for a key role, and a "warning" that the basic mistakes he sometimes makes need to be reduced. Last year, Davey took it easy with Darryl until August, when he cracked the whip. Darryl responded.

GAME 70—Cards 3
Mets 2

JUNE 29

A fun day with the kids, though exhausting. There's nothing fun about the ballgame tonight. We're never in it, the Cards bomb Rick Aguilera, we don't even manage an extra-base hit off Andujar. I'm hitless again.

At one point in the game I slip into the clubhouse for a soft drink and find Gooden, Fernandez, and a couple of other guys playing whiffle ball. I'm not the greatest in the world about staying on the bench, but I'd never horse around like this during a game, and I lose my cool at this flagrantly lackadaisical attitude, and blurt out, "Come on, Doc, there's a game going on out there."

I'm back in the dugout quickly, as are the guys from the whiffle ball game—all but Doc, who comes out five minutes later. I ask Charlie Samuels if Dwight is angry. Not so much angry, Charlie replies, as resentful that I singled him out.

Well, Dwight, that's the price you pay for being a superstar. But when I get the chance, I tell him I should not have singled him out. I apologize.

"Still my friend, Doc?"

Straightfaced, Doc replies, "You've never been my friend, Mex." Typical Dwight humor.

This game is the last straw for Davey. He calls a meeting afterward and isn't in a conciliatory mood. This is an ass-kicking. Somehow he found out about the clubhouse episode—and there may have been others I don't know about—so now the nonstarting players are required to stay on the bench. They won't be allowed in the clubhouse. The starting lineup can go down for a quick drink or something, but that's it.

"Maybe I should crack down," Davey wonders aloud.

I want to jump up and yell, "I agree! You should!"

The manager can lose the reins of his team. Once things are out of hand, more times than not you can forget it for that season. Almost every veteran ballplayer has seen it happen. In these special cases, my assertion that modern ballplayers care and care hard is invalid; a small percentage of the players will go through the motions.

The Mets aren't at this critical stage, or even near it—Davey would never allow it, and the guys on this team wouldn't give in— but we are suffering.

Doc tomorrow.

GAME 71—Cards 6
Mets 0

JUNE 30

This is terrible. With Gooden starting, we lose. Orosco is the victim in the eleventh inning.

For the three-game series, the Cardinals have six stolen bases, we have none. A little-noted point: All the Cardinal speed forces pitchers to hurry their delivery from the stretch. I'm not sure this is smart, because some runners—Vince Coleman, for example, and Tim Raines with the Expos—simply can't be thrown out unless they slip, and the speeded-up delivery helps the batters. Pitching from the stretch is less effective than a full windup in the first place; hurrying the motion to the plate can only exacerbate the problem.

Foster has taken over from Gary in this series as our designated hot bat, but his blows are isolated. We out-hit the Cards this afternoon, but leave everyone on base.

GAME 72—Cards 2
Mets 1

Stretching for the throw.

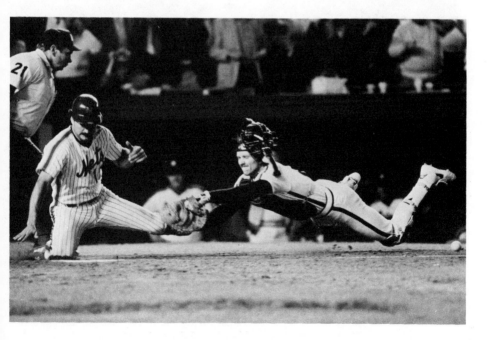

Reaching for the plate.

Dwight Gooden—the phenom.

Ed Lynch—following through.

Rusty Staub—on the move.

Darryl Strawberry—launching another rocket.

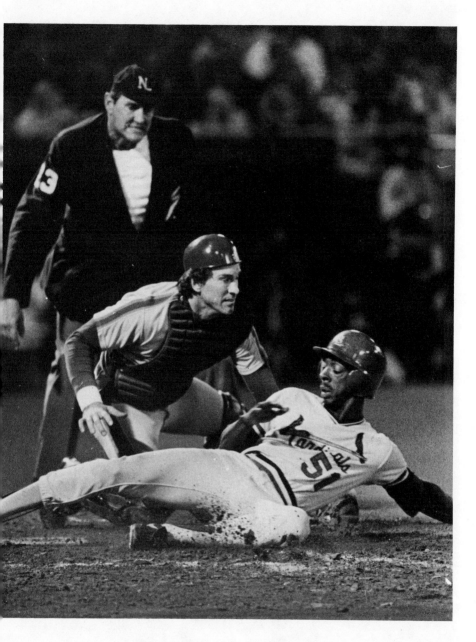

Gary Carter—blocking the plate.

Len Dykstra—taking a close one.

Ron Darling—firing the high, hard one.

With daughters Jessie Joy (on the left) and Melissa Sue.

Mom and Dad visit Shea.

Keith and his brother, Gary.

Doing the pregame crossword puzzle.

4. OVERNIGHT SENSATION

JULY 1—NEW YORK CITY

"I'm in a dark forest. I'm killing this team" were my exact words to the press, and they were quoted exactly right. Where no sunlight penetrates, without map or compass; a batter without a clue.

I hit .232 in June. For the last half of the month, .143. I would not have thought that possible.

The Mets were 11-and-18 in June. We're in fourth place, five games behind the Cards.

There's a hint of rain in the air this evening. The team reports to Shea scanning the sky. When you don't want to play baseball, the odds are good you'll lose the game. Right now, we don't want to play baseball. A rainout would be welcome.

Adding to the gloomy atmosphere is the fateful turn in the Mookie Wilson story: They're going to operate. Mookie will be out two months, at least. We might get him back for the last month. There goes our speed, but he's a bird with a clipped wing in the outfield, and he can't swing effectively left-handed, so why not?

The question remains: Will Davey and Frank Cashen give Len Dykstra a full shot at the job, or go with various combinations of Strawberry, Foster, Heep, Christensen, Hurdle, and Dykstra?

One decision has been made. Ray Knight is the starting third baseman—against all pitchers. The on-again, off-again platooning system with HoJo is discarded. It wasn't benefiting either player, or the team. Ray is happy, of course, and I think it's a good decision regarding Howard, too. He's young. Let him get away from the dismal season for a while. Ease his mind. Howard can play, but he may have to wait to prove it. That's all right. Most of us have waited.

About 20,000 fans show up for our return to Shea. I'm surprised that the boos are as scattered and half-hearted as they are. Nevertheless, I recall the sold-out standing ovation bestowed on the struggling Cubs in Chicago.

On the mound for the Pirates, the worst team in the league, is Rick Reuschel, whom the Cubs let go. He's good enough to beat us this night, combining with Candelaria for a shutout. In the second, three walks and a single off Fernandez give the Pirates a run and leave the bases loaded with nobody out. A blowout looms, but Sid shuts them down on a strikeout and two pop flies. Often enough, that kind of turnaround will spark a team. But we go quietly. Six subsequent good innings from Sid are wasted. A rejuvenated Ray Knight barely misses a homer to the opposite field in the ninth to tie the game, must settle for a double, and is stranded. The losing streak is now six. I have no idea what it would take to spark the Mets.

Sure, the players discuss our plight. We're in trouble, there's no use hiding it. Only our pitching has kept us afloat. We're stinking—but don't leave out the "t." We're not sinking.

If the Mets were an ordinary team, I'd say we have the two classic choices: give in and set ourselves up for an awfully long three months, or grab the season by the bootstraps, play hard, and—win or lose—the months will fly past.

If we were an ordinary team, we would have this choice, but no team with Gooden, Darling, Carter, Strawberry, Foster, Hernandez is ordinary. It's not possible for us to give in.

At the same time, it's hard to avoid—for me at least—the defensive posture: Hang on until the All-Star break, thirteen games away. Don't slip further back than the magic number, seven, which we're rapidly approaching. Come back with a fresh start.

GAME 73—Pirates 1
Mets 0

JULY 2

What a nice way to start a day. The Sarge himself, Gary Matthews, calls at noon from Philadelphia. He knows I had that court date in St. Louis on Friday. He saw the box scores for the weekend series. He's checking up on me. Thank you, Gary; I'm a lot better now.

Likewise, Sixto Lezcano of the Pirates offers encouragement during batting practice. Sixto and I go back a long way, to our Double-A minor-league days; I was at Little Rock and he was playing at Shreveport in the Brewers' farm system.

"Don't let this divorce fuck you up," he says bluntly. "Don't let her ruin your season. Be aggressive."

And a final pick-me-up: *The Sporting News* poll of 100 pitchers puts me in second place as the "most feared hitter" in the National League, defined as the hitter they would least like to face in the ninth inning, when a hit wins the ballgame. Twenty votes for Dale Murphy, sixteen for me, then down to four or fewer for everyone else. (In the American League, the choice is Eddie Murray. Who else?)

My choice for most feared hitter is Keith Moreland of the Cubs. Most feared pitcher in the ninth inning: John Candelaria, without a doubt. Least-feared pitcher: I'd rather not tell him!

The Sporting News poll encourages me. I've never denied that self-doubt and negative thoughts are my worst enemy. Look at it: I'm a career .300 hitter. There are only a dozen of us active in the major leagues today. Yet I'm capable of wondering if I'll hit again. I can even wonder how good I was in the first place. I can twist myself into a Gordian knot of doubts.

The bad left ankle is not my main problem, but the Mets order it x-rayed today. The trainers are worried about a possible hidden stress fracture, such as the one suffered by basketball star Bill Walton, which sidelined him for a couple of years. But the slides are clear. What this mechanism needs is rest and fewer games on turf.

The newspapers carry some unsettling remarks by Johnson and Carter delivered after last night's loss. They are not terrifically positive.

Carter: "We all had such hopes for the season. In spring training, I thought it'd be a matter of how many runs we'd score. I remember saying this is going to be a fun summer."

I don't like to hear it. This statement is a little too negative for me. On the other hand, look at our lineup tonight. It gives good cause for concern: Hitting one–two are Kelvin Chapman and John Christensen. Neither is hitting .200. Neither is a base-stealer. Among the Met heavyweights, only Foster is hitting the ball consistently hard right now; Carter has slacked off after a hot streak; Strawberry can't be expected to be totally sharp yet; I'm pathetic.

Before the game, I meet with Joey Fitzgerald for some serious homework. Joey tapes all of our at-bats at Shea, and I review my swings almost every evening. This afternoon, Joey retrieves the tapes of my at-bats in the first series of the year, when I hit the ball hard against the Cardinals. We compare those swings with last night's. The untrained eye wouldn't see any difference. I pick up two changes. I am now standing too upright. Sometimes I do this as a strategy, but last night I was upright and not aware of it.

More critically, I'm dropping my hands and moving them *toward* my body as the pitch is delivered, rather than sliding them straight *back* toward the catcher, by way of a gentle, controlled "trigger." The new down-and-in movement loses me a fraction of a second because I have to get the hands back up. I now have a hitch. A hitter can get away with one, but only with very fast, powerful hands and exquisite timing. (Christensen has a big hitch. Willie Mays had one.)

Dad has watched my initial hand movement closely for years; he considers it the key to my swing. Straight back, slowly—that's the key for Keith, he says. I know this, but sometimes, like the last few weeks, I don't feel the breakdown of this rhythm. It's not something that I can think about during the swing. In that moment, I can think only about the ball.

Dad and I have been talking regularly. He knows what's going on off the field. I imagine he has picked up this aberration in my hand action (I bought my parents a satellite dish after I signed with the Mets, so they watch almost every game). If so, he hasn't said anything. I haven't asked him. The slump eats at him as much as me, or more, but the days when he would try to lecture me are over. Now it's my turn to change: I need to be less stubborn about asking for advice.

After working with Joey, I concentrate in batting practice on that slow movement straight back with the hands. In the first inning of the game, Christensen doubles. Larry McWilliams with his goofy delivery misses with the first three pitches and I step out to check with Buddy in the third-base box. The light is green. Thank you, Davey. Show me some confidence. I sit on this pitch, a fastball right over the plate, and hit it against the wall in right field for the RBI—the game-winner, it turns out.

The next three trips are poor, but nobody is on base, and twice I'm leading off. I've been leading off so often that Bill Robinson pronounced me the best leadoff hitter in the league. Rusty rubbed salt in the wound by calling me "Pesky."

All things considered, I'm happy. A key hit, we get some others and score five runs on only nine hits, Darling hangs tough for eight innings before he gives out in the ninth, McDowell saves. We stop the skid at six. In the clubhouse, I spar with a pesky reporter. He's trying to entice me into admitting that I'm pressing at the plate because of Darryl's absence. I won't say it because it's

not true. I'm pressing, period. But I don't run him off with sur-
liness. I endure.

Tonight I can snicker at the "Curley Shuffle" picture hanging
on the wall of my cubicle, a new gift from a fan. Last week I felt
like I belonged with the Three Stooges.

GAME 74—Mets 5
Pirates 4

JULY 3

Can it be true? For the second night in a row, this time before a
full house of fireworks fans, I rap an RBI in the first inning, and
it holds up for the game-winner. In fact, despite my slump I now
lead the league in GWRBIs. What a joke—but I'm not laughing.
These hits with men on base the last two evenings are an im-
provement. The Mets are puttering along with two victories, and
this production from the number-three man has to be encouraging.

The real game-winner is Foster's subsequent three-run homer
in the first, giving Eddie Lynch something to work with. Lynch,
who seems to come up in the rotation on big attendance days and
national TV, goes the distance, scattering hits right and left but
escaping relatively unscathed until the ninth. I blame that Pirates
run on the giant firecracker booming while Eddie was batting in
the bottom of the eighth. He jumped. We all jumped. Then he
struck out and maybe was still shook up when he took the mound.

In the ninth, I have a long chat with George Hendrick at first
base. He's on with a single. George was the original "I don't need
no press now, man" ballplayer—before Steve Carlton, even. His
antipathy toward the reporters goes back to an episode in Cleveland, when he got burned on a story which misquoted him regarding a teammate, forcing him to apologize to that player. (A
situation not unlike my own earlier in the year, involving Ron
Darling.) George decided to hell with the press, and hasn't talked
since. Not in Cleveland, St. Louis, or Pittsburgh.

Our conversation tonight is all about divorces, court appearances, the nastiness of everything. George has just gone through
a bitter break-up. Ironically, perhaps, I've discussed my situation
with more opposing players than my own teammates. The league
is an extended family, and whatever close ties have been estab-

lished between teammates usually endure the separation caused by trades. Word of personal problems spreads.

On the Mets, Staub is my main listening board and crying towel—and he's a perfect one for me, because I get down on myself too easily and, as noted, Rusty disdains self-pity.

The Mets are feeling a little better tonight, and I don't believe the upcoming national holiday has anything to do with it. A ball season is a long series of sometimes subtle, sometimes dramatic shifts of mood. The Mets are picking up. We race through our showers in order to beat the crowd out of the parking lot. They're staying late for the fireworks. We're going to the airport. We win the race but have to wait for the airplane, a Delta charter. The Mets stalk into the hotel in Atlanta at three in the morning.

Four days here. Three in Cincinnati. Four in Houston. The mid-America swing, not my favorite, but it's vital in these ten games before the break to keep going whatever momentum we've established with our modest two-game streak against the modest Pirates. If we get some more timely hits, we'll make it.

Program note: Disregard a story in today's *Post* comparing the Walt Terrell for Howard Johnson trade with the Mets' infamous Jim Fregosi for Nolan Ryan deal years back. The Mets gave up Ryan. Enough said, but we're a long way from a verdict on Terrell for HoJo. Whatever happens, I admire Howard's straightforward, stoic attitude regarding his problems this season: never complain, never explain. One thing I would work on is his professed dislike of hitting against left-handers. You've got to go up there ready to hit whether the guy throws left or right or between his legs. Be a tiger. Right now, I'm working on this myself.

GAME 75—Mets 6
Pirates 2

JULY 4—ATLANTA

Fireworks indeed. Where to start? Start at noon, when I wake up feeling not good at all and peer out the window at the pouring rain. Keep pouring, I mumble, while punching the magic button on the phone.

"A pot of major-league coffee, please."

I don't want to play today. That sounds bad following my

homily about keeping things rolling, but I'm beat and it's wet and this is Atlanta.

I call Dad and we discuss my work with the trigger of the smooth hand movement. He pauses.

"Listen," he continues, "I've found something else."

Dad has tapes of Cardinal appearances on the "Game of the Week" going back to my first years with the team, in the mid-1970s. He also has a thirty-minute montage tape of Hernandez at-bats scattered through the past decade.

Studying these old swings and comparing them with my stance and swings this year, he has discovered that my stance has gradually opened, until now, he believes, it's too open. I don't buy it. I've always hit with my front foot, the right one, half a foot-length closer to the plate than my back foot. No more, no less. It's automatic by now. Nothing I have to think about. I tell him so.

Dad insists the old tapes show otherwise. They show a very closed stance, he elaborates, with my lead foot an *entire* foot-length closer to the plate. I can't believe it, but Dad knows batting stances. He's reporting what he sees.

And something else. From the center field camera position he could see all of the number 17 on the back of my jersey as I moved into the ball—in the old at-bats. This year he can see just the 7. I'm not closing my upper body as much now.

This observation in effect proves his other point. My right foot drastically closed in the old days would force my right shoulder more closed, thereby exposing the back of my jersey to the vantage point in center field.

"Do me a favor. Try it."

I'll never forget this final exhortation. Dad has been suffering right along with me these miserable six weeks.

He suggests that I overcompensate in batting practice; he has always believed in overcompensation. If I was swinging a little up at the ball as a kid, he had me hit down on it, as the best way to get back to level. Now he wants me to get as closed in the batter's box as, say, George Hendrick, who looks like he has just taken a full stride toward the third-base dugout.

I agree to try it—but I still hope today's game is rained out. It looks likely, but we board the bus and go to the stadium anyway. The rain slacks off enough for us to get in batting practice. The stance feels uncomfortable, and there's no immediate benefit. But no immediate falling off, either. I hit the ball okay. Some of the guys note the new approach. Bill Robinson and I discuss the strategy. Bill, our batting coach, has been working mainly with my attitude, not my mechanics. For one thing, he couldn't know about this business with the foot position. For another, he's well aware that coaches can get too technical on too many points. Correct one main thing with a talented hitter, and a lot of factors will fall into place. Like Dad says.

Rusty watches with great interest. Rusty and Dad know each other; they've discussed hitting a few times. Dad surprised Orange one night at dinner with this question: "Rusty, how can you start your swing from a dead stop?" Rusty just smiled. I don't know how he does it, either. Almost every good hitter has a release mechanism, a trigger. But watch Staub. He's a statue until the ball is thrown.

After an hour's delay this evening we start the game, and I'm still not anxious to play, not singing in this rain. My first time up I hit a rope off Rick Mahler to the wall in left-center for a double. It's a 3-and-2 change-up, outside corner, driven to left-center—all with my front foot closed to the hilt.

Dad, I'm dumbfounded.

In the third, I'm robbed. Murphy makes a diving catch in center—but the replay clearly shows the ball on the ground behind him! The umpire at second, Jerry Davis, can't see that, but he does see Murphy jump up and fire the ball to second base, a dead giveaway. When an outfielder catches the ball on a dive, he comes up waving it in the air. Davis calls me out, though, and he's not overruled.

I'm not pissed. Mainly, I'm absorbing the fact that I've hit two balls hard in consecutive at-bats for the first time in a long, long while.

It rains harder and they bring out the tarp, which spells out in large letters: "When It Rains, It Pours."

An hour and a half later, we're back on the field for the Braves' third inning, and the field is soaked.

Dwight has to come out of the game when he tightens up, and Roger McDowell, rushed into service, gives up a couple of runs. They're leading 3–1 and the omens are bad. Davey moved Dwight up in the rotation to pitch on three days rest, so he can get three starts before the All-Star break, with the last one the Sunday before the break, so he won't have to pitch in the celebrity classic. The season comes first—but rain tonight screws up the strategy.

In our fourth, with two on and one out, I drive the first pitch to right-center, where Claudell Washington loses his footing in the water and the ball in the lights, and the liner sails by him and all the way to the wall: a triple for Keith, two RBIs. Three good swings in the game; my first two-hit game in three weeks.

A mile-a-minute I'm talking to anyone who will listen. When I'm excited, I jabber. Umps, fielders, coaches, teammates, ground crew, everybody but fans. I'm a kid with a brand new pet—no, a pet he had lost but has now found after weeks of searching. The new stance is uncomfortable in that I'm aware of the extended right foot (ideally the hitter isn't consciously aware of anything mechanical), but nevertheless I'm swinging well from this stance, and I'm seeing the ball beautifully.

With four runs, we take the lead. In the sixth, I hit another liner to right. Claudell catches it. Big deal. It's my fourth solid contact of the night.

In the eighth, I drive a 2-and-1 pitch over the wall on a line. These are the Braves we're playing, so a little Indian slang is appropriate: "Keith hit 'em big fly."

"Big fly" is our new lingo for home run.

Keith very happy, except when I realize that I would have had the cycle if Davis had called the play correctly back in the third inning. That was my missing single! Touring the bases on the home run, I shout at Braves third baseman Ken Oberkfell, "I would have had the fucking cycle!"

Oberkfell played with me on the Cards. An old buddy, he wears the same world championship ring I do, from 1982. That ring assures a brotherhood for life.

"Fuck you, Keith," he says by way of commiseration.

We're leading 7–4 now, so I figure that's it for my cycle attempt. I won't come up again. Jogging out to my post at first, I look over and see Jerry Davis grinning. I flip Jerry the bird. And he grins back!

What, me mad? After five straight ropes, three hits, three RBIs? And with the game official, so it can't be rained out? I could hug the guy who messed up my cycle!

SPLAT! That's the Mets crashing in Atlanta's eighth inning, the ugliest thing this year. Leach, who has pitched four good innings, is lifted for Orosco. Jesse promptly gives up three walks, two in a row to load the bases for Dale "Most Feared Hitter" Murphy. Two outs. Davey walks to the mound and calls for Sisk—righty against righty—and Murphy drills a double to the wall, clearing the bases. Good Lord, we're behind by a run, and I can only think about what a nasty loss this will be.

Bruce Sutter comes in for the ninth inning, naturally, and damned if Johnson and Heep don't get pinch singles off him, with Johnson then scoring on an infield hit by Dykstra, tying the game.

I strand Heep on third when I fly to left for the third out. Against Sutter, I always move up in the box a little, hoping to catch his split-fingered fastball before the bottom falls out. I've had great success against him. He counters tonight by "Pearl Harbor-ing" me with straight fastballs, four out of six pitches—for the first time in all our encounters. Hand it to Bruce. He strokes Hernandez by naming him the most dangerous hitter in the league, then outsmarts him.

The Braves don't score off Sisk in their half of the inning. I single in the twelfth inning to complete the cycle, and Staub calls from the dugout, "Get the ball! Get the ball!" I hadn't thought about it. I get the ball.

We score two in the thirteenth. Terry Harper hits a two-out, two-strike homer off Tom Gorman to tie the game.

In one of the innings—I lose count—the guys on the bench get their rally caps on—that's a cap flipped inside out; old baseball tradition.

Around two o'clock, I announce to the team, "I'm ready! Let's play ball!" They look at me like I'm crazy, but if we can end it soon, I'll be in bed by three or shortly thereafter, up at noon—all standard for me.

We don't end it soon. An hour after my brave declaration, I've had it. An impulse leads me to call my new girlfriend in New York. "If I'm playing baseball at this hour, at least you can be awake," I laugh, and return to the fray.

We score one in the top of the eighteenth. Gorman is still throwing for us. The first two Braves are easy outs. Pitcher Rick Camp bats for himself. This is it. I go to the mound and tell Gorfax, "I know you've had trouble with pitchers, but that was last year. This is this year. Let's get him."

With the count at two strikes, I don't even get into my fielding crouch. No way he'll get anything to hit here. He'll swing at something bad and miss. This game is over. The next thing I know the ball is sailing over the wall, left fielder Heep is holding his arms over his head, center fielder Dykstra has collapsed on his knees, and pitcher Gorman, his face red as blood, has turned in utter shock to look at me. And I can't look back at him. I can't help you, Tom, I admit it. I have to turn away.

Stumbling back to the dugout after the next guy grounds out, Gorman mumbles, "I didn't know Garber had that kind of power."

Garber?! Tom didn't even know who was batting! Long night.

Well, we score five times the next inning and I'm not too unhappy to make the third out. Utterly bushed, I'm hitless my last three times up. What a nasty twist it would be to *lose* my groove in the same ridiculously extended game in which I *found* it. I also boot a grounder. I work hard to convince myself I'm just tired.

Surely, we mutter, these five runs will do it, even with the memory fresh of the Braves homers twice tying the game in the extra innings. Ron Darling, relieving for the first time in his career, shuts them off with only two runs. Ronnie is uncomfortable out there, and who wouldn't be, warming up and coming into the game a couple of hours before the sun is due on the horizon.

We hose down Gorfax something terrible after the game. A giddy post-game clubhouse, wrapping up almost a dozen hours at the ballpark. If we had lost—now that would've been different.

We're on the bus at four-thirty. Unbelievably, they're blasting off the fireworks for the few hundred fans who have spent the night at the ballgame.

A huge Shriners convention is sharing our hotel, and the festivities are highlighted (as they affect the Mets) by a steel band playing in the lobby at all hours. I have no problem with the Shriners or their hats, but some of the guys have had long, long waits for an elevator. On the bus to bed, they take out their frustration. "Kill the Shriners! Kill the Shriners!" is the chant. Crude, but all in good fun after a twenty-eight-hit attack that survives three come-from-behind rallies by the Braves.

At five, I'm home in bed, happy at last.

GAME 76—Mets 16
Braves 13

JULY 5

The wake-up call arrives on time at three in the afternoon. Normally I would lie around for a while, but not today. I know that if I close my eyes, I'll be out until six. Let's get the coffee and the newspapers up here and think about this.

For starters, each calf has a knot the size of a walnut. I'll need a couple of days of massages and heat.

Second, last night's game should have been suspended at some decent hour.

Third, I fibbed to all the reporters about my late-inning phone call. I told them I'd called my brother, and that's what the papers are reporting in their lengthy stories about the incredible game.

Fourth, the slump, I believe, is over. I can't imagine a four-hit night not bringing me out of it. Just call me the "Overnight Sensation" (a great album by one of my favorite groups, Frank Zappa and the Mothers of Invention). The new stance is still an effort, but I must be on the right track. And how many times in past seasons have I snapped out of a slump on a night I didn't want to play, a night I was tired or sick? Maybe that condition serves the same purpose as coming to the ballpark hungover.

It's important now to take each day one at a time. With an average flirting with .250, it's a disaster to try to get back to something respectable (.280 say) in one or two weeks. In a way, the numbers work in my favor, anyway.

I divide the season into groups of 100 at-bats. I expect at least thirty hits per 100. Any more is the bonus I strive for. I don't think most fans realize that over a period of 100 at-bats (about a month; 25 games), there is a difference of only six hits between .270 and .330.

Six, that's all. One hit every four games. That arithmetic lifts my spirits in a slump.

Steve Garvey told me early in my career that the main difference between a .280 and a .300 hitter is keeping the giveaway at-bats to a minimum—those times when the hitter goes to the plate in the ninth inning with his team winning or losing 10–0, and it's hard to concentrate.

Pete Rose says, "If you get one hit, want another. When you get two, want the third."

I say, more modestly, "A hit a day keeps the doctor away."

This is true, because there will always be the multiple-hit games. Cut out the 0-for-4s and a hitter has it made.

Tom Gorman gleefully reports on a phone call this morning from New York City.

"Hello? Tom Gorman?"

"Yeah. Who's this?"

"I'm a Mets fan. A fan of yours. *Rick Camp!!!* You gotta be shitting me!!!"

Slam!

I single in the first inning, score; line out to the shortstop in the fourth, yell "Fuck!" as I go back to the dugout; am picked off first after walking in the seventh. My evening doesn't matter a great deal because we're ahead 6–0 after three innings and Aguilera baffles the Braves with his fastball and hard slider and good control.

Four in a row. The mood on the team has turned completely around. A week ago I was worried. Worried. Now I have that old feeling again about this team and this season. The players are there when we need them. It looks like Dykstra can spark us at the top of the order. At long last we're hitting. The pitchers can give up a few runs and still feel they can win.

GAME 77—Mets 6
Braves 1

JULY 6

Go ahead, rain. See if I care. I'm not playing today, anyway. Davey told me after last night's game that my legs would get the game off this afternoon.

Now I'll just enjoy this whirlpool. Training facilities in the visitors' clubhouses at all the stadiums have taken a great leap forward in recent years. We have complete services everywhere. I'm happy to truck out to the park on a dead day to enjoy a bowl of major-league coffee, a little beneficial R & R, and the crossword puzzle.

"To break a slump." Three-letter word. Last letter "t."

I've got it, Eddie! I've got it!

JULY 7

Yesterday's rainout will be made up as part of a doubleheader today, Sunday. I only pinch-hit in the first game (without success), and despite my protestations it's probably smart of Davey to keep me out against a tough left-hander, Zane Smith. Playing both games after the marathon, even taking into account yesterday's rainout, might hurt me just as I'm coming out of the slump.

We win.

In the second game, we rack 'em up again, mainly with walks, but with Hernandez contributing a two-out, two-run double pulled down the right field line. An important hit for my confidence, which is much higher but still not 100 percent.

I should never have the chance for the RBIs. With first base open, I assume I'll be walked. I look over at the Braves' manager, Eddie Haas, expecting to see him flash the four fingers. Nothing.

Thank you, Eddie—but, frankly, I don't expect to see you managing this team much longer.

I shouldn't gripe about my series, but I'm griping. The Mets won all four games—six in a row now—but the six line drives caught off my bat still irk me. Instead of 6-for-18, with any luck I would be 10-, even 12-for-18. Does this complaint sound like I'm out for myself, a selfish player? Of course I'm selfish about my hits. When I'm hitting, our odds of winning increase exponentially. Bill Robinson conveys this thought to me this afternoon, working to keep me revved up.

How about Ray Knight's terrible luck? Awarded the third base job by Davey, Ray responds as he predicted he would, 5-for-8 in the doubleheader, 8-for-22 in the series. But he pulls a muscle and will miss some games.

The job goes back to HoJo.

GAME 78—Mets 4
Braves 0

GAME 79—Mets 8
Braves 5

JULY 8—CINCINNATI

"Personal problems," Jim Palmer says on the "Monday Night Game of the Week," may be partly responsible for my recent slump. I know about the remark only because Jay Horwitz rushes up to me in the fifth inning tonight at Riverfront Stadium, and says urgently that he has received a dozen phone calls from New York TV and radio stations wanting a clarification.

We know what the immediate suspicion is: something to do with drugs. That suspicion follows in the wake of the grand jury testimony in March. I ask Jay to call back every one of those stations and tell them that I'm going through a bitter divorce, and I'm not answering questions about the matter. When I next see Jim Palmer, I'll point out how his innocuous remark sets off a mini-firestorm of Big Apple media attention.

I see Howard Cosell before the game. He's interviewing the Reds' new owner, Marge Schott, as I walk by on the field. "Do you realize, Keith," he asks me rhetorically, "that you're hitting .065 against the Reds this season?"

I thank you, Howard, for that morale-booster. I didn't know the exact number, but I'm aware it's not very good. My average isn't very good against most of the teams. I also know that their pitcher Joe Price is a tough left-hander whom I've never hit well.

All of which makes my single, my double and my home run off Price very, very sweet. Then I get the fourth hit off Jay Tibbs.

With these hits off Price, I know I'm back. The stance—is it new or is it old?—feels very comfortable now. But I play it cool with the press. I just say, "I feel good." In my mind, though, I'm the overnight sensation.

Before the game I ran a hand in our clubhouse hearts game, for the first time in my card-playing life. The guys joke later, "Run 'em every day if it brings 4-for-5."

Thanks to our hitting, we get away with another subpar pitching performance, by Lynch this time. He deserves the break. Like almost all our starters, he has pitched better than his record (6–5). The pitchers have carried the hitters. Now it's our turn.

One thing, though. For the second time in as many starts, Eddie gives up a big RBI to the eighth-place batter, with two outs and first base open. I groan. Here's my explanation. Lynch, like many off-speed and control pitchers, fears being considered a wimp. Even these control pitchers need a macho attitude out there. At times, they'll want to throw to a given hitter rather than walk him. But they'll also want to throw it by the hitter. This is ruinous.

The only solution, I believe, is to order Eddie to intentionally walk the guy. Next time in this situation, Davey will flash four.

After the game I meet Jim Kaat in the hotel bar. Who else is there but Cosell, and we all have a good time until two o'clock. Howard congratulates me on my game; I remind him of his statistic. For all his chatter, I like Cosell. I chatter a lot myself. We exchange phone numbers. Let's have dinner.

Gary Matthews is on the disabled list for the Cubs. Now it's my turn to call him in his time of need.

Too bad for the Cubbies, huh?

GAME 80—Mets 7
Reds 5

JULY 9

We rough up Mario Soto, I belt a two-run homer. Mario, one of the finest pitchers in the league, must be hurting. I ask him, he insists he's fine, but the fastball is short a few critical inches. Funny about these pitchers. Jesse's not right, and he's not saying anything, either.

Doc isn't right, either, and I know it from the first inning. It's nothing obvious, but I can feel it. Trotting into the dugout after the third, I ask him. He says he's fine. After the fifth I ask him again. This time he says he'll talk to me after the game.

After the game he tells me. A childhood friend has just been murdered. Doc is hurting inside. Doc pitches eight innings of five-hit, two-run baseball. Does this tell you anything about Doc?

In the eighth we score four times without a base hit. This production might be a record: walk, walk, walk, walk (one run), sacrifice fly (another run), error on Dave Parker in right field (final two runs).

In the ninth we score four more times—the same four guys! Our eighth victory in a row is a joke, a laugher. There have been precious few of these.

The players are riding me hard now about my compulsive yakking. I guess they're right. I've gone from exhausted to strong as a bull in five or six games. I'm a front-runner, I'll admit it. I don't know a ballplayer who isn't. It's hard as hell to keep my head up when I'm struggling, leaving runners all over the place, the ballclub losing. I try hard to stay with the program, and do a damn good job, I think, but I can't really fool the guys. They know.

Ten days ago we were reminding ourselves we're not as bad as we look. Now we have to remind ourselves we're not as good as we look.

GAME 81—Mets 11
Reds 2

JULY 10

Okay, fellas, I'm going public. It's official. I'm hot. I'm on fire. I'm in heat. In a close game against Tom Browning, I hit a belt-high inside fastball into the left field corner, with ease. With ease, I tell you, on a bastard pitch. A bastard. The drive wins the game and convinces me. The stance is right. The ball floats to the plate. It looks as big as a balloon. How can I miss it?

Rick Aguilera throws his second complete game in a row. He ties up Rose with those sinking fastballs. It's a thing of beauty. It's also fun to watch Rick get the first three guys in the lineup— Milner, Venable, and Rose—in the first and eighth innings, so he doesn't have to go after Dave Parker with men on base. It's especially critical in the eighth inning; then he gets Parker leading off the ninth. This is Gooden-toughness on the mound. I mention this sequence to a reporter, an old hand at the game, and he says, "Gee, I'd never thought about that kind of thing. I wonder whether Aguilera was thinking like that."

"Go ask him."

Yes, Rick says, he was trying to bring up Parker in the lead-off position.

The bad news here is that Carter's knee is killing him, and I know it's affecting his stroke at the plate. Bad news, but we've been fighting problems all year, and here we are only two and a half games out of first, with the season half over.

"Is it discouraging to win nine in a row and only pick up two and a half games against the Cards?" the reporters want to know.

No.

I watch closely to see how everyone behaves tonight on the flight to Houston. Because it's a charter, the guys could really cut up if they wanted to. But the team is subdued. Business as usual, winning ballgames. Another day at the office. Memo to the staff: Avoid the emotional roller coaster.

We must also avoid becoming Nolan Ryan's 4,000th strikeout tomorrow night. The pitchers are already taking bets, teasing the nervous batters. Don't bet on me, fellas. I can go defensive, if I have to. Before I choke, I'll choke up!

GAME 82—Mets 2
Reds 1

JULY 11—HOUSTON

Before the Nolan Ryan drama tonight, a meeting with our commissioner. Peter Ueberroth is an impressive individual with a great deal to gain from a peaceful resolution of the contract talks between owners and players, so I am puzzled that he seems so standoffish right now. I hope it's shrewd politics. I fear it's symptomatic of "business as usual" in baseball: The owners' belief that they own not only the teams, but the game itself.

I like to believe there's a difference—but at the major-league level, perhaps there isn't. Just as the notion is ridiculous that fans would watch Triple-A players masquerading as the real Mets and Cards and Cubs, perhaps they would also reject the real major leaguers going off to "play by themselves" as the Firemen, the Falcons, and the Pups. The owners need us. We need them. Ueberroth tells the Mets tonight that nobody wins with a strike. He concedes that some of the owners' positions—especially the salary cap—are not viable. Behind all his remarks, I sense a little panic. He knows what we all know: The fans turned against his predecessor, Bowie Kuhn, when they felt he didn't do enough to avert the strike four years ago. After Ueberroth's success with the Summer Olympics, they'll be very disappointed with a strike. It will be perceived, wrongly, as his failure. He knows it; I sense that tonight. If he does indeed harbor the rumored larger political ambitions, they're at stake.

As happens so often, if you don't get to a great pitcher early, you're sunk. Tonight features a neat twist: If the Mets don't get to Ryan early, some batter is going to be famous on the sports pages for a day or two. Ryan only needs seven strikeouts. He'll surely get them if he goes into the late innings; he could get them early.

And we don't get to him early, leaving one, two, and three men on, respectively, in the first three innings of the game, while scoring only one run. There's a ballgame going on, but it's hard to get into it. The hitters watch and wait as the K total mounts. In the dugout not a word is said about the rising total, but everybody wants it over with—so long as it's someone else!

By way of distraction, home-plate umpire Dave Pallone gets a wake-up call—the worst I've ever seen. One of Ryan's fastballs is tipped beneath the catcher and caroms off the ground directly up into Pallone's jewels, splits his cup and he's down for the count. I can only guess at that agony, but he's ready to umpire after six or seven minutes.

After our fifth inning, which concludes with strikeouts by Strawberry and Carter, Ryan has six and leads the game, 3–1. He's throwing hard, his curveball is over the plate. It doesn't look good for the guys batting in the sixth—Heep, Johnson, Santana.

Poor Danny Heep: After two very quick strikes leading off, what chance does he have? Worst of all would be to take a called third strike, so the impulse to swing at anything will be difficult to resist. I know and Danny should know, too, that the next offering will be the biggest curve Nolan can break off, and that's a big one. It will be hard for him to keep it out of the dirt, but hard for Danny not to swing, anyway. The crowd (around 20,000, not bad for the Dome) is yelling and screaming. Around with the right arm—and Heep is already swinging when the ball leaves Ryan's hand. The bat never has a chance. I have a beautiful angle on the play—gulping a Coke in the clubhouse, watching on TV. Danny strikes out on a ball in the dirt.

"Mr. 4,000" is the needle after the game. The teasing Danny doesn't mind, but he is genuinely unhappy to be the 4,000th victim.

"It's not the end of your career, Danny!" I remind him. "Just the highlight!"

Just kidding. I know whereof I speak. Tom Seaver struck out his 3,000th man a few years ago. That was Keith Hernandez.

An overlooked irony is that Heep hasn't been playing much, since Strawberry is back and Foster, along with me, is carrying the team on this road trip. But tonight Davey loads the lineup with left-handed hitters, so Heep gets a shot. His part-time role has to be tough now, especially after playing well and winning games as a regular for over a month. I look at it this way, and so does Davey: With a left-handed hitting bench of Heep, Hurdle, and Staub, the opposing manager thinks hard about coming in with a right-handed reliever.

After the strikeout, the fans stop the game with a long cheer, then start leaving, even though we tie the contest with two tainted runs in the seventh. I'm not out for cheap shots, but the Dome fans are weak. Hell, even the cabbie who brought me to the stadium said the best night for him is a 4–0 game (either way) in the fifth inning. He'll get his first customer that early, and a steady stream will follow for the rest of the night.

Our man Sid Fernandez keeps up with Nolan in strikeouts, without walking anyone, but leaves after giving up a homer in the sixth. So I'm wrong: I thought before the game we'd win if Sid had his control. (Sid is still learning at the plate, too. In the fourth inning, he figures he's out on a third strike and heads for the dugout. No, Sid! Wait for the call! Pallone calls it a ball. Sid misses the next pitch, anyway.)

In the eighth inning, I get a little wake-up call of my own. Jose Cruz hits a line drive right at me and it hooks at the last moment. I catch the ball behind my right ear. I hear the draft from this shot! My ear is ringing from the *Pop!* for the rest of the game. A lucky catch? Only if you call reflexes lucky. I'm one of those perhaps unusual cases: not particularly quick afoot, but with great reflexes—legs included.

I spread a little mustard on the play, I must admit, lunging back to the bag to double off Phil Garner, then pausing dramatically as the crowd reacts. Rusty assesses one buck for showboating. Still, it's one of the three hardest shots I've ever caught, or missed, for that matter. Joe Morgan and Chris Chambliss hit the other two.

A line drive isn't an infielder's hardest play, not at all. The most difficult chance on a grass field is the hard ground ball directly at us which has to be fielded on the in-between hop. There's no time to shift up or back for a good bounce. On Astroturf, the toughest chance is the one-hop bullet, because the ball springs off the carpet. On wet turf, we're petrified by that unguided missile. You won't see many infielders hold their po-

sition in front of it. We'll jerk to one side and try to grab it that
way.

My favorite hardest chance is turning the sacrifice bunt into
a double play. It's not physically dangerous, but it's dangerous
for the team if I wheel the ball into center field.

The Astros have a way of making me look good in the field,
with all their line-drive hitters from the left side. Invariably they
smoke a couple of balls in my direction, more than any other
team, and I get the opportunity for some heroics.

Dykstra's heroics save the game in the ninth inning. He makes
a diving catch on the turf, and he'll have a nice rug burn to show
his grandkids. Then HoJo saves the game again with a diving
catch down the line.

Then we lose in the twelfth, anyway. Our streak ends at nine.
Not bad for the road.

It's official: I'm not on the starting All-Star squad. I don't
deserve to be, this year.

Tonight is my 300th at-bat, with eighty-one hits. I'm only nine
behind schedule. I can make that up.

GAME 83—Astros 4
Mets 3

JULY 12

I can't lift my right arm above my shoulder. Sliding head-first into
home plate last night, I somehow jammed the shoulder. Steve
Garland meets me early at the park this afternoon to work on it
with massage, ultrasound, and heat. Diagnosis: severe bruise, almost but not quite a separation. Close call, but with the lingering
fear that my swing, finally grooved, will jump the tracks again.
By game time I can swing easily enough. I'll play. Thank you,
Steve.

On the subject of diving plays: In yesterday's *New York Post*,
Dick Young wrote in his "Clubhouse Confidential" column: "Len
Dykstra's hustle is eye-catching, but I can't help thinking it's over-
done a little when he dives headfirst for a liner over second, and
catches the ball as it's about to sail over his head—a ball that could
have been caught knee-high if he had kept his feet." And there's
a picture of Dykstra with the caption "overdoes it."

Personally, I don't care how eye-catching his hustle is. I only care how game-winning it is, and Lenny's hustle has helped us win games on this road trip. He's a feisty guy, plays with abandon in the Pete Rose tradition, and can't play any other way. Why should he? Why criticize the rookie?

Tonight, Dykstra doubles and scores and we win in ten, but only after Darling has given up a two-out ninth-inning homer to Alan Ashby to tie the game—on a change-up. Davey can't be happy. Earlier in the year, he had some words for the Gooden-Carter battery after Dwight gave up a change-up homer to Greg Brock. The idea is to not get beat on your third-best pitch.

GAME 84—Mets 3
Astros 2

JULY 13

"Strange Brew" was the title of a great rock tune by Cream, and it's an appropriate label for this ballgame, marked by some of the best (by the Mets) and worst (by the Astros) pitching of the year; also by terrible calls, terrible plays, ominous plays, and a terrific final score.

Starting the game for the Astros is rookie Mark Knudson, making only the second start of his career. He doesn't have much going for him this evening, that's obvious from the get-go. And I have to help his cause by opening my big fat mouth.

"How's the kid throwing?" Cott Deal, the Astros' first-base coach, asks me in all innocence in the Houston third.

"That was a pretty good pitch I hit, a backdoor slider," I reply, referring to an RBI single in our third.

"You're hot, aren't you?"

"Kind of"—and now here comes my mistake—"but this kid doesn't throw hard enough. I can cover the whole plate."

Deal no doubt transmits this intelligence to Bobby Lillis, Houston's manager. When Dykstra leads off the fifth inning with a single, Lillis yanks Knudson. If I had told Deal that his pitcher is throwing like Nolan Ryan, the gamesmanship would have been too blatant, therefore counterproductive. But I could have said, "He's throwing pretty good. I'm just real hot. I can hit anything."

If I had worked it that way, maybe Lillis would have stayed with the kid and given us a chance to drive in more runs. As it turns out, the guy Lillis brings in, Madden, can't find the plate, walking Backman and myself. Then he gives up a single to Straw-berry and a bases-clearing double to Foster—on a 3-ball count.

Mets lead 7–1 after five. The game is getting out of hand, and that seems appropriate, because it started getting out of hand—from an aesthetic standpoint—in the second inning, when home-plate ump Paul Runge called one of the worst strikes against Strawberry I've ever seen. The ball was down at his ankles, and Darryl looked back in amazement. Davey must have shouted some-thing quite obscene from the dugout: Before we know what's happening, he's thumbed from the game.

For the rest of the evening, we're suspicious. In a funny way, the string of balls called against Madden, even though they netted us runs, may add to the suspicion. Veteran umps sometimes get pissed at pitchers having trouble throwing strikes, and perversely squeeze the zone—trying to get the guy relieved, I suppose. Is the plate wide, is it narrow? Who knows tonight? After the Straw-berry incident, Wally starts to dispute a called third strike, but I indicate from the on-deck circle that the ball was, indeed, over at the knees. In the seventh, I get irritated at a pitch outside that's called a strike.

A ballgame can lose its bearings, and it happens tonight. It's not consequential for the Mets; we're winning.

Lynch pitches his fifth complete game of the year and throws as well as I've seen him, against a team that always hurts him. It's his first win against the Astros.

The reason for his problem with Houston is simple. Lynch is nervous pitching against left-handed line-drive hitters. Eddie's best pitch, his slider, is "flat"—it breaks sideways, not down, and too often this movement merely brings the ball onto the meat of the bat of a left-handed hitter. Before the game, we discuss strat-egy, and Eddie decides to try a slight adjustment in his release, to get the ball moving down more. It works: He gets eleven ground-ball outs, and it's fun and satisfying to watch him work.

At long last, he benefits from the notoriously pitcher-favoring Astrodome. Besides the fact that the trapped air in the place is dead (even a ball hit on the nose sounds like it has broken the bat), the Dome also has a high mound, I'm certain. The same holds true for Shea and Dodger stadiums. The rule book dictates ten inches, but if they ever get out with a surveyor's transit, they'll find these three mounds are high. I know a light bat when I wield one and a high mound when I see one.

Conversely, the Wrigley Field mound is low. In fact, some of the pitchers were discussing before the Cub series two weeks ago that Roger McDowell might have trouble on that low mound, which would undermine his sinking fastball. The second game of that series proved them right. Roger was hit hard.

High or low, the mound in the Astrodome isn't a good place for the hometown hurlers tonight. This is a good game to shoot cripples against mop-up pitchers, supported by fielders who are back on their heels. I know this, and there's Backman on first base when I come up in the ninth, Mets leading by nine runs. Jeff Calhoun is pitching. Calhoun isn't a mop-up pitcher, but it's a mop-up situation, and it has to be hard for him to give it his best concentration. But here's the rub: It's hard for the hitter, too. I know Steve Garvey is right about the importance of these situations for the average, but I still have trouble digging in for a good set of swings.

The commentators note that Hernandez is a better hitter with men on base. I agree, but how is this a point of pride? Who wouldn't be able to concentrate with the winning run on third base?

I roll into a weak double play.

GAME 85—Mets 10
Astros 1

JULY 14

Not by accident did Davey wait last year until we were in Houston before giving Doc his first major-league start. The big field and the high mound should be perfect for him. Not much over a year later, he returns this Sunday night, already established as a superstar pitcher.

He pitches a beautiful game, following on the heels of last night's sloppy affair. Dwight has tremendous force in his pitches and fortitude in his character. Less than a week after a disturbing episode in his life, he produces his best game of the year. Maybe he has thrown harder, but I doubt it. His heater breaks eight bats in the early innings, by unofficial count. "Take it easy, Doc," I kid him. "You're going to force the Astros' clubbie to fetch a new batch."

His mound opponent, Bob Knepper, is throwing not as hard but just as skillfully. We're scoreless in the eighth. Ronn Reynolds, playing for Carter, whose knee is really a problem now, singles to open the inning, and Dwight, knowing that Ronn doesn't have much speed, tries to cut it too close with his bunts. They roll foul. He strikes out.

Reynolds moves to second on an infield single by Dykstra, and now comes the play that wins the game. It looks like a funky run in the scorebook, but give all credit, Dick Young, to a great hustling play by Dykstra. Chapman hits a double-play ball to Bill Doran at second, but Dykstra slams into shortstop Craig Reynolds on the pivot. Reynolds's relay throw hits Chapman in the foot as he crosses the bag at first, and the ball caroms way down the first-base line. Reynolds comes around to score. That's all we need.

Dykstra again: back in the fifth, a perfect Dykstra-to-Santana-to-Johnson throw nails Denny Walling trying to move to third on a long fly. A game-saving fundamental.

Where's the excitement in a 1–0 ballgame? Some fans have the nerve to ask.

The Mets conclude the most successful road trip in the twenty-four-year history of the franchise: eleven victories, one loss. Heading out of New York on July 3, I would have considered seven wins acceptable.

Foster and Hernandez provided the biggest lift in the hitting department. The big personnel keys were Dykstra's successful stand-in duty for Mookie Wilson, and Strawberry's return. Darryl has had a couple of homers and half a dozen RBIs in the fourteen games since his return.

Hand it to Foster. Just when his job appears in jeopardy and Davey is hinting that he'll find someplace to play Heep on Darryl's return, Foster starts hitting the ball hard and timely. Now he can get in some blows for the Mets at the player-rep meeting tomorrow in Chicago. He's replacing me because I have to go to St. Louis to consult with lawyers in the divorce action. What a pleasant way to start the three-day break.

But wait a minute! They want me on the All-Star team! Immediately after tonight's game in the Dome, Jay Horwitz rushes

up. The league office has just called. They want me to replace
the injured Pedro Guerrero.

"No," I say, and it doesn't take me long to arrive at this decision. I already have plans. Lawyers are waiting. Plus I don't want
to be an injury replacement. Pete Rose was chosen as the backup first baseman, and that's okay—he's a big star and having a
good season—but statistics dictate I should have been the choice—
as the back-up, not the starter. Do it right or not at all: That's my
attitude, and if it sounds like I'm pouting, so be it. I'm not the
only player with complaints about All-Star team selections. Jose
Cruz, one of the top hitters in the league for years, was chosen
this year for only the second time. It gripes him.

After the rest of the team loads onto the bus for the ride to
the airport and the flight to New York, I return to the hotel. I
have a drink. It hits me: I can't go to St. Louis tomorrow. I can't
get bogged down with the divorce case now. It can't be entirely
coincidental that I started to come out of my slump the day after
that disastrous weekend in St. Louis that began with the day in
court. That courthouse session was supposed to be the end of the
matter until the conclusion of my season. I want to keep it that
way.

I need the three days off. I call my lawyer and ask him to
cancel me out. He understands and agrees. I'll go home.

For the record, here are the two All-Star teams:

Position	Fans' choice	Hernandez's choice
First base	Garvey	Clark
Second base	Herr	Herr
Shortstop	Smith	Smith
Third base	Nettles	Nettles
Outfield	Murphy	Murphy
	Strawberry	Guerrero
	Gwynn	McGee
Catcher	Carter	Kennedy

So the fans got four out of eight right.
My pitchers: Jack Andujar, Doc Gooden, and Danny Cox for

the starters; Lee Smith, Ted Power, Jeff Reardon and Goose Gossage in relief.

Umpires: Harry Wendelstedt, Dutch Rennert, John McSherry and Doug "The Lord" Harvey call the best balls and strikes in the league. Frank Pulli, honorable mention.

GAME 86—Mets 1
Astros 0

JULY 15, 16, 17—NEW YORK CITY

I haven't enjoyed a more relaxing three days in my life. No baseball, no divorce, no lawyers, no book. Jim Kaat and his date join me and mine for a Broadway play and dancing afterwards at the Palladium. This is my night on the town, while the boys are playing showcase baseball in Minneapolis. I don't regret turning down the invitation to be Pedro's replacement. I don't even regret the five grand I thereby lost: $2,500 each from my glove manufacturer, Rawlings, and my shoe manufacturer, Adidas. Nor do I judge Andujar for refusing to show up because he wasn't selected to start the game. He doesn't have to answer to me or the media.

Interesting is an All-Star list selected in *The Times* by Tim McCarver, choosing among players he has seen. For first basemen, he gives a slight edge to Willie McCovey over Willie Stargell. Hernandez? "Not in this group," McCarver replies, and I agree. I also agree with his reasoning: Hernandez doesn't have the long-ball power of the other two. McCovey was awesome. Ted Williams said he had the sweetest swing in the game. "Now watch this man swing" was Dad's instruction. If Willie McCovey had hit for line drives all the time, and not homers, he would have batted .320 for his career.

Willie Stargell hit .260 for a decade, but with loads of HRs and RBIs; then he changed his style as he grew older and his bat a little slower, and he improved his average as his power production came down. Admirable.

JULY 18

The first game after the All-Star break is a mini-Opening Day. For a hitter or a team in a slump, the second half of the season represents a clean slate. For me and the Mets, we hope to keep a good thing going. Another factor looms this year: We have only eighteen games before the strike date, now set for August 6. This may be a shortened season. We're in good shape now, a mere one and a half games behind St. Louis (a triumph, when I was thinking two weeks ago in terms of six or seven behind), but we have to catch up now. There may not be time later on.

I have a new watch, thanks to the National League office, which has selected me as last week's Player of the Week, the third time I've won the award. It's a nice timepiece, with an inscription. This watch goes to Gary; Dad has one, I have one.

Changes: John Christensen, Mr. Warmth in the hearts game, has been sent down to Tidewater to make room for Tom Paciorek, acquired from the White Sox. This is optioning the future to make room for the present. John will be back late in the year. The pennant we want to win is this year's, and Paciorek is a veteran who can hit.

If "Wimpy" (named after his love of hamburgers, *a la* the Popeye character) doesn't locate in Manhattan, I'll be disappointed. A wild and crazy guy, he'd be a lot of fun in Rusty's van. Besides, he's perfect for the East Side, with his coiffed grey hair and middle-aged trim. Tom looks like he jogged out to the stadium with the New York Road Runners.

A much more important lineup note is Carter's absence from tonight's game. There's talk of surgery. He didn't play in the All-Star game, so that's three days' rest, and the doctors want him to have several more off before he gives the knee a test. If the joint fails, Gary's gone. And like Davey says, we don't want to contemplate the season without him. Frankly, I would be pessimistic—but I've been moderately pessimistic earlier, and we've proved resilient. The Mets have the horses for some surprises. Who thought that Dykstra would sub so well for Mookie, or Heep for Strawberry?

The Braves are in town to start the homestand—our longest of the year, beautifully situated in the schedule to get us off to a good start against the weaker western division teams, whom we've beat up on. Knock on wood. These statistics mean almost nothing, because nothing prevents a team you've pounded all year from bouncing you around with a sweep in September . . . or July.

A beautiful evening greets the ballplayers, and it's a pleasure to be back at Shea after two weeks away. My body feels great, better than it has in months. The ankles are okay, considering all the Astroturf games before the break. The tight muscles are loose.

My (illegal?) left foot becomes an issue immediately, with Terry Harper on first in the first inning. Terry Tata tells me to keep the foot inside the foul line.

"What are you going to call if I leave it outside?" I ask him. He doesn't know.

"Look, Terry, don't call it tonight. Go look up the rules. Let's get this straight."

While my foot remains outside the line, the game degenerates into something of a farce. It's not as bad as the debacle in Pittsburgh early in the year, but neither is it what Abner had in mind. It's amazing how a mere three-day break will undermine the skills. My timing is off: Nature calls right before we go onto the field for the first inning! The bowels know better than this.

Highlights: During my first at-bat, the applauding crowd directs my attention to the big screen. This is my 1,500th major-league game. I didn't know it. This means that my fly to left field is my 3,500th out, something like that. A sobering thought. I'm happy, though. It drives in Dykstra.

Backman is thrown out—way out—trying to steal on a slow curve, the perfect pitch for the runner. That's what I mean about sluggish following the break. Forget it, Wally.

Their man at shortstop, Rafael Ramirez, one of the best, boots two balls.

Our man at third, HoJo, makes three errors, two in the fifth inning, costing a run and earning some boos. He gets a round of applause from the third-base fans when he cleanly fields a roller in the seventh. He tips his cap. I don't believe the initial boos, anyway. Johnson is playing an excellent third base, he's coming around at the plate, and I think his uncomplaining attitude has penetrated the stands. There are boos and there are boos. These aren't real.

In the fifth, with the bases loaded and two outs, HoJo pops up behind the mound and the Brave infielders gather around. The ball drops untouched after Oberkfell makes a lunging try. This is a ballgame in disarray. I'm on third base and little more than walking down the line as the ball ascends and descends, so I'm barely across the plate ahead of Strawberry, who is running all the way from second base. A bad highlight for them is a good one for us: Darryl is for real this season. He also delivered a patient, two-out single earlier in the inning. And earlier he also initiated a big 9–4–2 play at the plate to throw out Ramirez trying to score on Murphy's double. He's hitting the cutoff man with much more regularity this year.

I give Darryl the game ball. He started off the season ready to play, but not hitting very well; he's come back from the injury even more ready to play. Give a piece of the game ball to Jesse. Darling and McDowell have suffered for eight and a third innings. Roger gives up a two-run homer to Horner that brings the Braves within one run in the ninth. Davey calls for Orosco.

Last year, I always told Jesse when he came in, "You're the best fucking left-hander in the league. Now show them." Something like that. It was true.

This year, for whatever reason, I had not been pumping him up as much, until I did it in a game in Cincinnati. He said to me afterward, "Keep telling me that." Tonight I tell him in no uncertain terms what he can accomplish with his talent—anything in the baseball world. Then he mows down Oberkfell and Hubbard with his nasty stuff.

So it's a good win. We gave them as many opportunities as they gave us (four errors each way), but the Braves are in fifth place and we're in second, and this game shows why: We capitalize just a little bit more, make a big play, get the final out.

After the game, HoJo is the first player the reporters besiege. He handles it well—helped by the fact that we won the game. Charlie Samuels takes offense and shouts out to one and all, "Hey, Wally had three *hits*." Sure, Backman, we'll get to you, but let's get the good stuff first.

The Mets post this victory before St. Louis plays Los Angeles on the coast. Matching our favorable homestand is an unfavorable road trip for the Cards. They're playing on the West Coast, where all three parks are grass, which cuts down the Cards' speed game. The Cards have veterans who normally wouldn't worry in July about what we're doing, but the strike threat changes matters. These may be "September" games. Scoreboard-watching starts early in 1985.

At 1:00 a.m., Dad calls with the Cards' score: Dodgers win. Dad also reports that, in his humble opinion, Jesse is definitely back. If you know a lot about hitting, and Dad certainly does, you know about the kinds of pitches that worry batters. He liked what he saw via the satellite tonight: handcuffed Brave batters.

GAME 87—Mets 7
Braves 6

JULY 19

While I'm enjoying the food at Rusty's restaurant and puzzling things out with Lynch early this afternoon, the red-haired boss informs me that my friend Paul Gleason, the actor, was waiting for me at the restaurant after last night's game. I stood him up— vapor lock. I've never figured this out: With baseball, I pride myself on always being in the game. I don't make many mental errors. But off the field, I forget things. I'm spaced out most of the time, utterly elsewhere. Still on the ballfield, perhaps.

Orange also kids me about another contradiction.

"On the field," he says, "you have the best hands of any living human being. Off the field, the worst." He delivers this reminder after I've just tumbled a glass of iced tea or fumbled my fork. He's right. My hands aren't good off the field. I even stumble around quite a bit.

Over the All-Star break my girlfriend and I watched Gleason shoot some scenes for the TV movie "Doubletake" on Second Avenue right across from my building. As a performer in one field, I enjoy watching performers in another genre. I'm glad, though, that I don't as a ballplayer suffer from the equivalent of stage fright.

Only one time have I been truly nervous on the field. That was in the ninth inning of the seventh game of the Series in 1982. My stomach was cramping so bad I couldn't stand upright; my crouched fielding posture was my only posture. I was begging that the ball go somewhere else. It did. I'll do better this October.

On a 1–10 scale, with 1 being perfectly relaxed and 10 bonkers, I'm a 1, maybe a 2, before the basic midseason game. I always have a nervous-energy buzz coursing through me, but this buzz doesn't contradict my feeling of being relaxed. However, the term "perfectly relaxed" for me might be another person's "off-the-scale 10."

A poet said, "If my devils leave, my angels might take flight as well." I like to believe that I transform my nervous energy into baseball energy.

Not unrelated to this discussion are the recent remarks in the newspapers by Neil Allen, now with the Bronx Bombers. Neil is quoted as saying that in New York, unlike St. Louis, he won't have to live up to the Hernandez trade. The equivalent with the Yankees, he says, would have been coming over for Dave Winfield. I take that as a major compliment because Dave is a great ballplayer, but if I were the Yankees, I would wonder whether that attitude is what I want from my short-relief ace. From this guy I want, "Give me the damn ball!" Like McDowell, like Orosco.

The umps tonight declare that my foot will have to be inside the line. The league has decided. After fifteen years, I have to change my style literally overnight. Thank you, Whitey. Now my back is partially to the infield, I don't get the same jump off the bag into fielding position, and I can't get the tag right at the bag.

"Bullshit," I tell the umps.

Against the Braves, it doesn't matter much. They're not a running club. For this game, they're a pitching club. Zane Smith, a left-hander, shows me more tonight than he has in the past. Carter's single in the second (Gary starts tonight; this is the big test) is it for us until I come up in the seventh. When the team is being bested, there's often a discussion among the more studious hitters: What he's throwing, what to look for, what might work against him? Some hitters think about these things, some don't. I don't necessarily recommend analysis; paralysis by analysis is a possibility. Some guys are better off if they just go up hacking, as Jose Cruz puts it.

I'm more inclined to analyze matters and perhaps even make an adjustment if the problem at hand is a lefty. Smith has a good inside fastball and, tonight at least, a great curve, with which he knotted me up in the first. In this seventh inning, I move back from the plate, ready for the fastball, still able to handle the curve outside. I'm rewarded with a single off the inside fastball.

(Against Steve Carlton I regularly moved in on the plate, because he threw me nothing but breaking balls away. Carlton was the only *breaking-ball* power pitcher I've faced. He threw his slider that hard. He doesn't anymore.)

Zane Smith isn't a power pitcher in Carlton's league, but he's plenty good for us tonight, with help from Sutter. Victimized is Aguilera.

GAME 88—Braves 1
Mets 0

JULY 20

Now my left foot is a national story. Joe Garagiola gives me twenty seconds before this afternoon's "Game of the Week" to explain the situation. I do my best. Davey has filed a complaint with the league office. Left-handed first basemen have been playing with a foot outside the line forever (the position is awkward for right-handers). Mattingly of the Yankees does it, and flagrantly.

I have the feeling in the first inning that we're in for a good game. For one thing, Doc is pitching. That gives us the odds going in. Then he intimidates the Braves: With two strikes on Murphy and Horner, their two power hitters, Dwight waves off Carter's first sign and fans both with great fastballs. That's a message: I don't need the curve or anything else to beat you guys. Try to hit my heater. Ironically, Doc gets only two more K's for the game.

In the meantime, we play long ball with their pitchers, including two dingers from Darryl, one a grand slam in the first inning. His thumb hurts—and it will until it gets a complete rest, after the season—but it hasn't affected his home-run power.

Dad recites Cookie Lavagetto's definition of "home-run power," and it's a good one: When your best shots are in the parking lot and your merely good shots are nevertheless over the fence, you have home-run power. When your best shots are over the fence, but your good shots reach only the warning track, you have warning-track power.

On the Mets, Straw, Foster, Carter, and Hernandez have home-run power—and Strawberry has something else besides. Maybe my name on the list raises a few eyebrows. It will without a doubt elicit some cracks from the squad next spring. I'll stick by the selection. I have home-run power, but a lot of my "home runs" are line drives, so they're not home runs. If I wanted to dial 8 more often, I would have to lift the high pitches. My instincts are to drive those balls into a gap.

I could also work with weights for the forearms, wrists, and hands. In my pro career I've exercised in the off season for strengthening (as opposed to remedial) purposes only once, prior to the 1977 season. It helped: I hit fifteen homers, but I haven't exercised since. I'm just lazy.

Straw's home-run power-plus has its best game of the year, before a national audience, and we pound the Braves' hapless bullpen for eighteen hits.

One of those hits almost costs me $250. Dykstra, on first base, is running on his own with the pitch, which I line into right field, near the line. I'm not running at full speed, since I expect the throw to come into second base, with the play ending with runners on first and third. It doesn't dawn on me that Lenny will try to score from first, but he does because he was off with the pitch, and he draws the throw to the plate from Claudell Washington. I figure that Washington's throw, coming almost right down the line, is an attempt to throw me out at first, after my wide turn. I still don't realize Dykstra is going home, so I skid to a stop rounding first and scramble back to the bag. Only now do I realize what has happened: Dykstra has scored.

Strawberry drives me in anyway with another homer, but in the dugout Davey seeks me out and mutters, "That's two-fifty."

"Why?!" I'm astonished.

"You should have been on second."

"I thought he was throwing behind me. I didn't see Lenny running with the pitch."

"Okay," Davey says. "I'll rescind it . . . this time."

Worse than the criticism, from my point of view, is the broken bat. Nothing but hits were in that piece of wood for several weeks. There's always brief anguish upon losing a favored bat—even though this was also the bat that betrayed me throughout my miserable slump. I never dump a bat during a slump—there's no use pretending that it's the bat's fault—but, perhaps illogically, I always regret the loss of a bat during a hot streak, as though the wood deserves some of the credit. I award this bat the Distinguished Service Cross.

Spikes, too. I usually go through four pairs of shoes a year, and my current pair is worn down to the nubs, way overdue for retirement, but I'm going to stick with these shoes until the bottoms are slick.

With a new bat, I double my next time up and drive home

another run. It seems like only yesterday when I had a measly 29 RBIs—and holding. Now suddenly I'm closing in on 50, and am on track for 90 for the year, maybe 100 if the team keeps on hitting.

I hope the Cards are watching this game, prior to their night game in L.A. I watch their game on the big screen at a new club downtown. John Tudor loses, and we're only a half-game back.

The bad news is that Ed Lynch is in the hospital.

"You're pitching tomorrow, Eddie. Coming to the big party tonight?" I was teasing him before the game.

"not tonight," he mumbled, "not feeling too well." Looking terrible, too. Still, it's a surprise to hear that he's down with food poisoning.

GAME 89—Mets 16
Braves 4

JULY 21

This is ridiculous and I've never seen anything like it. After five innings this Sunday afternoon, before 50,000 fans, we're ahead 9–1. This makes twenty-five runs for the Mets in fourteen innings. Then Atlanta comes back with seven runs in two innings and we're ahead only 9–7. Then we come back for six more, then they counter with three, and the final is a telltale 15–10. Bad pitching.

Lucky beneficiaries of our hitting binge are Terry Leach, guest starter for the day in Eddie's absence, Tom Gorman, who is shelled in the seventh, and McDowell, who takes his lumps in the eighth. There's no question that McDowell's right ankle is still weak and affecting his push off the rubber; his stride is shorter, and he's not getting much action on his sinker. The trainers have Roger on the same isometric program I follow. In time, he'll strengthen; in the meantime, he'll struggle.

Conspicuous in the Braves' production tonight is Dale Murphy's two-run homer. It's conspicuous only because our staff had shut him out in previous games, successfully working him as the book dictates: hard stuff inside. Anything out over the plate is endangered. Like Strawberry, Murphy can drive the ball as hard to the opposite field as he can pull it down the line.

I still have no complaints about my new bat, which has produced two doubles, a single, two RBIs. Davey lifts me in the eighth inning after Rick Cerone, formerly of the Yankees, accidentally punches me in the gut on a tag play at the plate. I'm an easy stand-up out. Why all the violence, Rick?

I don't recall playing in two such back-to-back blowouts. I continue to wonder about Eddie Haas, the Braves' manager. Three times he has pitched to me with an open base when an intentional walk wouldn't have hurt them; three times I've come through with hits. That's "airhead" managing, as we say. The lights are on, but there's nobody home. In today's blowout, the Braves have a man on third, with one out, when the game is still close. Davey plays the infielders back. Let 'em score; so will we. Last night, Haas ordered his infield to play *in* for a play at the plate— when the Braves were losing by ten runs! Damnedest thing I ever saw. It's just not done. Get the out, goddamn! Get the "contest" over with.

The Braves leave town in disarray. The Mets conclude ninety games with the same record as last year: 53–37; not bad considering our health problems and stagnant hitting for most of the season.

GAME 90—Mets 15
Braves 10

JULY 22

Before tonight's game against Pete Rose and the Reds, the Mets' A-ball team from Columbia, South Carolina plays a game at Shea. I don't attend: I've seen enough A ball in my lifetime, up-close and personal. If you haven't seen a game, however, I recommend an evening in the minor leagues. It's a great way to appreciate the quality of big-league play. There's just no comparison. I say this not to gloat in any way, because we've all played in the minors, but in order to put in proper perspective the suggestion that the owners might bring up Triple A players during a strike. The fans would accept that brand of baseball as the major leagues for about three innings.

How many guys from this Columbia team might make it to the majors? Just *might*? Four or so. That's all.

One of them is David West, the incredible twenty-year-old pitcher on the mound this evening. West is leading the game 12–4 when it's stopped, to make way for the major leaguers. The score is misleading: He's pitching a no-hitter. Occasionally a team will score one run, maybe two against a no-hit performance, but four?

The problem is, West is a wild left-hander. Great fastball, but wild—giving some credence, perhaps, to the theory that lefties are slower to develop than right-handed pitchers. Buddy Harrelson, who managed West last year, reports that he struck out the opposition in double figures in the championship game in 1984—but walked twelve.

Twenty-three-year-old Sid Fernandez is starting for us, one of those young lefties with control problems, at least until his last several games, when Sid has been on target. The fans are finally catching on that Sid is as strong a strikeout pitcher as Dwight. He's leading the league in strikeouts per nine innings (a little over one per inning); he just hasn't pitched nearly as many innings as Dwight; however, he might not be able to keep up the percentage if he did.

Sid throws pretty hard (88–89 mph) and he has a tremendous slow curve. His best weapon is the *difference* between the two velocities: The curveball is only around 65 mph. This big difference gives the hitters fits. In addition, Sid's curve breaks very late. Even Carter can't believe that some of the curves sweep in for strikes at the last moment.

Sid is a bona fide 15–20 game-winner. He's a steal from the Dodger organization. While the papers refer to Fernandez as *El Sid*, I prefer *Sid the Squid*. The batters get all tangled up in his pitches.

Tonight, he no-hits the Reds through six innings, striking out nine and walking only two. However, we're luckless against Mario Soto, so when Concepcion homers to lead off the seventh, we're behind, then they score two more times and the game gets away from us. Yet another hard-luck outing for Sid. Every team seems to have a hard-luck hurler. Last year it was Darling. This year, Fernandez.

But give some credit to Mario Soto. He was due. He does the job.

GAME 91—Reds 5
Mets 1

JULY 23

Welcome, everyone. Mom and Dad from San Francisco, the older kids Jessi and Melissa from St. Louis. They're in for a big week of baseball and the New York night life. I have it all worked out: Juan and Juana in my big bed, me and the kids on the hideaway couch. But Juan won't hear of it, so he and Mom have the couch, the kids and myself the bed. At any rate, my definition of "night life" differs from all of theirs by four or five hours. Needless to say, Keith will have to do the adjusting. Hell, I might see a sunrise. I might even get some sleep.

It's great to see them, and it's particularly sweet to have Dad in the stands when I'm hitting well, due in good part to his help.

Any apprehension before the game? Not really. When I'm hitting, I'm hitting, and I can handle those penetrating eyes. It's when I'm not hitting that I may tighten up and really stink—as I did on the West Coast. Speaking of the coast, the tables are now turned. Playing in San Francisco, St. Louis will post its scores in day games prior to our night games with the Reds. Today they post a victory.

It's satisfying to get a hit my first time up, off a tough lefty, too, Tom Browning. No complaints when I whiff in the fourth. It's a great breaking ball. Then I'm robbed by Rose's dive for a liner in the seventh, then by Buddy Bell at third base on another liner in the ninth.

Being robbed of hits is part of the game, but tonight is a little unusual in that of the Mets' last fifteen outs, with only one hit mixed in, fully half of them are hard shots right at somebody. You can't say the Mets aren't hitting the ball.

The last thing a batter can do, however, is try to aim the ball. We can go for left field or right field, or a hole in the in-field on a hit-and-run, but beyond that, aiming the ball while hit-ting would be as destructive as aiming the ball while pitching. The muscles tighten and the swing or throw isn't free and easy. It won't work.

The fans figure the robberies on hard-hit balls are offset by the bouncers that elude fielders and the bloops that fall in. For good hitters, they don't. To hit for a .300 batting average, my average of well-hit balls has to be considerably higher than that.

Closer to .400, I'd guess, especially considering my slow wheels. The super-fast guys like Coleman might be able to hit .300 with a well-hit-balls average of *under* .300. As I've said, those wheels would be worth thirty points to me. Imagine.

All credit tonight to Dave Parker, rejuvenated with the Reds. His homer wins the game, and his season, along with Rose's handling of his young ballplayers, is carrying the club. Dave has dropped his hands a bit at the plate because he's grown a little older and therefore a little slower in his reaction time. I notice the change, ask him, and he acknowledges it. Despite the fact that Parker was, in his prime, the greatest all-around player I've played against, he's not afraid to change with age. I respect that. I hope I'll have the courage to do the same, if it's required. However, I don't carry my hands that high to begin with.

Doug Harvey has announced that his crew will enforce the illegal left foot—but Eric Gregg tells me this evening that he isn't going to say a thing unless Rose gripes. Rose doesn't say a word. The foot stays out.

GAME 92—Reds 4
Mets 0

JULY 24

In the third inning of this rare midweek afternoon game, Santana is on second base with nobody out. He studies Harrelson as the coach flashes a long series of signs to Aguilera, who, after failing on his first two bunt attempts, is behind with two strikes. Nine-tenths of all that hand movement by the third-base coach is superfluous, but Buddy has to do something to divert the opposition, who enjoy trying to steal signs. In this case, the diversion backfires.

Santana picks up the bunt signal, which comes at the end of the sequence, but Aguilera misses it, so when he singles to left, Santana, looking for the bunt, is momentarily frozen by the full swing. He gets a late jump. Buddy waves him home and he's out by five yards on the throw from Max Venable.

Fans like to fault the coach on these plays—players sometimes do, too. But with a good jump Santana scores, and Buddy has had success with aggressive coaching at third. Though the Mets aren't all that fast, we've had very few guys thrown out at the plate—right now, I can't think of one. Plenty have been safe on close plays. The real cause of this lost opportunity was the missed sign by Aguilera, not the coaching.

Strawberry's base-running blunder in the sixth clinches the loss. Very briefly: He's out trying to steal third after being given the official "hold" sign. Beyond that, Buddy even motions for Darryl to "stay where you are." But Darryl has a love affair with third base. This ill-fated sally costs him $100—and his green light for the base. Now he'll have to wait for explicit instructions to go. If Darryl goes over there again without the sign, he'd better make it or he'll really pay—maybe $300. He still has the green light for second base, however, as do Backman, Dykstra, and Mookie. These three also have the green light for third.

"So what, with their salaries?" you inquire about the fine.

Well, there's more to those salaries than the printed figure (in other words, less). These fines are cash out of the pocket; they hurt. Moreover, they hurt the team.

Of more significance to the team than this one loss is Davey's announcement, via the press, that Backman is the full-time second baseman. Kelvin Chapman has lost his job as a platooning infielder. I still believe Kelvin's problems this year go back to spring training, when he started swinging up at the high pitches. He hasn't recovered.

Backman, on the other hand, has come back from a spring when he hurt himself by trying to pull the ball too much. He has added the bunt to his repertoire. He deserves the full-time job. The club will benefit.

In the losing cause, a homer for Hernandez, giving me twenty runs and twenty RBIs for my last twenty games, Jay Horwitz informs me after the contest. This is good, but the net result tonight is that we've slipped to three and a half games behind the Cards, who swept Frisco on the road while the Reds swept us here. This is very bad, with only eleven games to go until August 6.

The writers interrogate us about an alleged "inconsistency"— all those runs against the Braves, next to none against the Reds. Ridiculous. Winning fifteen out of twenty is inconsistent? We ran into good pitching from the Reds. They did the job. Give them credit, don't fault us for inconsistency.

In the evening I shepherd parents and kids to Broadway for

A Chorus Line, and everyone thoroughly enjoys the show, although Dad says he could have done with less of the homosexual business.

GAME 93—Reds 3
Mets 2

JULY 25

Kelvin Chapman has been sent down to Tidewater, in what Davey informs the press is his "toughest decision." I believe that, because Davey is loyal to the players he believes in, and he has always believed in Chapman. But Davey can also make the hard decision that's best for the team *this* year—not next. I'm not surprised at the decision, but the timing is unusual. Now we don't have a single backup middle infielder.

By the time I hear about the demotion, Kelvin has packed his bags and gone. There's not much to be said anyway. Good luck. Hope to see you back.

The Astros are in town for four games. They've been in a slump, and might be ready to break out. We've just lost three games to the Reds. I'm concerned about this series. Houston is a team you usually have to beat, they don't often beat themselves, although they did once or twice in the Dome. And we may be running out of time.

The Astros are my mystery team, and have been since they were in the playoffs in 1980. With a lot of good players, they haven't generated a solid winning team. Part of the problem is they've never had a real cleanup hitter. Jose Cruz, a great hitter, should be hitting third, not fourth.

Their slump continues tonight. Without great stuff, Dwight handles them easily enough—albeit giving up two solo homers in the seventh.

On the mound for them is Mike Scott, formerly a Met, rejuvenated this year with his adoption of the split-fingered fastball. Maybe the pitch is doctored, too. The Cubs found a little scrap of sandpaper behind the mound in the Dome earlier this year during a game Scott was throwing.

I handle the pitch: In the first, an RBI single to left; in the third, ditto to right.

This latter at-bat I consider one of my best in the big leagues, even though it produces only a single, even though it's only a midseason game. With the count full, Scott throws three nasty pitches on the inside black. I foul all three straight back. The next one is out over the plate a little, and I'm thinking home run for a split second before the ball takes a quick little dart down and away. Nice movement on that bastard pitch, Mike, but I still rip it hard to right. I get real pleasure out of this single, and I know Dad does, too.

A couple of innings later, Davey goes out to talk to home-plate ump John McSherry. The fellows in the dugout have found a scuff mark the size of a half-dollar in the same place on eight different balls. That's no coincidence. We, the jury, find Mike Scott guilty of doctoring the baseball, even if the judge ignores the prima facie evidence. Even if we get to Scott for five runs in six innings.

Three of these come on a shot by Carter (whose knee is holding up), after Scott has walked me intentionally, with first base open. That's the right strategy, but Carter rises to the challenge and almost knocks off my hand with his joyful high-five after the slam, and then almost flings his batting helmet into Bill Robinson.

With the addition of Dykstra to the lineup, Carter is no longer so alone as a demonstrative player on this otherwise low-key team. Dykstra is a pistol. On a long drive to right-center by Glen Davis, Lenny makes a diving try right at the wall, and slams headfirst into the barrier. He doesn't move. I think his neck or perhaps collarbone is broken, and race out to the scene. By the time Strawberry gets to the ball and relays it in, Davis is all the way around for a homer. Dykstra finally gets up, he's okay, but in a year or two, I'll bet he plays that ball off the wall—for his own sake and for the team's. However, I wouldn't want him to play *now* any differently than he does. Let his own learning pace him. You can't take the fire out of him any more than you can take it out of Gary, or Mookie at the plate.

Mentioning Carter makes me reconsider my prediction regarding Dykstra. Carter is a ten-year veteran and he would be diving into that wall, still, if he were an outfielder.

In the seventh, Mets leading 6–3, Davey orders Backman and Hernandez to try the always exciting "runners on first and third, two out" scam. I break off first, the Astros initiate the rundown, Wally breaks for home—too late. They throw him out.

The fans assume I blundered because they don't know I'm *supposed* to get caught in a rundown. They're not familiar with the plan. We work the play fairly well, actually, but Astros' shortstop Craig Reynolds plays it perfectly, to his credit; infielders are uncomfortable with the play, too, which is rife with potential for mistakes by runners and defenders. At any rate, it's not my fault that the Mets don't get the run tonight!

We need a shorthand designation for this play, it's becoming so popular. "Run-and-run"? "Go, man, go"?

"Steal a run" is an accurate description, but here's my name: the Curley Shuffle. This catches the flavor of it.

The big difference between this win and the previous three losses is simple: Tonight, our first two guys get on base five times and score three runs. Against Cincinnati, they were 0-for-25. That statistic says everything about table-setting.

GAME 94—Mets 6

Astros 3

JULY 27

Rained out last night, so this evening, Saturday, we play two. We were scheduled to be the "Friday Night Game of the Week," and NBC gave us a little coverage as they waited for the decision on the weather. Tony Kubek said we may be the only team in this division with a real chance to catch St. Louis. Amazing how everyone who overlooked the Cards in the spring is convinced, three months later, that they are nearly invincible.

May have a chance? Of course the Mets have a chance. In my mind, we're *favored*. Especially with Orosco and McDowell throwing well.

The network carried the backup game, and there was Dodger first baseman Greg Brock with his foot very clearly outside the line. So Davey and I decide to test the issue again, first thing tonight.

Randy Marsh is calling the plays at first base. Kevin Bass walks in the first inning off Fernandez, and I take my position with the foot outside the line. Marsh steps up and tells me to get it inside.

I ask whether the rule is for me or everyone, and ask him whether he saw the broadcast last night. He gets mad.

"Wait a minute, Randy, I'm not mad at you. But goddamn, let's get this straight. Is it or isn't it just for Hernandez?"

Tonight, it's for Hernandez *at least*. Marsh makes me move into fair territory.

In the seventh, with the Mets leading 4–1, Bill Doran is batting for Houston against McDowell, with two men on. McDowell is due up first in our half of the inning, so I don't understand why Johnson doesn't bring in the left-handed Orosco to make Doran hit from the right side (his worst), and also bring in a fielder for Santana who has just ended our seventh inning. Davey could flip-flop the two in the batting order, so the pitcher hits in Santana's place and the infielder leads off the eighth for us. This flip-flopping strategy, perfected by Whitey Herzog, is standard now.

Then I remember. We don't have anybody for the middle infield. Can this go on?

Doran hits a three-run homer. It's weird about Doran. He has pounded the Mets all year; overall average, .286, but against us, way over .400. The case of Jose Cruz, the Astros' best hitter, is even weirder. He's struggling down the interstate against the Met staff. I don't know why players get on hot or cold streaks against an entire pitching staff, and then maintain the streak even though games against that staff are separated by months.

Doran homers after Davey has been forced to stay with Roger, who's sinker doesn't sink. Some fans have the nerve to boo the rookie who was our savior for week after week.

Not to worry, Roger. The Mets tally six in the seventh, six in the eighth. Five Astro errors are involved, so, thanks to the way they figure these things, all twelve of these Met runs and the preceding four are unearned. The big blow: Knight, making his first start since he pulled a muscle a couple of weeks ago, hits the big fly for three runs.

A quick cup of coffee and we're out for nine more innings, and do another number on them. I'm a happy hitter, with three hits and five RBIs for the day. On the mound this game for the Mets is Bill Latham, brought up from Tidewater just for this occasion, in Lynch's continuing absence (he's out of the hospital, building up his strength). Latham was hit hard in a start early in the year, but he pitches fine ball for seven innings in this second game.

GAME 95—Mets 16
Astros 4

GAME 96—Mets 7
Astros 3

JULY 28

The kids fly back today to St. Louis, and Davey gives me permission to arrive late at the ballpark, so I can take them to the airport. I'll have the day off after last night's doubleheader, anyway. I dedicate it to Lou Brock, who is inducted into the Hall of Fame today.

Although my ankles need the rest, I have mixed feelings about not playing: Joe Niekro, the knuckleballer, is pitching for Houston. I gripe about the pitch, but it's also a challenge to dance with Astaire.

As the game rolls along, any regret turns to thankfulness. Paying us back for the two blowouts, the Astros finally hit. Darling is below his standard, and it's apparent early. In the second inning, he walks Niekro on four pitches, with first base open and two outs.

I'm observing from the bullpen, a first for me. Davey said it would be okay. Coach Vern Hoscheit and I sit in the little car that shuttles in our relief pitchers (although nobody uses it) and discuss baseball, life, and his liquor store in Nebraska, and we watch the game on TV. In addition to his bullpen duties, Vern is the coach who passes on to the players the scouting reports; who's stealing, who's bunting, what the pitchers are throwing and the hitters hitting. He has a hard-ass demeanor but Vern is a puppy dog at heart.

Relievers have a strange life. They have nothing to do until called on. Nothing, and they may not be called on for days. They can watch the game on TV in their little "office," or climb up to their special bleachers and watch the action live, or water their tomato patch, or wander back into the parking lot behind the scoreboard and count cars. How much of this can you tolerate, game after game? As a diet it would drive me crazy, but as a breather from the campaign on this warm summer afternoon, the bullpen is delightful even as the game is a disaster. The Astros score twelve times.

Danny Heep, who filled in for me at first base, informs me afterward I can have my job back. Santana makes two errors at shortstop. That's rare but no cause for alarm. By purest coincidence, I'm sure, the "Today in Baseball" item in *The Times* reports that on July 28, 1971, sixteen-time Gold Glove winner Brooks Robinson made three errors at third base in one inning.

Santana is a Dominican who lives in San Pedro de Macoris, the town that has produced a batch of major leaguers, mostly infielders. None could be any smoother with the glove than Rafael. His movements are liquid and he has an intriguing way of getting the ball to me not a moment too soon. Santana's throws are always close, but never late.

Look who's at "Rusty's" having dinner tonight: the players' union crew, including Donald Fehr, Mark Belanger, Gene Orza, Dick Moss. Their gut feeling, and now mine, too: Hang tough, players, the owners will come around.

We realize, as *The Times* survey published this morning indicates, that most of the fans support the owners. The fans don't understand the issue of the pension fund, or the fact that the owners are trying to scale back our free-agency system. We do have friends in high places, however. Mike Lupica has written a column in *The Daily News* that puts a fair light on our position. I post it on the bulletin board.

GAME 97—Astros 12
Mets 4

July 29

A story in *The Times* extols Carlton Fisk's weight program for building up his HR numbers. Fine. The story also reports that Fisk is laying off red meat, processed meats, salts, and fats; his new staples are salad, fish, chicken, and pasta. The diet I can't go along with, either. For one thing, it would mean giving up the ribs at "Rusty's," a step I'm not prepared to take at this time. Perhaps in six years when I'm thirty-seven, like Fisk, I'll consider such serious regimens.

It's interesting that both *The Times* and *The Daily News* today feature large photos of Foster dropping a foul pop yesterday, with the bases loaded and two outs. The runners subsequently scored. The *News* picture is a full page with the huge caption, FOSTER'S FOLLY.

No. That is *The News*'s folly. George raced his ass over to get to the ball, was looking up into the glare, and had to try for the catch with his glove extended in front of him, waist high. Catchable, yes, but no folly when he didn't pull it off. The reporter on duty knows this, but his newspaper is more concerned with the catchy alliteration.

This may be the most important week of the year for the Eastern Division. While we entertain the Expos here for three games, St. Louis is in Wrigley Field starting tomorrow, then we go to Chicago for four games later in the week. We're in second place, three and a half behind the Cards; Montreal is a game behind us. With all their injuries, the Cubs are foundering, eight and a half back. We have to take this series against Montreal. It would be nice if the Cubs can do something against the Cards.

Chasing St. Louis is getting a little frustrating: We win, but can't gain ground. However, they must be thinking the same thing in reverse: The damn Mets, we can't shake them.

I'll go out on this limb: If the Cubs are wiped out by the Cards, then by us next weekend, they're through for the season. So much for my prediction that the Expos would be the first to drop back.

Frankly, I'd like to do especially well against the Expos in this series because I have a chance for my best month ever, and a chance to be named National League Player of the Month. Right now I'm hitting .411 with twenty-seven RBIs for July, and eight game-winners.

My best previous month was August, 1979, when I hit .385 and drove in twenty-eight. I don't have to look up those numbers. I remember them. I won the award, a beautiful action photo with an engraved plate. Now I'd like to have one in my Mets uniform. I hope they haven't changed the prize.

The beat writers in all the cities vote on Friday—all the writers. For the annual Most Valuable Player award, each city is limited to two writers. I don't know how they're selected. To be in the running for the grand prize, I'll have to have a great August and September, too.

The self-proclaimed "Gangster of Love," Expos shortstop Hubie

Brooks, greets me during batting practice. Hubie is a single guy who enjoys his love life, and life in general. Feeling fine, he reports, but his batting sucks: 3-for-27. He can't get comfortable in the cleanup position, where Buck Rogers is hitting him. There are horses for courses; there are hitters for positions in the lineup. He may adjust; he may not. I would be much less effective batting fourth, because I'd feel obliged to swing for more homers. I'm perfect for the third spot. Hubie has always hit third or fifth, I believe.

His slump is fine with me because it hurts his team, but I think it's a grave mistake to hit Hubie fourth. The Expos' real problem is that they don't have a legitimate third-place hitter. Andre Dawson, hitting in that position now, should be batting fourth in this lineup, followed by Dan Driessen and Hubie. I'd hit Tim Raines third because he hits for a higher average than Dawson, who's playing on bad legs. Granted, some of Raines's speed would go to waste in the third position.

My theoretical point: It's conceivable that Team A with weaker hitters could have a better lineup than Team B, if the batters on Team A were perfectly suited to their positions in the order.

We're on the national tube tonight, and before the game Jim Palmer apologizes for his reference to my "personal problems" a couple of weeks ago. He heard from Cosell about the burst of curiosity that those two words triggered, and he offers to make a clarification on the air. I want to drop the matter. It's a no-win situation.

I've had good luck on televised games this year, and tonight is no exception—at least in the first at-bat, when I lace a pitch into the corner in left, driving in two runs. Now I need just one more for thirty for July. I want it.

Aguilera throws another splendid game, a one-hitter going into the eighth inning. He has something of Dwight's composure. Orosco comes on in the eighth to get Rick out of a jam, and completes the game in the ninth with great pitches—all but one, which Tim Wallach hits out, breaking up the combined shutout.

"What was that pitch?" I demand of Jesse on the mound. "A change-up?"

"Yeah."

"What the fuck? Give 'em your best."

I hate to see a pitcher get burned on his third-best pitch, but the homer doesn't bother the Mets. We saw the rest of the pitches—the real pitches. Jesse, you're back! You're the best damn left-handed reliever in the league!

GAME 98—Mets 3
Expos 2

JULY 30

At Rusty's prompting, I find Frank Cashen for a heart-to-heart before tonight's game. It seems that we're always getting into problems with our flights to and from California, and it's not too early to worry about the schedule as it stands now for September 8. The last game of our next West Coast swing is in the afternoon, but we're not scheduled out of Los Angeles until 10:30 p.m., on a commercial flight—the red-eye, for chrissakes!

Here's what this means: about five hours in the airport, drinking; arriving home about 8:00 a.m., wasted. Forget about a relaxing day off before the most important series of the year—with the Cards!

It's no good, I explain to Frank. Arthur Richman said he couldn't find a charter, but I ask Frank to look harder, and he says he'll see what he can do. A 6:00 p.m. charter would get us home at 3:00 a.m., a more reasonable hour, and save the day off for making the time-zone adjustment.

The best example in my experience of matters getting out of hand while waiting for airplanes was an episode when I was with the Cards, some years back. We were supposed to make a connection in St. Louis with a flight due in from Kansas City—within an hour, TWA officials assured us. The plane showed up eight hours later. We waited all night in the ambassador class lounge the airline was kind enough to provide. They pulled one of those accordion dividers across the space, separating the jocks from the other passengers.

I'll relate a few of the incidents that ensued: Ken Reitz ran headlong through the divider; Silvio Martinez ripped a pay phone off the wall; Keith Hernandez yanked the *T* off the *TWA* sign on the wall. These three did most of the damage, but just about the whole team was drunk. Eight hours, remember!

Complaints were lodged from the other side of the divider, and when the team returned home from the road trip, the three main culprits had to publicly apologize, on television. I said something like, "I think this apology is ridiculous. Hit us with a fine and to hell with it."

If I treat this St. Louis episode lightly now, it's not because I condone drunken behavior, nor because I think jocks should get special treatment. Jocks should not get special treatment. Joe Blow doesn't apologize. He pays for the damage and that's that.

Tonight's game is a mismatch, as Dwight makes clear in the opening frame, striking out the side on ten pitches—nine swinging or called strikes, one foul ball. As Davey tells the reporters, the superlatives on Gooden have run out. Opposing managers grant him their ultimate respect: They play for one run in the first inning. When they get a baserunner, they don't want to risk losing him. Tim Raines reaches first base twice tonight, but doesn't try to steal.

Against Dwight, every inning is the eighth. Time is running out with his first delivery. Only one other pitcher in the league merits such respect: Valenzuela.

Remember when George Brett played in very close at third base against Mickey Rivers during one of the Yankees–Royals playoffs, taking away the bunt, daring Rivers to hit the ball past him? The strategy wiped out Mickey for the series. Buck Rogers has Tim Wallach playing in almost that close against Dykstra and Backman tonight. In the third inning, the ploy backfires as Backman drives the ball past Wallach. Surely these little things are as interesting as the progress of the previous or the next wave.

Fourth inning: With runners on first and second, Dan Driessen hits a sharp grounder to the right of second base—directly at Backman, who is playing him perfectly, but also right at umpire Joe West, who doesn't get out of the way. The ball caroms off his shin and we can't make a play. Bases loaded. That should have been the third out. We squawk briefly, but the rule is clear: A ball hitting an umpire is in play. There is no presumption that the fielder would have made the play. If this ball had bounced into the short outfield, the Expos would have scored.

Does Dwight mind? He gets Wallach to bounce out to shortstop. West is red-faced the rest of the game. Rusty quips, "I wish he had been so slow on his feet against the Braves." West leaped over a hard shot by Rusty that the Braves converted into a double play.

In our half of the fourth, Bill Gullickson fires a two-strike pitch over Carter's head—his former battery mate, no less. Gary takes affront.

Maybe I'm naive, but it doesn't occur to me that something might happen in the fifth inning, when Gullickson comes to the plate. On the first pitch, Dwight sails one over his head. The Expos bench is up on the steps. So are we. Frank Pulli jumps out from behind the plate and issues the mandatory warnings.

After the game, before Dwight goes on Ralph Kiner's TV show, I remind our pitcher: "I don't know what happened, Dwight, but the pitch got away from you."

Fines have been levied *ex post facto*, when a player has confessed to throwing at a hitter. Dwight tells Ralph that the pitch got away from him; something about a little moisture. Somehow, I don't think the Expos . . . or the umps . . . or the Mets . . . or anyone else who saw Dwight's control this evening believes him.

I approve of throwing at a pitcher in retaliation only to the extent that I *disapprove* of throwing at a *hitter* in retaliation. That happens. They throw at our slugger. We throw at theirs (speaking hypothetically, of course). I don't buy it. Their slugger didn't do anything. Send the message to the right party: their pitcher. At any rate, the practice is way down from ten years ago, when I came into the league. Old-timers will tell you that throwing at hitters was epidemic thirty years ago. The good old days, you know.

Frank Pulli has a great night. He loves the drama behind home plate, and there's plenty of it this evening. In the sixth, scoreless game, Backman is on first, I'm up. On a 1-and-1 pitch, Wally breaks on the hit-and-run. The Expos have read the play and called for a pitchout. My job in this situation is to protect the runner. I do—by throwing my bat at the ball and hitting it out to shortstop. I also hit the catcher Fitzgerald's glove. This is catcher's interference, but I still race to first base, where I'm safe by half a step. Eric Gregg calls me out. Irate, I begin the argument with him, until both of us look over to see that Pulli has already punched me out—for interference: stepping on the plate to hit the ball. But I didn't have time to step on the plate.

The TV replay backs me up. I step on the plate *after* I've thrown the bat. The play is catcher's interference. And I'm clearly safe at first on the other play. So I'm arguing with two umps on two calls on one play, and I'm safe on each of them. It's not my night. Plus, Backman has to go back to first because of the interference call. He eventually scores on Foster's single, winning for the Mets.

This game was a lot of fun.

GAME 99—Mets 2

Expos 0

JULY 31

Interesting reading into today's papers. First is the report that Curtis Strong, the Philadelphia caterer indicted on drug charges, is going to trial in Pittsburgh on September 6. Strong is the fellow about whom I testified before the Pittsburgh grand jury. His lawyer says that ballplayers will be subpoenaed to testify in the trial.

Second, the owners' offer of the day asks the players to fund our own pension program: As our salaries go up, the owners' contribution to the plan goes down. I believe this scheme would be a first in the nation's history, but of course it won't be a first, and the owners know it. We'll strike first.

And two more items, proving that much of a baseball game is in the eye of the beholder. The ground ball I hit to shortstop on the bogus interference play last night is described by Joe Durso in *The Times* as a "hard grounder." Filip Bondy in *The Daily News* calls it a "slow grounder."

I recall that the ball was fairly well-hit. But writers and announcers sometimes see what they want to see, or report what they want to report regardless of what they see, or don't see the play at all.

A classic example: Jack Buck told me this story about announcer Harry Caray, who was working the St. Louis games at the time, and Ken Boyer, one of the Cardinal stars. The two men were at odds, and Boyer at one point told Caray that he could place his microphone where the sun don't shine. After that, Buck told me, most balls hit to the outfield by Boyer, no matter how hard hit, were a "lazy fly" in Caray's broadcast of the game.

Before this afternoon's senior citizens game, Pulli has the nerve to send a baseball over to me for an autograph for some friend. Pulli's a good guy, so along with the signed ball I send a note back: "Thanks to you, dickhead, I wasn't 3-for-4 last night!" I wouldn't take such liberties with every ump.

The way I figure it, and I do figure it, I need one measly hit today to stay above .400 for the month and, less important, extend my hitting streak to twelve games. And I need one RBI to make thirty. It's a high number, but would nevertheless only tie me with Foster's figure for the month. My stats are getting more play in the press, thanks to the batting average, but give George equal credit for leading the way this month. And Backman, too, who has been getting on base at a .400 clip. Everybody, really, has been producing in July.

So I'm mad in the first inning when, with Paciorek running from first on the pitch, my line shot is caught by the third baseman. If it goes over his head that's my hit and RBI. As it is, Tom is doubled off and I throw my bat. Damned game.

This afternoon is Eddie Lynch's first start on the homestand, thanks to the salmonella bacteria picked up on a (carrier-unnamed) flight from Miami to New York at the conclusion of the All-Star break. A tough break for Eddie, losing two starts when he's pitching so well. His last start, in the Astrodome, was a career effort. He pitches well today, too, even though he gets into trouble in the fourth. I think he's tired but he comes out in the fifth and retires the top of the order on easy plays, striking out Andre Dawson.

Lynch is a helluva good guy. Humorless on the mound—who isn't, come to think of it?—he has a sly sense of humor at all other times. A while back, he and I were leaving my building. The doorman was caught out of position as we emerged from the elevator, but he sprinted the width of the lobby to spin the door for Lynch, who was leading the way.

"Nice hustle, Rudi," Eddie deadpanned as he walked through.

Two fine, hustling plays help out Eddie today. In the third, Foster plays Dawson's double off the wall perfectly, throws a strike to Gardenhire, and holds the runner on third. (Hammie has returned! We have a backup middle infielder!) Brooks pops up for the final out (he has no RBIs for the three games). Run saved.

Then, in the fourth, with runners on first and second, pitcher Dan Schatzeder up, a good-hitting pitcher, I signal to Davey that I want to play back a little—even with the bag—for just one pitch; it's a bunt situation, but I have a hunch that he may swing away on the first strike. Davey signals okay. And damned if Schatzeder doesn't rifle a grounder to my right. I dive for the stop, get the runner at second, and Lynch covers first for the double play to end the inning. Big cheer from the crowd for my stop and the ensuing double play, but the point easily missed is why I was in position to make the play in the first place. If I'm in on the grass, playing for the bunt, I don't have a chance on that ball; RBI single, big inning brewing.

I play a hunch. Davey goes along. Despite his reputation for working with computer records, Davey is more of a "hunch" manager than any I've played for or seen. Davey loves to roll the bones, seven come eleven. Take chances. I like it!

I would put in this category Davey's decision to bring in McDowell in the sixth. Lynch can only go five in his first start back, but I'm looking for Terry Leach, who has been effective in the middle-relief roll. McDowell has been struggling, and he gave up that homer to Doran of the Astros his last time out.

But Davey hears a voice I don't, and Roger throws better than he has in weeks. I feel good things from the first out, a grounder to Backman on a pitch that dips down. "You're back!" I yell over. Roger blows another bubble. He's the only player I've seen who will blow a bubble during his delivery. For me, that would be rubbing the stomach while patting the head.

Carter gets his revenge in the sixth for last night's bean-ball episode. He homers. On his curtain call, he exults before the fans, thrusting his arms high and punching the air. Nothing self-effacing about The Kid. As Pete Rose said, he plays with a Little Leaguer's gung-ho enthusiasm. I'll ditto that. I couldn't carry on this way (oh, I might get out of hand if I hit a slam in the ninth inning of the seventh game this October), but Gary couldn't play my way, either.

In the eighth inning I still need that hit and that RBI, but I'm leading off, so only a homer will do it now. The Mets are ahead 5–2 and rain is coming in. Umpires will take liberties in such circumstances, expanding the strike zone to speed things up. Eric Gregg does, calling a high strike. This has been the best game Fat Albert has called in years, so I'm surprised, then mad. Then I break my bat on a roller to second base and that's it for the month.

Backman teases me, "You're just not as consistent as me, Mex," referring to his own recent twelve-game streak.

I don't make my goal, but how can I complain? In the whole month, I didn't have half a dozen at-bats that displeased me. If I go to the plate with a positive thought and maintain it for all the pitches, have the good eye, and get the good cuts, I won't complain regardless of the result. I may throw my bat at the time, but that's just competitive fires, not anger at myself.

In the ninth, we have a problem. Roger has been breezing along, throwing mostly ground-ball outs, but now there are two on, one out, and left-handed Dan Driessen the tying run at the plate. After getting a foul ball on the first pitch, Roger shows a pitch I didn't know he had, something off-speed on the outside corner. Strike two, but that pitch is like stealing third base: You'd better make it. If it's out over the plate against Driessen, the ball is very likely out of the park and we're hurt by another off-speed pitch in the late innings. But it's in a good location, Driessen takes it, and then grounds out. Nevertheless, the sinker is really your pitch, Roger. You know that.

We win and sweep the series and then enjoy the Cards–Cubs game on satellite TV in the clubhouse. "Who would have imagined," Staub asks, "that on July 31 we'd be rooting for the Cubs to win?"

The reporters ask if I'm sad to see July end. No way. I'm happy with my contribution and our 21–7 record. We've just swept the Expos and perhaps buried them. Why shouldn't we do as well or better in August? I point out where we would be if we had had just a fairly good month, 17–11, say, instead of four games better. We'd be six back of the Cards.

In the evening, Rusty, myself, actors Paul Gleason and Len Cariou and our four dates head out for the latest superstar restaurant, "K-Paul's." The chef/owner, Paul Prudhomme, has opened his place on the West Side for just six weeks this summer. Then he and the crew will return to New Orleans. Rusty knows Prudhomme and has cooked with him.

Four hundred dollars for eight is almost a moderate sum for dinner in New York City, East Side or West, and the blackened redfish is a lot of excellence.

GAME 100—Mets 5
Expos 2

AUGUST 1

Lay day, as they say in sailing. I read where McDowell told the press after yesterday's game about my shouted encouragement, "You're back!" I didn't realize it had made much of an impression on him, but I'm not surprised. These guys need the boosting. Relief pitching is a fragile livelihood.

And here I am on the culture pages of *The Times*, for a change, mentioned in an interview with novelist and Met fan Philip Roth. He proves what I've been arguing all along: The fans don't understand the Curley Shuffle play.

Recall when Backman and I were ordered to try to pull it off against the Astros exactly one week ago. Well, the interview with Roth gets around to his baseball book, *The Great American Novel*, and his attendance at that Mets game last Thursday. In the course of a dissertation on the relationship between this game and the novel, he says:

"It was a beautifully bizarre night. The center fielder [Dykstra] slid into the wall and almost knocked himself out. Between innings, on the big television screen in left center, they played a 'Three Stooges' movie to amuse the crowd. Meanwhile, the cops were throwing somebody out of the stadium, and everybody stood on their seats to watch that. Then the P.A. announcer asked us all to stand and sing 'Take Me Out to the Ball Game' to welcome a contingent of visitors from India. Pure American Dada. Finally, when even the great Hernandez got trapped off first base, I thought, 'Well, "The Great American Novel" is not such a bad book.' "

Thanks for the modifier, Philip, but dammit, I wasn't trapped off! That's the play!

I feel badly that I haven't read his novel. It may be right on the nose, but to ballplayers much of the writing about the game seems beside the point. On one end of the scale is all the junk, on the other is a vision of the game too romanticized or intellectualized, or both.

Baseball is just baseball. We play the games. Winners and losers are designated. We come back next year. A lot of the stuff written about the "flawless symmetry" of baseball etc., etc., etc., falls on deaf ears with the players, and not because we can't understand it. Because it seems overblown, if not misguided.

I have a weakness for analysis, too, but it's usually confined to the game itself. I keep the mysticism to a minimum. In my view of things, it has to be brought into the stadium by an outside agent; by a large white owl, say.

So you understand, Mr. Roth, why I haven't read your baseball novel. Nor do you care.

I digress as I sit here in "Rusty's," enjoying a fine dish of seafood pasta, sipping on another frozen margarita with extra salt, waiting to ride out with Orange to the airport for the flight to Chicago for the big series with the Cubs. During the second drink, I grow gloomy and change my mind: The players are going to have to strike. The owners didn't believe we would strike in 1981, and they don't believe it this time. We'll have to prove them wrong again. Florida, here I come. Got the poles ready, Eddie? I'll bring my sticks, too. No way am I going to sit around the city and mope.

Two bad omens reinforce my premonition. First, a big guy comes up and asks me if I have a minute. "Yeah," I reply, expecting an autograph.

"It's about the strike, Keith . . ."

"Hey, no, man. Forget it! I'm not talking about the strike."

The strike! Give me a break, fella. I'm supposed to sit here and discuss the strike with some guy just in from left field?!

Rusty! Escort this guy back to the bar!

Next, a guy sitting at a nearby table stands up and walks over, autograph material in hand. Fine. This I can handle.

"Mr. Hernandez? Willie Hernandez?"

He's in the other league, bub. Last year's MVP.

5. STRIKE TWO

AUGUST 2—CHICAGO

Today's *Chicago Tribune* carries a piece by sportswriter Bob Verdi citing the opinions of the pro golfers regarding the looming baseball strike. The golfers are playing the Western Open nearby. One J. C. Snead is vociferous in his denunciation of the ballplayers. Golfers, he says, pride themselves on being "independent contractors." Tennis players, too. No performance, no pay.

Well, fine, if that's the way they want to organize their professional game. J. C. Snead plays a game in which the professional structure has no bosses. He's an independent contractor, and more power to him. I, however, have a boss. I must negotiate.

Not long ago the players were chattel. Now we have a limited free agency and enjoy greater negotiating leverage with the owners. This means longer contracts and higher salaries. Are they too long? Too high? In this country, impossible.

Does the plumber want the opportunity to open his own shop and have ten guys working for him? Does he want the opportunity to negotiate with these ten guys to establish employment terms— the best he can get, the best they can get? Okay. This is what the owners and ballplayers are doing. It's not the players' fault that salaries are high. No one forced Gene Autrey and George Steinbrenner and Ray Kroc and Ted Turner to pay high sums. Is the ballplayer or the plumber supposed to turn down a million bucks, if that's what the market is offering?

I can talk about it all day, however, and make no dent in the public's opinion, which is set in concrete. The fans have no sympathy for players threatening to strike while making the well-publicized average salary of $362,000. The number has stuck; forget the fact that it's misleading. A more important figure is the median: $220,000. Half of the major leaguers make less than $220,000. But to the public, only guys earning $25,000 should strike.

By way of contradiction, it seems to me, the public does not resent the great wealth of many of the club owners, some of whom make it clipping coupons and collecting interest, others by changing the face of the world—Ray Kroc, for example, the recently deceased founder of the McDonalds chain, owner of the Padres. Apparently, it's okay for capitalist moguls to pile up the wealth, but ballplayers should be limited. Wrong. Neither moguls, ball-players, nor plumbers should be limited.

More power to the owners, I say, to make their millions, but grant us, the players, the legitimate right to negotiate for a fair share of the baseball profits.

"But we're losing money!" the owners cry.

Who really believes it? The owners are wolves in sheep's cloth-ing (to indulge in a little hyperbole). They know the public is on their side, and they know our side of the issue is more difficult to explain than their ridiculously simplified "average salary" prop-aganda. I'm afraid they're willing to force a strike because of this public-relations advantage, hoping that the fans will force the players to cave in.

Perhaps it's strange, but as the Mets' "shop steward" I haven't discussed these matters with Nelson Doubleday or Fred Wilpon or any of the other Met owners. I use the term "wolves in sheep's clothing" as a collective "negotiating" term, and certainly intend no disparagement of the Met owners. From all I've seen, they're good baseball men, devoted to the success of the team, willing to spend money to bring that success to New York City. Nelson sometimes hangs around the batting cage before games at Shea; Fred, too. They're open and accessible and supportive. They have their negotiators; I have mine. This leaves us free to be friends.

On this positive note I conclude my lobbying. Depending on events, there may be other harangues.

Here's Bob Verdi now, at batting practice before today's game with the Cubs. Verdi is a good writer, a guy you can deal with (just about the only one about whom I've heard Bruce Sutter talk highly). Therefore, I inform him that his piece with the golfers is horseshit.

"Lay off," he snarls with a grin. "I just got aired out in the Cubs' clubhouse."

Hanging around the cage, I also catch up with the current rumor, a week old by the time it reaches me (where have I been?): We're trading Dykstra, Calvin Schiraldi, and Bill Latham to the Red Sox for Tony Armas. Good Lord! Another awesome power hitter, to go with Gary, Straw, and George. My question is: Who joins Backman at the top of the order? Who will be the men on base?

In the clubhouse, around the batting cage, I sense a teamwide doubt going into these four games with the Cubbies. I hope I'm wrong, but nobody on this team can forget the one-sided demolition derby at Wrigley a year ago.

Pitching for them this afternoon, a gorgeous one with the wind blowing in, is Dennis Eckersley. We haven't faced him since he came to the Cubs from Boston early last year. Somehow, his rotation has always missed us.

A good thing, perhaps. He's tough on us for six innings today. So is Warren Brusstar for three.

As so often happens, the really intriguing plays, the ones the players enjoy so much, won't show up in the box score or, in all likelihood, the stories in the papers. Here are three:

1. In the first inning, Ryne Sandberg makes it to third base, one out. Gary Matthews is on first. Keith Moreland is hitting. Moreland is, as they say, slow afoot, and he hits a grounder to Johnson at third base. Sandberg should break for home on the play, but he doesn't. Johnson looks at him, then throws to Backman coming across second. Backman checks Sandberg, still at third, and throws on to me for the double play. It's a thing of beauty, the work of HoJo and Wally watching Sandberg while executing their plays, but the DP is possible only because last year's MVP makes a base-running error. Or maybe he was told to hold. Either way, it's the mistake of a team not playing well.

2. Sid Fernandez throws seven straight slow, slow curves (the only kind he has, and all he needs) to Davey Lopes on two consecutive at-bats. To everyone else, Carter has Sid mixing in the fastball. One of the curves to Lopes is a ball outside, six are strikes painting the outside black. An experienced, smart, good hitter, Lopes takes all seven pitches. Clever play-calling by Carter, wonderful pitching by Sid. Batters expect the catcher to mix 'em up, utilizing the whole repertoire of the pitcher, in, out, up, down. But mixing 'em up can be *not* mixing 'em up. The same pitch, the same location. The repetition starts working on the batter's head: "Well, he can't throw it again." But he can, and Sid does. One stipulation: The offering had better be a bastard pitch in a bastard location. Sid's curve on the outside corner against right-handed hitters is both of those. It starts out about four feet beyond the strike zone and just nips the corner as it dives into Carter's mitt.

If the right-handed hitter knows it's coming, he might be able to poke it on the ground to my side of the infield, that's all. If he's not looking for it, he'll be frozen in time and space.

3. In the sixth inning, with Bowa on third base and the Mets down 2–1, Lopes (against Terry Leach now) hits a hard ball to me. I knock it down, spin, and throw home. But Bowa isn't going home. All hands safe. I look dumb. However, I made the right play, because I don't have time to look—only time to throw. Down by a run against good pitching, we can't give up a run without a play. Somebody in the infield should have yelled at me, perhaps. Perhaps they did. I wouldn't have heard the warning cry over the noise from the stands.

Back in the dugout, Davey suggests that I had time to look. I don't agree, but fortunately don't have to say so. I have a better reply: "Well, at least they didn't score."

That particular play has happened only three times in my career, that I recall. The first was in Tulsa in 1974. Ken Boyer, managing us, defended my going home with the throw. The second time was last year . . . at Wrigley . . . Bowa on third. He eventually scored.

GAME 101—Cubs 2
Mets 1

AUGUST 3

I called Dad last night. The July hitting groove is wearing at the edges. The writers first put the thought in my head when they asked if I was sad to see July go. I know better than to divide up the season like that, but I did pause. Will August be different? I was hitless yesterday in Wrigley under my favorite conditions. I went hitless the last game in July, too.

"What do you think, Dad? I don't feel too good now."

"Your front foot is pointing out at the pitcher. Aim it at the plate." The answer is out before I've finished the question.

And so I do, and so it's nice to get an opposite field single in the third inning on a two-strike count. I'm seeing the ball better, again. August is declared officially "open."

I have also dropped down a half-ounce in the weight of my bat, as I usually do about this time of year. I'm a little slower with

my swing and need to compensate. I started off the season at
32½ ounces, so now I'm down to 32.

During the 1982 Series, I abruptly changed my bat model and
weight. I was 0-for-12 in the first three games, arguing with Dad,
and generally miserable. During batting practice prior to the fourth
game, I took a swing with one of Willie McGee's stock—the Louisville Slugger C-271, 34½ inches long, 32½ ounces, cupped. I liked
it and borrowed it for the game. I went 0-for-4 but hit ropes. I
was back. I hit the ball hard for the final three games of the Series,
and I've been with the C-271 since.

There are two main differences between this one and my many
earlier models (among them, the R-43, K-75, M-110 and M-159).
This bat is cupped: The tip of the barrel is hollowed out, so that
more of the weight is in the meat of the barrel. This style is almost
standard now. Also, the flange at the bottom forms a sloping joint
with the handle; with the other models, the flange is an abrupt
protrusion that can cause blisters.

At 32½ ounces the C-271 felt great that day in Milwaukee. A
half-ounce lighter, it feels pretty good today.

What if Dad had had the satellite dish my whole career, so he
could see me every game and always be ready with a suggestion?
Would I be a career .310 hitter, .320, instead of .300?

It's a bad question. There's no answer. Besides, that question
gets mixed up with the other question: Why is this year the first
time I've really been able to openly ask Dad for advice, and willing
to listen to his answer? With all the crap coming down this year,
and more on its way, Dad has been totally understanding; Mom,
too, but that goes without saying. Maybe the separation of my
kids from their father has served to bring closer together their
father and *his* father. It's a pat explanation, but it feels right.

These ruminations aren't in my mind during this game. This
game is big. If we lose again today, the Cubs-at-Wrigley-Field
doubts will really come to the front, and the pressure on Doc to
win tomorrow will be enormous.

It's big, too, because Ron Darling on the mound needs a solid
game after a couple of shaky ones. Everyone knows what happened last year—Ronnie's semicollapse after the All-Star break.

What a game it turns out to be.

In the fourth, an error by Ray Knight puts Cey on base, an
error by Santana scores him; a walk puts Jody Davis on base, a

wild pitch scores him. We are not amused, but how bad would the inning have been if pitcher Dick Ruthven hadn't been thrown out stealing third on ball four to Davey Lopes? You heard right. Ruthven, on second base after the Santana error, is running when Lopes receives his walk. With Ryne Sandberg coming to the plate! Carter easily throws the pitcher out, and the Mets are fortunate to be out of the inning. Otherwise, Sandberg bats with two men on, two already in. I understand that the hometown fans are getting restless concerning Jim Frey's managing, and they have good reason to be grumbling on this play—if Frey ordered it. But I can't believe he did. Ruthven must have thought there was a man on first. This is not a vapor lock. This is a major-league fuck-up.

We get an unearned run of our own in the sixth and are leading 3–2 going into the bottom of the eighth—an inning to remember. With one out, Hebner walks, Cey singles, Davis walks. Bases loaded. Frey brings in Chris Speier to bat for Larry Bowa, a veteran for a veteran. The fans are going crazy.

A digression: How does the frenzy of the fans relate to the excitement felt by the players on the field? Are the fans as excited? More excited? I think they may be more excited, because they don't have anything else to do. We have plenty to think about. On the field, our only salvation lies in keeping our minds on the situation, the tactics, and the baseball.

Back to the game, and the fans are still going crazy. A bunt is a possibility, so I watch Jim Frey before every pitch to Speier. I don't know the Cubs' signs, but I don't need to know them. *Any* sign will be the squeeze sign in this situation, except with the count two- or three-balls, or with two strikes. First pitch, second pitch, third pitch: Frey sits on the bench with his arms folded across his lap. He doesn't move. Now, with the count 2-and-1, he touches the bill of his cap with his right hand. No preliminaries, just the artificial movement. What else can it be? I don't need to watch Don Zimmer relaying the signs from the third base box. The squeeze is on. I ease in. Davey motions me back. I signify "negative" with a shake of the head, but still retreat a step. I can't call time for a conference. That would clue Frey that I've picked up his sign.

Speier drops his bat for the bunt. When Hebner on third base breaks for the plate, third baseman Knight automatically breaks.

I'm breaking in, too, and cleanly field the bunt—a good one—but nevertheless I don't have a play at home. I wheel and throw to first. But Wally has vapor locked, the base is open and my throw is headed for right field—until it hits Speier on the back of his helmet. Cey follows Hebner across the plate, but if the ball hadn't hit Speier, Davis would have scored from first base and Speier would have ended up on third, pretty much putting us out of the game.

The play is a sequence of good sign-stealing by Hernandez, bad brain work by Backman, good fortune on my throw. Davey and I are probably the only ones in the park who know that if I had held my ground before the play, instead of moving back that one step, I would have had Hebner at the plate.

Yes, the fans get as or more excited than the players, but I don't see how they can be having as much fun. In many situations they can't know what has really happened.

We're still in deep trouble in the inning, with only one out and Davis on third, Speier on second. Gary Woods is batting. With the Cubs leading 4–3 now, figure on another bunt. Since I know the sign, I can do better than figure; I can know. Frey tips the bill of his cap, so I'm waiting in front of the plate when Woods squares to bunt—and pops it up to me. Davis off third base is easy to double-up.

Three outs, at last, but when the dust has settled, the Mets still find themselves down a run going into the ninth, and still down that run two outs later. Now we get a break. Wally beats out a slow roller to shortstop. We *manufacture* a break, Cardinal-style.

Wally's hit brings me up against Lee Smith, the best reliever in the league last year. He throws as hard as anybody and has always been trouble for me, but he's overworked, perhaps, this year, with two months of baseball left to play. This is a moment for me to practice what I preach. Keep the head in the game; ignore the screaming throng and high stakes.

The outfield swings around to the left, so Smith is going to pitch me outside. He usually does. With the outfield alignment, I have little chance for an extra-base hit, unless it's against the wall in the left field corner. I'm thinking, "Single. Don't try to take what isn't here."

Smith's first offering is a fastball, outside. I'm looking for it and foul it back. My assumption regarding their strategy is confirmed. Now he shakes off a sign. This might be disapproval of the catcher's selection, or it might be a ploy. Sometimes pitchers shake off a sign before the catcher has even flashed one, trying to confuse the batter. If the pitcher shakes off a couple of signs, I'll step out of the box to clear my head and forget it. Nine times out of ten, the catcher will then flash the previously agreed-upon pitch, the pitcher won't shake it off, and I can get settled without having to endure a series of proposed and rejected choices.

Smith, however, is ready to go after one shake-off. Surely Davis flashed the fastball, with a one-strike count, a great fastball on the mound, and the outfield swung around to left. I don't know why, but I decide it's an honest shake-off from Smith. He has dictated his own pitch—the slider. I *know* it. And I know he always throws the slider on the inside edge to me. And I break a rule: I anticipate against a right-handed pitcher. I look slider. And here comes the slider, not on the corner but the inside half of the plate, and I pull it down the right field line, all the way to the beautiful ivy-covered wall. With the right fielder Moreland way around in right-center, Backman, running on the pitch, scores easily. Tie game. Smith and catcher Jody Davis, and probably manager Jim Frey, will talk after the game about that pitch selection.

The Cub fans are silent, the scattered Met enthusiasts are vocalizing their joy, and I feel an immense satisfaction, standing on second base. The clenched fists of the Met dugout are pumping in confirmation of my own exultation.

After the game, Rusty says it's the biggest clutch hit in August he's seen. Rusty knows ballplayers, he knows me: I need the stroking.

Orosco sets the Cubs down in order. In our tenth, Howard Johnson hits a homer off George Frazier. This is the same Howard Johnson who couldn't get the ball out of the infield until six weeks ago, the third baseman about whom Clint Hurdle got off the quip of the year, "He's writing a book: *The Summer of Four-to-Three.*" I heard that poisoned barb with a wince. Back in June, I could have coauthored the tragicomedy. Now HoJo and I are working on a new project, as yet untitled.

The dugout is joyful. In their last chance, the Cubs go down— with a whimper, I'm afraid. Richie Hebner gets thrown out of the game by Harry Wendelstedt for arguing over a called strike—strike two, so Steve Lake comes in to finish the at-bat. Strike three.

Oh, what a game. We win most of our games by scoring early and staying ahead. It's the best and safest way to win, but it's not the most exciting. This afternoon is the most exciting way to win.

GAME 102—Mets 5
Cubs 4

AUGUST 4

With only two days remaining before the strike deadline, I believe the owners will make us walk. They simply don't believe that the older players, who really aren't affected by the main issues of this strike—arbitration and salary cap—will hang with the younger players who stand to benefit in the future by our determination to protect free agency now.

What are the players talking about, the games or the strike? We talk about both, especially the latter with me, since I'm the player rep, the pipeline to the negotiations. Any news? Anything new? What's the plan? If I'm the pipeline, the well has run dry. Nothing is flowing. I have no answers.

The Mets have the answer: Doc is throwing and now all the pressure has flipped over to the Cubs. If they can't beat him, they're down for the count. They have looked shaky the first two games, with those base-running lapses, Hebner losing his cool on the last out. Today Jody Davis gets thrown out for arguing about a strike, but at least it's the third strike, and Hebner runs into a putout at third.

On the other hand, the Cubs could come up with a list of their own: shaky Met plays. It's a big series, and the strike is on everyone's mind; I'm not surprised by what we've seen in Chicago this week.

Hebner tells me at first base that Gooden's curveball is the best he's ever seen, and he's been playing professional baseball for over twenty years.

Dwight wins his eleventh game in a row, eclipsing Tom Seaver's Met record; this evening, Seaver wins his 300th game, pitching for the White Sox against the Yankees. There's a note of irony here: If the Mets hadn't given away Seaver after the 1983 season,

I don't think Dwight would have started 1984 with the Mets. He would have been at Tidewater and come up later in the year.

Don't ask me what "really happened" regarding Seaver, because I don't know; it was such a sore subject in spring training last year his name wasn't even mentioned. Frank Cashen was one stride in front of the posse. I know this: Tom would have helped thé Mets last year. I also know that the furor that erupted when Tom got away, timed as it was with the beginning of the Hernandez contract negotiations, made my agent's task easier. For better or worse, Frank had to sign me.

For better: In the third inning today I get my 60th RBI on a bloop to left field, and the stats reveal something interesting. The Dodgers' Pedro Guerrero and I are tied with those 60 RBIs. Guerrero, however, has twenty-six home runs. I have seven. This probably means that Pedro's RBIs have come in bunches, while mine have been more scattered. Take your choice, but I'll stick by my oft-repeated feeling that it's RBIs, not HRs, that count for the ballclub. Or put it this way: A home run is only as good as the runs it drives in.

Our pitcher doesn't buy it. One of Doc's main concerns this year is hitting his first big-league homer.

GAME 103—Mets 4
Cubs 1

AUGUST 5

Dave Kingman was the last Met so honored, in 1975. Ten years later, Keith Hernandez is voted National League Player of the Month for July. Jay Horwitz reports the news to me in the clubhouse before the game. You bet I'm happy. I knew the writers voted last Friday, with results to be announced today. Teammates congratulate me and Hurdle adds, "Don't be afraid to win it again in August."

The thought has crossed my mind, Clint. The news leaves only the question of the strike hanging over me.

The poor Cubs, down 2–1 in the series and with Trout and Sutcliffe still on the disabled list, have to bring up a rookie to pitch today. Derek Botelho is his name, and he lasts four and two-thirds innings, giving up eight hits and six runs. Lynch, just about at full strength now, pitches seven fine innings and gives up only one homer with the wind blowing out. As the big guy would say about another pitcher, but never about himself, "He toed the slab and threw a gem." Eddie enjoys delivering classic baseball lingo with curling lips and sardonic twist.

The game, however, belongs to Strawberry. The Cub fans are cheering for him to hit his fourth homer of the game in the ninth inning. Even the infamous bleacher bums have converted to Darryl's cause for the day. They accorded him a standing ovation after his third HR in the seventh—a monster almost out of the park in dead center field—and now they're booing as Warren Brusstar goes 3-and-0 on him in the ninth.

The fans have given up on the 7–2 game, and more. If the Cub players didn't know it earlier, they do now by watching their fans: Eight games behind us, they're out of the race in 1985.

Brusstar responds to the derision and throws three strikes in a row, the third of which Darryl lines for a single.

The fans cheer. I've never seen anything like this reception at Wrigley, but the fans here know a great performance when they see one. There's hardly any comparing Darryl this year and last, as a hitter or a player. The main reasons: He's more patient with the outside pitch and isn't trying to pull it; he's more effective with two strikes because he's not trying to hit a homer every time up; he got injured and couldn't play and came to appreciate more his talent for the game; he has a wife and baby.

I know Darryl is excited about his day, too, because he thinks there are two outs, not just one, when he catches Bob Dernier's fly in the eighth inning. He starts trotting in while Dykstra yells that the runner on second has tagged up—and is going all the way home! A little embarrassing for Straw, and I don't look for that mistake again. (I pulled something similar in 1980. With runners on second and third and two out, I played *in* for a play at the plate. Nobody on the bench caught the mistake before it was too late: A ground ball slipped past me and two runs scored.)

After the game there's elation—we've taken three out of four at Wrigley, dispelling the nightmarish memory of last year—and dismay—because this is it. The strike deadline is tonight, and to outward appearances nothing is happening. I tell the guys they don't have to fly to Montreal for tomorrow night's game if they don't want to. But everyone goes. Met management has retained the charter flight north, and will pick up tonight's hotel bill in Montreal, even if we go out tomorrow.

The flight to Montreal is a boozy gambling party. We lead the Cards by a half-game.

GAME 104—Mets 7

Cubs 2

AUGUST 6—MONTREAL

"Hello, Keith Hernandez?"

"Who's calling?"

"This is Lance Lancelot from WIOU. Any comments about—"

Slam!

There must be a hundred of these phone calls today. I hang up fast, which isn't good PR, but what am I supposed to do? We have spokesmen in New York, and I'm waiting in a hotel suite in Montreal for the official call. Do we strike? I call in every forty-five minutes. No news.

At one o'clock, a dozen players are milling around, playing cards, jumping up at every ring: "This is it! This is it!" But it isn't.

At two, Rusty announces he's leaving town. It's too late, now, he says. We're striking. He's right. Half an hour later the call comes through. The players should go home. The initial feeling is relief. At least we know. This relief overwhelms any feeling of regret, and I have a strong feeling that we won't be out for long. Not long ago, I thought any strike might last a month. Now I believe it will be much shorter.

On the Eastern flight to New York with Rusty and a bunch of the other Mets, one of the flight attendants conveys the information from the captain that La Guardia is packed with reporters waiting for our arrival. Therefore, the airline is going to try a last-minute gate switch. Rusty, taking charge as usual, seeks a special routing for us out of the terminal. The Eastern people agree to help, but we still have to go through the waiting area.

I've never seen reporters as frantic as this mob. The gate switch hasn't worked. The newshounds are going crazy; it's as bad as that mob fighting for answers from the airline hostages in Lebanon a couple of weeks ago.

No comment.

No comment!!!

No comment!!!

I shout that I'll see them at baggage claim. Hah! As the other players plow on through, Staub and I divert straight down to the baggage-handling area beneath the terminal. We get our bags pronto while a couple of dozen Eastern employees come over to shake hands. Union solidarity and all that. I wish. Celebrity-ogling, more likely. Nice guys, though, and I don't hear any threats of a fan boycott once we return to the playing field. Eastern brings up a taxi and we're on our way. I don't mean this as an advertisement, but the airline has been awfully good about these arrangements. Why did the other guys decide to tough it out upstairs?

I eat in. The phone is ringing nonstop. Rumors are flying. I unplug the phone.

'Night, all.

NO GAME
TONIGHT

AUGUST 7—NEW YORK CITY

I stink bad in the big Backman and Hernandez versus Staub and Gardenhire golf match at Rusty's club in Westchester, north of the city. I do have the excuse that it's hard to concentrate. On the first fairway we're interrupted with a message for Rusty to call Frank Cashen. "That's it," Orange says. "It's over, but we won't play tonight, so we're golfing now."

Other foursomes on the course shout over at us as we play along. "The strike's over! The strike's over!" Their excitement is contagious. The strike is over! The short strike says one thing to me. The owners were testing us, we called their bluff, and they came to a quick settlement. The crucial meeting required all of an hour and a half! Don't tell me the agreement couldn't have been settled last month or last year.

I also have it straight from a horse's mouth that, despite all the hosannas for our commissioner, Ueberroth had little to do with the settlement, which was a *fait accompli* when he entered that now-famous apartment on the East Side.

I don't begrudge Peter the good publicity, but I hope he puts it to good use. I hope he follows through on his intention of assuring that any renewed contract with him as the commissioner will be with the players' consent. Let's all select the commissioner.

When you get right down to it, baseball is one of the last major holdouts for the old-time robber barons' way of running things.

But, back to the business at hand. This is a tough game. My god-awful 64 for nine holes assures my team of defeat. I'm not this bad a golfer. I'm not a good golfer, but I can hit the ball well on occasion.

At the turn I call Cashen and he asks for me to get everyone back to Montreal. We'll play baseball there tomorrow night: one game, the first and last of the series.

The guys know. I don't have to call them. On the last night of my summer vacation, I escort my girlfriend to *Silverado*, a rare Western (I missed *Pale Rider*). I have trouble recalling a worse movie. She wants to leave early, but I argue that it's got to get better; then I want to leave but she argues that it can't stay this bad. I'm afraid we're whispering in the stands. We're there for the last lousy frame.

NO GAME
TONIGHT

AUGUST 8—MONTREAL

Nobody needs to be told to forget the strike. It's history, it didn't last long enough to be a disruption. Despite sitting on the runway for an hour at La Guardia, arriving at the hotel here at 2:30 p.m., grabbing lunch, napping on the training table in the clubhouse but arising still tired, I have three marvelous rounds of batting practice. We all look sharp in the cage. I see and hear a lot of line drives sizzling off the bats—although hits sound different in practice, because we use taped bats or bats with bad wood. We don't want to break good bats before the game; the idea is to make solid contact, which we can do just as well with weak timber.

The Mets are sharp, the Mets are ready. Frank Cashen says on the pregame radio show that he considers us the favorites, and I agree. We're good, we're veterans, we're leading. John Travolta agrees, too. He's ushered into the clubhouse by Arthur Richman and shakes hands all around.

The hitters are tuned up, but the pitchers aren't. With two of the best rookies in the league pitching—Aguilera for us, Joe Hesketh for the Expos—the score is 10–6, Mets, after four innings.

My first at-bat, an RBI single to left field. Feels good. Next time up, a helicopter (*lingo:* hanging curve) looks so big and is approaching my bat so slowly that I have time to flash, "Don't get greedy and try for the HR; just hit it." I hit it into the right field corner for two more RBIs. Here's a good example of how my approach at the plate differs from that of a real slugger. Strawberry tries to murder that ball, and he should. Carter or Foster would try to murder it, too. Batting third, my job—my instincts— are simply to hit it hard. A double in this situation produces two RBIs, a HR three—but the odds for a double from my bat are a whole lot better. Which strategy makes the most sense, behind 3–2 in the second inning, with two outs?

The final score is 14–7. Memo to the Expos: Turn the page. Memo to Keith in the ninth inning: This is one "meaningless" at-bat when you should be able to bear down. You're 5-for-5, only the second five-hit game of your career. How often will you get the chance for six?

I am bearing down against Tim Burke. On the first pitch I almost do it, lining the outside offering down the left field line— just foul! *Ouch!* Then I line out to the left fielder.

Hurdle after the game: "Gee, Mex, you couldn't get a break!" Clint is referring to what the box score doesn't reveal: My third hit, up the middle, was fairly cheap. My fourth hit was really cheap, looped into short left. I was beaten on the pitch.

The excellent evening means something else: I'm back at .300 for the year. It has been two and a half months; a fifty-point hike since June 30, when I was down to almost .250. The Irish say it's a long road that has no turning. This hybrid Spaniard understands what they mean.

At Little Rock in 1973, when it took me two months to climb from .179 to .300, I got back to my apartment, figured out my average and then slipped into a hot bath. I dozed into some state of semiconsciousness—and something . . . a spirit? . . . a second body? . . . what? . . . rose out of my body. I started awake and it fell back into my body. A breakdown or a vision? I don't know. I may have been in a state of nervous collapse; perhaps it was my very own out-of-body experience. Whatever. It comes to mind as I lie in my tub tonight, twelve years later, hitting .300 once again.

GAME 105—Mets 14
Expos 7

AUGUST 9—NEW YORK CITY

About 45,000 fans turn out for this first game at Shea following the strike. Boycott be damned. However, many of these tickets were purchased early. This is the long-awaited August series against the Cubs, the series that starts the pennant drive. Alas, the Cubs are out of it, but they're a prideful team and will want revenge for last weekend at Wrigley.

The game begins in standard fashion for the Cubs. Their scheduled starter, Dennis Eckersley, misses his turn with a bad shoulder. They substitute Dick Ruthven. In the first inning I ram a liner off his big toe. He hops around, gives up a run, gets a single in his at-bat—then leaves the game. I regret the injury, but at least we won't have to watch that strange stretch of his for the rest of the evening. Ruthven doesn't bring his hands to his body as he checks the runner. He holds them out in midair. The first few times a batter faces him, the batter waits for him to complete the damn stretch—even though completion after that halt would be a balk. The batter's timing is mixed up. After all these years, I can handle it. (The stretch that still bothers me is Scott Sanderson's, Ruthven's teammate. It's a regular stretch, but he thinks nothing of holding it for five seconds, sometimes longer. Drives me crazy.)

Either Darling or Gooden could go for us tonight, because both are rested after the two-day layoff. You have your choice of two theories in this situation: Go with Gooden, win the first game—what I call the World Series theory; always go with the ace in the first game of the fall classic. Or go with Darling, decreasing the odds a little, but maintaining good odds—and if they pay off, Gooden is ready to ice the series tomorrow night.

Dad has called with his advice. "Go with Dwight," he urges. Davey goes with Darling. Roll those dice! And seven comes eleven. Davey's a genius.

We win despite Dutch Rennert's blowing two different calls at first on pickoffs of Sandberg. Replays clearly show Sandberg out each time; still, Dutch is one of the best, especially on balls and strikes. Sandberg doesn't score.

We win despite Jody Davis's two home runs, which follow hard on one of those batting tips that turn a player's career around—

for a week or so, maybe a month. Johnny Bench suggested that Jody hold his hands farther away from his body.

We win because manager Frey orders first baseman Durham to hold McDowell on first base in the seventh inning. Exacerbating the situation for the Cubs is Durham's limited range with the glove. Dykstra singles on the ground right through the hole where Leon should have been posted. A double-play ball, all the way.

The win tonight is important, and the way we win is important. Back and forth, punch and counterpunch, with us landing the last one. Cheap psychology: Sometimes this kind of victory is better than a blowout, especially in the first game of a series. Let them think they can win, then slip by on the rail. The next game or the final game, run them into the ground. Blow 'em out.

On the other hand: A first-game blowout might take its toll on their bullpen for the rest of the series.

Conclusion: A win is a win is a win.

GAME 106—Mets 6
Cubs 4

AUGUST 10

John Vukovich, first-base coach for the Cubs, informs me that my liner off Ruthven's toe pushed the nail halfway under the skin. Make me wince! Yet Ruthven jumped off the mound and threw me out. That took balls. Dick should have been writhing in pain as the ball kicked into left field and I sped around to second!

Backman is in trouble with the Cubs—again. This time it involves his negative judgment (dutifully printed, of course) regarding Frey's decision to have Durham hold McDowell on first base. Frey is all over him in batting practice, indirectly.

"Keith," he calls to me, "I see you still haven't taught Wally to keep his mouth shut!"

Before I can retort, Bill Robinson interrupts. He's observing his batters' practice swings from his favorite post, right behind the cage.

"Lay off, Jimmy. We've handled it."

"You telling me to shut up?" Frey demands.

"No. I'm just telling you we've handled it." Bill is pissed.

Now Wally pipes up. "Fuck you, Jimmy."

Frey explained to the papers that he was playing against the bunt possibility last night. That excuse doesn't hold water. Looking for the bunt, Durham simply plays in front of the runner instead of behind him.

Some of the Cubs have expressed the opinion to me that their manager is a great winner but not such a great loser. I like Frey, but I'm beginning to understand what his players mean. However, would I want a manager who is *fun* to play for when his team is losing? That doesn't sound like the right stuff.

Besides, the string of bad luck the Cubs are enduring is incredible. All five of their starters are now on the disabled list: Sutcliffe, Trout, Sanderson, Ruthven, and Eckersley. No club could survive that misfortune. The Mets would be in fourth and fading fast, too.

Frey's feisty mood carries over into the game. In the second inning, he complains to the umps about my "deke" of Bowa at first base in a bunt situation. You know the deal: I start in, then come back to the bag to take the throw from the pitcher. I've been called for an infraction once this year, the very rare first baseman's balk. Now I have to ask every ump what the rule is—more precisely, how he interprets the rule as it's written.

Some say, "Step off the dirt and onto the grass and it's balk." Others say, "If you're already coming back to the bag before the throw over, it's okay."

May we please get this straight before I retire? My famous left foot, too. Even the announcers on the "Game of the Week" wonder aloud whether mine is not a special case. Scully and Garagiola see all the teams, and they see protruding left feet from a lot of the first basemen.

In our half of the second inning, Foster surprises their man on the mound, Fontenot, with a Pearl Harbor attack. George almost never swings at his first pitch of the game—like me in this respect. He doesn't even pretend to be interested in the delivery. This afternoon, he swings. The ball flies over the fence for two runs. Sweet, George. I'm going to try that before the season is over.

Fontenot is a tough left-hander when he's on; today he is, and he handcuffs me. It's nice to see him depart for a pinch hitter in the seventh, then even nicer to come up in our half of the inning, bases loaded, nobody out. A hitter's dream and I get a pitch to hit from George Frazier for a simple single, two RBIs and a four-run lead.

Credit Davey for getting the big inning rolling. With Dwight hitting, Gardenhire on first, and nobody out, Davey took off the bunt sign, replaced it with the hit-and-run, and Dwight bounced the ball through the vacated left side of the infield. We were only ahead 3–2 at the time. Most managers, especially with Gooden on the mound, would play for one more run, but not Davey today.

The four-run lead is more than enough for our pitcher. The Doctor with a big lead in the late innings is the surest bet in baseball.

Then there were three in the National League East. I say "three" out of politeness, or caution. The Expos aren't out of it, but I don't believe they are realistically in it, either, seven games behind two good teams. Climbing over one team is one thing, but two? Most unlikely. I was wrong in declaring that the Expos would be the first team to fall back, but how could I take into account the spate of Cub injuries? The Expos will still be the first *healthy* team to fall.

GAME 107—Mets 8
Cubs 3

AUGUST 11

Amazingly, we now have a chance for the second sweep of the Cubs at Shea this year. The Cubs are throwing Derek Botelho, the young guy we jumped on in Chicago. Perhaps they should try this fellow Ty Stofflet, from Pennsylvania, the subject of a profile in today's *Times Magazine*. The piece reports that Stofflet throws his softball at 104.7 mph, much faster than any major leaguer has been clocked.

This is hard throwing, but the story should mention that the pitching rubber of the softball diamond is only forty-six feet from home plate, compared with sixty feet, six inches in hardball.

While we're reading the paper, I should comment on another story, this one about the poor hitting in the minor leagues. Two explanations are put forward: the use of aluminum bats in college, and the too-swift promotion up the minor-league ladder. Both arguments make sense. I've hit with an aluminum bat—and what a joy it is. You can't get jammed. A ball hit on the hands is still a line drive. Therefore, the college batters aren't disciplined to hit on the sweet spot. When they graduate to wooden bats in the minors, it's a tough adjustment.

Aluminum bats are used in amateur baseball because they don't break; they save money. Why not convert professional baseball to aluminum? Hitting would improve. Great for the game, right? No way. Line drives off aluminum bats would rip gloves and extremities right off the fielders, and maybe a few heads off the pitchers. There's a straight analogy with the new metal woods in golf. They hit the ball harder—but nobody is standing at the front of the tee trying to catch it.

Concluding our review of the big *Sunday Times,* here's yet a third piece of note, this one a large, full-blown profile—the apotheosis of Darryl Strawberry. A bit premature, perhaps, but I hope not. I hope it's an understatement.

It's funny what has happened in New York City this year. There was a piece recently about Don Mattingly, the great young first baseman for the Yankees. His numbers smother Darryl's, with or without the latter's injury; Mattingly leads the major leagues in RBIs. But Straw gets the greater acclaim. Rickey Henderson is having a super year, too, but rather quietly. And Ron Guidry may win twenty games, but who other than a diehard Yankee fan is aware of it? Dwight is the only pitcher in town.

The Mets are *the* team this year; we're outdrawing the Yankees by over 5,000 fans a game, even though the Yanks are in contention, playing good ball.

We win pretty easily today, rapping Botelho for eight hits and six runs in six innings, but I'm worthless at the plate. A "comfortable" 0-for-4, as we say. Hitters aren't baffled or intimidated on these days, as we might be against a Gooden or a Ryan or a Valenzuela. We're at ease at the plate—just hitless.

Consider Ed Lynch, who throws a complete-game seven-hitter for us. He's a "comfortable" 0-for-4 pitcher. He strikes out only one guy today—Bob Dernier, the first man up in the first inning— so he's far from overpowering. Eddie just has good stuff (primarily a much better slider than last year) in good locations. Leon Durham enjoys a comfortable 0-for-4 against Eddie today; Bowa a cozy 0-for-3.

This designation is not a slight. It's a paradoxical compliment.

Other comfortable 0-for-4 pitchers in our league are Lamar Hoyt of the Padres and Rick Reuschel of the Pirates. There have been many fine ones over the years.

Eddie and some other pitchers like to be pumped up and reminded of the situation. "Come on, Eddie. Two strikes! Your pitch!" I'll be after him the whole game with exhortations. But unlike any other pitcher on our staff, Ed doesn't look at me. He just nods his head. Lately, Eddie's best pitching has been against the toughest hitters. In the seventh, with two men on and two out, Sandberg's hitting: ground ball to end the inning. It's fun to watch Ed work now.

I'm aware of omens, and I like this one. In the seventh inning, during the required singing of "New York, New York" by Sinatra, the scoreboard flashes the St. Louis loss to the Phillies. The Cards, I'm convinced, were helped by the strike break. They had lost five of six going into the layoff, and regrouped. They came out smoking, now they've finally lost again. Spurred by the good news from Philadelphia, the 40,000 leather lungs at Shea this Sunday afternoon serenade Eddie through the eighth and ninth innings: "Sweep! Sweep! Sweep!"

GAME 108—Mets 6
Cubs 2

AUGUST 12

Cosmopolitan has left me off its list of the ten most eligible bachelor athletes. I console myself with the knowledge that technically I'm not yet eligible—but I'm as eligible as Ronnie Darling, who's pretty close to a marriage decision, and he's one of the honorees. Ronnie has the magazine stowed in his locker.

Another magazine making the rounds is *Sports Illustrated*. A house ad in the magazine is supposed to feature a batter's-eye picture of Gooden in his windup, with the caption, "What does it feel like to look down the barrel of a loaded gun?" Tom Gorman insists they have the wrong man, and Gorfax has somehow manufactured a picture of *himself* in the exact same point in his windup, and is arguing vociferously that *this* is really how it feels to look down the barrel of a loaded gun. I laugh until I cry. Typical 'fax humor.

The clubhouse and the dugout are in great shape. The team

feels good. We believe we'll win every game; it's in the air. The other team scores first. Big deal, we say in the dugout. Hold 'em, we'll get ours. Against the Cubs, we put the games away in the eighth, seventh, and sixth innings, respectively.

The Mets will not crack come September. That's a given. We may not win it all, but we won't crack.

Here's a batting note I hadn't thought about until today, when I read that Wade Boggs hasn't popped out to the infield in three years. And Rod Carew can only recall popping out three times in his nineteen-year career!

I can't match Carew, but I don't hit many pop-ups, either. No good disciplined hitter does. The only one I recall this year was the one to third base in Philadelphia that I didn't even run out— the one I woke up recalling in the middle of a dream.

The pop fly as a clue to hitting is easy to explain. The good line-drive hitters are swinging level at the top half of the ball. If they miss the mark on the low side, they'll still get enough of the ball to send it to the outfield as a fly. Rarely will they just nick it underneath. Watch next time at the ballpark. Which hitters are popping out? The weaker hitters and the sluggers, the former because they're not that good with the bat, the latter because the towering pop-up is the price they're willing to pay for the power swing that also produces home runs.

Thirteen Phillies strike out in eight innings tonight against Sid the Squid. In a year or two, *Sports Illustrated* may be able to use a picture of Fernandez in their ad. Sid has one asset on the mound that Dwight doesn't share, that little hesitation in his delivery just before he releases the ball. It must throw the internal timing mechanism of the hitter just slightly ahead of the delivery. Then if that delivery is the slow, slow curve, the hitter is way early with his swing. Tonight, the Phillies can't hit the pitch. Literally, they can't put the bat on the curveball. They may hit the fastball somewhere, but the curve hardly at all.

Early in the game, the guys on the bench speculate why the crowd, a good one for Monday night, seems so laid back. The consensus is that the fans are tired from a big weekend in Manhattan. As the K total mounts, the fans get into it. By the ninth, when Sid's total is thirteen, with only two hits allowed, they're bellowing.

But Rick Schu hits a double, and Mike Schmidt a single. Despite our 4–0 lead, Davey comes out of the dugout. The fans protest. They want the complete game and some more strikeouts. When Davey's arm goes up for McDowell in the bullpen, they really let him have it. Sid gets a standing ovation, of course, as he trudges across the grass, but Davey is booed again—hard—when he retreats to the dugout. He derisively tips his cap. It's a tough decision, but the idea is to win ballgames. Sid has gotten into very quick trouble quite a few times. We're leading, he'll get credit for the victory. He can record his first complete game some other day. I go with Davey.

As Roger takes his final warm-ups, the crowd continues to roar for Sid to take a bow. Finally he does and the fans are satisfied. McDowell delivers to Glenn Wilson, who has murdered us all year—and Wilson drives a three-run homer over the center field wall.

First, silence. Then, "We want Sid! We want Sid!"

Oh, the fickle fans, they forget that Roger saved our collective ass early in the summer, when Jesse was struggling. The players don't forget, but the homer is a little disheartening. A solid game such as Sid has pitched deserves a nice, solid conclusion. Instead, it's now messy; more messy, when Greg Gross singles with one out. Here comes Davey again. I don't carry a boo meter, but I believe this is the hardest the fans have gotten on him all year. Nor is Roger blowing bubbles as he walks briskly off the field, but maybe the fans haven't completely forgotten his contributions: The boos are faint. Had it been Doug Sisk, you could have heard the boos in The Bronx. They may be able to hear them over there as Davey leaves the mound for the second time in the inning.

I make certain tonight that Orosco believes he's the best goddamn reliever in the hemisphere. I give him no choice. He saves it. The Cards lose. We lead them again.

GAME 109—Mets 4
Phillies 3

AUGUST 13

The car pulls up at 8:30 this morning to carry me across the river into New Jersey, where I attend a style show for the new spring line of clothes by Adidas. I'm on the Adidas payroll so I don't mind the work, but I can't understand how some other players do a lot of these promotions. Just a little wears me out.

Earlier this year Carter made some remarks to the press about his disappointment with the commercial opportunities coming his way in the Big Apple. I feel differently. I don't want to see my picture plastered everywhere. I value my privacy. Believe it or not, I'd prefer anonymity to the shouted greetings on the streets. But at least these are recognition for my play on the field. Capitalizing on that acclaim in other ways is a little unsettling for me. This has been my feeling; it may change.

The Adidas connection is a good one, and they're talking about working with me this winter on more promotional work. Apparently Michael Jordan did great things for a competitor, Nike, with his "Air Jordan" shoe campaign. Adidas is mulling a similar big campaign with some of their jocks.

If I'm so wary of self-promotion, why am I writing a book? That's a tough one, but as the guy said, it seemed like a good idea at the time.

Of course, I'll have to suffer the consequences at Shea next year. I can hear the new chant now.

"Author! Author! Author!"

I'll deal with it then. I have another problem today. As never fails, this day when I have an outside obligation is one day I really need to sleep in. The night was a bad one. I get to the ballpark worn out. This will have to be one of those kick-it-in-the-ass, mind-over-matter games.

I don't pull it off. Bad night at the plate.

Also to be factored in here is the month of the year: These are the dreaded dog days of August. We've turned the corner on the schedule, but the end is not yet in sight. And it's hot. On a losing team, the dog days can eat you alive. On a good team, they're not nearly as bad, because the anticipation of the upcoming pennant race carries us through them. (August isn't the pennant race, despite what we sometimes say.) As a unit, the Mets have none of the symptoms of dog days, but every player, believe me, will have a struggle once or twice during the month.

The baseball season goes on and on and on . . . and then on some more. The fans move in and out of it, as they desire, giving their favorite team only as much attention as their time and interest dictate. But the players live the season, like it or not, and there's just no way to be ready and willing for each one of the 162 games. Without having first-hand experience, I assume the same is true of any job. Some days at the office it must be a hard struggle going in. Drink an extra cup of coffee, spend a little longer with the *Wall Street Journal*, stay out a little longer for lunch, run an errand, talk on the phone, tour the offices of underlings, swap jokes. Get through this day.

I give it my best, but look at me tonight: ground ball, ground ball, fly ball, ground ball—and not because the Phillie pitching is superb. Bad day at the office. Maybe Pete Rose and Lee Iacocca don't have them, but I do.

And my legs are gone. I ask Davey before the game for a day off sometime. He'll try to find one—probably against the next left-hander. Are Hernandez's legs the only ones on the team that give out from time to time? I suspect not.

Charles Hudson's pitching isn't superb, but I feel overmatched tonight for only the second time since the first of July. I'm not baffled—just defensive. He jams me all night in the *cocina*, my kitchen, where we hitters keep our pots and pans. He beats me inside. Next time, though, Charles "I Don't Like Charlie" Hudson, I'll be lying in the weeds.

Something else never fails: After an interview exploring some baseball virtue, the virtue vanishes. Mike Lupica interviews me before the game on my prowess as a clutch hitter. I've been red hot in this regard for the past month. So not only are my four at-bats tonight miserable; runners are in scoring position for three of them.

Last night it was Fernandez with his slow curve from the left side. Tonight, it's Aguilera with his hard slider from the right side. Inspired by Sid, Rick sets his own personal high for strikeouts, with eight in seven innings. Orosco saves beautifully. My little dog day is irrelevant: The Mets are cruising—nine wins in a row, 30 in our last 37—on the strength of veteran bats and the best young pitching staff in the National League.

GAME 110—Mets 4
Phillies 2

AUGUST 14

Where's the carcass? Apparently, under the stool in front of Hernandez's locker. Why else the clutch of vultures, waiting to pick it clean. Well, fellas, you'll have to wait a little longer. This carcass doesn't mind talking, but neither does it entirely appreciate the fact that for six weeks while I was driving in runs almost daily, you came by for visits rather lackadaisically, but tonight when I lose the game in the bottom of the ninth, you're swarming. So wait.

I go back into Fig's office and call brother Gary in San Francisco. How's the new baby? ... The weather? ... Your golf game? ... When are you coming to town? ... etc., for ten minutes.

"Mex! A couple of friends outside!"

The way outside is past my locker, so I apologize as I walk by. "Sorry, fellas, got to see these friends for a minute. Be right back."

Good friends, too—Lee and Erica Lipton, he a clothes designer, she a model. Lee is planning a shopping trip to acquire for me all the latest in fall threads at good prices. Wait a minute! Hernandez needs discounts?! I don't *need* them, but who would turn them down?

My friends know better than to pick the bones. We discuss this and that, but my conscience finally catches up with me. It's time to play "Carcass for a Day."

Sitting on my stool, fresh beer in one hand, cigarette in the other, waiting. These tired bones are all yours. Silence. I look up.

"Okay, I'm ready."

And what can I say? *Mea culpa.* I stank, stranding a host of runners, with the ignominy culminating in my last at-bat: bottom of the ninth, one out, bases loaded, Mets one run behind; one of the ultimate goat-or-glory situations the game offers. A good hit and we score twice and win. A double-play ball and we lose.

Hell, a fly ball ties the game. A high hopper scores the tying run if the fielders don't have time to turn the double play. Even a strikeout isn't fatal; Carter batting behind me gets a chance. In other words, almost anything will do except the grounder right at the infield playing halfway (corners in for a play at plate; shortstop and second baseman back for the double play).

I hit the grounder right at the second baseman. Score it 4–6–3.

Well, look at it this way: We're fortunate to even get a chance in the inning, which featured three walks and an error by the reliever Don Carman. But a lot of victories require help from the other guys. "Capitalizing on mistakes" is the phrase. I couldn't do it, tonight. I stank. Enough, fellas? I need a shower.

The newsies with the microphones are the ones who try my patience. There are a lot of them and each needs his thirty seconds or a minute. The regular beat writers, fine, but the guys with the microphones, the ambulance-chasers—occasionally I have no time for them and tell them so. I tell them so tonight.

The ballplayers are quietly respectful—tonight. "Fuck it, Mex; next time." "You've carried us for a month, Mex, can't do it every night." Tomorrow, after I've had a night to sleep it off, they might sharpen the needles. I expect someone to dub me "Mr. August"; Hurdle, most likely.

Before Staub, Lynch, and Heep carry the remains out to the van, Davey tells me the day game tomorrow will be the sought-after day off. He undoubtedly wishes it had been tonight!

GAME 111—Phillies 2

Mets 1

AUGUST 15

Once again, I enjoy the early innings today in the comfort of the bullpen, chatting with the guys and their coach, Vern Hoscheit.

Noteworthy is Dwight's lack of success on the hottest day of the year. It's obvious from the get-go that the Doctor isn't making a house call today. Paciorek, Carter, and Knight hit first-inning homers for us—but the game is tied 6–6 after four innings. After one more, Davey lifts Dwight, who has thrown almost 100 pitches and lost several pints of sweat. It's awful today.

As previously mentioned, the one thing a player wants on his day off is his day off. The whole day. This isn't going to be that day for me because the game is too screwed up. Somebody will win but nobody will do it going away. After we achieve a little lead, Davey inserts me for defense. Still leading by one in the bottom of the eighth, I'm due to hit seventh and would just as soon not, thank you. I'm never ready to hit for the first time late

in a game. I'm a lousy pinch hitter. Damned if we don't manufacture some action, though, bringing up Strawberry with two on,
two out. I'm next. Darryl lifts a high, high fly to left field and Von
Hayes loses the ball in the sun. Two runs on the error, great! But
now I have to bat. Not so great. We need the runs to pad the lead,
but I also feel a visceral displeasure with Hayes. I roll out to second
base.

We take the series, three games to one; it's another boost for
the Phillies' reputation as the most disappointing team in the league.
Any team with some pretty good pitchers and Schmidt, Wilson,
Hayes, Ozzie Virgil, and Juan Samuel should be competitive. They're
fifteen games behind us! Something's wrong down there.

Something is also wrong with Gardenhire's entire muscula-
ture. I've lost count of the pulls he has suffered. Usually it's the
hamstring, today it's the groin muscle, injured while chasing a fly
in the second inning. So, once again, we don't have a spare middle
infielder. Kelvin Chapman down on the farm can't help out; he's
hurt, too. However, Larry Bowa is available. Now that the Cubs
have capitulated (they've released Bowa to make room for Shawon
Dunston, the shortstop in their future who wasn't ready earlier
in the year), I'm sure Cashen is talking to Bowa.

GAME 112—Mets 10
Phillies 7

AUGUST 16—PITTSBURGH

What is a "flat" ballclub? The phrase is used all the time, but it's
hard to define. In August, it's tempting to blame an unlucky coincidence of individual dog days landing on the same day; or
maybe something does happen to the chemistry of the team, another nebulous, commonly used term. Whatever, it seems beyond
our control. If I were into such matters, I'd check the star charts
for tonight.

A more mundane explanation would be that the Mets are
listless following yesterday's three-and-a-half-hour ordeal in the
heat and humidity of Shea, and this morning's flight. However,
I'm flat and I didn't play much yesterday, flew over last night,
and got a good night's sleep here. Lynch did, too, and he doesn't
have it tonight. Sisk doesn't have it, the hitters don't have it. Even
the F-Troop Irregulars, led by Staub and Hurdle, are out of it.

Clint is one of the best on the bench; always in the game, chatting it up, prodding and provoking. Tonight, Clint is on sabbatical, too.

And here we are against a team with a nine-game losing streak, thirty-five games out of first place, returning home from a sweep (on the losing side) in St. Louis. And they whip our butts, led by Bill Madlock, the fine hitter who stands way up in the box (unlike most fine hitters) and is suffering through a .235 season.

In the second inning I read the tea leaves: While we're plodding around, the Pirates' Marvel Wynne in center field makes a great diving catch on the rug against Santana. That says something to me: Terrible team, etc., and here Wynne is, playing his heart out.

With more evidence, it would be interesting to speculate on the effect the Pirates' big trade has had on the team. They got rid of two high salaries, John Candelaria and George Hendrick, who openly proclaimed they didn't want to play in Pittsburgh, in exchange for some young guys. The trade may have helped Pittsburgh: How can they suffer from the loss of players who didn't want to be here, no matter how good they are? Wynne's exemplary hustle may reflect uplifted spirits.

Billy Martin asserts today that his Yankees will be in the World Series. They're "the best team in baseball," Billy says. That's an idle boast, but they are playing well. New York is beginning to buzz about the prospect of a Subway Series. First, however, the Mets must pick up the pace.

GAME 113—Pirates 7
Mets 1

AUGUST 17

Flat again, but saved by Strawberry's big fly and a two-run triple by Paciorek in the seventh inning, just when we're about to squander another fine job by Sid, who has a triple himself in the inning.

GAME 114—Mets 4
Pirates 3

AUGUST 18

In fact, if it hadn't been for the two big hits yesterday, we would have lost three straight to these Pirates. This afternoon's game is another abysmal affair. You would think that yesterday's come-from-behind rally would stir us. Uh-uh. Our showing over the weekend proves to me that we're just flat, without excuses.

Madlock is quoted as saying that some of the Mets have mentioned to him how hard it is to play in Three Rivers Stadium before 10,000 mute fans, after the zealous nights at Shea. Madlock suggests that the Mets are a club with rookies and sophomores, who should be excited anywhere, and veterans, who should know how to handle any situation. He's right, and we have another series here in the middle of September, when a repetition of this weekend's debacle could prove fatal.

Carter is off today with a stiff neck. He was also missing behind the plate the day before yesterday. That's three recent losses when Gary wasn't catching. After the game today I tell him he's just too valuable behind the plate—taking nothing away from Hurdle and Reynolds. "We have forty-seven games to go, Gary. We need you in forty-five of them."

Gary promises. We're half kidding around, but only half.

We charter out of Pittsburgh to Montreal for a one-game stand to make up one of the two games lost to the strike. The original plan called for spending the night in Pittsburgh, proceeding to Montreal tomorrow. I talked to Arthur Richman shortly after that plan was announced and requested this charter. We get it and are in the hotel by seven in the evening.

We also have a charter set up for the flight out of Los Angeles on September 8, the one I've been lobbying for for weeks. That one is costing the Mets $47,000, Arthur informs me, but it's also saving the Mets' day off, in effect, before the biggest series of the year.

If there were ever any doubt, it's wiped out now. The management is doing everything it can to win this year: the acquisition of Paciorek, last-minute charters to ease the travel. Now it's up to us to get this series out of our system.

GAME 115—Pirates 5
Mets 0

AUGUST 19—MONTREAL

Huge game. The Expos are coming home after victories over Tudor and Andujar of the Cards. Bryn Smith, their ace, is going tonight. They trail us by only four games: I may have been premature in my assumption just a couple of weeks ago that they were almost out of it. Four games behind is not out of it by any means.

We're coming in after looking bad against the Pirates, and here's our almost-ace, Ron Darling, dead asleep on a trainer's table when I show up at the park at 4:15, and he's still asleep at 7:00, when they have to wake him to start his warm-ups. Major-league toothache.

But maybe it takes the importance of this game and Darling's dangerous tooth to wake us up, because the flat feeling is gone. We're back, ready to play ball again.

This does not mean, however, that we're ready to hit. The 3-through-6 hitters in the lineup, in fact, are 0-for-14 for the game. But as Darling's good pitching and our good fortune would have it, the heart of the Expos' order is not much better, with 1-for-14. That one hit is Andre Dawson's triple in the sixth with one out. Darling proceeds to get Hubie Brooks on a check-swing strikeout (for the second time in the game, and for the second time the Gangster of Love disputes the call) and Terry Francona on a comebacker to the mound.

Close plays, tense situations all over the place: Dykstra thrown out at home by left fielder Tim Raines on a Hernandez fly ball to short left (too short, as it turns out, but Raines' arm is as weak as his legs are strong, so it's a worthwhile gamble); Foster thrown out at home trying for an inside-the-park-homer on a fly to right misplayed by Dawson (George, logically enough, pulls up coming into third base, thinking he'll never be waved home, but he is waved on and would have made it if he hadn't slowed down); Dawson and Brooks thrown out on Expo baserunning blunders in the same inning.

So the game is scoreless in the eighth, and Darling is pulled for Heep, who hits a double off the wall. Then Dykstra does what Dykstra has done ever since he came up: another little thing to win. With two strikes, he gets the ball to the right side of the infield, moving Heep to third with one out. The outfield comes in for a play at the plate and Backman, who has been about as hot as me since July, doubles over Herm Winningham in center field. Without Dykstra's ground ball moving Danny to third, the outfield isn't pulled in and Herm catches Wally's ball.

If they want to keep a truly meaningful stat, they should keep track of the times the first and second (particularly) and seventh and eighth hitters advance a runner to third, setting up the sacrifice fly. Dykstra's ground ball tonight, followed by six straight outs from a rejuvenated McDowell, wins this game for the Mets and Darling.

Nothing was prearranged, of course, but the clubhouse after the game is a celebration—the biggest of the year by far. Earlier in the season I watched closely to see whether victories were taken in stride; they were. Tonight, well, count the ways this is a big victory. To hell with taking it in stride. We have a party. As luck would have it, Ronnie is celebrating his twenty-fifth birthday, and his girlfriend has loaded up his locker with helium balloons. They go everywhere, naturally, and the funny gas into the lungs of Hurdle, Lynch, and McDowell. Caution: Men at Play.

GAME 116—Mets 1
Expos 0

AUGUST 20—NEW YORK CITY

"How about our 'perfect pitcher for an eighty-one-game season'?"

Prior to tonight's game with the Giants at Shea, I direct this question to Mike McAlary, the *Post* writer who described Darling as such about a week ago.

The statement was bullshit at the time, because although Ronnie took the loss in that ballgame, he gave up just five hits and a walk in seven innings, and struck out five. After last night's effort with a toothache, I decide McAlary should hear from me.

"That's a horseshit thing to write," I add.

He stares in response, then replies, "Well, what was his record at the All-Star break, and what is it now?"

"But you don't write something like that now! Wait till the end of the season. Then make an evaluation. You're putting a gun to his head."

I don't tell McAlary, but I believe Darling took that slur as a challenge. He read it, or was told about it, I'm sure.

Also on the journalism front: *The Post* today reports its telephone poll asking readers to vote for Mattingly or Hernandez as the city's best first baseman. Mattingly beats me by twelve-plus thousand to ten-plus thousand. Somebody from the paper asked me yesterday for my reaction, and I told him the truth. I vote for Mattingly. Look at his numbers this year, look at his age (Don is twenty-four years old).

And also on the journalism front, and significantly, *The Times* is in the middle of a multipart series about drugs and baseball. Front page stories! The media boys are gearing up for a major offensive on this issue; the shit may hit the fan in Pittsburgh.

At the ballpark, the Mets are joined by Larry Bowa, recently of the Cubs. I knew it! It's a good move. Perhaps the fans wonder whether a late-season addition to the lineup is fully accepted as a member of the team. You bet. The acceptance is instant and total. A Cub one day, a Met the next. Who cares? Team allegiance is very strong and yet easily transferred.

Gooden does exactly what I expect tonight, coming off his bad outing against Philadelphia. After a dangerous first inning in which he gives up two singles and two walks but no runs, he burns the Giants. Maybe the key is the third out in that inning. Joel Youngblood batting, bases loaded: Doc fans him on three pitches.

Over the next eight innings, Youngblood is followed into the K-Korner by Brenly, Gott, Gladden, Wellman, Brown, Youngblood a second time, Brenly a second time, Uribe, Gott a second time, Wellman a second time, Driessen, Uribe a second time, Roenicke, Brenly a third time, and Deer.

Sixteen in all. The umpires finally direct the Mets to cease and desist from flashing on Diamondvision a cartoon of a shark with gaping jaws about to gulp the cowering batter. No matter; the fans are in a feeding frenzy.

Only one Giant, Chili Davis, doesn't strike out, and he gets three of their six hits. Chili hits Doc as well as anyone, with a couple of other three-hit games to prove it. Go figure.

The Astros nuke the Cards tonight. We move ahead by one and a half.

Meanwhile, I've been stuck on 69 RBIs for about a week. Granted that RBIs run in streaks, and 69 is a fine number, but I'm tired of it after seven games. May we please try something new?

GAME 117—Mets 3
Giants 0

AUGUST 21

From the "Metropolitan Section" of *The Times*:

> Our friend the stockbroker and sometimes-Mets fan was working late the other night, and before he left his office, he telephoned his wife to ask if there was anything he could pick up on his way home. She said she had a craving for Häagen-Dazs vanilla-orange swirl. A block from his office he purchased a pint of the ice cream and then hailed a cab for the short ride home.
>
> "Quick, get in," the cabbie instructed. "Hernandez is up, bases are loaded, it's the bottom of the ninth, there's one out, the score is Phillies 2, Mets 1." The driver's statistics tumbled out even as he turned up the volume of his radio.
>
> Strike one, strike two, a foul ball on the next pitch, then another foul—even the sometimes-fan found his pulse racing, his palms getting sweaty. By now the cab had reached its destination. "Hey, you can stay till the game's over," Louie, the driver, told his passenger as he pulled up to the curb. "Hernandez is gonna get a hit; the Mets are gonna take it." Then he said: "Listen, if they do, the ride's on me."
>
> Caught up in the excitement of the moment, the stockbroker held up the paper bag with the container of ice cream in it. "O.K., if they lose I'll give you this."
>
> The next two pitches: ball one, ball two. Then the sound of bat and ball connecting, a ground ball and, the unthinkable, a double play! Hernandez had failed to come through. The game was over. The Mets had lost.
>
> "Oh, no!" shouted Louie.
>
> "Oh, no!" said the stockbroker, paying the fare and handing over the paper bag.
>
> When he walked into his apartment, his wife was waiting for him. "Where's my vanilla-orange swirl?" she wanted to know.
>
> "Ask Keith Hernandez," her husband responded.

Ma'am, I owe you.
Despite the riveting subject matter of the aforementioned story,

the big news around town today is LOTTO, the New York State lottery with a jackpot this week of $41 million. That's a lot of glue. Everyone on the streets is buying and talking LOTTO. I'm tempted to get in line myself—but don't.

At the ballpark, Lynch tries again for his career-high eleventh victory; like Dwight yesterday, Eddie is coming off a bad outing last week.

Great, agonizing game. It's tied at 1–1 in the bottom of the seventh when I lead off against LaPoint with a single. Carter follows with another. Strawberry at the plate. Yes, I am surprised to see the bunt sign flashed. But he bunts, and LaPoint throws me out at third. Foster flies out. Knight grounds out. After the game, Davey is defensive with the reporters on that play selection. Strawberry had homered his previous at-bat, but Davey points out that if Darryl had bunted well and advanced the runners, nobody would say a thing.

It's a great situation for analyzing the choices and calling the strategy:

Pro-bunt: If successful, runners are on third and second, less than two outs.

Anti-bunt: 1. With first base open after the bunt, the Giants would walk Foster to face Ray Knight, who is as good a double-play hazard as there is on the team; 2. Because Darryl is almost impossible to double-up, a ground ball gets me to third base anyway; 3. The bunt might fail.

I wouldn't have had Darryl bunting, but as Davey said, what if Darryl had done the job? Once again, Davey proves that he'll try the unconventional.

I've been asked to bunt just one time since I established myself as a third-place hitter, years ago. Herzog put on the play, and it worked. I've never bunted with the Mets. I don't look for Darryl to be ordered to try many more.

The whole episode might have been moot if HoJo's dramatic pinch homer in the eighth had held up, but McDowell returned the favor, serving up one to Bob Brenly in the top of the ninth, with a man on. Brenly had struck out in four of his previous seven at-bats in the series.

From ecstasy to dismay just like that. A tough loss, but I don't think it will undercut the momentum we've built. We'll be in the race until the last days. We know it. Turn the page. It's just a novel for light summer reading, yes?

GAME 118—Giants 3
Mets 2

AUGUST 22

It's official, according to *The Post*. Davey has informed Doug Sisk that it just isn't the reliever's year. All relievers have these years, Davey says, and he's right. Nevertheless, we hate to be going into a stretch drive with a reliever having an acknowledged off-year.

Pitching tonight is a reliever having a fine year. Terry Leach is working on short notice for Fernandez, who has a dizzy spell before the game. Terry responds with a three-hit shutout. Going for the Giants is Vida Blue, who by ill luck was featured in yesterday's installment of the drug series in *The Times*. (Vida is, so far as I know, the only player with his *first* name stitched onto the back of his uniform.) He pitches pretty well tonight, without a lot of success. And finally, I get my 70th RBI (and 20th GWRBI).

In the early innings it seems that the fans are in a surly mood (perhaps because they came to see Sid throw K's), but they relent as our lead mounts and Leach throws well with his submarine motion. The fans are paying attention, too. Twice Terry fails to get down a sacrifice bunt, then in the eighth he pulls it off and they reward him with a standing ovation, which he acknowledges with a lighthearted shrug. What the hell. We're ahead 7–0. The runner, Santana, gets to third before I come up. Here it is, a "meaningless" situation for the game but a chance to fatten the stats. Mark it 4–3 on your scorecard.

After our victory, we watch the Astros and Cards, and for the second time in two days the Astros blow the game in the ninth inning. In the first game of the series, the usually reliable Doran let a hard grounder get through his legs at second and the ball rolled all the way to the wall on the glass grass at the Astrodome, scoring the only runs the Cards got all night. The Mets can't really gripe, however. We cleaned up on the weaker Western Division teams, too, and got a lot of gifts in the process.

But how the Astros blow the game tonight is infuriating: Bob

Lillis pulls Joe Niekro after he gives up—what?! A grounder that's booted by the first baseman! That's all. Niekro is working on a four-hitter, a shutout.

Dave Smith strikes out Jack Clark, terrific, but then Lillis takes him out to bring in a rookie, left-hander Jeff Calhoun, to play the lefty–lefty game against Van Slyke. But Herzog counters with Tito Landrum. He walks. Finally another pitcher walks another pinch hitter with the bases loaded, forcing in the losing run.

This is overmanaging. Leave Niekro in. But if you do take him out, leave Smith in. He's the only reliable reliever Houston has. To hell with all the lefty–righty business. The Mets yell and scream and moan throughout the disaster, then we retire to "Rusty's" for a drink to forget it all.

Montreal, meanwhile, has lost its fourth in a row following the 1–0 defeat to us in the one-game stand. Their subsequent slide after that game verifies our spontaneous, uncharacteristic celebration: It was a big, big victory—and defeat—in Montreal.

GAME 119—Mets 7
Giants 0

AUGUST 23

No, I don't mind that *Post* story pitting Mattingly against myself—except when it's the instigator for tonight's abuse from the fans. From the first to the eighteenth inning of this doubleheader with the Padres, I catch crap from two guys with blond hair, about my age, seated in the first row of the stands, right off first base. In the early innings, they're the only people in the stadium saying a word. It's always an eerie silence for the first innings of 5:30 starts, when most of the people aren't off the freeways; like a golf tournament where the marshalls hold up signs: QUIET. Most inappropriate for a baseball game, however, and bellowing through the silence are these two pricks.

"Who's the best first baseman in New York, Keith? *Mattingly*!!"

"You're dogging it, Hernandez, ya bum."

It starts off bad and gets worse, and my hitting doesn't do much to let the air out. My at-bats in the first game read 3–1, K, 3–U, K. Two grounders, two strikeouts—and one each against Mark Thurmond, what we call a cunnythumber (*lingo*: junkballer).

There are your "comfortable" 0-for-4s, guys like Lynch, and then there are your cunnythumbers, guys who have the minimum required for survival in the big leagues. They throw junk, sometimes well-placed, and can be especially effective as relievers, because the hitters see their stuff only once in a game. Bill Campbell of the Cards is an example. He had great stuff with Boston before he hurt his arm. Now he throws effective junk as a middle reliever.

We're leading 1–0 going into the sixth, when San Diego raps five consecutive two-out singles and scores four times. It could be that it took this long for them to get warmed up. Somebody goofed for the Padres, forgetting about New York City traffic on a Friday afternoon, perhaps; the team bus arrived at Shea only half an hour before the game. No time for batting practice.

Aguilera, our starter, hasn't been releasing the ball well in his last couple of starts, especially in the middle innings. Everything about his delivery looks fine until the last moment, when the hand doesn't really snap through. He's aiming instead of throwing. His confidence has dropped a notch.

Our manager isn't around to watch this loss. I'm swinging my bats in front of the dugout before the bottom of the first inning when Johnson strides past me to talk to Bruce Froemming, behind the plate. The next thing I know, Froemming has yelled that Davey is kicked out of the game. I look around and ask, "What happened?" It turns out that Napoleon (Froemming's nickname) had yelled at Aguilera in the top of the first for giving him a look after a pitch was called a ball. Umpires can be touchy. They don't mind the catchers giving them some grief, as long as it's from behind the mask and without turning around—not showing them up, in other words. They don't want to see or hear a thing from the pitchers.

Davey doesn't like the umps getting on his players and tells Froemming so—in too many harsh words, I guess. No matter. In these televised days, the manager thrown out of the game is still managing. Extension 381 at Shea rings Davey's office. He'll call the plays from there. There aren't any to call in this game, however, which turns on a Padres' bloop single and a Mets' line-drive out—the bloop scoring their third and fourth runs of the sixth inning, the line drive off Paciorek's bat leaving the bases loaded in our fifth. How many ballgames turn on such inequities? Too many to count, and that's why we play so damn many games: hoping that the injustices balance out, giving way to skill and performance.

In the seventh inning, Steve Garvey and Greg Nettles rock Tom Gorman for long homers. Two of Greg's sons are helping the bat boys in this doubleheader. They're cute, running in and out with bats about as big as they are.

We're way behind, but the ninth is an exciting inning anyway. We load the bases on a hit and two walks, and Hernandez comes to the plate. I hope that lady hasn't ordered any ice cream from her husband. I'm jinxed if she has. Down five runs, we have a chance to tie the game; Carter, hitting behind me, is the tying run. But Santana pulls a terrible blunder, getting himself picked off third base on a throw from the catcher Kennedy, for our twenty-seventh and final out. That's a fine-able offense.

Hurdle murmurs to me after the game, "Took you off the hook, didn't he?"

Yes, he did. Let me explain this cowardly sounding remark. I do love runners in scoring position, I do love these clutch situations—but I love them more when I'm swinging the bat well. I'm not tonight, although I did line a pitch just foul before Rafael's mistake. I'm mad that the game ends this way, when we do have a chance. But, yes, there's a faint whiff of relief in the air around me. A month ago, I would have been madder. Today, well, Hurdle's remark says it all. Ballplayers are like everyone else. A challenge is great, but failure in front of 45,000 fans isn't. We can get mixed emotions in these situations.

So Santana does the dirty work for me and we troop into the clubhouse for a twenty-minute break, then troop back out to face the throng again. The two guys in the front row are still there. I'm still not hitting, either—even off Roy Lee Jackson, who used to pitch for the Mets and against whom I iced my batting championship in 1979, with two, maybe three hits off him on a 5-for-5 night.

In the fourth this night, I hit a sharp ground ball to the left of Kurt Bevacqua, playing third base. He reaches but can't come up with it. A hit! These days, I'm doing well to get a hit a game. I need them. I'm not looking at the scoreboard, but I catch out of the corner of my eye the big "E" flash.

Error! That's bullshit. This isn't even a "home book" question. Yes, Bevacqua might have stopped the ball but it slipped just past him. A clean hit—a bullet. I tell Kibler umpiring at first, "That's a hit!"

"Yeah," he agrees. "Send the scorer down to us. We'll correct it." So I'll ask Jay Horwitz to send the guy down and the umps will instruct him on the play. Umpires overrule scorekeepers, when there's a blatant mistake. Alas, scorekeepers can't overrule umps on *their* blatant mistakes.

Do I protest too much? In a way, yes. I'm struggling, the hits aren't coming easily, and I don't want anybody to take away the few I do ring up. My touchiness is glaringly proved in a later inning, when HoJo tells me after another fruitless at-bat, "You're pulling off the ball a little bit, Keith."

"Yeah, no shit, HoJo!"

The dugout stops talking. I run out to my position.

All in all, a tough night as we're shut out in this second game by Jackson, Lefferts, Walter, and McCullers. The Squid strikes out nine in six innings but gives up a two-run homer to Garvey. Enough.

GAME 120—Padres 6
Mets 1

GAME 121—Padres 3
Mets 0

AUGUST 24

Arguably, this is our third pre-pennant race "critical" game of the season. The first was here against the Pirates in early June, when we were down, just wiped out by the Cardinals in St. Louis, shut out by Pittsburgh in the first game of the series, and about to go on a long road trip before the All-Star break. Darling won it. The second was the make-up game in Montreal after the strike, when again we were hurting. Darling won it. The third is tonight, coming back after a doubleheader loss at home. Our "perfect first-half pitcher," as Ronnie was described, wins this one, too. Case closed.

Two marvelous plays in the eighth inning save the game. Darling gives up a walk and two singles to load the bases, none out. We're ahead, 3–1. Davey brings in Orosco to face Nettles, who hits a looping fly to short left-center. Pure trouble—but Santana races back, looking for the ball first over one shoulder, then the other, turns at the last split moment and catches it on his left side, back to the infield. Heart-stopping.

Terry Kennedy up next. This play Bowa calls the finest first-to-short-to-pitcher double play he's seen. Kennedy hits a sharp ground ball to my right. The ball is loaded with top spin. I'm playing deep because Kennedy is slow, and the ball is hit too hard for me to come in for the short hop or drop back for the long one. I only have time to react a few steps to my right, snap up the ball on the in-between hop, a bad one at that, and throw to Santana covering second. Rafael drags his foot across the bag with Garvey charging into him, leaps out of the way and throws to Jesse, right there at first for the return throw. The ball is in the dirt but Jesse digs it out, breaks from the bag, and jerks back to look at the umpire. Dick Stello pumps the air. Double play! The fans erupt and the fielders race into the dugout and a thumping greeting from the bench. It's fun to make these plays; this one sparks the team. It sparks me! I rip a single to lead off the eighth, we score twice and win.

This game is hard work for all of us, but we show that we can hang in to win a close struggle after the doubleheader loss.

I go to Vern Hoscheit with one piece of information after the game. On the double play, Tony Gwynn was sprinting all the way from second base. Jesse should have come off the bag throwing to the plate, not looking back to the umpire for the call. His reaction was understandable, with all the excitement, but if the call had been safe, he would have been too late with the throw home. Gwynn would have scored the tying run.

Vern says he'll point this out to all the pitchers. But what a marvelous play . . . two plays . . . three plays . . . four plays! Santana's catch, then my stop and throw, Santana's coverage at the bag, Jesse's coverage and scoop at first.

GAME 122—Mets 5
Padres 1

AUGUST 25

Strawberry took himself out of yesterday's game with a sprained middle finger. Darryl, I told him afterwards, you can't miss any more games. I'm a lot older than you and I don't intend to miss any more games this season. You'd better not. We have to have you.

Today, Darryl is hot: 3-for-3 with a homer and four RBIs. We're hot, rapping sixteen hits altogether. Even the stagnant Hernandez is semi-hot, with a couple of late-inning hits that might get me back on track. I expect to be lukewarm after those hot weeks, but the cooling-off period is now a little prolonged, and too cool. I'm ready to go again. HoJo was absolutely right about my pulling right shoulder, but it's not as easy to correct as telling myself, "Don't do it anymore." I'm working on it in batting practice, but I can't effectively concentrate on a technical point during the game.

Padre manager Dick Williams doesn't hurt my rehabilitation by leaving Tim Stoddard in to die in the eighth and ninth innings. I've had trouble with Stoddard in the past, but he has nothing tonight. We nail him for eight hits in the two innings. These episodes make me glad I'm not a pitcher. Batters don't know an equivalent misery. We usually get to wait a couple of innings before looking bad again. The pitcher in trouble has no such reprieve. An equivalent torture for the hitters might be this change in the rules: If you strike out, hit again; strike out again, hit again; do it till you get it right.

No, thank you.

The game demonstrates the importance of inspiration for a ballclub. The double play in the field yesterday unquestionably carried over into our half of that inning, and into our attack today. We've bounced back from that doubleheader. We're resilient, but this I've known since early in the year.

Mike Lupica in the *Daily News* calls Davey's controversial decision to have Darryl bunt the other night "dumb." That's the general public assessment. My last word is this: Don't hold your breath waiting for Darryl's next bunt.

GAME 123—Mets 9
Padres 3

AUGUST 26

It just goes to show. Up against Fernando Valenzuela, resilience doesn't have a prayer. Freddie will win every time. I finally get a hit off him in the ninth inning; the pitch is only the second strike to me all night that's not on the black, and if he didn't have a 6–1 lead at the time, this strike would most likely have been on the black, too. Fernando has better control of more pitches than any pitcher in our league. I don't say better pitches. Dwight's curve and fastball are better, but he doesn't have Fernando's variety of pitches, all thrown where he wants them. Valenzuela is the left-handed Juan Marichal. He and Gooden are the two pitchers in the league to whom the batters doff their caps and say, almost with pride, "Here's to you." If the Cards' John Tudor keeps up the remarkable control next year he has exhibited this year, he'll become the third pitcher in this elite.

"Your friends are back." Bob Davidson, the umpire at first, points them out for me. Ah, yes, in the stands enjoying the contest are my two pals from doubleheader night. Smarter by two days, I don't make the mistake of acknowledging their presence, and they wind down as the innings roll past. My concern now is that these yahoos are season ticket holders, and intend to use their tickets most of the remaining games. I don't remember when a belligerent fan has rankled me as effectively as these two did the other night, to the point where I wondered whether they were disrupting my play.

Program note: Eddie Haas is finally fired by the Braves, after they lose twelve of thirteen games. I saw this coming way back.

GAME 124—Dodgers 6
Mets 1

AUGUST 27

Suddenly, our resilience has evaporated. Jerry Reuss does a number on me, on us. We just can't hit the ball until the ninth inning. I lift one almost to the wall in left-center for an out, then Strawberry hits it over that wall. But it's not enough.

I know I'm swinging fairly well, but doubt—anxiety?—is

creeping in. I need to get hot again. The club is muddling along. We're heading for the dangerous West Coast.

GAME 125—Dodgers 2
Mets 1

AUGUST 29—SAN FRANCISCO

Dad says there's nothing wrong with me technically—I'm a little too crouched, a little too tense; that's all. Be like a tiger, Keith; poised, yes, but not paralyzed. Rip the bat.

I tell Aguilera the same thing before today's game. Throw the damn ball, Rick. Cut it loose. You've got eight good fielders out there. And Rick does throw well for his six innings. McDowell pitches well. Orosco pitches well. HoJo pinch-hits a triple in the ninth inning and scores on Backman's fly to tie the game at three. That makes two games in ten days that HoJo has saved with a late clutch hit. But Leach doesn't pitch well and we lose on a homer by Chili Davis in the bottom of the tenth. That makes two games in ten days we have lost anyway, after HoJo has saved them with late clutch hits.

We achieve this outcome despite numerous doubtful Giant plays on the bases: Playing for one run in the first inning, Trillo bunts after Gladden leads off with a double (playing for one run early against Gooden makes good sense; otherwise?); Gladden trying to steal home in that first inning, and Aguilera calmly throwing a strike to Carter for the tag; Youngblood, not a really fast runner, is caught stealing in the second; Youngblood is picked off second by Carter in the fifth.

Meanwhile, Aguilera gets down the sacrifice with two strikes in the second, and Santana then scores on Backman's single.

The point: As of the fifth inning, the Mets have executed better and capitalized on opportunities and lead 2–0. We're playing well and leading; we should take the game. But the Giants score twice in the sixth and go on to win.

In the seventh, with Frank Williams pitching, we get a rally going and I come up with runners on second and third. Manager Davenport brings in a fresh lefty, Mark Davis, one of the tougher relievers around, averaging almost eleven strikeouts per nine innings. His curves eat me alive. I'm an average strikeout.

My battle with the bat this afternoon is a rough one, 0-for-5, two strikeouts, only one well-hit ball. Their starting pitcher, Atlee Hammaker, is the seventh left-hander of the last nine starters against us. Why kid myself? Despite my confidence against left-handers, right now they're giving us trouble—me and the team. I'm not handling the curveball because I'm not waiting on the pitch.

GAME 126—Giants 6
Mets 3

AUGUST 30

The sixth inning tonight in the wet cold at Candlestick may be one of those I look back on after the season and label "crucial." I drive in Backman with a single to right. Normally not that exciting, but special tonight because I have, for the second time in two months, made a radical modification in my stance. Mike Krukow, the Giant starter, is a right-hander with a wicked off-speed curve. The pitch is the equivalent of Sid's, but from the other side. As an adjustment this at-bat, I move up in the box, with my right foot about an inch in front of the plate. The catcher Brenly can't miss this maneuver; plus, he might have read or heard that I move up in the box against Sutter, to catch his split-fingered fastball before the break. I hope he sees my adjustment; I hope he believes I'm ready for the curve and will call fastballs and sliders. That's what he does. I see all sliders and hit a bastard on a 1-and-2 count for the RBI.

Brenly, I deked you out? Maybe. The curve is the one pitch I didn't want to see in that situation.

Is this another crucial game? We certainly can't afford to let this road trip get off to an 0–2 start. Who's pitching? Darling. And with the Mets ahead 2–1 in the ninth, thanks to another HoJo clutch hit in our half of the inning, Darling gets out of a bases-loaded jam with nobody warming in the bullpen. I'm shocked that the bullpen is quiet. Davey must be telling Ronnie something: Mature as a pitcher right now. Our manager is according Darling the Dwight Gooden honor: total confidence—this in a game in which Ronnie has walked six batters.

This is beyond rolling the dice. This is brinksmanship. After the game, Dad and Gary inform me that the many Met fans were murmuring throughout the inning, "Why isn't anybody even warming? What's going on?"

But Davey's gutsy confidence in Ronnie pays off, and who knows, it might make Darling an even better pitcher. It can't hurt. At any rate, it's the fourth big game he's won for us this season.

GAME 127—Mets 2
Giants 1

AUGUST 31

And today, enthusiastic about my new position in the box, I stink against Jim Gott and strike out twice. Come on!

We get only six hits. Dwight loses his fourth game, shocking the nation. The Mets are treading water.

Steve Marcus writes in *Newsday*:

"Backman has temporarily replaced the slumping Keith Hernandez as the team's chief spokesman. Hernandez has not set an example worth following, with one hit in thirteen at-bats, and one RBI in his last seventeen games. When Hernandez was having a great season last year he was in a better position to speak out. At this point he is trying to discern his own flaws."

Keith Hernandez writes in his book:

Wally is talking more, and more cogently, because he's feeling more like a veteran on the team. He's more secure. He understands more. I have talked to the press every day of the season, giving them whatever they've asked for. I'm responsive and seldom surly. They ask for more when I'm hot; they pay less attention at other times—until I really stink and they're attracted to the carcass. I'll get hot again this season and they'll climb back on the bandwagon.

Marcus's paragraph is a cheap shot, and I don't like it.

I'm convinced that the writers this week are itching to report back to Gotham the demise of the Mets on our West Coast swing. It's in the air (the itch, not the demise), mainly because it would be the juiciest story at the moment. However, should we revive and stomp everyone in the rest of the games out here, the writers will report this turnaround just as enthusiastically because they'll be able to fan the "pennant-contending" fires.

It's not their fault. They're not paid to give a damn about the Mets. They're paid for their *stories*. They also sense that a second story is developing out here, and they're already searching for tidbits. It looks like I'm going to Pittsburgh soon to testify in the drug case.

GAME 128—Giants 3
Mets 2

SEPTEMBER 1

I hit .265 for the month of August, with most of that production in the first two weeks. My batting season shapes up thusly:

April:	.309,	12 RBIs
May:	.241,	10 RBIs
June:	.232,	7 RBIs
July:	.392,	29 RBIs
August:	.265,	11 RBIs

Because there's a 160-point difference between my high and low months, does it follow that I'm a streak-hitter? No. Prior to this year, I have been a consistent hitter who enjoyed some very hot streaks but none of the horrendous slumps that plague the true streak-hitter. My June slump this year was a new experience. Never to be repeated, let's hope.

I'm on the bench today, and not happy about it. Davey says I'm slow with the bat and need a day off. Maybe I do, but I'm working on this new position in the box, and I can't work on it if I'm not playing. When Darryl comes down with this flulike bug going around and has to be scratched, I go to Davey again and ask him to put me in.

"No. Take the day."

He has in mind that we face yet another left-hander, Dave LaPoint, and Davey has witnessed my difficulties with lefties recently.

Joining me on the bench this afternoon are Mookie and Bruce Berenyi, activated because this is September 1, the date when rosters can grow from twenty-five to forty players. Bruce is the forgotten man on the club—after starting the season as our third starter. The shoulder is fine, he and the doctors report, but I don't think he'll start any more games this year. Relief, maybe. Mookie's shoulder is much better, but he still has to be worried about it.

Should it recover completely, Met management has a very tough choice next year—perhaps even this month. Will they platoon the two center fielders, Wilson and Dykstra? Trade one of them? It's a difficult decision, from one point of view; a luxury, from another.

I know this: Neither man will ever be happy on the bench as a "role player." Dykstra is frustrated now because he's being platooned with Paciorek, and we're facing so many left-handers Lenny is sitting a lot. A reporter asked him why he's not playing more against left-handers. Dykstra replied, "I guess he [Davey] wants to make the race as close as possible." That remark can be read three ways: Playing Paciorek keeps us close, or not playing Dykstra keeps us from running away with it, or Lenny was misquoted. He's brash; he probably said it. No big deal.

The biggest problem with platooning Paciorek and Dykstra, in my opinion, is the weakening of the right-handed-hitting bench when Paciorek starts. It is not stupid to say that some players mean more to their team on the bench than on the field. I'd start Dykstra against all but the toughest left-handers.

The ballgame. Nothing wrong with us that some hitting wouldn't correct, but we can't generate hits when we need them. In the eighth inning, with the first two men on base, Davenport brings in Scott Garrelts to relieve LaPoint and Garrelts merely strikes out the side—the side being our three power hitters, Carter, Foster, Strawberry. Whew!

It's not often that I get the perspective from the bench. Today, it's not an enjoyable one. We're looking at leaving San Francisco 1-and-3 for the trip and heading for the tough clubs in San Diego and Los Angeles trailing St. Louis by three or four games. I can hear the big black birds circling overhead right now.

The luxury their two relievers—Garrelts and Davis—give the Giants cannot be overestimated. But their miserable record goes to show that short relievers aren't effective if you don't have the lead in the late innings. No matter how well they pitch, it's too late to help. Atlanta and Bruce Sutter are proving the same thing.

It hasn't been pointed out by the press, at least not very strongly, but the truth is the Mets are by far the best team in the National League with questionable relief pitching. Our relievers' ERA at this point is one of the highest in the league. The work out of the pen has been spotty; brilliant in streaks, then so-so. The work in the batter's box has been spotty. Starting pitching has carried the Mets this year.

Today, the relieving is okay. Sisk is an interesting choice to take over from Lynch in the seventh inning, considering the importance of the game, McDowell's freshness, and Davey's recent statements about Doug. But Sisk holds the Giants for two innings. We enter the ninth down 3–1.

HoJo pinch-hits a double, a blooper. Staub, also pinch-hitting, drives him home with a hard double in the gap. Mookie now comes off the bench for only his second at-bat in two months, and he bloops the ball down the left field line for a wind-blown Candlestick hit.

But on the play, Larry Bowa, running for Staub at second base, rounds the bag at third too far and is thrown out trying to get back. Bowa and third-base coach Harrelson feel like shit right now. The comeback is in jeopardy.

Runner on second, one out, one run behind. Davey sends up the third pinch hitter of the inning: me. Davenport goes to the bullpen for Mark Davis, who has handled me twice in the series on a strikeout and a weak roller.

I have no explanation for what happens next. Let's face it, the odds aren't good for me: I'm struggling at the plate, facing a good pitcher, an important game on the line. However, I'm fairly loose as I approach the plate, formulating my plan. The plan I come up with is simple: Get a hit, tie the game.

I get looser with every pitch, and even with the count 2-and-2, I'm still loose. The laws of nature dictate that with two strikes I should get antsy. Instead, I go the other way. No explanation. And I decide to take a page from Davey's book. I'll roll the dice. I'm going to look for the curve on this pitch.

Davis throws a curve. From my hiding place in the high weeds, I swing. The result is one of the three longest home runs of my career—the only ball I've hit into the upper-deck seats anywhere. (I've reached the facing of the upper deck in St. Louis twice, once off Orosco, once off Mike Scott.)

Ah, the joy in Mudville this day. The Mets escape from the city by the bay with a split of the series.

Can one swing turn around a season for a team? I don't know, but I do know that every championship team has to have a couple of come-from-behind victories in September. In this one, four guys came off the bench—Johnson, Staub, Wilson, and myself—and four guys delivered. It's a great win for us.

Can one swing turn around a hitter? Absolutely. I've come out of slumps or minislumps with just one correct swing. The swing today may be the best I've ever executed. The day off may have helped. What if I had talked Davey into letting me start the game? Would I be writing a different story right now? Yes. Would it be as satisfying? Probably not.

Jerry Azar, the sportscaster on Channel 7 (ABC) in New York, is traveling with the team, and in the general crush after the game he asks me about Davey's recent remark to the effect that as Keith Hernandez goes, so go the Mets. I'm humble in my reply, naturally. The key point is that I'm the no. 3 hitter. Any no. 3 hitter is the most important hitter in the lineup, for reasons explained earlier. I extend rallies or slow them down, but the success of the Mets does not revolve around me or anyone else—among the starting eight. Without question, we couldn't win the pennant without Doc.

Harrelson and Bowa tease me about saving their asses after the baserunning mistake at third base. I call Larry "Angry Man" because he never smiles during the game. I've warned him that I'm going to get him to smile on the field one day. Angry Man insists on treating me to dinner this evening in San Diego, after the carefree flight down from San Francisco. And a satisfying meal it is after a satisfying and surprising day. I have just one regret: Due to circumstances beyond everyone's control, my parents and brother weren't in the stands to see the home run. They suffered with me through three days of frustration. I wish they could have witnessed my rebuttal.

GAME 129—Mets 4
Giants 3

SEPTEMBER 2—SAN DIEGO

My concern going into tonight's game against the Padres is remembering the feeling of that one swing yesterday afternoon. Batting practice is fine, but that doesn't necessarily translate. As it turns out, I have no cause for concern. I've never felt better at the plate. I know the mold, I step inside and close the door behind me and lock it and throw away the key. The mold is as comfortable as a rocking chair. The rocking chair is moved up in the box, with my right foot in front of the plate an inch. I rock gently as I wait on the pitch with the Buddha's patience.

Dad's message has made it through loud and clear: Just relax, Keith.

Another factor working for me in the game: Last night I was sick as a dog with chills and flu misery—they could have used me for the TV ads—and I still am. I've picked up whatever knocked out Straw in San Francisco. I know, however, that feeling lousy works *for* me as often as not (the hangover syndrome). Tonight, it certainly does. And another thing: My brother is in the stands.

First inning, single off Thurmond (last week at Shea, he got away with his junk; tonight we bomb him out with four ropes in the first inning). Second, single off DeLeon for an RBI. Fourth, single off Walter. Seventh, single off Patterson. Eighth, home run off Patterson, two RBIs. All five hits are about as hard as I can hit the ball. Hurdle tells me it's the greatest performance he's seen against left- and right-handed pitching, better even than anything he witnessed from George Brett while Clint was with Kansas City. Frankly, I'm not inclined to doubt it. As a hitter this one evening, I feel practically perfect.

The team is not far behind, as we explode for eighteen hits and twelve runs. Seven of the hits, six of the runs come off left-hander Bob Patterson, making his major-league debut. Last week Dick Williams left Tim Stoddard in to die, tonight Patterson is the sacrificial victim; dubious strategy, to me, when dealing with a guy just starting his big-league career; there's such a thing as shell shock. But the bombardment is just what the Mets need. We scrounged out two wins in San Francisco, now we need an explosion and get it.

We're also inspired by another Cardinal loss, which we watched on the tube during batting practice. The Cards have dropped four of five, proof that they're missing Jack Clark, who's out for a couple of weeks at least with rib problems. We're only one behind. Right now, I ask one thing of this season. Let it stay close enough so it will mean something when the Cards lose a couple in a row this month, as they will, as the Mets will. Then we'll see whether the orifice on their backsides puckers. Ours won't.

The beneficiary of the hitters' largest tonight is Sid the Squid

Fernandez, operating with a sizable lead for the first time this year, I believe. When the score climbs to 10–1, I ask him how it feels. A huge grin spreads across his face as he replies, "Great." Some pitchers would try to be tough in the situation: It's not over till the fat lady sings, the last man is out, and all that. Not Sid. He's happy and why hide it? He coasts to the checkered flag and his first complete-game victory.

Bowa wants to treat me to dinner again, but I have to decline. I have other things to do. I return to my room, don my long-sleeve warmup jersey, turn off the air-conditioner, crack the window and sweat out this fever. Yet another remedy from home. The fever was great for one game, but I'll be worn out tomorrow if I don't get rid of it.

GAME 130—Mets 12
Padres 4

SEPTEMBER 3

Better, but still lousy this morning after a wet night. And the die is cast: A series of phone calls verifies that I have to testify tomorrow in Pittsburgh. The prosecutor won't let me wait until Thursday, our day off out here. So I'll fly across the country tonight, go straight onto the stand, and fly back to Los Angeles, missing our final game here tomorrow evening. I'll feel shitty if we lose. Nor do I want to have two days off in a row, not when I'm red hot, not when we're due to face Roy Lee Jackson, who pitched well against us at Shea. I'd like another shot at him.

I believe I'll keep the groove even with the disruption. I can pretend we've been rained out. Acts of God. The truth is, however, I'll miss the game because of the acts of Hernandez three years ago, and now I have to wash that laundry in public. Fair enough.

At the ballpark, we're still hot. Carter is on fire as he hits three long homers his first three at-bats, Strawberry adds one. I love it. With two outs in the first, left-hander Dravecky blatantly pitches around me, the left-handed hitter he should prefer over Carter. Gary takes him over the wall. Don't the Padres know he hit three homers in San Francisco? They forget sometimes, these pitchers, but not often: My walk total is way down this year (I won't be near my usual 100 or so), because the hitters behind me are too good. I should get 600 official at-bats for the first time since 1979.

And with Carter and Strawberry hitting homers against these left-handers, the managers may change their strategy about hoarding left-handers until the Mets come to town. Hell, ten of the last fourteen starters have been southpaws. The managers are thinking that lefties make Backman bat from his weaker right side (it's so weak, he'll try hitting left-handed against left-handers in spring training next year), get Dykstra out of the lineup, confront Hernandez and Strawberry with problems. It all makes sense— but we're 34–19 against left-handers. When we're hitting, it doesn't matter. That's one of the major assets of our left–right–left–right batting order in the three-through-six slots.

In the last inning, I'm the third out on a 3-and-2 strikeout. A reporter asks, "Do you feel bad Gary didn't get a chance at his fourth homer?"

I hadn't even thought about it! It never crossed my mind he would have had the opportunity. If it had, I don't know what I could have done. I was going hard for another hit, anyway. I wanted to head out on a good note.

GAME 131—Mets 8
Padres 3

6. HARDBALL

SEPTEMBER 4—PITTSBURGH

Leave San Diego at 11:30 p.m., lose three hours to the clock, arrive in Chicago at 5:00 a.m., lay over until 7:00, arrive Pittsburgh 9:30 a.m. Find out immediately that I won't get called today, after all. They're still selecting the jury. Wonderful. I'll miss tonight's game for nothing. If I had known, if they had told me, I could have played in San Diego tonight, flown out, and been here ready to testify tomorrow.

As it is, I kill the day in my hotel room, where I'm registered under the name Keith Thompson. Despite being dead tired and still fighting the flu, I stay up late for the baseball scores on television.

Truly, my main concern about giving this testimony is what the Mets do in the game I miss (or games; there's no guarantee I'll testify tomorrow), and how these lost days will affect my groove. What if we lose a game or two in my absence, and then lose the division by that same number of games? To say that I'd feel badly is not to say that I believe I would have made the difference in the losses. But I am swinging well now and should be able to help the team. I urge the Mets to win tonight!

What about my reputation? Psychological effects of all this publicity on myself? On the team?

I'm not worried about it. I've made a mistake; many, many other decent people have made the same mistake. I'm going to wear the hair shirt in public; they're not. I'm not ashamed of myself for what I've done. Using cocaine in the early 1980s when it was the drug of choice in the United States—just as pot was ten years earlier—is not the gravest of sins, I believe. Getting involved was a bad, bad mistake. It was stupid. It hurt me and, indirectly, other people. I surely have nothing to be proud of. However, there are matters more grievous for myself and issues on the national scene of more importance than first baseman Keith Hernandez's flirtation with cocaine three, four, five years ago.

Mom, Dad, and Gary know what happened. They're prepared for the firestorm of publicity that's about to engulf me, and they can handle it. Jessi is the only one of the kids old enough to understand what's happening. In fact, I am concerned about her.

The Mets won't be affected at all by this publicity, except to the extent that it affects me. They—we—are trying to win a pennant, period. I've told quite a few of the guys what to expect. I've told Davey Johnson. Frank Cashen knows.

At last. The sportscaster comes on . . . and the Mets won big tonight, with two more homers from Carter. I heave a sigh of relief and turn off the TV. Tomorrow is the day.

GAME 132—Mets 9
Padres 2

SEPTEMBER 5

No, it's not. I'm at the courthouse at 10:00 a.m., sitting in an office, waiting. Seven hours later, I'm still in the same office, still waiting. I don't get called to the stand today.

So there goes the plan to give my testimony, fly to Los Angeles tonight and get some rest before the first game tomorrow night against the Dodgers. The question now is whether I'll finish testifying tomorrow in time to make it to the game at all. The enforced layoff is now two days.

Back at the hotel, I watch the evening news. The lead story is Lonnie Smith's testimony today admitting that he used cocaine, in the company of Keith Hernandez, among others. According to NBC, CBS, and ABC, this revelation is the most important news happening anywhere in the world today.

Well, if there's nothing worse going on than my own and other professional baseball players' problems with cocaine several years ago, the planet is in better shape than I thought it was.

Don't get me wrong: I'm not downplaying the importance of assuring the integrity of the game, or the importance of baseball players as role models for kids. I'm merely pointing out, in this context, that neither of these issues is the reason the Pittsburgh trial is the biggest story of the day. If these issues were the reason for the coverage, the networks and newspapers would put the story in context. Instead, they'll wring it for all the juice it might contain, and then drop it.

SEPTEMBER 6

On bright days, I usually wear sunglasses. I have them on this morning as I approach the federal courthouse. Turning the corner of the building, I see the security cops, the pack of reporters and photographers. Is the whole world watching?

Wait a minute. I take off the sunglasses. Here you go, fellas, it's Keith *Hernandez* of the New York Mets. Keith *Thompson* just checked out of the William Penn hotel.

The photographers tumble back on themselves as I advance down the sidewalk. They fall back as though I were a tidal wave. Watch carefully on your VCR tapes of the footage of me walking alongside the building—all the networks used the same shot. See me glancing quickly to my left, and slightly behind, and notice just the hint of a smile, perhaps a smirk? Two photographers are arguing over turf, and they've started fighting—actually exchanging punches, right at the edge of the sidewalk, as I stride past them into the courthouse. Here I am, very, very tense, about to raise my right hand and swear on a Bible in public for the first time in my life, about to be made a spectacle of before the country, and the scene that ushers me in is like a sudsy Friday night at Shea. The main difference is, these two guys are fighting over a piece of *me*.

Why did I use cocaine?

The standard answers play a part: I had more money than I had ever known; I had a lot of free time; a baseball season is an emotional roller coaster; my marriage was in trouble.

I also think my basic personality might have led me to try cocaine: I was never one to look before I leaped, and this impulsiveness got me into trouble as a kid and in the minor leagues, several times, and it did so again in 1980.

It's this simple: The drug was there, I tried it. That sounds awfully stupid, and it was. I was a young man making a young man's bad mistake.

I have two regrets about my testimony in the courtroom.

First, I regret my use of the words "massive" and "demon." I have no idea why I said them. My use of cocaine was never massive. If the phrase I used, "a demon within me," is interpreted to mean I was addicted—well, I never should have used it, and don't know why I did. The clinical term describing my cocaine abuse in 1980, '81 and '82 is "recreational use," unfortunate and self-serving as the connotations may be. It makes me wince even to think about the harsh description invoked by the defense attorney: I was not, by any stretch of any imagination, a "junkie." I could not have hit .321 and almost won the batting title in 1980 if I had been using large amounts of any drug. I hit at least .300 every month of that season.

The next two years, 1981 and 1982, were the most difficult of my professional career—and, perhaps, of my life off the field, too. My marriage, never strong to begin with, was disintegrating. The strike in 1981 disrupted the year and sapped me of some of my ballplaying desire. But I hit .306.

While 1982 was a great year for the Cardinals, culminating in the World Series victory, it was tough for me. But I hit .299 and drove in 94 runs in that championship season.

My second regret from the testimony is the "40 percent" figure I used to describe the number of players using cocaine in the romance period, the early 1980s. I believe that I testified to something like "40 percent, probably less," but "40 percent" is the figure that sticks with the public. How could I know what the percentage was?

Whatever the number of users, I was one of them. Should I therefore be suspended from baseball?

I agree with Peter Ueberroth, who says he is out to end the use of drugs, not to punish people. The use of cocaine in major-league baseball was way down before these Pittsburgh proceedings. Lee MacPhail, the labor negotiator for the club owners and formerly president of the American League, acknowledged this point in a small box attached to the long stories about drugs in baseball in *The New York Times*. If I hadn't finally realized the jeopardy in which I was placing myself, the prison sentences handed down in 1983 would have done the trick. I believe they opened a lot of eyes around the league.

One final point: Let's not hold professional baseball to a higher standard than everyone else is subject to. As a ballplayer, that's all I ask. Yes, baseball is a national pastime, but there are others; yes, the players serve as role models for Little Leaguers, but so do many other figures in our public life. Let's not get too hypocritical as we beat up on baseball in the coming weeks and months. The drug problem in America is across-the-board.

Major-league baseball has provided the fans with over a century's worth of entertainment, with only isolated embarrassments, and it will continue to do so.

I walk out of the courtroom at 2:30 p.m., catch the four o'clock flight to Los Angeles, ride to Dodger Stadium with the Dodgers' Enos Cabell (also in Pittsburgh testifying, also on the same flight). I thought an eighteen-inning ballgame was tough on mind and body, but it pales in comparison to my three hours on the stand in Pittsburgh. Together with the two long plane flights, the lost day waiting, the lingering flu, and the emotional pressure throughout, it all adds up to an utterly drained Keith Hernandez.

I walk into the Met dugout in the bottom of the fourth inning.

Hey, Keith. You okay?

Everything okay?

Welcome home, pilgrim.

With these brief encouragements my teammates greet the return of their first baseman. Then the subject is dropped. We're playing a baseball game.

However, I can't pretend that my mind is 100 percent back into the game at hand. But it's close, and it's helped a great deal by the game itself: Gooden versus Valenzuela, scoreless when I arrive, scoreless when Gooden departs in the ninth, Valenzuela in the eleventh.

Paciorek saves the game in the eighth inning with a marvelous diving catch on a ball over his head, off the bat of Mariano Duncan. In the ninth, Dwight's last inning, he fans Pedro Guerrero on a 3-and-2 pitch, and Carter throws out Mike Marshall, running on the full count. Strike 'em out, throw 'em out, guys!

My turn for heroics comes in the tenth, pinch-hitting for Doc, with Santana on first and one out.

"Think I'll get booed?" I ask Mel Stottlemyre.

"Fuck those people!" he replies. I appreciate this.

But I'm nervous, with no idea what to expect in Los Angeles. Fifty-fifty: some cheers of encouragement, some boos, most of the people sitting on their hands.

What are my chances in this situation? I haven't swung at a ball in three days. I'm still sick. I'm facing Tom Niedenfuer, who throws hard.

When I say I'm seeing double at the plate, it's no metaphor.

I am seeing double. Niedenfuer is *here*; a blink of the eye and he's *there*. I hit into a double play.

After the Dodgers squander good scoring chances in the eighth, tenth, and eleventh innings, we win in the twelfth when Darryl hits a ground-rule double to the opposite field. Even though I'm on base after only a fielder's choice, scoring the winning run is a gratifying way to return to the action.

Forty—no less than forty—reporters are waiting in the clubhouse. I take one look at the horde and head the other way. They're not interested in this great ballgame; they want the nitty-gritty regarding Pittsburgh. I'm not giving it to them. He'll have no comment tonight, fellas: Jay Horwitz conveys the bad news.

(What does this say about it all: My testimony today is dropped to second billing on the network news; an airplane crash is the lead story.)

GAME 133—Mets 2
Dodgers 0

SEPTEMBER 7

Clearly, I have to make some statement to the fans. I want to. The Mets want me to. Jay suggests a meeting with the New York reporters in a room in the hotel. I'll make a statement but answer no questions. In Pittsburgh I answered all the questions I intend to for a while. I'm not going to let this drag on and on. I write the statement myself—not my lawyer or agent or anyone else. I say what has to be said, what I want to say, and all I feel I should say.

Quote:

There was a time in my life when I did a stupid thing. In 1980. This was when I was separating from my wife and went through a crazy period in my life.

I'm sorry if I caused any embarrassment to the Mets or the St. Louis Cardinals and to baseball fans in general, particularly Mets fans.

I was never an everyday user, never enough to have to check into a rehabilitation center. I corrected the problem myself in the early part of 1983. Since early 1983 I have not used the drug.

It's a chapter in my life that is closed, one that I'm not proud of.

All I'm concerned about now is winning a division title for the Mets and the New York fans.

Cocaine is a dead-end street. If I can be an example for young kids, as far as drugs are concerned, then don't mess with them. They're a dead-end street. It took me two-and-a-half years to get away.

My advice to everyone is to stay away from drugs.

Today's game—nationally televised, just my luck—is set for a 1:20 start. The team bus leaves the hotel at noon. I walk into the dugout forty-five minutes later to find three camera crews set up on the field right in front of the dugout. All they want is to shoot me, sitting there. Thanks anyway, guys. Jay Horwitz runs them off.

Vin Scully of NBC reads a large part of my statement during the broadcast, and I thank him after the show.

Joe Garagiola is another matter: He observes that Hernandez is a good "contact" hitter who "sprays" the ball to all fields.

I don't "spray" the ball with good "contact," Joe. I *drive* it. Kick a guy when he's down!

Batting practice today tells me one thing: The "perfect" swing I had is gone. I feel alright, but the rocking chair is creaking. In fact, Garagiola may be right for a day or two—I hope no longer. I may have to settle for decent contact, and not worry much about driving the ball.

The game is rolling along in the sixth inning, Mets up 4–2, when Mariano Duncan comes up for the third time. During his second at-bat, he was wolfing Lynch, our starter.

"Throw something hard, Lynch."

"Throw the ball, Lynch."

Eddie heard Duncan's taunts, and blew them off. It's bush and stupid to harass the pitcher from the batter's box (from the dugout is less hazardous to your health). But Duncan is in a bad slump and these "comfortable" outs off Lynch are all the more frustrating.

This third time up for Duncan, Lynch strikes him out and makes him look bad. As Duncan heads back to the dugout, Lynch can't resist a taunt. Hell, the kid deserves it. He can dish it out. Let's see if he can take it as well.

"Grab some pine!" Eddie hollers.

It's an old baseball phrase, and a good one, even though now an anachronism because the benches are padded.

Duncan jerks around and cusses Eddie. Eddie cusses back and adds, "Come on out!" and gestures with his hand.

This is too much. Duncan charges. All I can figure is he doesn't know that Ray Knight, playing third base and moving to quickly intervene, was a Gold Glove boxer. Ray can tap dance all over your face. (I've heard he did a number on Cesar Cedeno.)

Knight grabs Duncan, a major-league mismatch. The benches clear. For some reason, Strawberry goes bananas, and I have to restrain him. After five minutes of milling, everybody goes back where they belong.

Fights between baseball teams are an interesting phenomenon. With hockey, I can understand it, given the level of violence in the game itself. By the same token, I don't understand why there aren't more fights between football players.

Baseball is such a genteel game by comparison. Ballplayers are friendly with opposing players, chatting with them before, even during the games, and dining with them later. So why the bench-clearing brawls? Where does the animosity come from?

There is no animosity, with rare exceptions. If beanballs have started the episode, the batter involved is genuinely mad, but the benches clear mainly for reasons of peer pressure—team solidarity. We don't want to fight the other guys. "Bench-clearing brawl" is almost always a misnomer. The benches cleared, but there wasn't any brawl. Just a lot of milling around.

There are, however, on every team, a couple of guys who just like to fight, and they come out wild-eyed. The rest of us try to protect these guys from hurting themselves or anyone else. This said, I should add that there are a few players around the league I wouldn't mind punching if they gave me a good reason.

I was caught in the middle of a fight in 1975, when I played the first half of the year with the Cardinals before being sent down. Lynn McGlothen was pitching for us, the benches cleared following a series of brushbacks, and Dave Kingman charged McGlothen. Our catcher, Ted Simmons, dove after Kingman, but Dave ducked under him and kept coming. I stepped in next and grabbed his shirt as he bowled me over. By myself I was doomed but reinforcements soon arrived.

This afternoon in Los Angeles, Lynch is truly angry with Duncan, who was bush all the way. It's no secret: Eddie is sensitive to the charge that, for being such a big guy, he doesn't throw very hard. He would have fought Duncan, gladly, if Knight hadn't intervened.

No punches are thrown, but the scuffle somehow wrenches Eddie's back. Davey takes him out after he finishes the inning. The Dodgers bang McDowell for three runs. Strawberry homers in the ninth to tie it. Then the Dodgers score one off Terry Leach to win the game. It's the fourth ineffective short stint by Leach since he threw the three-hit shutout as a starter about a month ago. Terry is not a short reliever. He's not geared to these situations. He's an ideal middle-inning man and spot starter.

The proof that my sweet swing has deserted me comes in the eighth inning. I pop out to the infield. It's been about three months.

GAME 134—Dodgers 7
Mets 6

September 8

Mookie Wilson is starting in center field—his first start since returning to the roster. Mookie, I believe, is the center fielder again. As good a job as Dykstra did filling in, Davey apparently feels that center field is Mookie's job. I concur. And Lennie can't gripe. He is, after all, a rookie. It won't hurt him to pay some dues.

Orel Hershiser for the Dodgers has the consistent sinker that McDowell seeks. Combined with a curveball, the pitch makes Orel as tough as any right-hander in the league, except Gooden. When I hit a double off him in the seventh, I can feel a semblance of the good swing returning. One good swing, that's all it may take; off a good pitcher, it's even more of a confidence-booster. The next inning, a hard single for an RBI proves my hunch. I'm okay. Yesterday's pop-up is history. Now we need to get this team rolling.

We get two runs in the eighth to go ahead, but Mike Marshall hits a two-run homer off Orosco to tie it. That's a homer off Jesse in each of his last three outings. He's lost his hard stuff. Thank goodness for the great breaking ball; but it's not enough, that's obvious.

Sid the Squid really has the buzzard's luck, doesn't he? Seven innings, five strikeouts, three hits, one run; that performance should be good for a victory, but it's another no-decision.

I fail to contribute in the tenth and eleventh innings, striking out against Powell and Diaz. Diaz, a left-hander, makes me look bad on three pitches, the first two, curveballs. Diaz is one of those rare pitchers against whom I have to look for the curve, he throws it so often, and effectively. I have to take my chances if he slips in a fastball. On a two-strike count, that's just what he does. I'm frozen. Caught looking. (If Mark Davis had thrown a fastball for a strike in San Francisco, instead of that curve I was betting on, the scorecard would read K instead of HR.)

Mookie homers in the top of the eleventh, and Sisk gets the victory with three ground balls in the bottom half.

Another storybook ending, for Mookie, for Doug. I've been urging Sisk to throw strikes, demanding that he throw strikes. Today, he throws strikes.

And kudos for Rick Aguilera, established now as a starter, thinking and preparing as a starter, but called on by Davey to pitch the ninth and tenth innings. Three strikeouts, no problems. I make it a point to detour past Rick's locker to congratulate him.

Now we can enjoy that charter back to New York. Seven wins out of ten on the West Coast is perfectly acceptable, especially considering that Doc didn't win a game. He had one loss, one no-decision.

Coming up, three packed-house games at Shea with the Cardinals. We're dead even, 82–53. This will be fun.

I hope. How will the fans at Shea greet their prodigal son?

GAME 135—Mets 4
Dodgers 3

SEPTEMBER 10—NEW YORK CITY

I thought I was ready for anything. Then most of the 50,000 fans in the stadium rise in a standing ovation. Some boos would not have surprised me. Encouraging applause, that I could understand. But as they rise and cheer, I'm stunned. Also, I'm trying not to pay much attention. We've got a ballgame here: on the mound, Danny Cox; on first base, Mookie; the score, 1–0, Cards. But the cheers are hard to ignore.

I don't believe the fans are saying with their greeting, "Well done, Keith, we approve."

They're saying, I hope, "You made a mistake. It's over. Some of us have made that mistake, and worse, and we're not subjected to this public scrutiny. We're okay, you're okay. Play ball."

This encouragement from the fans is greatly appreciated, to put it mildly. I need it! Thank you, New York. I have to take the first pitch in order to collect myself. Fastball, strike one. Now I get down to business.

What a thrill to be able to repay the fans with a hard single, driving in our first run with an assist from Vince Coleman, who slips in left field.

With two outs, I'm on second base. Cox pitches carefully to Strawberry with first base open. After two balls, Whitey holds up the four fingers. Put him on. This brings up Foster. Good strategy. George has been cold lately, Whitey knows. And Cox throws right and George bats right.

George is famous for his dawdling at the plate, holding up the pitcher before finally stepping into the box, suddenly stepping out just before the pitcher starts his windup. In this at-bat, he carries his behavior to extremes. He may be doing it on purpose to rattle the young pitcher. At any rate, Cox is rattled, angry, and throws his first pitch right at Foster and hits him on the ass. George usually flips the bat away disdainfully after being walked. But now, he carries the bat with him and points it at Cox. The umps rush in, some of the players rush out, but a brawl is defused before it gets going. The bases are now loaded for a left-handed batter, and a dangerous one: HoJo. Cox has made a terrible mistake. Retaliate for George's tactics later, if at all. Not now. He'll hear about it from Herzog.

The count on Johnson goes to 1-and-1. This is the key pitch in the game, as it turns out. Johnson is a dead fastball hitter. As ballplayers say, he can turn it around as well as anyone. Cox can throw the fastball or come in with the slider, and try to make it a strike. Standing on third base, I figure he has to throw the slider and hope hard that it's a strike. The slider misses high and away. Now on the 2-1 count, he must throw the fastball. A few pitchers in the league might throw their breaking ball on this count, but Cox isn't one of them, not in this situation. The pitch must be a strike.

No need to stop the game to tell Howard this. He knows the fastball is coming. I watch as Darrell Porter, the catcher, sets up on the outside corner. The ball, however, arrives on the inside half of the plate, and low. HoJo creams it for a grand slam.

The place goes wild. The fans are yelling again as we head onto the field for the second inning. Even one of the two guys who was berating me so unmercifully a couple of weeks ago is cheering me tonight as I trot to the bag. He holds up one finger in salute—the index finger.

Alas, few things come easy for the Mets these days. An hour's rain delay after the second inning deflates the tension of the game—before that, every pitch merited a cheer or a moan—and the Cards get back into it with three runs in the middle innings off Darling.

Darling, of course. If it's a big game, it's his turn—amazing how that has worked out this year.

(Coincidentally, Ronnie takes a turn in *The Times* today, authoring a brief guest column on the Op-Ed page on the subject of how to improve New York City. Among other measures, Ronnie proposes a domed stadium for Manhattan, perhaps downtown in the Wall Street area. Obviously, he doesn't feel as I do about domed stadiums, but pitchers have always liked the Astrodome, a paradise for them because it's so bad for hitters.)

Ronnie pitches a good game, McDowell saves beautifully. Roger comes on in the middle of the seventh inning and Davey makes a flip-flop in the lineup, bringing in Ray Knight to play third. It's the obvious move, allowing Roger a couple of innings on the mound before he comes up in the batting order, but the fans aren't happy. Ray is replacing the man who hit the grand slam. The fans aren't happy with Ray, period, and they let him know it when he strikes out. He's the designated goat this season. It has been a tough go for him, but it's not too late to contribute. He has contributed. Even with an average barely over .200, Ray has won some games with big hits. All in all, though, the year is tearing him up.

This game pretty well sums up the season of the two teams: the Mets with the long ball, getting ahead, the Cards coming back with singles, doubles, stolen bases, and scratched-out runs. They miss Jack Clark, who's still out with pulled rib muscles. Darrell Porter batting fourth against right-handed pitching will not win the pennant for them. Porter is batting like Knight: on the feeder, heading for the interstate.

Mets up by a game, but Cards battling.

I wonder what Whitey was thinking, sitting in the St. Louis dugout while the fans in New York cheered me. He took a great deal of heat for trading me, and now everyone seems certain that he made the trade because of my drug use. They congratulate him for never saying a word in his own defense, taking the heat in noble silence.

That's bullshit. I don't believe Whitey traded me because of my cocaine use. Two reasons:

1. If it was because of drugs, why didn't he trade Joaquin Andujar, who has been named by at least two players testifying in Pittsburgh as having used cocaine? If Whitey knew about me, he would have known about Joaquin. If he traded me on principle, that same principle would have dictated that he trade Joaquin. The fact of the matter is, you just don't trade twenty-game winners. They're too hard to come by.

2. He tried to trade me every year after he joined the club, in 1980. Bobby Valentine, former Met coach, told me that Herzog always tossed out my name in the winter meetings as a negotiable commodity. However, when Whitey called Frank Cashen in June 1983 to talk trade, he was not *dealing* Keith Hernandez. He was *seeking* Neil Allen. Cashen informed me later that their conversation went something like this:

When Whitey expressed interest in Allen, Frank asked, "Who for?" Whitey mentioned a couple of insignificant names. Cashen wasn't excited. Herzog said, "I'll get right back."

He called back in fifteen minutes. "How about Hernandez?"

Cashen almost fell out of his chair, literally, and then replied, "Let me call you back." Five minutes later Frank called Whitey and said, "You've got a deal."

If Whitey's primary goal was to trade me, why didn't he seek better personnel in the deal? He probably could have gotten them. No. He wanted Neil Allen, in a major error of judgment, it turned out. By offering Hernandez, he knew the trade would be made.

In fact, the White Rat got rid of me because he didn't like me. I didn't behave as he thought his ballplayers should, and I wasn't going to change for him. Whitey got rid of all the independent thinkers on the club. Jim Kaat and Gene Tenace, clear winners but guys who wouldn't march to Whitey's drummer: They were the first to go after the World Series in 1982.

And, as I have explained, 1981 and 1982 were difficult years for me, even though I performed well. Without my personal problems, maybe those seasons could have been even better, but Whitey drew a rash conclusion. Any way you look at it, that was a horseshit trade.

GAME 136—Mets 5
Cards 4

SEPTEMBER 11

I'm pissed at Dick Young. He can write whatever he wants about me—who gives a damn—but leave my family out of it. I don't appreciate his writing today, "He [Hernandez] was lucky to get away with only his family destroyed, not his career."

My personal life and my family are not your beat, Dick.

Word spreads in the clubhouse that Herzog fined Cox $1,000 for hitting Foster last night. It's the largest fine I've heard of; too large. Take it to the grievance committee, Danny. (Lynch has been fined $200 by the league office for his part in the fight in Los Angeles. He doesn't want to pay.)

Whitey sends up a brilliant batting order tonight against Dwight: Coleman, McGee, Herr, Van Slyke and Pendleton, one through five. All speed, contact hitters. Get on the bases and steal. In the absence of Clark, to hell with finding a substitute cleanup man. There won't be any cleaning up against Gooden, anyway. Hustle hard for one run at a time—especially when you've got John Tudor going. Right now, he's as likely to throw a shutout as Dwight.

The Mets counter with—high grass! I've never seen the lawn this high at Shea; it's as high as the infields at Wrigley and Candlestick. The idea, of course, is to slow down the ground balls, keep them in the infield—the opposite effect of artificial turf.

Also, the dirt around my base seems soft and loose, to keep the Cards from getting firm footing. Good going, groundkeepers. Is this unfair? Not unless Astroturf is.

In the bottom of the fourth inning, Diamondvision shows a replay of Pete Rose's record-breaking 4,192nd hit, and the fans give Pete a long-distance standing ovation. Even the Statue of Liberty goes down for maintenance and repairs, but Pete, he's eternally burning. The rest of us are not in his league.

Meanwhile, "uneventful" great pitching dominates at Shea. Dwight has command of his fastball and curve, Tudor has his uncanny control and change-up pitch. Against right-handed batters, I'm convinced he throws his fastball deliberately inside on a 1-and-1 count. Show the batter the hard stuff inside, keep him honest, but never give him that pitch to really hit. In his current groove, Tudor knows—he just knows—that he can paint the outside corner on the 2-and-1 count.

Recall Danny Cox's dilemma last night against HoJo on the 2-and-1 count: Cox had to throw the fastball for a strike, any strike. Tudor throws whatever pitch he wants for a strike on the corner at any point in the count. This, in a nutshell, is the difference between good and great major-league pitchers.

Tough as he is, I enjoy hitting against Tudor. He always has something in mind. But, like most pitchers (and their catchers), he can fall into patterns. Batters try to discern them. Even if we're successful, it doesn't mean we'll hit the good pitch. Tonight we don't. Pitching as he has for the last several months, I rate Tudor with the best left-handers I've faced: Rudy May (the best), Jerry Reuss when he was traded to the Dodgers, John Candelaria, and Jon Matlack with the Mets.

I've said it before: Good pitching is a challenge I enjoy; nevertheless, it's no fun getting beaten by these guys time after time. The writers ask me if tonight's almost-perfect Tudor is the same pitcher of recent years. I reply, "Ask Paciorek. He saw him in the American League, pitching for Boston."

Paciorek's answer is, "No. He's not the same."

As a bunter, however, Tudor still has something to learn. Witness the interesting eighth inning in the scoreless game. Gooden walks the seventh and eighth batters, Mike Jorgensen and Ozzie Smith, with nobody out. Uncharacteristic and unfortunate. Tudor comes up in this definite bunting situation. Without qualms I come down the line to within fifteen feet of the plate.

Only in September would I risk getting this close. I reason this way: In September, in a pennant race, neither Herzog nor Tudor (acting on his own) is going to risk hitting into a double play. Any other month, maybe; in September, they'll go with the "correct" percentage play, especially with all the Cards' speed and the top of the order coming up.

Tudor fouls Dwight's first pitch. Now Herzog has seen that I'm practically in front of the plate waiting for the bunt, but I still don't believe he'll take the bunt off. Tudor studies the signs at third base. If he's trying to deke me out, I don't buy it. At any rate, he squares too soon on the next pitch—just before Dwight begins his delivery. Then again, what is "too soon" against Gooden? Wait until the last moment and the ball will be in the catcher's mitt. I charge down the line again, watching the position of his bat. He might try to push the ball past me, but I can read the bat position easily: angled toward me, watch out; angled down the third-base line, that's where he's going with the bunt. Tudor aims the bat at third, so I keep coming. He gets the bunt down, but not hard enough to get past me. I'm almost waiting for it, right on the third-base line. Easy force at third.

A satisfying play and lots of fun. Tudor, standing on first after the fielder's choice, says, "Great play."

"You squared around too soon," I reply.

Now Ozzie Smith tries to steal third—and is out, or at least is called out on a close play. Card fans might question this strategy, but as I remark to the Cards' first-base coach, Nick Leyva, who played with my brother in the minors, "Why not? You guys live by the steal. Sometimes you'll die by it. Most of the time you'll live."

Leyva agrees. So does Whitey, I'm sure. But as a result Vince Coleman's double doesn't score anything. Then McGee walks, but Herr bounces out. The Cards end up the inning with three walks and a double, five total bases, and no runs. I'll bet that hasn't happened often to them this year.

We can't score either, and Dwight comes out after nine innings; Davey is always careful with Doc's twenty-year-old arm. Jesse serves up a homer to Cesar Cedeno, whom the Cards have just acquired from Cincinnati. This isn't the first game he has won for his new team. The homer comes on a two-strike count, and this isn't the first homer the opposition has hit off Met relievers on an 0-and-2 or 1-and-2 pitch. These mistakes (if they're mistakes; Cedeno hit a pretty good pitch, low and away) anger the fans more than the players. The players have sympathy. If someone pulls a mental boner, we might get a little mad, without saying anything. But on a pitch that gets away, well, it happens. Nobody intends to throw the ball squarely over the plate on a two-strike count.

Dwight, for his second consecutive outing, pitches nine scoreless innings and doesn't get a victory. For the record, I would have left him in, matching Tudor inning for inning. To hell with the number of pitches he had thrown. This is important; Dwight's arm can handle it. I'd say this even if we had won the game.

It's a difficult loss, but we're not gnashing our teeth and yanking our hair. Good game.

GAME 137—Cards 1
Mets 0

SEPTEMBER 12

Super Thursday, when the Mets play for the pennant against the Cards in the afternoon at Shea and the Yankees start a four-game battle for first place with Toronto tonight in The Bronx. Speculation about a Subway Series fills the papers again. I make this prediction: Either the Blue Jays or the Yankees will win three of their four games and go on to clinch the division fairly easily. Their series won't be an inconclusive 2–2 split.

For those readers with good memories: I acknowledge that my earlier assertion that the Yankees "aren't too good" was misinformed. I was also mistaken about the Padres, who have turned out to be less than the best in the West.

The three-game series between the Mets and the Cards, on the other hand, will not have a climactic impact on our pennant race. Going into the series, a 2–1 outcome was likely; now it's a certainty. Our race will go to the wire. If I ever believed the Cards would fold up, I don't anymore. They don't have that look, and their game is too resistant to slumps. On Astroturf, they'll get their ground-ball and high-hopper hits, then they'll steal, then they'll score. They manufacture runs like no team I've seen: walk, steal, steal, fly ball.

In this afternoon's first inning, Mookie, by working out a walk, verifies something I was just about to conclude anyway: He's more selective at the plate since his return. He saw Dykstra help the team with some strategic leadoff walks, and he realized he would get better pitches to hit by getting ahead in the count.

This ballclub had forgotten how valuable Mookie is. We thought choosing between Dykstra and Wilson might be a tough decision, but as good and invaluable a job as Dykstra did for us for almost two months, he's not Mookie Wilson; not yet, anyway.

And Mookie is strong and fresh. For him, this is July.

Five hits off Andujar follow Mookie's walk, and we score four times in the first. Wilson and Backman get hard hits in the second and Joaquin is gone—the worst performance I've seen from him since he became a true pitcher, in 1982. No thanks to me, we score twice more and lead 6–0 after two innings.

But Lynch also pitches the worst game I've seen from him, including several bad pitches on two-strike counts, and the Cards are back in the game, 6–5, after four innings. There's no getting around it: St. Louis is a dangerous, frustrating team to play. They keep coming; they never die.

I believe St. Louis would score more runs over a season than a lineup of the eight best home-run hitters in the game.

After our success off Andujar, we do nothing off one Pat Perry, in his first major-league appearance after a half-dozen years in the minors. Two hits in four innings off him, no runs. This newness actually gives him an advantage: We have no idea what to look for. How about Herzog pitching the rookie in this of all games? Despite our many differences, my admiration for Whitey as a field manager—and for putting together a practically new team after winning the World Series three years ago—knows no bounds.

Ninth inning. Jesse pitching with the Mets still leading by a run. Vince Coleman is out bunting to third—but the replay shows the ball bouncing off his helmet, then onto the field. Foul ball, but the umps don't see the ricochet. I don't see it. Herzog argues to no avail. Strange play. One out.

Two-ball, two-strike count on Willie McGee, switch-hitter batting from the right side, the batting championship sewed up, strong candidate for MVP. Carter sets up inside and I mutter, "Shit." If this is the fastball, Jesse had better get it in there, or we've got trouble.

In 1982, St. Louis catcher Gene Tenace told me he would never call for the inside pitch in a late-inning, potentially game-losing situation. Here's why: The pitcher is more likely to miss any pitch "away" from the batter. If he's aiming at the outside corner and misses away, it's a ball outside—and unhittable. Fine. But if he's going for the inside corner and misses away, the pitch is over the middle—a pitch that can beat you. Makes sense.

Also, Jesse's fastball runs away from right-handed hitters. For it to be on the inside corner as it passes the plate, it has to start two or three inches *inside* that corner, before running out to the inside black. If Jesse starts it off over the corner, it ends up toward the middle of the plate. Boom!

The pitch is the fastball. McGee hits it over the wall in left-center field. The game is tied on his ninth homer of the year. And another homer off Jesse. He's struggling.

Well, let's win it again, fellas. Mookie singles. Backman bunts him to second base. Hitless since my single in the first at-bat of the series, I have a chance to redeem myself. Ozzie Smith at shortstop is swung way over by second base, holding Mookie close. Pendleton at third is playing deep. The hole between short and third is big enough to accommodate the proverbial Mack truck. Coleman's position in left field says as much. He's shallow, hoping for a play at the plate if I single through the hole.

I'm looking for a pitch on the outer three-quarters of the plate to drive through that hole. The pitch I'm likely to pull off left-hander Ken Dayley is his curve, which I could hit hard. Porter and Dayley know this and would like to avoid it. Anyway, Dayley's best pitch is his ninety-plus heater. So I'm most likely to hit the ball to the left side, yet the Cards are giving me that side of the infield because of Mookie's base-stealing threat.

I stand more erect in the box than usual. When I'm having a bad day, I do this to help release some muscle tension and slow things down. Relax, relax, relax. Crouching has the opposite effect.

I swing through the first pitch for strike one. Dayley shakes off the next sign, but I don't believe him. I think Porter is crouched behind me shaking his head, an indication to Dayley to shake *his*. Porter has played with me; we've talked a lot. He knows how I enjoy the cat-and-mouse and Dayley isn't likely to shake off his veteran catcher's selection. I decide Porter is trying to deke me out.

I don't think Porter is going to call for a curve on the 0-and-1 pitch. Get the fastball over, maybe I'll foul it off, you're up two strikes. Then maybe waste the hard curve in the dirt, hoping I'll swing. I don't believe he'll throw the curve on the 0-and-1 count. And I agree with your strategy, Darrell: fastball on the outer three-quarters.

Dayley throws the fastball right where he wants it, but right where I'm looking, too. I hit it through the gaping hole on the left side, Coleman charges and can't make the play, Wilson scores standing up.

Curtain call for Keith, and sweet it is, coming after eleven hitless trips to the plate, following the single in my first at-bat of the series. I began and now I conclude this series receiving an ovation. Best of all, we finally win a game we almost blew.

Immediately after the game, SportsChannel interviews me for the New York City cable-TV broadcast, St. Louis radio and TV ask for and receive time, then finally I go into the press room to meet the writers. To accommodate the overflow covering this series, the Mets have set up a separate press room in what used to be the Jets' clubhouse. As a result of all the interviews, I miss celebrating with the team, and I'm unhappy. It should have been a sweet moment to share with them, but by the time I show up for a shower, most of the guys are gone.

This has happened to me before, but the inappropriateness had never struck me as fully as it does today. I mention this to Rusty and he says that next time I should simply tell everyone to wait a few minutes. Go up and share the moment with the teammates in the clubhouse, then meet the press. I'll do that. I hope I have the opportunity soon.

We have every reason to feel pretty good this evening, winners of four of six games against the two other top teams in the league, Los Angeles and St. Louis, and all of the games settled in the last inning. We're ahead of the Cards by a game, with twenty-four to play.

GAME 138—Mets 7
Cards 6

SEPTEMBER 13—MONTREAL

Charlie Samuels has rushed an order for $31\frac{1}{2}$-ounce bats for Hernandez. For the first time in my career I'm dropping to this weight; 32 ounces feels too heavy. What a difference from May, when I was complaining to Fig that my bats were too light!

Until the new ones arrive, I'll choke up an inch or so. I've never choked up, but I need the bat speed now.

Doubleheader tonight in Montreal; one of the games is the last make-up for the strike. Davey has informed me that I'll play all four games; in fact, he says I'm the only guy who will automatically play all remaining games until we win it or lose it. I expect that, Davey, and I'd go to the whip with everyone. Give Gary a break in one of these two games tonight. Otherwise, it's everybody all the way.

We lose the first game, 5–1, in straightforward, lackluster fashion. Bryn Smith, their ace, throws a fine game. We're a little flat and we can't blame Olympic Stadium, which, like Three Rivers in Pittsburgh, is one of those venues that doesn't generate a lot of excitement even when the stands are full. Tonight they're not.

For one thing, the fans are a long way off. For another, their knowledge of baseball is suspect. The people are enthusiastic, but their zeal is misplaced when they boo the Expo pitcher for a successful sacrifice bunt—because *he* was thrown out—and cheer him when the defense gets the runner at second—because *he* was safe at first. This is all wrong.

In the second game, Larry Bowa gives us a big lift with a two-RBI double in the gap in left center. No one knows more than Larry, a great student of the game, that he should never have seen the high fastball on the first pitch, with our pitcher, Terry Leach, coming up next. The league knows Bowa is a high fastball specialist when he's batting from the right side. Dan Schatzeder has a mean curve, too. Throw it! Why let the eighth man beat you on his pitch?

Fans blame hitters for making an out when, sometimes, credit should be given pitchers. Likewise, they credit hitters without realizing that sometimes a dumb pitch has helped his cause. But the hitter still has to hit the dumb pitch, and Bowa does. Carter hits yet another September homer to ice the game in the ninth.

I'm on base at the time with a single—but the pitch I'll remember was the preceding one.

I lined a foul right over our visiting dugout on the third-base line, and the ball struck a lady in the forehead. With her hands in the pockets of her jacket, she never had a chance. The blow knocked her out cold for about a minute. I've seen people hit hard, hurt even, but never knocked unconscious. They carried her off. After the game, I ask the officials to let me know how she is.

GAME 139—Expos 5
Mets 1

GAME 140—Mets 7
Expos 2

SEPTEMBER 14

Eddie Lynch has been with the Mets for several of their most dismal years, so when Eddie says today's game is the worst performance by a Mets team he has ever seen, he's saying something caustic. We're showcased on national television, to boot.

The Mets used to have a big fan who was a professional sign painter. I saw him in the stands while I was with the Cards. He had beautiful messages prepared for almost every eventuality. Today would have been an appropriate time to flash my favorite: WE ARE NOT AMUSED.

Neither the fans, nor the players, nor the manager, nor the general manager is amused today. I don't know. Is it worth going into? Sure, if for no other reason than to defend Carter's reputation.

Gary is victimized by the scorekeeper, who must feel as some of the players and fans in Montreal do. They're out for him. Carter is assessed throwing errors on a steal of third, when Johnson simply lets the ball get by him, and a pickoff throw to me, which I simply don't catch. After the ball sails through me, I inspect my glove to see if perhaps the webbing has, at long last, broken. Otherwise, I have no explanation. It hasn't.

Hell, let's talk gloves. They're more interesting than this ballgame. This is the first year one mitt has lasted this long. I suppose it will make it through the season, but my second one is ready, just in case. I always have one ready to go, already broken in. Ron Fairly taught me how to do this properly, how to tighten certain laces before I soak the stiff, new leather in lukewarm water. Then I put two baseballs deep in the pocket and wrap the glove tightly with tape, thumb side out, until it dries. This technique lets the fingers stay stiff while the thumb side gets loose and flexible. After I've soaked and molded the glove, I massage it, keep a baseball in the pocket, and sometimes warm up with it. Net result: The transition from worn to new glove will be a smooth one.

The mitt is the "Big Dipper" model made by Rawlings. Insiders will know that MacGregor made the real Big Dipper model, so I'll explain. In emulation of Willie McCovey, I chose the Big Dipper in my early years in the minors. But I thought then, and still do, that Rawlings has the best leather and webbing. Rawlings wanted to sign me, but I told them I liked the design of the Big Dipper. They offered to make the Big Dipper model—or something very close to it—with their leather. So today I play with the Rawlings version of MacGregor's Big Dipper first baseman's mitt, model no. CMH-C. It's one of the bigger mitts, and many first basemen use it.

The lady knocked out by my line drive yesterday is still in the hospital.

GAME 141—Expos 5
Mets 1

SEPTEMBER 15

At the last minute, Darryl scratches himself from the lineup, in a game we must win. The Cards haven't lost since they left Shea; we've lost twice, so we're a game behind now. Strawberry's thumb is really hurting at times; it's apparent on certain swings. But we need you in the lineup, Straw. You're not a one-dimensional player.

You can help us in the field even if your hitting is bothered. The doctor has assured you that the pain isn't a danger signal. The thumb won't get worse, nor will it get better before the long rest at season's end. Take some Ascriptin, Darryl, and play.

Darryl may still be concerned that this injury poses a threat to his career, despite medical assurances to the contrary. Who am I to tell him to brush this fear aside? I don't have Darryl Strawberry's future in front of me.

Yet I urge him to play through it. I remind him that an injury can help a player concentrate. I hope I'm not screwing up.

Today, the point is moot: Danny Heep, taking his place, hits a three-run homer in the first inning. Johnson homers in the fifth, Wilson in the ninth.

Once again an important game falls to Darling, and he responds with seven strong innings. Jesse breaks out of his home-run slump with five straight outs to save it.

GAME 142—Mets 6
Expos 2

SEPTEMBER 16—NEW YORK CITY

So far I'm right. One of the two teams—Toronto, it turns out—won three of the four games. I'll stick with my prediction: The Yankees don't get close again.

At Shea, the grass has been mowed for the series that starts tonight with Philadelphia. The long stuff was reserved for the Cards.

John Christensen is back with the club, now that Tidewater has won the Triple A championship. "I missed bitching you," John tells me by way of greeting. Mr. Warmth left me the queen of spades when he was sent down, with a note, reading, "I'll be back. Hold onto this. I'll slap it on you."

John didn't have a good year in the minors, but maybe he'll have some productive at-bats with the Mets before the season is over. He won't be eligible for post-season play, regardless, nor will any of these guys who joined the club after September 1. With the roster limit expanded to forty, our dugout is packed. Where will we all fit next week in the tiny dugout and clubhouse at Wrigley Field? With only two toilets for the team (five is standard), we'll be standing in line. Boot camp.

After the barely acceptable split in Montreal over the weekend, we arrive at the park and learn that the Cards have won the first game of their doubleheader against the Pirates. We counter with a blowout—and with Dwight on the mound, a safe blowout. Davey pulls the regulars in the middle innings, and some of the Tidewater boys get into the game. During the game the Cards post a victory in their second game in Pittsburgh. It's important for the Mets to remember that we have our shot at the Pirates later, and the Cards have a bunch of games left with the Expos, who have beaten them nine out of twelve, and with these Phillies, another fast artificial-surface team who can give them trouble.

Our blowout gets a big lift from faulty Phillie pitch selection in the third. I fault their ace pitcher, Kevin Gross, and the catcher, Darren Daulton. They know how hot Carter is and they know they're not going to score many if any runs off Gooden. So why throw Gary a high fastball on the first pitch with two men on? The Kid whales it over the wall.

The next inning, Gross's last, he starts Johnson off with fastballs on three of four pitches. The third one HoJo hits to the wall for a double. Gross has a great curve and Johnson is a dead fastball hitter. Where's the logic?

In the happy clubhouse, Dwight, who has merely struck out eleven and run his scoreless-inning count to thirty-one, wants to talk only about his hitting: a single, a double, two RBIs. He's not kidding when he says he'd rather hit a homer than throw a no-hitter. To that degree he takes his pitching excellence for granted.

When Dwight does hit his homer, we'll never hear the end of it. We'll hear about his prowess tonight for a couple of days. Doc loves to saunter around the clubhouse waving his bat, talking about hitting. Takes nerve to be so talented and so secure within that talent.

GAME 143—Mets 9
Phillies 0

SEPTEMBER 17

In today's *Post*, Dick Young castigates the Shea crowd for giving me that standing ovation. It doesn't bother me. He can write what he wants. He has the last word, by definition. So does *Sports Il-*

lustrated, but I am curious why editors and everyone else seem to have chosen me as the *symbol* of the drug problem in baseball. Hey, we need a picture. Get Hernandez's. In *Sports Illustrated*'s editorial on the subject, they run one picture. Mine.

Hell, Dave Parker is leading the league in RBIs. He, too, has won the MVP award and is one of the frontrunners to win it again this year if the voting isn't affected by Pittsburgh. But who even knows Dave Parker testified?

Joe Niekro has been traded by the Astros to the Yankees, who sorely need pitching for what's left of their pennant drive. I'm not unhappy about that deal. I'll never have to dance with his knuckleball again, and now the National League is without a knuckleball pitcher, believe it or not.

Eddie Lynch is still bothered by back spasms caused by the fight in Los Angeles. Including a couple of starts before that game, tonight marks his sixth consecutive ineffective outing. He doesn't have his pinpoint control. Shane Rawley for the Phillies has his, however, and gets by tonight even though he's not throwing hard. Usually he throws bullets. He doesn't throw me one pitch inside. I don't know why. He gets me out four times, and the next time we face him he may try the same tactics. I'll be waiting.

Our record for the past month reveals something I don't understand. With the exception of that short streak on the West Coast, when we swept San Diego, the Mets have posted a rhythmically mediocre record: win, lose, win, lose, win, lose. We'll hit hard for a game, maybe two, then go cold, then hit hard again. I've never been on a team that turns hot and cold with the bats as suddenly as this one.

On the other hand, we're remarkably stable as a team—in the dugout and clubhouse. Almost subdued, I would say, and that very likely comes from the personalities of the team veterans. Staub, Foster and Wilson are all essentially quiet guys. Doc is a quiet guy; Darling, of course. Carter and myself are the only exceptions.

But while the team stays calm, the fans are getting more excited by the day. Staub reports this. Rusty is probably the most visible and recognizable of the Mets and he moves around Manhattan, so he would be the one to pick up on new developments. I haven't perceived any such upsurge—maybe because I'm traveling incognito, cap pulled down, collar turned up, sunglasses. Folks are nice, but I'm being careful anyway.

No disguise will do me any good in St. Louis. Old friends there inform me that the press is pounding out a drumbeat of antagonism. The theme is one I dispute: Whitey knew why he traded me but didn't say a thing; he took the heat to protect Keith. The papers are running letters calling me a coward. A columnist writes that New York fans would give a standing ovation to the Night Stalker if he produced clutch hits.

Meanwhile, what about Andujar, my old friend? He has said only, "I'm embarrassed," but he hasn't apologized or anything else. The St. Louis fans are cheering him. The media is silent on the subject. Joaquin is still with the team, helping it chase a pennant.

What's the "moral" difference between this silence and the ovation at Shea? None. Each is a form of boosterism.

I'll return to St. Louis next month as some kind of traitor. My only answer will be a series of ropes strung around the unfriendly confines of Busch Stadium. I hope I can do it. I'll be nervous. I'm already a little nervous at the prospect. No way will I walk without an escort from the hotel to the stadium right across the street. I want the big guys at my side, Lynch, Staub, Carter; and Knight, the professional.

These are the only nerves I have right now. I'm calm regarding the pennant race. In 1982, I was much less so. We needed to play merely .500 ball for about ten days to clinch the pennant in mid-September, and those days were the slowest of my life. I asked Gene Tenace if it was always so. He said, "No. The first time is the worst by far. It gets easier." Tenace knows what he's talking about, with all his experience with the great Oakland teams of the early 1970s.

Not many players in the future are going to get his kind of post-season experience. These days, dynasties last exactly one year. The competition is too good. Look at the Tigers.

GAME 144—Phillies 5
Mets 1

SEPTEMBER 18

Now they tell us! Doug Sisk is going to be operated on for bone chips in his throwing elbow. Apparently Doug informed somebody in Montreal that it was hurting and x-rays found a pool of chips floating around. Something is wrong here. Doug should have said something earlier or the team should have ordered x-rays earlier.

Jesse Orosco should be getting treatment, too. Is or isn't his elbow hurting him? Find out. Order Jesse to have ultrasound therapy every day and fine him when he misses; $100, $200, whatever it takes.

This whole business of our pitchers and their arms may cost us money—and the money for the World Series this year will be substantial, maybe $70,000 per player. For the first time, the Commissioner's office has said it doesn't need the 18 percent of postgame revenues Bowie Kuhn always collected for his bureaucracy. He wouldn't give up that money but Ueberroth has said he doesn't need it, so the funds go into the pool. Is Ueberroth a good politician?

Last year, it was a 4-for-4 day early in the season against the Cubs' Steve Trout that got me going. A similar day would help me now. I'm just puttering along, feeling fine against left-handers but only so-so against right-handers. We'll see. Trout's a lefty.

In the third inning, with Davey Lopes on second base, Keith Moreland fouls off eight or nine pitches in a row. Gary goes out to the mound to change signs with Aguilera. Everybody knows the Cubs steal signs. Bowa, the former Cub, tells us later how they transmit the information. On the slider, Lopes would look back toward second base; on a fastball, he'd stare straight ahead. Moreland puts the information to good use until Carter changes signs, then he hits into a fielder's choice. But the Cubs score a couple of runs on weak hits.

In the fourth we come back with three runs of our own on weak hits, including my bouncing-ball double over the third-base bag, and one solid blow—Knight's two-run double against the right field wall, one of the gratifying hits of his and our year. Standing on second base, Ray is not cheering or pumping his arms or saluting the dugout; nothing like that. Ray is staring straight ahead, tense, pumped up, vindicated, but still angry, perhaps, about what has been a bad year for him.

He and I had a discussion recently, all about hitting on the 1-and-1 count and how differently we attack it in a hot streak and a slump. In a slump, we feel we have to swing at the pitch if it's a strike, to avoid getting behind in the count. Because we're not sure we'll hit any pitch at all, we have to swing at more of them, helping our odds. But of course this really *hurts* our odds, because we're swinging at worse pitches. It's a cruel dilemma. When we're confident, the tables are turned. We'll take that 1-and-1 pitch. We're willing to go behind 1-and-2 or even 0-and-2, if it's not our pitch to hit. If we get another tough one, well, it's no worse for us than the one we took, and we feel we'll be able to get a piece of it, foul it off, stay alive.

In the fifth, for the first time in his career, Wally Backman bats left-handed against a left-handed pitcher. So he's not going to wait until spring training. I agree: Why not give it a try now? Wally's batting average has fallen about thirty points in recent weeks; a good bit of that is certainly due to the batch of left-handers we've faced.

In the beginning of this experiment from the left side, the left-handers will throw him curveball, curveball, curveball, breaking away from him on the outside corner. It's the Achilles heel of any batter, certainly a man new to one side of the plate. They'll throw it until he hits it.

His left-handed debut is a bunting situation, and he's successful.

George Foster is hitting the ball hard now, going 3-for-3 today. If he gets hot, watch out. If any of us get hot, watch out.

GAME 145—Mets 4
Cubs 2

SEPTEMBER 19

A couple of months ago they were hammering away on the floor of the apartment above me. This week they're pounding on the walls of the adjacent place. Don't they realize a pennant is hanging in the balance?! Building management replies that the rules permit work to begin at 8:30 a.m. This morning, work begins at

8:30 a.m. I seriously consider heading out to the streets for some peace and quiet.

Ahead 5–1 after three innings tonight over the increasingly hapless Cubs, we run out the string on our game—Fernandez in complete command—while paying almost as much attention to the Cards' game in Philadelphia. A third contest is also monitored on the TV in Davey's office, the Bears versus the Vikings.

We win. The Phillies win, breaking a six-game streak for St. Louis. The Bears win.

The Yankees lose. They're out of it. I called it. From this vantage point, it seems in retrospect that the Yankees had two problems this year that proved insurmountable: their starting pitching and their owner. What does George Steinbrenner expect the reaction of his players to be when he remarks about Dave Winfield, his main man, "Do we have a Mr. October? I've got a Mr. May"?

The surprise for the Yankees tonight is that Joe Niekro gets bombed in his first start. Coincidentally, and just when I'm certain that our league is now knuckleball-free, a knuckleball from Larry Sorenson gets me out in the seventh inning tonight. I had read in *The Sporting News* last spring that the Cubs liked the knuckler Sorenson was developing at the time, but six months later I'm not thinking about it. The first one he throws I take with a frown. The second one I knock on the ground to second base.

Sid the Squid registers eleven strikeouts and allows one lone hit (a homer) in eight innings. At first base, Moreland, who bats right-handed, tells me he'd rather face right-hander Gooden than left-hander Fernandez! Sid's fastball can't touch Dwight's, but to the hitters it seems just about as fast. I have the same trouble with Tudor. When he pitched against us last week, I would have bet he was throwing in the low 90s. The radar gun recorded 87, tops.

In the showers, I relay Moreland's compliment to Fernandez. Sid doesn't say anything. Ten minutes later, in the clubhouse, he walks by my stall and exclaims, "Did he say that about me?!"

He did. On the less positive side, Sid, I must say that you have officially joined that select group of pitchers who can turn a one-hitter into a three-hour ballgame. (Orel Hershiser is the charter member.) It's because you throw so many balls and so many high-rising fastballs that are fouled off. By the seventh inning, I'm exhausted. We fielders have to prepare for every one of those pitches. It's mental work. But I wouldn't change a thing.

My new bats are here, the $31\frac{1}{2}$ ouncers, and the difference is immediate. I feel that I'm controlling the bat again (a feeling I didn't have while choking up), and I hit three balls hard.

We go into the weekend trailing St. Louis by one game, sixteen to go. They entertain the Expos at home, we host Pittsburgh. If we don't gain ground now, we have no one to blame. The writers point out the Cards' advantageous schedule, with mostly home games remaining. I counter with the observation that they have six games remaining with the Expos, while we have six with the Pirates.

Fans wonder how teams in the spoiler role might play favorites coming down the stretch. It's a touchy question, for obvious reasons. My honest belief is that no team would play favorites in terms of trying to *lose*; but some teams, some managers, might try just a little bit harder to *win* against certain teams.

There's no doubt that the Expos, as a team, would prefer that Gary Carter's team not win the pennant. The Expos will try hard to beat the Cards, and I think they'll have some success; they'll play their asses off to beat the Mets. Hubie Brooks may be the one Expo who would like the Mets to win. He wishes he were back with us. Nevertheless, he'd love to beat us with a homer. It's the way athletes are—competitive fire.

Jim Frey of the Cubs wants badly to beat the Mets. There has been some bad blood during the year, we've swept them in Shea Stadium, the two teams were co-favorites in April, and the Cubs haven't had a fair chance this year, really. In our last two games, Frey tried everything he could think of. He'll try harder next week in Wrigley. However, the Cubs and the Cards are traditional rivals. Frey would love to play the spoiler in St. Louis if the race comes down to those final games of the year.

Prediction: The Mets will go into the series in St. Louis on October 1 leading the Cards by two games. We're hitting now, and we don't lose many games when we're hitting. We'll pop the champagne in my former hometown. Oh, how I would enjoy that tumultuous celebration on the mound, in full view of the 50,000 paying fans who will have booed me unmercifully.

GAME 146—Mets 5
Cubs 1

SEPTEMBER 20

Too many mistakes, a terrible break, and we fall to the Pirates, giving them their longest winning streak of the year—three miserable games. Darling, coming into the game with an outside chance of winning twenty on the season (sixteen now, four starts remaining), just doesn't have it. Rick Reuschel, the former Cub who started the season in the minors but has six straight complete games coming into this game, has his sinking fastball working.

The killer is R. J. Reynolds's bad hop, two-out single over my glove in the tenth. That pebble loses us the ballgame—and Shea has the smoothest dirt infield in the league. I'll remember this bounce if the season comes down to a game or two, which I'm sure it will.

But our bad luck is far from fatal. We still have time, or at least the fans must think so. There are only 30,000 in the stadium on a Friday night in the middle of the pennant race. I'm a little surprised.

GAME 147—Pirates 7
Mets 5

SEPTEMBER 21

Give a lot of credit to Bill Robinson, our man in the first-base coach's box who rides the Pirates' Rick Rhoden hard and early this afternoon. Rhoden is one of the better surgeon's in the league: An emory board tucked into one of the fingers of his glove is reputed to be his secret for doctoring the ball. Home-plate ump John McSherry finally checks the ball, and even though he doesn't find anything, the damage is done. Rhoden is rattled. He gives up two walks and four hits in the first inning.

The last of the hits is memorable. Dwight finally gets his homer, a solid wallop over the left field wall. In the dugout, he's speechless. A big grin wraps his youthful face. We're all happy. We already have seven runs, and with Doc on the mound and the Pirates at the plate—we'll win.

The Cards do, too, as the Expos blow a 6–1 lead. *Aaaaggghhhhhhhhh!!* Now it's pissing us off, these victories they manufacture. They're like a colony of ants chewing away at a big mammal. A run here, a run there, and pretty soon there's nothing left of the carcass. And it makes me mad that the other teams help them by issuing four, five, six walks a game. You can't do that against St. Louis! At least make them hit the ball.

The Cards have showed a lot more come-from-behind capability this year than we have. The Mets have to rely on long extra-base hits, which are harder to come by than singles, harder yet in the clutch. We're more of a get-ahead, stay-ahead team. Today is a good example.

GAME 148—Mets 12
Pirates 1

SEPTEMBER 22

Last year we lost eight of twelve games to lowly San Francisco. This year, it looks like the Pirates are serving in that role of Met-spoilers. They're eating us alive. Terry Leach takes an inning to get settled down and they score twice in the first inning, and add three in the sixth. Their Bob Kipper, a rookie making only his second major league start, is a "comfortable" 0-for-4 type. He keeps the ball low and gets us out; three of our five hits are infield models, and two of those are mine. A first for me? Could be.

I realize now that we're not playing with the intensity we achieved in August. Not just against these Pirates are we operating at a lower level. Against everyone. Even when we win. I don't know why.

Baseball is not like football or basketball, in which the superior team has a good chance of enforcing a victory if it absolutely must have one. Those teams meet in actual physical combat, and it's possible to literally run over the weaker opponent. Baseball teams can't do this. Though there's no question that we're a superior team, the Mets can't enforce this superiority over the Pirates on any given day. We can't make our hits fall, or keep theirs from falling. And the key to the game, pitching, is entirely out of the control of the team.

Now beaten by the Pirates two out of three, most of us gather in Davey's office to watch the Cards and the Expos on the "Game of the Week." We see Tommy Herr hit a two-out, two-strike, two-run homer to win the game for the Cards in the bottom of the ninth.

"Oh, too bad!" is not the phrase I hear muttered as Herr trots around the bases. "Fuck!" seems to be the expletive of choice. It is too bad that Jeff Reardon, the Expos' ace reliever, happens to be injured for this series in St. Louis. In all three Cardinal victories they came from behind. A healthy Reardon would have saved one or two of those games for Montreal.

GAME 149—Pirates 5
Mets 3

SEPTEMBER 23—PHILADELPHIA

Three games down, thirteen to go. Forget Pittsburgh. Forget everything except tonight's game and tonight's score. You'll notice that the dispatches from the front get more terse as we drive deeper into September. That's because there is, ironically perhaps, less to say. It's really too late for psychological boosts and letdowns, good signs and bad signs, the finer points of the game—even though I'll pass some on.

Do we win or do we lose? It's all that matters now. We don't care how.

We win.

The Cards win against Pittsburgh. R. J. Reynolds, the guy who beat us with the bad bounce RBI over my glove Friday night, drops a fly ball, allowing the Cardinals to score and win.

And already, a finer point I can't resist. It's instructive and makes me look good. In the sixth inning, Mets up 4–1, Juan Samuel is on third base when Mike Schmidt bounces the ball to me. I throw out Samuel going home, Carter blocking the plate. Great play, Hernandez, the announcers are no doubt intoning, while wondering, perhaps aloud, whether it's a *smart* play. With a three-run lead, why not take the sure out and give them the run? My reply: The play at home is a sure out. The key is my picking up that Samuel has broken late from third base. I see this out of the corner of my eye as I advance on the bouncing ball. Just before the ball gets to me, I throw another glance at Samuel— yes, all you Little Leaguers, I take my eye off the ball, in defiance of the rules; don't try it until you're my age. With this second look, I know I have the runner cold. So I throw home. I don't think, "I have him cold *if* I make a good throw." That doubt can't enter the mind of a fielder. Assume good execution and make your decision on that basis.

GAME 150—Mets 4
Phillies 1

SEPTEMBER 24

Keith Hernandez gets his 23rd game-winning RBI this evening. It's a new major-league record for Mex.

The fine print reads: first inning, sac fly. In fact, eleven of my GWRBIs in 1985 have come in the first inning, seventeen in the first four innings.

Credit tonight goes to Larry Bowa for his game-winning over-the-shoulder catch in the third inning. Making his first start in a Mets uniform (and out of position, too, at second base), Larry sprints into short right field and makes the wonderful catch with two on and one out, then spins and doubles off the runner at second. This catch turns the game around. It is as clear a case as I recall of a pitcher getting a big boost from a defensive play. Fernandez strikes out six of the next nine batters, and shuts the Phillies down. It's too bad he loses his shutout on a lousy homer in the eighth.

The Phillie Phanatic is an entertaining fellow, but he goes too far tonight when he hops on the roof of the Mets' dugout, reaches down and grabs the cap off Dwight's head, then takes it into the stands for an auction. This isn't a prepared stunt. Dwight gets upset, and I don't blame him. That cap hasn't given up an earned run in about a month.

(I use two caps a year, switching usually at the All-Star break, and death to the mascot who swipes my worn-in cap. Way back when I was eighteen years old and wearing a funky cap in the Instructional League, Lou Brock said, "You're too good a player to wear a cap like that." He gave me his. Still, I prefer a well-used one; Charlie Samuels has to make me switch, for the image of the team.)

Yet another fine point, instructive of how a ballplayer can look brilliant though he's merely lucky. In the eighth inning, Backman on first base, I suggest to Davey that we hit-and-run. Their pitcher,

Shipanoff, is usually around the plate. I'll make contact. Davey puts the play on. Backman breaks and I hit the ball through the vacated hole on the left side, reading before the pitch that the shortstop has covered.

In the next inning, Backman again on first, he breaks, the second baseman covers this time, and I hit the ball through *that* vacated hole. "How did you know!?" the reporters demand after the game. I didn't know. That second hit wasn't the hit-and-run. Wally was stealing and got a late break. I hit a weak ground ball; my luck that the second baseman was covering.

GAME 151—Mets 7
Phillies 1

SEPTEMBER 25—CHICAGO

Reggie Patterson, the fourth pitcher in a row about whom we know next to nothing, opposes us today in Wrigley. It's standard in September to see new pitchers as they're brought up by the noncontenders, and it's a disadvantage for the hitters. He marches through the Mets until Carter hits a grand slam in the sixth. Because Gary had struck out twice in the game, they walked me intentionally with first base open. Several times this year Gary has made the opposition pay for this strategy.

A 4–1 lead and Darling pitching. We're in good shape, yes? Yes, but they get their second run in the sixth, two more in the seventh and the game is tied going into the ninth. After striking out the first two batters, Orosco walks Lopes—but then picks him off—but I can't find the handle in my glove and throw a palm ball to Santana at second, and Lopes is safe. He scores.

This is the second game in the last six in which I was involved in the critical play that helped us lose; the first was the bad hop against Pittsburgh. It makes me wonder. I should be the guy in the infield who we want to handle the ball, but one time it bad hops me, the next I can't get it out of my glove. Things are not going our way now.

GAME 152—Cubs 5
Mets 4

SEPTEMBER 26

Thank you, Doc.

GAME 153—Mets 3
Cubs 0

SEPTEMBER 27—PITTSBURGH

A homecoming, of sorts. No assumed names this time; no sunglasses. Can it get any worse than it was in Philadelphia, where guys behind the dugout were urging me to "Guard that line," or in Chicago, where two louts were parading around our bus after yesterday's game with dollar bills stuck up their nostrils?

In other circumstances, these people are rabid fans asking me for an autograph. In the safety of a stadium, they change their stripes. It's all good training for me, however. Cultivate equanimity. St. Louis is coming up next.

Without a change of Met fortunes, that series is going to be meaningless. Our pitching is bad tonight in Pittsburgh. Lynch's back spasms, pinched nerve, whatever, takes him out of the game after two innings and the Pirates score six in the third inning off a collection of Met hurlers, including two just up from Tidewater. Our 5–2 lead is wiped out. The *coup de grace* is a slow roller that doesn't get out of the infield but scores two runners.

The game shows perhaps the main difference between the Cards and the Mets: the superior performance of their middle relievers.

In the sixth inning, R. J. Reynolds makes a great running catch off Christensen to save one run and perhaps more. Reynolds again! Is this the same guy who dropped the two-out fly in St. Louis to lose a game?

A team record of twenty-three players used by Davey isn't enough for the Mets; nor are our fourteen hits. We're four games behind now, with only eight to go.

Four!

Eight!

The days dwindle down, and all that. So much for my hunch

that we would be leading by two going into the St. Louis series. We'll be doing well to trail by two.

If we lose one more game, we're finished for 1985.

GAME 154—Pirates 8
Mets 7

SEPTEMBER 28

Strictly in the "for what it's worth" department, I'm back at .300 again, thanks to going 4-for-5 in last night's losing cause.

In an effort to get Backman's average moving up, I suggest to him—strongly—that he give up for this season batting left-handed against left-handers. He's not effective. The experiment is going to take time—the off-season and spring training.

"You think so?"

"Yes. Bat right-handed."

In the eighth inning tonight, coming up for the first time with a left-hander on the mound, he ostentatiously juggles the left- and right-handed batting helmets. Finally he selects the right-handed one. The squad cheers. We're hurting, but we can enjoy a light moment. Moping won't do any good, although there was some of it after the 8–7 loss last night.

This afternoon, a lovely one, the Mets are ahead 3–1 in the ninth inning, but the bases are loaded for the Pirates, one out. Henceforth, every one of these situations represents the season.

Davey brings in Orosco to face Sixto Lezcano, and Jesse gets him on a called third strike. The pitch is several inches outside but, damn!, we deserve a break. R. J. Reynolds should have been batting, though, to even things out.

But R. J. bats next. If he gets an extra-base hit to win the game, I'll drop in my tracks on the infield and bow down before the will of Higher Authorities. I'll head for the nearest chapel.

R. J. strikes out swinging.

GAME 155—Mets 3
Pirates 1

SEPTEMBER 29

How's this for a switch? A couple of Hell's Angels types are berating me this afternoon.

"Snitch!"

I have concluded that the fans riding me with taunts are my
age and younger, and male, without exception. In my mind, they're
guys who are most likely to have tried cocaine themselves.

The harassment, while not disruptive or widespread, has made
what should be the most enjoyable part of the season, the pennant
race, somewhat less fun.

Playing the Pirates has been no fun at all. Almost every game
of the last three or four series has been sloppy. Our pitchers can't
hold them. Give the Pirates some credit, too; they're playing hard;
the new blood coming over in the trades has helped them. Today
they take the lead in the eighth inning off McDowell and Orosco.
This is the season, folks—until HoJo dials 8 in the eighth to tie
the game, and Carter gets on the phone in the ninth to win it.

What a fitting end to the month for Gary, who will win Player
of the Month honors. Thirteen homers, thirty-four RBIs in twenty-
seven games. All on a terrible knee. An awesome month.

I'm not ashamed of my performance for September, especially
considering the circumstances: a .373 average, two homers, sixteen RBIs.

As I thought very possible, the Cards lost two of three to
the Expos this weekend, so we go there for the big showdown
three behind, six to play. We have to sweep. If we come up
short, we'll look back with chagrin at our record against the weakest team in the National League. The Mets are only 10–8 against
the Pirates, a difficult 10–8 at that. The Cards are 15–3 against
them.

GAME 156—Mets 9
Pirates 7

OCTOBER 1—ST. LOUIS

When Whitey saw that Davey had Gooden scheduled for tomorrow night against John Tudor, Whitey moved Tudor to tonight's
game. I tell the reporters that I'd go with Doc tonight against

Tudor, if I were the manager. Davey sticks with Ronnie in the rotation we've been following for a while: Darling, Gooden, Aguilera. That's showing confidence in Ronnie, and it has to help him in the long run. In the short run? As Davey points out, we have to win all three games anyway. And, if we beat Tudor tonight, with Dwight waiting in the wings for the second game . . .

I've changed my plans. I'm not bunking at the hotel across the street. Instead, I'm in seclusion at good friend and ex-teammate Ted Sizemore's house, and I drive to the stadium. No way am I going to walk the couple of hundred yards from the hotel to the clubhouse door and back again. I've had enough abuse in Philly, Chicago, and Pittsburgh. I know I'll catch it in the stadium here. St. Louis is a conservative town that the papers have been whipping into a frenzy regarding the Hernandez "betrayal." Some guys with too much of the local brew might get out of hand.

So, I'm hiding, and I'm not happy about it, but it makes sense. So far, however, it seems unnecessary. Around town, the little I have been out, people have been nice, not that much different than they were before.

"We miss you, Keith."

"You're the best, Keith."

Not a single confrontation—but the big one is sure to come: my first at-bat.

Bases empty, two outs. The boos start as I walk toward the plate, even before the PA announcement. The fans are getting into it. If I am officially introduced, I can't hear the name over the noise.

As nervous and pumped up as I am, I'm also feeling much stronger now. I'm back with the 32-ounce bat. The cool weather is the reason. I welcome it, and I'm the only guy on the team in my shirtsleeves. I walk on a 3-and-1 count. Tudor continues through our lineup, pitching on the corners, but not hard. He must be tight. The whole night he comes inside on me only twice.

In my second at-bat, the booing is a little diminished. I line out to left field. In the sixth, I single. That should help my cause. In the eighth, I strike out. That makes their day; cheers resound through the stadium.

Nothing the Cards have done has given the fans much to cheer about. Quite simply, Darling pitches the game of his career. He's in complete command after giving up a leadoff walk to Vince Coleman in the first inning—exactly what he didn't want to do, but he gets out of the inning.

Alas, his bunting isn't quite as good, as he misses the ball on a suicide squeeze in the seventh inning (on a tough pitch, granted). Will the season turn on a missed suicide squeeze? It certainly might. Everything in baseball turns on the little things. Before the screwed-up bunt play breaks the spell, we might have thought that the couple of little hits we managed in that inning were turning the game, and hence the season, to our advantage. Ray Knight bloops a single, then Santana hits a ball off Tudor's foot that bounces into right field for a double. But it goes for nought.

A chance here, a chance there for each team, but no reward, so Ronnie is out after nine innings, and the season rests with Orosco (McDowell has been working hard; he'll get a couple of days off, if at all possible). I'm on Jesse hard tonight. Every pitch.

In the tenth inning, Cedeno walks and steals second on a close play. Ozzie Smith takes a called third strike on a full count—on a close pitch. Smith, who has an excellent eye, glances at the umpire in bewilderment. Whitey says, "Fuck!" I read his lips. He's not mad about the strikeout itself; rather, about how his choices for subsequent moves are messed up. He was ready to send up Clark for Tudor, but Clark would now be walked intentionally, with first base open. So Whitey has to use, and perhaps waste, another hitter, Tito Landrum. Davey has a choice of pitching to Landrum or walking him. He tells Jesse to walk him. Now Whitey comes in with Clark, pinch-hitting for Coleman! I don't know whether Davey expects this. At any rate, Clark hits a line shot foul before flying out to Strawberry to end the inning. Fun cat-and-mouse strategy between managers.

In the eleventh, I look at a called third strike from Dayley, a nice curve that fools me, and the crowd goes wild again. Gary also takes a third strike and they're howling with joy. Then Darryl hits the ball as hard as it can be hit. His homers are usually these outrageously long, high punts. This line drive over the wall and against the scoreboard *beyond* the bleachers has a hang time of no more than 1.5 seconds. Only later, when Mike Lupica informs me, do I know that a deathly quiet has settled over Busch stadium. To me, it seems like a volcano has erupted, the Mets make so much noise.

We escape a fumbled fly in the bottom of the inning and win. *Whew*! Two games down, five to go.

The most exciting game of my career? Along with a dozen others, yes.

The clubhouse is a madhouse. It's like the World Series. Strawberry is pinned in. I'm surrounded. During batting practice, while talking to a group of writers, I had noticed one guy with a beard hanging around the perimeter, taking notes. Now, after the game, here he is again, hanging back, taking notes, but not asking anything.

"What's your name?" I call out.

"John."

"John Sondregger?"

"Yes."

"Beat it."

I realize I hereby violate the guy's First Amendment rights, but I don't give a damn. Sondregger is the bearded columnist for one of the local papers. Not long after the Cardinal series at Shea, he wrote a column about the movie *The Natural*, in which Robert Redford portrays a ballplayer who becomes a star, gets shot by his girlfriend (who then commits suicide), but returns to win the big game. Last scene: Redford playing catch with his son in the wheat field.

According to the column, I am somehow the natural who betrayed St. Louis. The point was fuzzy in my mind, but the insult wasn't.

Why should I give this guy the time of day?

GAME 157—Mets 1
Cards 0

OCTOBER 2

On the other hand, Steve Jacobsen of *Newsday* is a writer I enjoy talking with, although sometimes he gets carried away with all the heavy psychology. He's heading that way as we chat this evening. I'm not up to it. I feel strong physically, but uneasy in my head. Given the unpleasantness of my personal situation here (including another long meeting with lawyers) and the importance of this series, I'm having a hard enough time keeping myself together for the ballgame. I can't handle any more head trips.

I ask Steve to hold off on the extraneous questions. What does it all mean? Is there life after baseball? Frankly, I don't give a damn tonight. I just want to play the game.

I may be wrong, but I've decided that the booing in St. Louis is somewhat artificial. The animosity in the stadium certainly stands in contrast to the greetings I receive around town. The papers report today that last night's first boo was twenty-eight seconds. Could be. It seemed like a long time.

While the situation is getting to me, the Mets are relaxed this evening. We believe we'll win and take it to the Cards for the final game. Then the pressure will be on them. I don't think it helps the Cards to come into the series knowing they need to win only one game. In a way, it's better for the Mets to know that we have to win *every* game.

Dad is in daily communication with his analysis of the action. He says that Ozzie Smith was called out on ball four in the tenth inning last night. I suspected as much. We agree that the key tonight is to come out smoking against Andujar. Get them down three or four runs against Dwight and that should be it. And we do—but we don't. We come out smoking, with hits by Wilson, Hernandez (after another prolonged greeting), and Carter, but we don't get them down. Only one run scores. Toward that end we get a nice break on an attempted steal of second by Backman, when umpire Fred Brocklander is hit by Porter's throw. The play would have been close. Brocklander is the ump who called Danny Heep's homer in San Diego a foul ball. Fred is having trouble keeping his eye on the ball. Strange; he's a good ump.

Speaking of umps: Behind the plate tonight is Lee Weyer, the big guy with the biggest strike zone in the league. With Gooden and Andujar, I don't think Weyer's big zone will favor either pitcher. Last night, with low-ball ump Dutch Rennert, the advantage was Tudor's.

Porter hasn't had a hit off Gooden in fifteen or so tries, but he rips a triple to score Van Slyke and tie the game in the second. That's the first earned run Dwight has given up in forty-nine innings. With Porter on third, Smith grounds out to Johnson at third.

"Get to the bag, Keith! Get to the bag!"

HoJo has been concerned for two games that I won't get there in time. I assure him that I will. I do.

Dwight allows some more baserunners but, as usual, gets tougher as the evening wears on. I'm surprised Whitey hasn't tried a suicide squeeze in these first two games. He's had the opportunities, including two tonight. I'm watching him closely, staring straight ahead at the plate but with my eyes aimed to the left, into the Cards' dugout. I can see him even if he goes behind the barrier to hide from the Mets' dugout. If Whitey flashes any sign at all, it will be the squeeze sign. But nothing. No squeeze. No runs, either.

We add some runs, Foster hits a homer, and the Mets lead 5–1 going into the ninth. Then, with two outs and nobody on, a four-run lead and the fans streaming up the aisles, Dwight walks Ozzie Smith on four pitches.

"Don't let them make a run at us, Doc," I urge him on the mound. "Don't let 'em go to the clubhouse thinking at least they made a run."

But he walks the pinch hitter Ford, Coleman bounces an RBI single through the middle, McGee (who is still batting that .360) bounces an infield hit on which Santana and Backman collide lightly behind second base, and suddenly the bases are loaded with the tying, speedy runs. At the plate, Tommy Herr is the winning run. Is there a Met in whose mind doesn't flash a quick picture of Herr's homer ten days ago?

Davey sticks with Dwight. Herr hits a hard line drive—right at Backman. One game behind, four to go.

GAME 158—Mets 5
Cards 2

OCTOBER 3

I haven't spoken a word to Whitey, nor he to me. He's doing all his talking in the press, suggesting that the Pittsburgh Seven be held hostage: If the players' union doesn't agree to a testing program, suspend us. He also goes into great detail in an interview in the *Washington Post* about drug use on the Cardinal team in the early 1980s. He exaggerates.

The local St. Louis writers, and a lot of others, too, accept as gospel anything Whitey espouses. With his gruff manner, he has them intimidated. He's in charge, and he's helped along by the instinctive boosterism of the press and media in the Midwest. I doubt that he would be able to pull off this act in New York, where it often seems that the press is instinctively antagonistic.

The writers are with us all the way, now, however. All of New York is, apparently, with record television ratings for the past two games. I can't imagine that tonight's rating will go down. With Aguilera going against Cox, I rate the game and the season as "pick 'em." If we win tonight and tie the Cards, it's still "pick 'em." If we lose, it's theirs unless they blow it.

Two things need to happen early tonight: Rick needs to stop them in the first inning, and we need to score fairly early.

We try. In the first, Mookie singles, goes to second on Backman's ground out, I hit the ball off the wall in right to score Wilson (but can't get to second myself), Carter singles in the infield, Strawberry laces a single to right. One run in, bases loaded, and the Cardinal infield is staring at the ground. They can't hide the dejection. We're this close—*this close*—to running their asses out of here.

Foster is batting. Late last night, long after the second game was over, Davey and I were in the showers. "You going to start Danny or George tomorrow?" I ask him. I'm just curious. It wouldn't be illogical to play Heep against the right-hander Cox; on the other hand, George did have three hits in the game, including a homer. Davey said he wasn't certain.

George hits into a force play at home.

Johnson is batting, two outs. After HoJo hit the grand slam off Cox at Shea Stadium three weeks ago, Cox boasted that Johnson would never get another hit off him. Before the game tonight, I remind HoJo of the insult. But he grounds out. Cox wins round one.

What could have been an early big inning for us becomes instead a lift for the Cards.

During my next at-bat, in the third inning, with the count 2-and-2, Porter asks Ed Montague to check the pine tar on my bat. A pine-tar episode of my very own! Montague takes my bat and lays it across the plate. If the extent of pine tar is wider than the plate, I'm in trouble. It's not. Why now? On whose orders? I rip a single to right.

Porter reaches first base on a walk in the fourth, and I demand an explanation. Darrell says he was just kidding around, but Montague took him seriously.

The Cardinals' game:

In the second, they score after Pendleton goes from first to third on a wild pitch that Gary can't locate. Speed.

In the seventh they save a run when Coleman races to the left field line to intercept my double into the bullpen, holding Dykstra on third. Speed.

HoJo drives in a run in the eighth (but not off Cox), so we go to our last chance trailing 4–3. With two outs, it's up to me. The booing has tailed off; in this third game I have finally accomplished what I wanted and needed in the first one: a series of hard hits. They make me happy but one more is now required. I get it, cheap as it is: a bouncer to deep short. From the Cardinal dugout comes good-natured razzing. Cedeno holds his nose and makes a "blooping" motion. From Hernandez on first, a good-natured, inconspicuous tug at the crotch.

If it has to be a losing effort, I'm glad I don't make the final out in this particular game, giving the fans still more to gloat about. I'm sorry that Gary does.

Two games down, three to go.

We've played hard, loose, and well. We've just come up a little short. Recalling this game, I'll rue the missed opportunity of the first inning.

The Mets and the Cards have treated the fans to the best-played series of games I've seen or participated in in my career; fine baseball. Compare the slipshod performances on both sides in the Mets' recent games with the Pirates. We're talking about two different sports!

Still, unless the Cubs handle the Cards and we sweep the Expos, our season is over. To do my part in the Cub cause, I leave for good buddy Gary Matthews an envelope of local clippings about the Chicago "Flubs."

We fly home. There's no anger. There's no disgust. We've played good ball and we know it. In the Show-Me state of Missouri, we almost did. Our disappointment is tinged with pride.

GAME 159—Cards 4
                       Mets 3

OCTOBER 4—NEW YORK CITY

Before last night's game in St. Louis, I asked Met partner, my landlord Fred Wilpon, who was in attendance, if he could keep the workmen in our building quiet this morning until noon.

I arrive home at 3:00 a.m., get up at noon and all is quiet. I'm not surprised. It's Fred's building.

We beat Montreal handily tonight, but the Cards do the same to the Cubs. They've cinched a tie. The gloomy, foggy weather in New York is appropriate. My three hits aren't, somehow. They make eight in a row, tying a Met record, but who really cares?

I'm embarrassed to report, after declaring the Yankees goners, that they almost have a better shot than we have because they're playing the team they're chasing, Toronto, while we have to depend on the Cubs. The Blue Jays did romp away weeks ago, but then they collapsed. How could I know? What a joke it would be if the Yankees should sneak into the playoffs after we've dominated Big Apple baseball all year. But it wouldn't be a funny one for the Mets or, I suspect, our fans, 45,000 of whom have come out for this dreary game.

Two late-breaking notes on the five-hit game last night:

I was told by New York writers that Whitey said, in effect, "Well, why not, with his salary? But he isn't a Don Mattingly or Jack Clark."

I call this kicking a guy even when he's *up*, but the White Rat did go on to concede that I'm the best-fielding first baseman he knows. Don't do me any favors, Rat.

And this point of history turned up by the indefatigable Jay Horwitz: The game was my third five-hitter of the year, and I am the first National Leaguer to record three such games in a season since Eddie Waitkus did it in 1950, playing for the Phillies.

Eddie Waitkus was the real-life basis for *The Natural*.

GAME 160—Mets 9
Expos 4

OCTOBER 5

I receive a nice, semi-standing ovation as I come up in the first inning, seeking the new Met record of nine consecutive hits. Before the game, a friend passed me a note: "The whole world is watching."

I do believe he's kidding. I don't see the networks hanging around. Nobody gives a damn today what Keith Hernandez is doing. One month ago, now that was different.

For the record, he strikes out.

The Mets lose this afternoon, but long before our game is completed, the Cards beat the Cubs. They are the champs in the Eastern Division, but the throng gathered on Fan Appreciation day at Shea accepts the news with goodwill. They cheer our every play. Looking bad, we can do no wrong.

Toronto finally beats the Yankees today; so much for a Subway Series, on either end of the line.

For the second year in a row, the Mets finish second. We have won more baseball games over the past two years than any team in either league (188) and have nothing to show for it but a team attendance record.

More games than any other team. That's hard to believe. Except for the streak in July, this season has been a struggle. We were bedeviled by individual and team slumps, both on the mound and at the plate. Gooden, Darling, Fernandez, Lynch, and Aguilera—our starters—were the strength of the Mets in 1985.

Next year is the critical one for this collection of talent on the Mets. Last year, we surprised people. This year, we had a great season but not great enough. Next year, we'd better do it. Otherwise, I expect some changes.

A sequel: "The Mets Try Harder"?

It's not a matter of trying harder. We just have to win more games.

GAME 161—Expos 8
Mets 3

OCTOBER 6

Our season ends on this beautiful sunny afternoon as it began 181 days earlier, in a shower of confetti. Over 30,000 fans show up on this perfect day for football to wave goodbye to the baseball-playing Mets. It might have been Broadway, three weeks from now, with a bigger crowd by a factor of 100.

If today's game counted, Gooden would be pitching. As it is, he's through for the year. The Mets won twenty-eight of the thirty-five games Doc started. My good friend Jim Kaat believes we would have won the division if Dwight had started on three days rest over the last month. It's a thought.

1985 is history. For a ballplayer, the year doesn't end on December 31, but in October. It doesn't begin on January 1, but in April. Next April. Whether we like it or not, the season defines our lives.

I suspected going into this season that all would not be good cheer at *Chez* Hernandez. So it has turned out. But I'm a professional ballplayer, and I'm proud that I hit .309 for the campaign, sixth highest in the league.

From July 1, I hit almost .350, and I hit over .360 in the thirty games following my testimony in Pittsburgh.

The breakdowns of my batting average:

Home,	.284;	road,	.331.
Grass,	.283;	turf,	.364.
Versus lefties,	.315;	righties,	.303.

The high road average reflects, in part, the fact that most of my big multi-hit games were on the road. The high average on turf makes sense. What doesn't make sense was *last* year's turf average: .230. The leftie's/rightie's breakdown? As it should be: .300 against both.

I was down a little in the home-run department, with only ten, but ninety RBIs is my minimum goal for any year, and I made it with one to spare. I finished in the top ten in on-base percentage, hits, doubles, and walks.

Truly and with rare exceptions, on the ballfield, I'm free—and Lord knows I need to be.

Elsewhere, I'm not.

Divorce negotiations proceed; lawsuits are flying.

What does Peter Ueberroth have in store for me? I don't know. Something, he promises.

In a way, however, my chosen profession has prepared me well for uncertainty. Who knows what will happen at the baseball game?

After this afternoon's nine innings, a special video is shown on Diamondvision, a montage of the season with cameo shots of the Met players and Frank Sinatra singing "Here's to the Boys." The fans watch from their seats and cheer, the boys watch from the dugout, and after a final wave on the big screen from the greatest pitcher in baseball, Dwight Gooden, we step onto the field and raise our caps in salute, and toss them into the stands.

GAME 162—Expos 2
Mets 1